HANDBOOK
OF MODERN
CONSTRUCTION LAW

Jeremiah D. Lambert

and

Lawrence White

PRENTICE-HALL, INC. • *ENGLEWOOD CLIFFS, N.J.*

Prentice-Hall International, Inc., *London*
Prentice-Hall of Australia, Ptd. Ltd., *Sydney*
Prentice-Hall of Canada, Ltd., *Toronto*
Prentice-Hall of India Private Ltd., *New Delhi*
Prentice-Hall of Japan, Inc., *Tokyo*
Prentice-Hall of Southeast Asia Pte. Ltd., *Singapore*
Whitehall Books, Ltd., *Wellington, New Zealand*

© 1982 *by*

Prentice-Hall, Inc.
Englewood Cliffs, N.J.

"This publication is designed to provide accurate and authoritative
information in regard to the subject matter covered. It is sold with
the understanding that the publisher is not engaged in rendering
legal, accounting, or other professional service. If legal advice or
other expert assistance is required, the services of a competent
professional person should be sought."

*—From the Declaration of Principles jointly adopted by a
Committee of the American Bar Association and a Committee
of Publishers and Associations.*

Library of Congress Cataloging in Publication Data

Lambert, Jeremiah D.,
  Handbook of modern construction law.

  Includes bibliographies and index.
  1. Building—Contracts and specifications—United
States. 2. Construction industry—Law and legislation—
United States. I. White, Lawrence. II. Title.
KF902.L35   343.73'07869   81-11941
                   347.3037869   AACR2
ISBN 0-13-380436-4

Printed in the United States of America

In memory of Clara Lambert and Miriam White.

Happy he
With such a mother! faith in womankind
Beats with his blood, and trust in all things high
Comes easy to him. . . .

ALFRED, LORD TENNYSON

ABOUT THE AUTHORS

Jeremiah D. Lambert is a Senior Partner in the firm of Peabody, Rivlin, Lambert & Meyers in Washington, D.C. A graduate of Princeton University and the Yale Law School (where he was a member of the Board of Editors of the *Yale Law Journal*), Mr. Lambert has practiced law in New York and Washington for over 20 years and has specialized in construction contract law, among other areas. He has been Adjunct Professor of Law at Georgetown University Law Center and has written and lectured widely on financial, managerial, and regulatory topics. His articles have appeared in *The Business Lawyer, Federal Banking Law Review, Real Estate Review, Public Utilities Fortnightly,* and many other periodicals and trade publications. Mr. Lambert is a member of the District of Columbia and New York State Bars and is also a member of the American Bar Association, the Bar Association of the District of Columbia and the Association of the Bar of the City of New York.

Lawrence White is an attorney in the firm of Peabody, Rivlin, Lambert & Meyers in Washington, D.C., where he has specialized in construction contract litigation. Mr. White was graduated from Harvard University and the University of Pennsylvania Law School. He is a member of the District of Columbia Bar and the American Bar Association.

Why and How to Use
This Handbook

The *Handbook of Modern Construction Law* is a comprehensive guide to the many different legal problems that may arise before, during, and after the construction of a major building project. Although construction work is infinitely varied, all construction projects share common characteristics. Our primary purposes are, first, to show you how your construction problem will be classified and treated by the judges, arbitration panels and contract appeal boards to which construction disputes are referred for resolution; and, second, to share with you the lessons we have learned from experience on how, through careful legal planning, construction problems can be anticipated and minimized.

But it does not stop there. The need for a one-step sourcebook is more acute today than ever before, as the extraordinary growth in the American construction industry during the last two decades grudgingly yields to tight money, high interest rates, and slower growth in public and private construction spending. Therefore, the handbook will consider many contemporary topics besides the traditional ones, such as:

— Strategies to prevent construction litigation and to minimize the disruptive effect of litigation once it commences;

— The critical risk-reducing roles of sureties, bonding companies, insurance companies, and indemnification plans;

— Modern construction management techniques, including sophisticated computer applications;

— Labor-management relations;

— Practical advice on selecting and utilizing attorneys;

— Trends in the construction industry;

— Special problems associated with public contracting.

Building professionals reach for a book such as this one only when something has gone wrong. They are often relieved to learn that construction problems are predictable and of a pattern. Intelligent planning can substantially reduce the likelihood of their occurring; if problems do arise, there are conventional steps that can be taken to prevent disruption on the construction site while problems are peacefully resolved. Our focus, then, is on the real world of building and construction. Our goal is to give you perspective on your own problems by showing you how they fit into the broad mosaic of statutes, regulations, court decisions, standard-form contracts and industry practices that together constitute the law of building and construction.

As readers will see, our approach to the subject reflects one distinctive bias. Experience has taught us the value of an integrated approach to construction problems. We view contractors, subcontractors, construction managers, design professionals and attorneys as members of a team, the role of each player affecting and depending on the conduct of the others. Thus, the contractor must understand the constraints operating on the design professional, and vice versa. The subcontractor must know the terms of the general contract, even though the subcontractor may not be a party to that contract. Each team member must, of course, understand his own legal rights and obligations; but it helps immeasurably if he also comprehends the connection between his work and the work of others.

The interrelationship of roles is one of our paramount concerns in this handbook. We do not include separate discussions of engineering problems, architectural problems, and contracting problems. Rather, we treat discrete subjects—for example, the competitive bidding process (Chapter 2), the negotiation and drafting of construction contracts (Chapters 3 and 4), bonding and insurance requirements (Chapters 8 and 9), and construction litigation (Chapters 12 and 13)—from the unified perspective common to all members of the construction team. We also note, as appropriate, problems that are particular to one profession.

This handbook, in short, is useful as both a comprehensive guide to the field of building and construction law and a source book for engineers, architects, contractors, subcontractors, suppliers and attorneys confronted with specific legal and contractual problems.

HOW THIS HANDBOOK IS ORGANIZED

This handbook's 13 chapters are functionally divided into five parts, corresponding roughly to the chronological segments of an ongoing construction project.

Part I: Forming the Contract. The first three chapters discuss the procedures by which the industry's basic contracts—general contracts, design and engineering contracts, subcontracts, and supply agreements—are negotiated and drafted. *Chapter 1* provides a broad overview of the industry itself and introduces the members of the construction team. *Chapter 2* discusses the elaborate pre-contractual process of competitive bidding, and *Chapter 3* focuses on the closely related topic of subcontracting.

Part II: Substance of Construction Contracts. Chapters 4 through 7 constitute the heart of this handbook. They classify and discuss the major provisions in standard-form construction contracts, and treat in considerable detail the most common contractual problems. *Chapter 4* describes the many separate documents that, taken together, comprise the modern general contract. The chapter also reviews the standard clauses that appear in these documents. The next three chapters focus on three common problem areas. *Chapter 5* describes problems arising from change orders. *Chapter 6* examines the legal liabilities associated with construction delays and other timing problems. *Chapter 7* covers payment and financial problems.

    Part III: Others Involved in Ongoing Construction Projects. The legal relationships between owner, contractor, design professional and subcontractor are not the only ones that matter on an ongoing project. The members of the construction team also negotiate important subsidiary contracts, and the next three chapters discuss three of them. *Chapter 8* describes the role of the construction surety, who, by providing the protection of payment and completion bonds, promotes the financial stability of large-scale construction. *Chapter 9* describes the many different kinds of liability and property insurance policies that members of the construction team must purchase and maintain. In *Chapter 10*, we describe the collective bargaining agreements that define the legal relationship between the general contractor and the labor unions whose members perform the actual construction work.

    Part IV: Construction Management. One chapter of this handbook—*Chapter 11*—is devoted to a brief examination of new trends in construction organization, including the role of the construction manager and the use of computerized, "critical path method" management techniques.

    Part V: Dispute Resolution. The last two chapters are devoted to two related topics: the do's and don'ts of construction litigation (in court, before arbitration panels, and in other forums), and some practical suggestions on how to avoid disruptive lawsuits. *Chapter 12* offers a step-by-step analysis of construction litigation. *Chapter 13* offers tips on how to avoid litigation, and also describes how the prudent construction professional can best prepare for nasty disputes by maintaining careful construction records and anticipating problems before they arise.

    The text is supplemented by three additional sources of information. Illustrative legal cases are cited and discussed in each chapter; these provide a head start for attorneys who wish to investigate a particular topic in more detail. Each chapter concludes with a section entitled "Additional Source Materials," designed to refer the reader to the leading treatises, law review articles, and extended treatments of points discussed summarily in that chapter. Following the text, we have appended copies of some of the widely-used standard forms for construction contracting published by the American Institute of Architects (AIA) and the Associated General Contractors, Inc. (AGC). These are the most commonly used forms in the construction industry, and rare indeed is the large-scale construction project that does not utilize these forms in one adaptation or another.

    Many people have labored to bring forth this handbook, and we wish to express our gratitude to all of them for their contributions. We owe a particular debt of gratitude to Jeanne Carpenter and Susan Rogers, whose legal research enriched our text and gave substance to our generalizations; to Don Wallace, Jr., a professor at Georgetown University Law Center, who provided helpful guidance and assistance; and to Sonia Tenney and Anne Saulsgiver, whose superb organizational skills kept us from foundering in a sea of papers. Finally, we wish to express a special word of appreciation to the attorneys at our law firm, who graciously gave us the time and resources to finish what we started.

Jeremiah D. Lambert
Lawrence White

CONTENTS

3. Subcontractors and the Subcontracting Process (*continued*)

8. Construction Default: The Contractor's Bond (*continued*)

9. Insurance in the Construction Industry 154

10. Labor Relations in the Construction Industry 167

HANDBOOK
OF MODERN
CONSTRUCTION LAW

PART I

Forming the Contract

CHAPTER 1

The Construction Industry

1.1. INTRODUCTION

Compared with other sectors of the American economy, the construction industry is an extraordinary anachronism. In an era of corporate consolidation in which an ever-decreasing number of American companies owns an ever-growing share of the nation's business assets, the construction industry today is much the same as it has been for more than a century—a highly decentralized industry made up of a large number of small and medium-sized firms. Despite the recent emergence of national and even multinational businesses, the construction industry has a pronounced local orientation; most construction companies serve a single metropolitan area, and very few engage in business ventures that are regional or national in scope. Although vertical and horizontal integration has made business firms interdependent in other sectors of the economy, construction firms remain predominantly, even fiercely, independent. Very few large-scale construction companies are owned by larger corporations, and very few have wholly owned subsidiaries engaged in non-construction-related activities.

Competition is the hallmark of the construction industry, and competition is vigorously fostered by the unique structure of the industry. It is an industry of enormous size and breadth. In 1978, one out of every 18 people employed in the United States worked in the construction industry, more than in any other non-manufacturing sector. Almost a quarter of a trillion dollars' worth of new construction was commenced in the United States during calendar year 1980. Yet despite the huge aggregate size of the construction industry, individual construction companies are very numerous and comparatively small. There are almost half a million companies engaged in various aspects of the construction business in this country. The average number of employees per company is less than ten. The typical company is family-owned, operates in a single geographical area, and grosses between $50,000 and $200,000 in business receipts annually. It obtains some or all of its business by bidding against competitors, and its profit margin is correspondingly low. It suffers more than other companies from vagaries in interest rates and inflation. Construction projects are costly and take a long time to complete; construction companies, therefore, have always been high-risk, low-profit ventures.

From this combination of economic decentralization, a highly competitive market structure, and chronic financial fragility, the modern law of construction contracting has evolved.

1.2. THE INDUSTRY IN PERSPECTIVE

Before describing the principles of law that will occupy most of our attention in this handbook, we pause to take a backward glance at the construction industry as it has evolved during the last half-century. Construction is traditionally divided into two categories, on the basis of funding sources: *private construction*, financed by private investors, and *public construction*, financed by federal and local governments. As Table 1 shows, private construction has always accounted for roughly four out of every five dollars spent on construction in this country.

Indeed, it comes as something of a revelation to discover that public construction, despite its explosive growth in absolute dollar terms since the end of World War II, actually accounts for the same proportion of the total construction budget today that it did 30 years ago. Since 1950, public construction has grown from $6.9 billion to $47.5 billion (in 1980), almost a sevenfold increase; over the same thirty-year period, private construction has kept pace, growing from $26.7 billion to more than $175 billion. In 1950, private construction accounted for 79 percent of the nation's expenditures for new construction. In 1980, it accounted for exactly the same percentage.

The largest component of private construction has always been *residential construction*, accounting for approximately half of all private construction and about 40 percent of total construction. In recent years, the fastest growing construction categories have been privately financed *commercial construction* (office buildings, factories, plants, and particularly shopping malls and other regional marketing centers) and *public utility construction* (generating stations, coal- and oil-powered plants and—until recently—nuclear plants). In 1977, these two categories accounted for 32 percent of all private construction; by 1980, they accounted for over 40 percent. (See Table 2.) With housing starts particularly vulnerable to the tight money and high interest rates that will mark the early 1980's, it is safe to assume that non-residential construction will receive a growing share of the total spent on private construction. Some experts, in fact, predict that residential construction will dip below 50 percent of private construction by 1982, an event that has occurred only twice since the end of World War II.

Public construction is, in a sense, much more diversified than the private-sector

TABLE 1

New Construction, By Major Category
For Selected Years Between 1915 and 1978

(in billions of dollars)

	PRIVATE CONSTRUCTION					PUBLIC CONSTRUCTION			
	TOTAL	Total	Residential	Commercial	Public Utilities	Total	Buildings	Water and Sewer	Highways
1915	3.2	2.5	1.2	0.2	0.5	0.7	0.2	0.1	0.3
1920	6.7	5.4	2.0	1.7	0.8	1.3	0.3	0.1	0.7
1925	11.4	9.3	5.5	1.5	1.3	2.1	0.6	0.3	1.1
1930	8.7	5.9	2.1	1.4	1.5	2.8	0.7	0.3	1.5
1935	4.2	2.0	1.0	0.4	0.4	2.2	0.3	0.2	0.8
1940	8.7	5.1	3.0	0.8	0.8	3.6	0.8	0.3	1.3
1945	5.8	3.4	1.3	0.8	0.8	2.4	1.0	0.1	0.4
1950	33.6	26.7	18.1	2.5	3.0	6.9	2.7	0.6	2.1
1955	46.5	34.8	21.9	5.6	3.8	11.7	4.5	1.1	3.9
1960	54.7	38.9	23.0	7.0	4.6	15.8	5.5	1.5	5.4
1965	73.7	51.7	27.9	n.a.	5.8	22.0	7.9	2.4	7.6
1970	94.9	66.8	31.9	16.3	11.0	28.1	10.7	2.6	10.0
1975	134.5	93.6	46.5	20.8	17.4	40.9	15.5	6.6	10.9
1976	151.1	111.9	60.5	19.9	20.3	39.1	13.8	7.0	9.7
1977	174.0	135.8	81.0	22.5	20.3	38.2	12.8	10.7	9.4
1978	206.2	160.4	93.4	30.0	24.1	45.8	15.2	13.9	10.7

n.a. = not available.

Source: Industry and Trade Administration, United States Department of Commerce, *Construction Review* (Dec. 1979).

analog. Only one-third of the nation's public construction budget is used to construct buildings, the oldest and most traditional form of large-scale construction. The lion's share of the budget is devoted to the construction of water and sewer systems (30 percent of the public construction budget in 1980), and highway construction (23 percent). Other federal construction monies are spent on dams, irrigation, water diversion, other resource conservation projects (10 percent), and military construction (4 percent).

With the exception of privately financed commercial and public utility construction (which have grown fairly steadily and predictably over the last two decades), the construction industry has been extraordinarily susceptible to vagaries in the economic climate since the end of World War II. Residential construction, for example, went through a period of rapid expansion in the early 1970's, growing by more than 150 percent between 1970 and 1977. In the last three years of the decade, the residential construction industry grew by only 3 percent annually—an actual decline in real-dollar terms. Public

TABLE 2

New Construction, By Category, 1977-80

(in billions of current dollars[1])

	1977	1978	1979[2]	1980[2]
TOTAL NEW CONSTRUCTION	174.0	206.2	222.5	223.0
Private Construction	135.8	160.4	176.3	175.5
Public Construction	38.2	45.8	46.2	47.5
PRIVATE CONSTRUCTION	135.8	160.4	176.3	175.5
Residential	81.0	93.4	97.5	89.5
Commercial	22.5	30.0	38.3	42.1
Public Utilities	20.3	24.1	26.3	28.5
Institutional	6.2	6.7	7.2	7.8
Farm	4.6	5.3	5.7	6.3
Other Private	1.3	1.3	1.3	1.4
PUBLIC CONSTRUCTION	38.2	45.8	46.2	47.5
Buildings	12.8	15.2	15.0	15.4
Water and Sewer Systems	10.7	13.9	13.9	14.4
Highways	9.4	10.7	11.0	11.0
Conservation and Development	3.9	4.4	4.7	4.9
Military	1.4	1.5	1.7	1.9

[1]May not add up in every category because of rounding.

[2]Figures estimated by Bureau of Domestic Business Development, United States Department of Commerce.

Source: Industry and Trade Administration, United States Department of Commerce, *1980 U.S. Industrial Outlook for 200 Industries, With Projections for 1984* (Jan. 1980).

construction has also felt the bite as increases in government spending have slowed (and in some instances stopped altogether) in the late 1970's and early 1980's.

1.3. THE INDUSTRY TODAY

What is true of American industry in general is also true of the construction industry: it has evolved into a confederation of highly skilled specialty companies. Today, two out of every three construction companies (and one out of every two construction workers) are engaged in a "special trade"—plumbing, electrical work, masonry, carpentry, plastering, excavating, or any of a score of other specialties. (See Table 3.) The relatively recent emergence of these special trades has profoundly changed the legal and

TABLE 3

Construction Firms, By Category and Number of Employees, 1977

(in thousands)

CATEGORY OF FIRM	NUMBER OF FIRMS IN UNITED STATES	TOTAL NUMBER OF EMPLOYEES
ALL CATEGORIES	472.5	4,212
General Building Contractors	154.1	1,163
Heavy Construction Contractors	29.8	890
Special Trade Contractors	288.6	2,158
Plumbing, heating, air conditioning	56.5	458
Electrical	36.8	366
Painting and decorating	27.3	133
Masonry and stonework	24.8	152
Carpentry	24.3	124
Roofing and sheet metal work	20.6	172
Concrete	18.4	139
Plastering, drywall and insulation	16.8	186
Excavation	16.2	103
Floor laying and tiling	9.0	41
Water well drilling	4.3	22
Terrazzo, marble and mosaic work	3.9	22
Glass and glazing	3.2	24
Structural steel erection	2.6	48
Wrecking and demolition	1.0	9

Source: Bureau of the Census, United States Department of Commerce, *Statistical Abstract of the United States* (Sept. 1979).

contractual relationship between the owner of a construction project and the men and women who actually do the construction work.

These men and women were at one time employed by *general contractors* who provided laborers and organizational support for entire construction projects. Under the traditional approach, the owner and the owner's design professionals would deal directly—would have "privity of contract," in lawyers' parlance—with the general contractor only, who in turn would either provide construction services directly or make arrangements to *subcontract* portions of the work to special tradesmen. Today, the general contractor serves more of a coordinating function. The general contractor seldom performs the work himself (or if he does, he performs only an unspecialized part of it); his principal contribution is to supervise the work of the dozens, even hundreds, of subcontractors who actually construct the project.

General contracting firms today tend to be small, management-oriented concerns with accounting and computer capabilities. Much of the work that was once performed by general contractors is now done by subcontractors. The equipment and building material once supplied by the general contractor are now provided by independent suppliers and producers. Once upon a time, a construction project could be built pursuant to a single contract between owner and contractor. Today, it is not unusual for a good-sized construction project to require dozens of contracts—between contractor and subcontractor, contractor and supplier, owner and surety, owner and architect, owner and insurer. This handbook will explore all of these contractual relationships in detail.

1.4.   OWNER, CONTRACTOR, ARCHITECT AND ENGINEER

To the extent that one can generalize about a multi-billion-dollar industry, most construction projects share a common cast of characters and a fairly normal sequence of initial events.

Construction projects almost always involve four principals[1]: the *owner*, the *design professionals*, the *constructors*, and the *providers of subsidiary financial and real estate services*. The owner, as we have seen, can be either a private investor or a governmental entity. The design professionals are the *architect*, who creates and prepares the project's plans and specifications, and the *engineer*, who often coordinates with the architect and is responsible for the physical integrity of the structural and mechanical systems that comprise the construction project.

The constructors are the firms that engage in the actual work of construction. The general contractor, subcontractors, suppliers, material producers, and building tradesmen fall within this category.

Finally, construction projects depend on a long list of subsidiary players who provide financial assistance, indemnification, and other technical services. Chief among these are the standard mortgage and financing agencies—banks, savings and loan associa-

---

[1]The analysis and terminology in succeeding paragraphs are suggested by the American Institute of Architects, *Architect's Handbook of Professional Practice*, ch. 2, pp. 3–5 (Sept. 1969 ed.).

tions, and other institutional investors—that provide backing for privately financed projects; insurance and bonding companies, which provide indemnification and risk protection in a notoriously risky industry; real estate brokers, promoters and appraisers, who match investors with construction sites; and, least of all, construction lawyers, "a sort of people whose profession it is to disguise matters," in Sir Thomas More's felicitous phrase.

The interrelationship between the various players is accurately (if somewhat self-servingly) described in a passage from the *Architect's Handbook of Professional Practice*:

> In the normal building procedure the prospective owner selects an architect who, without ties tending to bias, will guide him skillfully through the intricate building process. In solving his client's problem, the architect may secure the collaboration of engineers and various other consultants and assistants and may obtain advice, data and assistance from mortgage and finance agencies and real estate services. When the contract documents are completed, the architect assists the owner in the selection of the contractor, who in turn, with the assistance of the suppliers, producers, and the building trades, performs the actual construction. During the construction phase the architect administers the construction contract and interprets the contract documents.[2]

In general, construction projects go through three distinct stages: an initial stage, when financing is secured and the details of the project are worked out with design professionals; a drafting stage, when plans and specifications are reduced to writing, contracts are negotiated, and contractors are selected through competitive bidding; and a construction stage, when the project is built. Even on a small project, many years may elapse between first conception and final construction, and much can happen during that time. Interest rates can soar, greatly increasing the projected cost of construction. Contractors and subcontractors can go bankrupt, in the process defaulting on contractual obligations and ruining a carefully coordinated construction schedule. Public officials can change their minds and reduce or cancel projects in midstream. From such vagaries of finance and fortune, litigation is born. There is no sector of American enterprise in which lawyers play a more ubiquitous role.

1.5. STANDARD FORMS

One reason for the prevalence of lawyers is the enormous number of contracts that must be drafted and negotiated during the lifetime of a construction project. Like commercial contracts in other fields, construction contracts are designed to achieve two goals: to define the practical and legal responsibilities of the contracting parties (often in cumbersome technical language that itself reflects generations of litigation and judicial precedent), and to shift common-law risks and liabilities in favor of the party with the

---

[2]*Architect's Handbook of Professional Practice, supra* n. 1 at 3 (lower-case letters substituted).

greater amount of negotiating leverage. Parties, of course, seldom see eye-to-eye on either of these goals.

Over the years, standard-form contracts have assumed an increasingly influential role during the negotiating process. One obvious reason is that the use of contractual "boilerplate" reduces the likelihood of costly litigation and results in greater certainty of meaning and interpretation on the part of both contractual parties. Another more important reason is that the standard forms themselves have been refined with the passage of time and now reflect several decades of experience and fine-tuning.

Two organizations in particular—the American Institute of Architects and the Associated General Contractors of America, Inc.—have each developed a carefully integrated series of standard forms that are widely used in the construction industry. The forms are revised periodically, and are explained and annotated in handsome, bound volumes. Lawyers frequently begin with these standard forms when they are tailoring a contract to the particular needs of their clients, and it is no exaggeration to say that a construction lawyer must be thoroughly versed in the scope and meaning of the standard forms if the client is to receive first-rate representation.

1.6. THE ROLE OF THE CONSTRUCTION LAWYER

As this handbook will show, the construction industry has two distinctive characteristics: its high risk and its extraordinary expense. The lawyer's role is simply expressed and rarely achieved: to minimize risk, and to do it as inexpensively and nondisruptively as possible.

Everyone knows what a lawyer is, but fewer people know what he or she is supposed to do or how much the services of a lawyer should cost. It is said with some justification that a client has delayed too long if the lawyer is hired after the lawsuit is commenced; this is another way of saying that one can most effectively use a lawyer to *prevent* litigation, which should rarely occur if lawyers have done their jobs properly. Lawyers should be involved in contract drafting and negotiating. (In our experience, some of the worst problems arise when owners or contractors use unmodified standard forms.) They should be consulted immediately when minor problems crop up; there is nothing more discouraging to a lawyer than a small problem that needlessly mushrooms into a major catastrophe and is brought to the lawyer's attention when matters are beyond the point of no return.

A lawyer's role, in short, should resemble the role of a trusted counselor rather than the role of a fireman summoned only in emergencies. Experienced construction lawyers can often anticipate problems before they arise. They can save their clients aggravation and money by avoiding litigation through the judicious use of protective contract language and the restraining influence of careful organization on the job site.

For their services, lawyers expect to be compensated. There are many kinds of compensation formulas, and clients—even those who are used to driving hard bargains with their peers in the business world—often seem reluctant to ask for explanations or negotiate over the cost of legal services.

Fee arrangements usually take one of three forms (although to complicate matters, these forms are often combined). A *flat charge* is the simplest, but is also the rarest in complex cases since it is very difficult for a lawyer to predict the amount of effort a particular case will involve until the case has actually begun. By far the most common mechanism for determining fees is the *hourly charge,* pursuant to which the client agrees to pay a negotiated fee for each hour of time spent by the lawyer on that case. The hourly rate varies considerably according to the lawyer's experience, the complexity of the case, the relative wealth of the client, and the prevailing rates in the geographical area in which the lawyer practices. Finally, in some litigated cases, plaintiff and attorney negotiate a *contingent fee.* This is ordinarily a predetermined percentage of any recovery; if there is no recovery, then the lawyer is paid nothing.

Under any of these fee arrangements, clients are responsible for paying out-of-pocket costs, such as filing fees, bills for photoduplication, telephone and postage, deposition expenses, witness fees (including the often substantial fees of an expert witness), and travel expenses. Litigation is terribly expensive. A complex case will require a battery of lawyers and the services of other technical experts, and can take many years to try. Construction companies too frequently underestimate the cost of litigation. They also fail to realize how disruptive a complicated case can be; company officials must take time off to have their depositions taken, to prepare their trial testimony, and to worry about the effect of mounting legal bills on shareholder confidence.

Effective use of an experienced attorney can prevent litigation, or at least minimize its impact if it should occur. Construction companies should observe at least these rules. They should pick their attorneys carefully. They should not be afraid to ask for a full explanation of all legal fees and costs. They should insist on cost-cutting mechanisms where appropriate, such as the substitution of paralegal assistance for higher-priced lawyers' services. And most important of all, they should involve their lawyers at all stages of a construction project, remembering the cardinal rule: it is often better to avoid litigation than to win a costly battle in court.

CHAPTER **2**

Awarding the General Contract:
The Refined Art of
Competitive Bidding

2.1. INTRODUCTION

Nothing has altered the construction industry more fundamentally in the twentieth century than the emergence of the subcontractor specialist and the corresponding change in the function of the general contractor.

Where once the general contractor was a master builder who employed his own construction workers and provided labor and materials directly to the owner, most construction work today is performed by subcontractors who are specialists in their fields—electricians, roofers, plumbers, excavators, and so forth. A modern construction project may involve as many as a hundred subcontractors, sub-subcontractors and suppliers.

The role of the modern general contractor is predominantly supervisory. The general contractor must assemble the constituent parts of the construction "team" by soliciting bids from hundreds of competing subcontractors, and must then coordinate on-site activities to ensure that subcontracted work is performed properly and in timely fashion.

Before construction begins, two processes are undertaken virtually simultaneously. First, the owner selects a general contractor to supervise and coordinate construc-

30

tion. The usual process for selecting a general contractor is competitive bidding, and the highly refined art of submitting and assessing competitive bids is described in this chapter. Second, each general contractor who bids on a particular project assembles a team of subcontractors to perform the bulk of the actual construction work. The process by which subcontractors negotiate with general contractors is described in Chapter 3.

2.2. COMPETITIVE BIDDING: AN OVERVIEW

General contracts in the construction industry are most commonly awarded through the process of competitive bidding. The process is distinguished by the requirement that sealed offers (also called proposals or bids) be submitted by each bidder at a specified time and place and in a specified form. The owner solicits such proposals from prospective bidders by issuing invitations for proposals or, in the case of contracts for public work, by advertising for them. Contending bidders are issued the necessary construction documents and related information and instructions about the project at hand. Typically, bidders then submit their proposals on proposal forms furnished by the owner.

At the place and time specified in the invitation, the sealed proposals are opened and evaluated by the owner's design professional. The proposal lowest in amount is ordinarily accepted by the owner, subject, however, to the constraint that the proposed amount does not exceed the amount budgeted for the project. Upon execution of a written contract incorporating the terms of the accepted bid, the low bidder becomes the general contractor for the project.

2.3. THE ADVANTAGES AND DISADVANTAGES OF COMPETITIVE BIDDING

The major theoretical advantage of competitive bidding is that it enables an owner to build a project at the lowest possible cost. Competitive bidding permits determination of a fair market price for the services and materials required. Competitive proposals generally provide a clear indication of actual cost, including allowances for overhead and profit. In addition, competitive bidding is thought to purge construction procurement of unfairness and favoritism. It is required by law in connection with most public work.

Competitive bidding is not without inherent limitations. It is premised on the unrealistic assumption that projects are built in sequential stages. It is ill-adapted to high-technology projects where the requirement of proprietary know-how may severely limit the number of eligible bidders. And it does not necessarily insure that the lowest bidder will also be responsible and competent to perform the work properly and in timely fashion. The lowest bidder may, for example, lack the necessary expertise, organizational ability or capital resources. The competitive bidding process rests, of course, on free bids and true competition, conditions that bidders may defeat—in violation of the antitrust laws—by bidding pools and turn bidding. Finally, the fixed-price lump sum contract, a central feature of competitive bidding, may encourage general contractors to submit unrealistically low bids with a view to squeezing subcontractors and obtaining increments to the contract price through change orders and claims.

Notwithstanding such difficulties, competitive bidding is relatively simple and inexpensive to administer. Institutional safeguards, such as prequalification requirements and careful bid screening, are easy to implement. Competitive bidding will very likely continue to predominate as the most common method of construction procurement.

2.4. PREQUALIFICATION

To protect against unskilled, financially unstable or irresponsible general contractors, owners frequently seek to prequalify prospective bidders by obtaining relevant information from them in advance of the submission of proposals. The AIA has systematized such information gathering in its Contractor's Qualification Statement (AIA Document A305), which contains questions concerning a potential bidder's organization, past history, experience level, operational methods, capital equipment and financial references. The form also inquires whether the contractor has ever failed to complete a job, what major projects he has completed or is in the process of completing, and in which states the contractor is certified or registered.[1] After evaluation of this information, the owner and his design professional can determine which contractors should be permitted to bid.

The preparation and evaluation of cumbersome financial statements, equipment and personnel lists, previous projects completed and similar data can require the expenditure of considerable administrative time and effort for both owners and potential bidders. Furthermore, it may be difficult for the owner to use such information, even though unfavorable, as a means for withholding an award, particularly on public work. A preferred method of prequalification, therefore, involves establishment of a contractor's prequalification list, consisting only of those contractors meeting minimum standards of size, financial strength and capability in specified fields of construction. Establishing and maintaining such a list is, however, a major task, usually undertaken only by public bodies.

General contractors often subcontract as much as 90 percent of the work to be performed on a project to various trade subcontractors. Prequalification, in order to be meaningful, must provide the owner with some way of prequalifying or otherwise approving the subcontractors whom the general contractor will employ. The owner may thus seek to extend prequalification to major subcontractors. The owner may also incorporate in the instructions to bidders a provision permitting rejection of proposed subcontractors *before* the award of contract, although a change of any proposed subcon-

---

[1]Like all AIA and AGC standard forms to which reference is made in this handbook, AIA Document A305 is reproduced in the Appendix.

tractor previously accepted may result in an increase in contract price. Conversely, a general contractor, if he is awarded the contract, may be bound to use a subcontractor whose name he has submitted and whose price for the subcontracted work he has included in his proposal.

2.5. INVITATIONS TO BIDDERS

An owner formally solicits bids by sending or publishing invitations to potential bidders. An invitation to bid is not itself an offer which a bidder may accept but is instead, legally, only a solicitation of offers. Nonetheless, the invitation to bid incorporates important procedural decisions by the design professional and the owner which will shape the course of work on the project. Although the formality of invitations to bid will vary with the type and scope of the work to be performed, an invitation to bid will commonly include the following basic items of information:

> — The name and location of the project;
>
> — A brief description of the work;
>
> — Whether the contract award will be by single or multiple contracts;
>
> — The time and place for receiving bids;
>
> — A statement whether opening of bids will be public or private;
>
> — The location where plans and specifications may be examined and obtained for bidding purposes;
>
> — Whether bid bonds or security deposits must be posted; and
>
> — A statement concerning the owner's right to accept or reject bids and whether bids are revocable.

In recent years, the process by which an owner invites bids has grown more formal. The widely used AIA form (AIA Document A701, "Instruction to Bidders") was first promulgated in 1970, and includes the invitation to bid as one of a half-dozen separate bidding documents an owner must circulate to potential bidders.

There is one major difference between invitations solicited by a private owner and those solicited by a municipal or governmental authority. Bidding procedures on privately financed projects are ordinarily governed by rules unilaterally established by the owner. The rules usually favor the owner and operate to the legal and practical detriment of bidders. By contrast, public contract bidding procedures are generally subject to statutory requirements designed to redress, at least minimally, the negotiating imbalance between owner and bidder.

The laws governing public construction may impose additional requirements on bid invitations. They may require, for example, that legal notice be given to prospective bidders by advertisement in designated newspapers or trade media. The information required to be included will usually cover the items listed above. In addition, however, state or local law may provide that award of contract be made to the lowest responsive and responsible bidder; that bids be irrevocable for a stated period; that bids may not be changed, corrected or withdrawn after submission; that withdrawal of a mistaken bid renders the bidder ineligible to rebid the job; that the bidder certify that he has not paid any government official on a contingent fee basis to assist in obtaining the contract; that minority group representation in employment be assured; and that other similar legal conditions be observed. Statutory requirements in connection with public contracts are strictly enforced.

Bid invitations almost always require that bids be submitted within a prescribed period of time or by a specified deadline. Courts once construed these time limitations liberally. The unmistakable modern trend, however, is to insist on timely submission of bids and to tolerate no excuses for bids submitted after expiration of the bidding period. This is particularly true on public projects, where statutes and regulations impose seemingly immutable time limits. In one recent case, for example,[2] a low bidder was disqualified because its bid was submitted four minutes after the deadline established in the bid invitation.

2.6.   INFORMATION TO BIDDERS

Once an owner invites bids for a particular project, he is obligated to make information available concerning the nature of the construction. Such information includes plans, specifications, drawings, contract terms and conditions, soil boring test data (where applicable), and any other documents to be part of the contract. AIA Document A701 contains a standard format for Information to Bidders, which has also been approved by the AGC.

Information to bidders amplifies the project data contained in the invitation in sufficient detail to permit bidders to submit intelligent proposals. It also elaborates on bidding procedures. It may provide, as AIA Document A701 does, that all bids be submitted on forms provided by the owner and that a bid, once submitted, cannot be modified, withdrawn, or canceled, in whole or in part, for a specified period after the time designated for receipt of bids.

Information to bidders also commonly prescribes a procedure for dealing with apparent discrepancies and ambiguities in the plans and specifications. Usually, a bidder is required to make a written request for clarification to the project architect. Replies are issued as addenda and sent to all bidders of record. A cutoff date for receiving requests for clarification is established prior to the date for the receipt of bids in order that all bidders may receive the last addendum within a reasonable time before that date.

A similar procedure is often adopted when substitutions are to be considered during the bidding period. Requests for substitutions are required to be made within a specified period before the date for receipt of bids. When requested substitutions are found acceptable, notice is given to all bidders of record through issuance of an addendum to the original invitation for bids.

Substitutions can become troublesome if contract specifications use the phrase

---

[2]*William F. Wilke, Inc. v. Department of the Army*, 357 F.Supp. 988 (D.Md.), *aff'd*, 485 F.2d 180 (4th Cir. 1973).

"or equal" with regard to materials or equipment to be incorporated in the work. As a general rule, courts will not find a breach of contract where a contractor uses equipment or materials different from, but equal in quality or performance to, those indicated in the specifications. To meet this problem, architect approval of equivalents is usually required.

A contractor planning to use less expensive equipment or materials under an "or equal" clause and to submit a lower bid based thereon must then assume, unless substitutions have been approved before bidding, that the project architect will be reasonable in determining whether the equipment and materials he proposes to use are the equivalent of those designated. Both the AIA and AGC recommend that the "or equal" usage be eliminated in favor of specific lists of products and brand-name equipment. It is conceivable, however, that such insistence can impose higher costs on the owner; contractors frequently complain that architects and engineers specify brand-name equipment and materials largely because manufacturers' representatives have provided free engineering services.

2.7. DISCLAIMERS IN BID INVITATIONS

It is commonplace for an owner to include disclaimers in information to bidders. An owner may, for example, include a provision warning each bidder to inspect the site himself, to make his own soil tests, or to verify the accuracy of his bid when submitted. Disclaimers are inserted to shift certain risks to the bidder and to preclude subsequent contentions of mistake in computation, unknown subsurface conditions, and other similar matters.

The most common disclaimer is the site investigation clause. One such clause is contained in Article 1.2.2 of the AIA's General Conditions (AIA Document A201):

> By executing the Contract, the Contractor represents that he has visited the site, familiarized himself with the local conditions under which the Work is to be performed, and correlated his observations with the requirements of the Contract Documents.

The site investigation clause has proven over the years to be one of the general contractor's worst enemies. It is often asserted by the owner as a defense to a contractor's claim for "extras"; courts have generally invoked site inspection clauses against the claiming contractor when the owner has made no affirmative misrepresentation of fact upon which the contractor reasonably relied.[3] It is also reinforced in many owner-drafted contracts by other provisions indemnifying the owner for unanticipated expenses resulting from undetectable variations in soil or subsurface conditions.[4] In general, and for good reason, owners are very reluctant to bargain away a protective site inspection clause. It is

---

[3]*Department of Transportation v. Brayman Construction Co.,* 382 A.2d 767 (Pa.Cmwlth. 1978); *Burke v. Allegheny County,* 336 Pa. 411, 9 A.2d 396 (1939).

[4]*See, e.g., Wrecking Corporation of America v. Memorial Hospital for Cancer and Allied Diseases,* 63 A.D.2d 615, 405 N.Y.S. 2d 83 (1978).

absolutely essential, therefore, that a contractor inspect the site with considerable care before submitting a bid, even if this means hiring special consultants or incurring other potentially unrecoupable expenses prior to the award of the contract. Courts are notoriously sympathetic to owners who argue that contractors inspected or should have inspected the job site before bidding.

In the absence of valid disclaimers, the contractor is entitled to rely on the accuracy of plans and specifications and any soil report which the owner may furnish. The owner is deemed to have warranted, if only by implication, that the information furnished is accurate. If the owner is not culpable of fraud or bad faith, however, disclaimers will ordinarily be upheld and are thus almost universally included in information to bidders in connection with soil tests.

In a leading and much-cited case, *Wunderlich v. State of California*,[5] a contractor alleged breach of warranty related to the composition of compaction material where the state, as owner, had furnished samples of the material and suggested certain conclusions to be drawn from it. The contract required the contractor to examine the site and stated that the accuracy of preliminary investigations was not guaranteed. The case turned on the question of whether the state had represented that sufficient suitable compaction material extractable at a reasonable cost would be available. Largely because of the disclaimers included in the contract, the court in *Wunderlich* decided against the contractor, finding that "[t]here was no representation as to quantities in the source, or that a consistent proportion of materials would be found throughout the source."

An opposite result was reached in another case, *E. H. Morrill Co. v. State of California*,[6] decided in the same year by the same court that had decided the *Wunderlich* case. In *Morrill* the state as owner represented that boulders encountered at the site would be of a certain size and dispersion. The boulders were substantially larger and more concentrated than represented. Although the contractor had visited the site, the court permitted him to recover for extra cost incurred despite a general disclaimer as to surface and subsurface conditions contained in the contract. The court distinguished the *Wunderlich* case, noting that the disclaimer in that case appeared in the contract together with the alleged representation. In *Morrill*, on the other hand, the disclaimer was general and did not overcome the positive assertion of fact which the state had made.[7]

2.8.   REJECTING AND WITHDRAWING BIDS

Information to bidders commonly provides that the owner may reject any bid that does not conform to the bidding requirements and may also waive any irregularity in a bid. The owner will also usually retain, and clearly state, his right to reject any or all bids.

---

[5]65 Cal. 2d 777, 423 P.2d 545, 56 Cal.Rptr. 473 (1967).

[6]65 Cal. 2d 787, 423 P.2d 551, 56 Cal.Rptr. 479 (1967).

[7]Disclaimer clauses are frequently ignored as superfluous in the United States Court of Claims and federal contract administration boards, on the ground that the general site inspection clause is more than adequate to shift the pertinent risks to the contractor. *See, e.g., Morrison-Knudsen Co. v. United States*, 184 Ct.Cl. 661, 397 F.2d 826 (1968).

Bids may thus be regarded as options which the owner may accept during whatever period of irrevocability has been stipulated in the bidding procedures.

AIA Document A701 requires a selected bidder, within seven days after a request by the project architect, to submit information as to (1) costs for each portion of the work, (2) designation of the work to be performed by his own personnel (as opposed to subcontractors) and (3) the subcontractors proposed for the principal portions of the work. If either the owner or the architect then has a "reasonable and substantial" objection to any of these items, the architect will so notify the bidder *before* the award of contract. The bidder will then be permitted to withdraw his bid without forfeiture of bid security (see §2.9.3) or to propose alternatives, which the owner may reject if they entail an increase in price.

2.9. BIDS AND PROPOSALS

An executed bid or proposal constitutes an offer by the bidder to the owner. It is commonly submitted on a proposal form provided by the owner to insure that competitive bids can be properly compared and that all bidders are proposing to do the same work under the same terms and conditions. In addition to specific identification of the project, four principal elements are ordinarily covered by a properly submitted bid: the bid items or price, undertakings or pledges, acknowledgements, and, if applicable, bid security.

2.9.1. Bid Items

In the simplest case, bid items consist of a lump-sum price for constructing the project in accordance with the contract documents. The lump-sum price reflects the general contractor's best estimate of the costs of material and labor involved and other related items, including:

— General and administrative expenses;
— Equipment costs;
— Utilities;
— Engineering costs;
— Interest;
— Insurance;
— Surety bond premiums;
— Taxes, permits, and fees;
— Legal expenses;
— Contingency allowance; and
— Profit.

After these items are taken into account, the contractor must determine whether the tentative bid will be competitive; whether the bid amount exceeds any arbitrary limitation imposed by the invitation to bid; and, in the case of public work, whether the contracting authority has appropriated sufficient funds for the work at hand.

In determining his bid amount, a contractor will routinely rely on bids submitted to him by subcontractors and material suppliers. These bids will ordinarily cover a large percentage of the work. They are, as a consequence, a critical feature of the bidding process and have occasioned significant litigation as to the degree of reliance a contractor may properly place on them. (See §3.2.)

2.9.2.   Undertakings and Acknowledgments

In submitting his bid, the bidding contractor undertakes or pledges that he will, if he receives notice of acceptance of his bid within a specified time after the opening of bids, (1) enter into a contract with the owner and furnish performance and payment bonds as required; (2) commence work within a specified time after execution of the contract; (3) complete the work as required by the contract; and (4) accomplish the work in accordance with the contract documents. The last three undertakings are, of course, also obligations of the contractor under the contract awarded.

The bid form will also commonly require the contractor to acknowlege that he has examined the drawings, specifications, and other contract documents as well as the conditions at site. If addenda to the information to bidders have been issued, it is customary to provide space for the bidder to enter the identifying number of each addendum received. The bidding contractor will also be required to represent that all work covered by the addenda is included in his proposal.

2.9.3.   Security

Bid security will usually consist of a bid bond or a bid deposit, determined as a percentage of the base bid amount or as an arbitrary lump sum. Bid security assures the owner that the selected bidder will execute a construction contract and furnish a performance bond, if required, within a stipulated period of time, failing which the bidder will be required to pay to the owner the difference between the amount of his bid and the next lowest acceptable bid amount up to the amount of the bid security. (See §2.12.)

2.10.   BID OPENING; EVALUATION OF BIDS; AWARD

Bids are usually submitted to the owner's design professional in sealed envelopes and are opened only at the time and place specified in the invitation to bidders. Award of contract, however, is not made at the bid opening but only after the bids have been evaluated and reviewed. Bid evaluation and review must take place within a period of time specified in the invitation to bidders.

When the bidders have been prequalified, the contract will usually be awarded to the lowest bona fide bidder. When bidders have not been prequalified, the contract award will be made to the lowest *responsible* bidder. In either event, the bids will be evaluated for responsiveness to the invitation. A bid offering performance not called for in the invitation will be rejected. Nonconformity of bids may relate to the work, time of completion, bonds submitted, or other similar matters.

In determining the lowest responsible bidder, absent prequalification and assuming the existence of a responsive bid, the owner and his design professional will consider the bidder's expertise, financial capacity, general reputation, past performance on similar jobs, and other comparable factors, all with a view to selecting the contractor who will do the job properly at the lowest price and with least administrative cost to the owner. Refusal to award a contract to the lowest bidder, however, must rest on substantial grounds. Otherwise, a defeated low bidder may lodge a bid protest and seek, legally, to compel award of the contract. In such litigation the owner must offer persuasive reasons for refusing to award the contract. The bidder's default on a previous construction contract constitutes the strongest grounds for disqualification, although other reasons, if provable, may be used by the owner.[8]

When the owner has determined the successful bidder, he must then provide appropriate notification. The mode of notification is critical. If the owner wishes to accept the successful bidder's proposal, he will issue an official notice of award, constituting an acceptance of the proposal and creating, under conventional principles of contract law, a legally enforceable agreement even though formal contract documents are not yet executed. If, on the other hand, the owner wishes to express his intent merely to execute formal contract documents at some future date, he will style the notification a "letter of intent" or "notice to proceed." Such notice can, even in the absence of a binding contractual commitment, permit the work to proceed.

There are obvious legal dangers inherent in a letter of intent. To protect the owner, a letter of intent must prohibit the general contractor from entering into any subcontracts or placing orders for material beyond the immediate scope of work authorized, other than on a contingent basis. In addition, the letter of intent must incorporate explicit provisions to cover settlement costs in the event a formal contract is never executed and to assure immediate insurance coverage while operations continue under the interim authorization. When the formal contract is executed, it will supersede the letter of intent, and payments made under the letter of intent will be credited against the contract sum.

Whether or not a notice of award or letter of intent is used, an owner must provide notification to unsuccessful bidders. Unless the owner intends to release them, the notification will advise unsuccessful bidders that their bids still remain available for acceptance for the period of time specified in the invitation to bid. The owner will then have an alternative to rebidding the work in the event the selected bidder fails to enter into a formal contract.

---

[8]The modern trend is to permit a frustrated low bidder to recover, at a minimum, his bid preparation costs. *Scanwell Laboratories, Inc. v. Thomas,* 521 F.2d 941 (D.C.Cir. 1975), *cert. denied,* 425 U.S. 910 (1976).

2.11. ERRORS AND WITHDRAWALS

Construction cost estimating is at best an imperfect process. Great variations in bid amounts are possible and even common. The complexity of assembling into a single proposal many "bits" of pricing data can lead to computation and clerical errors as well as fundamental errors of judgment with respect to quantities, labor costs and other components of the bid price. In addition, a contractor may seek to disobligate himself because a subcontractor, on whose sub-bid he has predicated a portion of the bid price in his own bid, has revoked the sub-bid or has, in turn, claimed mistake.

Courts vary in their willingness to relieve a contractor of the consequences of his mistakes. Once submitted and selected by the owner, the contractor's bid is regarded as an offer that has been accepted. Rescission of the contract so created may then be denied if the mistake is deemed to be unilateral (specific to the contractor) rather than mutual. However, relief from mistaken bids will be allowed where the owner knows or has reason to know of the mistake, as would ordinarily be the case, for example, if an entire item representing a substantial portion of the bid price has been omitted. In order to support rescission under these circumstances, a contractor must show (1) that the mistake is material; (2) that it was not the result of negligence; (3) that enforcement of the contract as made would be unconscionable; and (4) that the owner has not relied on the mistaken bid to his detriment.[9] He must also give prompt notice of intent to rescind and to restore any amounts paid on the contract. Normally, courts will not permit a withdrawing contractor to correct his mistake and rebid.[10]

In *M. F. Kemper Construction Co. v. City of Los Angeles*,[11] a leading case in which rescission was permitted, a contractor mistakenly omitted a $330,000 item from its bid, which was, as a result, approximately $250,000 lower than the next lowest bid. The contractor discovered its error several hours after the bids were opened and immediately notified the Board of Public Works as the awarding authority, a few days thereafter submitting evidence of the unintentionally omitted amount. The Board nonetheless accepted the contractor's erroneous bid. The contractor then refused to enter into a formal contract. Without readvertising, the Board awarded the contract to the next lowest bidder and demanded forfeiture of the contractor's bid bond. The contractor then commenced legal action to cancel its bid and obtain discharge of the bid bond. Notwithstanding a statement in the invitation to bidders and the official bid form that bidders "will not be released on account of errors," the court permitted the contractor to cancel its bid. In so doing, it noted the distinction between errors in judgment, for

[9]*Town of La Connes v. American Construction Co. Inc.*, 585 P.2d 162 (Wash.Ct.App. 1978); *John J. Calnan Co. v. Talsma Builders, Inc.*, 367 N.E. 2d 695 (Ill. 1977).

[10]The Michigan Court of Appeals, however, has recently suggested that a contracting body may have the authority under certain circumstances to accept a corrected bid. *Department of Public Works v. American Bank & Trust Co.*, 268 N.W.2d 367 (Mich. 1978).

[11]37 Cal.2d 696, 235 P.2d 7 (1951).

which relief would not be allowed, and clerical or mathematical mistakes, for which it would:

> Where a person is denied relief because of an error in judgment, the agreement which is enforced is the one he intended to make, whereas if he is denied relief from a clerical error, he is forced to perform an agreement he had no intention of making. The statement in the bid form . . . can be given effect by interpreting it as relating to errors of judgment as distinguished from clerical mistakes. If we were to give the language the sweeping construction contended for by the city, it would mean holding that the contractor intended to assume the risk of clerical error no matter in what circumstances it might occur or how serious it might be.
>
> Such interpretation is contrary to common sense and ordinary business understanding . . .[12]

The AIA's recommended procedure for dealing with mistaken bids accords with the *Kemper* case:

> If, after bids are opened, the low bidder claims he has made an appreciable error in the preparation of his bid and can support such claim with evidence satisfactory to the Owner and the Architect, he should be permitted to withdraw his bid. His bid guarantee should be returned and he should be disqualified from again bidding on the Project in the event additional bids are requested.[13]

State statutes may also provide relief. A Massachusetts law permits a bidder to withdraw and his bid deposit to be returned to him if there has been a "bona fide clerical or mechanical error of a substantial nature." California law similarly provides a relief if "the mistake was made in filling out the bid and not due to error in judgment or to carelessness in inspecting the site of the work, or in reading the plans and specifications." Under California law, however, a public agency does not have authority to disobligate a bidder; he must instead file suit to obtain relief.[14] A Pennsylvania statute also adopts the distinction between clerical and judgmental error and permits relief from an "unintentional" clerical error of sufficient magnitude to affect the bid price.[15].

The hazy distinction between "clerical" and "judgmental" errors thus assumes considerable legal significance, despite imprecise use of the terms by courts and commentators. A clerical error is normally an error relating to the transcription and copying of numbers, rather than their calculation. An error is judgmental, on the other hand, if it involves calculations or estimates that turn out to be wrong—for example, an estimate of the number of hours necessary to complete a job. In recent years, the distinction has lost

---

[12]235 P.2d at 11-12. *See also Elsinore Union Elementary School District v. Kastorff*, 54 Cal.2d 380, 353 P.2d 713, 6 Cal. Rptr. 1 (1960).

[13]AIA, *Architect's Handbook of Professional Practice*, Chapter 16 ("Selection of Contractors"), at 10 (1971).

[14]Mass. Gen. Laws, ch. 149 §44B(2); Cal. Gov't Code §14352 (West).

[15]Pa. Stat. Ann. tit. 73, §§1601 *ff*.

some of its importance. One court has suggested that characterizing an error as "judgmental" or "clerical" is less important than deciding whether the error is "objectively verifiable."[16] Another has declared that the distinction is worthless and should be disregarded.[17]

The clearly indicated avenue for the mistaken contractor is thus the equitable remedy of rescission. He cannot claim the existence of a genuine mistake, perform the contract, and then ask a court for reformation of the contract terms to those he originally intended. Just this procedure was followed in *Lemoge Electric Company v. County of San Mateo,*[18] where a contractor accidentally included a $10,000 electrical item as a $100 sub-item. The contractor notified the Board of Public Works of the mistake. The Board nonetheless accepted the erroneous bid. The contractor then proceeded to perform the contract, thereafter bringing suit to reform the contract to provide for the correct bid amount and to recover the amount of the mistake as damages. In rejecting reformation, the court noted that the contractor could have rescinded the contract without incurring liability on its bid bond and should have done so.

Once a bid is submitted, it cannot be withdrawn or modified for the period of time (usually several weeks) specified in the invitation to bid.[19] This is to allow the owner time to sift through and compare the sometimes numerous and frequently technical bids received from hopeful contractors during the bidding period. If bids are not accepted or rejected before the specified date, then the offer expires and is no longer binding on the contractor. An interesting question—and one that, thankfully, arises infrequently now that standard-form contracts are widely utilized—is how long a bid must remain open in the absence of a controlling provision in the contract. If the contract does not specify an automatic expiration date, then bids are considered by courts to have a "reasonable" lifetime and may not be modified or withdrawn during that period. What constitutes a "reasonable" period will be determined on a case-by-case basis, and there is no dearth of case law on the subject.[20]

2.12. FORFEITURE OF BID SECURITY

Bidders are often required to furnish a bid deposit or bid bond in connection with competitively awarded contracts for construction. If a selected bidder refuses, without

---

[16]*Balaban-Gordon Co. v. Brighton Sewer District No. 2,* 342 N.Y.S. 2d 435 (App.Div. 1973).

[17]*Wilfred's, Inc. v. Metropolitan Sanitary District,* 372 N.E.2d 946 (Ill.App. 1978).

[18]46 Cal.2d 659, 297 P.2d 638 (1956).

[19]Under Article 4.4.1 of AIA Document A701, all bidders must pledge to observe any time period specified in the invitation, and not to modify or withdraw their bids until the time period has expired. Significantly, however, Article 4.4.2 permits contractors to withdraw bids prior to the closing date for bid submission—an important "out" for contractors who discover mistakes in their bids prior to that date.

[20]*See, e.g., N. Litterio & Co. v. Glassman Construction Co.,* 319 F.2d 736 (D.C.Cir. 1963); *Truscon Steel Co. v. Cooke,* 98 F.2d 905 (10th Cir. 1938); *Loranger Construction Corp. v. E. F. Hauserman Co.,* 384 N.E.2d 176 (Mass. 1978); *Construction Supply Co. v. Brostrom Sheet Metal Works, Inc.,* 190 N.W.2d 71 (Minn. 1971); *E.A. Coronis Associates v. M. Gordon Construction Co.,* 216 A.2d 246 (N.J.Super.App.Div. 1966).

legal justification, to enter into a contract after it has been awarded, the bid bond or deposit will then constitute a fund on which the owner may levy for protection against damages suffered as a result of the bidder's failure to go forward. In such cases, the question arises whether the bid bond or deposit is in the nature of security or whether it is a means of liquidating the owner's damages.

If the bid bond or deposit is in the nature of security, the owner is required to prove the damages to which he is entitled, usually the difference between the amount of the bidder's proposal and the next acceptable bid. If the damages exceed the amount of the bid security, the owner may then retain that amount and seek recovery of the balance from the general contractor. If damages are less than the amount of the security, the owner must then return to the contractor the unused portion.

If the bid bond or deposit seeks to liquidate damages, however, the amount thereof will be retained by the owner even though actual damages suffered may be less than the bond or deposit amount. Conversely, the owner will be precluded from recovering any amount in excess of the bid bond or deposit amount even though actual damages suffered are greater.

A bid bond or deposit may validly liquidate damages only if the amount of damages is difficult to ascertain at the time bids are solicited and the bid bond or deposit amount is not disproportionate to actual or anticipated damages. Courts will otherwise regard liquidated damages as a forfeiture. Damages will then be assessed only if provable. In a competitive bidding context, it is, of course, not possible to establish a bid deposit or bond amount with reference to anticipated damages since the bid amount of the selected bidder and that of the next lowest bidder—the usual principal measure of damages—is not known until the bids have been opened. Only when the selected bidder has refused to enter into the contract awarded are damages ascertainable. The order of magnitude of damages may nonetheless be estimated in relation to the size of the project and the administrative expense involved in rebidding, should that be required.

On public work, statutory provisions may empower the public agency awarding contracts to recover, at most, only the difference between the selected bidder's low bid and the next lowest bid if the selected bidder defaults. In that event, the bid bond or deposit is regarded simply as security to the extent the amount is greater than the difference between bids and as a limitation on recovery to the extent that amount is less than the difference.

Finally, it should be noted that in most jurisdictions there is no pecuniary liability for mistakes due to clerical errors, provided that the errors were not deliberately made,[21] are insignificant in size,[22] do not prejudice the owner except pecuniarily,[23] and are promptly brought to the owner's attention as soon as they are discovered.[24]

---

[21]*Puget Sound Painters, Inc. v. State,* 278 P.2d 302 (Wash. 1954).

[22]*Rhode Island Tool Co. v. United States,* 128 F.Supp. 417 (Ct.Cl. 1955).

[23]*Scottsbluff School District v. Olson Construction Co.,* 45 N.W.2d 164 (Neb. 1950).

[24]*Kutsche v. Ford,* 192 N.W. 714 (Mich. 1923).

2.13. ADDITIONAL SOURCE MATERIALS

General:

AIA, *Architect's Handbook of Professional Practice*

— Chapter 2, "The Construction Industry" (1969)
— Chapter 16, "Selection of Contractors" (1971)
— Chapter 17, "Owner-Contractor and Contractor-Subcontractor Agreements" (1973).

C., J. C., Jr. "Another look at construction bidding and contracts at formation," 53 U.Va.L.Rev. 1720 (1963).

Cushman, Kenneth, *et al.*, "Rights and responsibilities of the general contractor, subcontractor and material supplier," reprinted in PLI, *Construction Contracts 1979*, at 155-327.

Hohns, H. M., *Preventing and Solving Construction Contract Disputes* (Van Nostrand Reinhold Co., 1979).

Lederman, Lawrence, "Once around the flag pole: construction bidding and contracts at formation," 39 N.Y.U. L.Rev. 816 (1964).

Oertli, Richard A., "Construction bidding problem: is there a solution fair to both the general contractor and subcontractor?", 19 St. Louis U.L.J. 552 (1975).

Sweet, Justin, *Legal Aspects of Architecture, Engineering and the Construction Process* (West Pub. Co. 1970).

Bid Mistakes:

Berger, "Mistakes in Bids—Edition II," *Government Contractor Briefing Paper*, No. 76-5 (1976).

Fields, R. W., "Relief from mistake in bids," 32 Ins. Counsel J. 259 (1965).

Grime and Walker, "Unilateral mistakes in construction bids: methods of proof and theories of recovery—a modern approach," 5 B.C. Ind. & Com.L.Rev. 213 (1964).

Hume, "Mistakes in bids and bid bond liability," 35 Ins. Counsel J. 36 (1968).

R., J. "Forfeiture of construction bid bond denied because of unilateral mistake," 6 Utah L.Rev. 578 (1959).

Jones, Kenneth H., Jr., "Building and construction contracts—addition mistake in submitted bid is not necessarily the kind of negligence that will bar equitable relief," 39 Texas L.Rev. 497 (1961).

Bid Protests

Cass, Ronald A., "Government contract bid protests: judicial review and the role of the court of claims," 39 U. of Chi. L.Rev. 814 (1972).

Comment, "The role of GAO and courts in government contract 'bid protests': an analysis of post-Scanwell remedies," 1972 Duke L.Rev. 745.

Promissory Estoppel Doctrine

Gaides, John B., "Firm offer problem in construction bids and the need for promissory estoppel," 10 Wm. & Mary L.Rev. 212 (1968).

Stuntebeck, Clinton, "Construction bidding—firm offer—UCC §2-205 and promissory estoppel," 18 Maine L.Rev. 297 (1966).

"Contracts—promissory estoppel and the UCC statute of frauds—subcontractor is not estopped to assert the statute of frauds despite general contractor's reliance on oral sub-bid in calculating the prime bid," 48 Miss. L.J. 883 (1977).

Anno., Promissory Estoppel, §12—"Relations among contractors: contractors' financing," 48 A.L.R. 2d 1069, 1085.

Public Authority Contracts

Pierson, "Standing to seek judicial review of government contract awards: its origins, rationale and effect on the procurement process," 12 Boston College Industrial and Commercial Law Review 1 (1970).

Anno., "Constitutionality, construction, and application of statute providing for correction or relief from consequences of error or mistake in bids for public contracts," 126 A.L.R. 837.

Anno., "Contract for personal services as within requirement of submission of bids as condition of public contract," 15 A.L.R. 3d 733.

Anno., "Differences in character or quality of materials, articles or work as affecting acceptance of bid for public contract," 27 A.L.R. 2d 917.

Anno., "Liability of municipality on quasi-contract for value of property or work furnished without compliance with bidding requirements," 33 A.L.R. 3d 1164.

Anno., "Recovery from U.S. of costs incurred by unsuccessful bidder in preparing and submitting contract bid in response to government solicitation," 30 A.L.R. Fed. 355.

Anno., "Revocation prior to execution of formal written contract of vote or decision of public body awarding contract to bidder," 3 A.L.R. 3d 864.

Anno., "Right of municipal corporation to recover back from contractor payments made under contract violating competitive bidding statute," 33 A.L.R. 3d 397.

Anno., "Right of public authorities to reject all bids for public work or contract," 31 A.L.R. 2d 469.

CHAPTER 3

Subcontractors and the Subcontracting Process

3.1. INTRODUCTION

Construction contracting proceeds simultaneously on two levels. While the owner solicits competitive bids from companies wishing to supervise the project as general contractor, each prospective general contractor engages in its own negotiations with the dozens or even hundreds of subcontractors and material suppliers who will be responsible for the actual construction work.

The evolution of the subcontracting system has generated an intricate web of legal relationships that did not exist as recently as a few generations ago. Construction contracting, once a relatively simple matter between an owner and a general contractor, is now immensely more complicated. The general contractor must commonly enter into many contracts with subcontractors, who in turn may enter into contracts with lower-tier subcontractors and suppliers. The contractual rights and obligations of the participating parties frequently conflict and require delicate coordination by the general contractor, who is normally the only contracting party in privity with the owner and all the first-tier subcontractors. Delay or default by even the smallest subcontractor can be amplified to create intractable liability problems for other subcontractors and the general contractor.

Modern construction contracting, therefore, requires close adherence by contractors and subcontractors to three operating precepts. First, subcontracts must be negotiated and drafted with care. Second, the general contractor must recognize and devote considerable attention to his obligations as project coordinator. And third, the parties must be able to resolve inevitable disputes without delaying or jeopardizing the course of construction.

3.2. NEGOTIATING THE SUBCONTRACT: THE SUBCONTRACTOR'S PERSPECTIVE

Subcontracting differs in critical respects from other forms of contract negotiation. Ordinarily, one contracting party manifests his intention to accept or reject the offer of another party, and the contract is not formed until the offer is formally accepted. In the construction context, however, the normal process of offer and acceptance is interrupted by the general contractor's own participation in competitive bidding for the prime contract.

When an owner advertises a construction project, general contractors solicit bids from subcontractors. The bids are, for legal purposes, equivalent to contractual offers to provide specified services for a quoted lump-sum price. The general contractor, however, cannot accept the bid until he is awarded the prime contract, for the obvious reason that he does not wish to bind himself if he does not receive the contract.

The general contractor, therefore, neither accepts nor rejects the subcontractor's bid when it is tendered. Instead, the general contractor calculates his own bid for the prime contract based on the bids he has in turn received from subcontractor solicitations. If he is awarded the prime contract, he so notifies the subcontractors whose bids formed the basis upon which his own bid was submitted, and formally accepts their offers—offers which may have been extended weeks or even months earlier.

In the context of competitive bidding, subcontracting thus presents certain unavoidable problems. The subcontractor is free to modify or rescind his bid at any point up to the moment at which the general contractor accepts; if the subcontractor modifies his offer *after* the general contractor has submitted his own bid based on the subcontractor's original terms, the general contractor may be faced with greater than anticipated costs for the work (see §3.3), although nothing requires the general contractor to use the services of the subcontractor whose offer was the basis upon which the general contractor's own bid was calculated. Once the general contractor is awarded the contract, he is free to solicit additional subcontractor bids and accept the lowest offer he can find.

"Bid shopping," as this latter practice is known, is, from the subcontractor's perspective, one of the most troublesome aspects of subcontract negotiation. The general contractor's bargaining position is improved substantially when he is awarded the prime contract, and the temptation is great to press would-be subcontractors for lower prices or more advantageous terms.[1]

---

[1]The prime contractor is in a peculiarly favorable position to impose upon those who would enter into subcontracts with him burdensome agreements as to arbitration. The number of subcontractors from whom the prime contractor may choose is limited only by the scope of the industry, while would-be subcontractors must seek the nod of a single prime contractor, who is in that respect a complete monopolist.

Electronic & Missile Facilities, Inc. v. United States ex rel. H.W. Moseley, 306 F.2d 554, 559 (5th Cir. 1962).

Bid shopping distorts the contract negotiating process in several ways. It decreases the accuracy and reliability of bids at both the prime contract and subcontract levels; general contractors are encouraged to underestimate their bids on the theory that offers from subcontractors can be lowered by judicious bid shopping; and subcontractors are encouraged to overestimate their bids so that they will have room to reduce their offers later. Bid shopping may also reduce competition between subcontractors by discouraging some subcontractors from participating in the bidding process and can actually lead to higher prices when one subcontractor or a small number of subcontractors control business in a single area. Finally, bid shopping can force subcontractors into submitting irresponsibly low bids and then sacrificing quality or skimping on safety or inspection procedures, to the detriment of the public and the industry as a whole.

For more than three decades, bid shopping has been condemned by the Code of Ethical Conduct of the AGC. The practice persists, however, due in large part to judicial reluctance to condemn it, and in smaller measure to its advocacy by economists who view it as "the purest form of competition" in the construction industry.[2]

Initial efforts to curb excesses associated with bid shopping focused on the creation of so-called "bid depositories" to monitor subcontract awards. Bid depositories were created and managed by trade associations. Member subcontractors submitted sealed bids directly to the depository, which, on a specified day, opened, tabulated and printed all bids. Today, bid depositories have disappeared, largely as the result of antitrust prosecutions.[3]

In recent years state legislatures have attempted to prevent the most serious abuses by enacting remedial legislation. In several states, "bid listing" statutes require general contractors to provide the names of all subcontractors whose bids were used in figuring the prime bid and to limit the circumstances under which a successful general contractor may replace listed subcontractors or modify the terms of subcontracts.[4] Bid listing is also required for most federal civilian contracting.[5]

A recent development in the field of public construction contracts is the enactment of legislation requiring general contractors to file all solicited bids from subcontractors with a state awarding agency. The agency is authorized to reject non-responsive bids. From those deemed responsive, the agency forwards to the general contractor a list of acceptable subcontractors' bids, determined on the basis of price and other objective criteria. The general contractor then picks from the acceptable subcontractors and prepares his prime bid in accordance with the sub-bids he has chosen. If the general contractor is awarded the prime contract, he may substitute subcontractors only with the

---

[2]*See, e.g.*, Orrick, "Trade Associations Are Boycott Prone—Bid Depositories as a Case Study," 19 Hastings L.J. 505, 521 (1968).

[3]*See, e.g., Mechanical Contractors Bid Depository v. Christiansen*, 352 F.2d 817 (10th Cir. 1965); Schueller, "Bid Shopping and Peddling in the Subcontract Construction Industry," 18 U.C.L.A. L.Rev. 389 (1970).

[4]*E.g.*, Cal. Gov't Code §4104 (West); Mass.Ann.Laws ch. 149, §44A; N.Y.State Fin.Law §138; N.J.Stat.Ann. §52:32-2.

[5]Regulations of the General Services Administration (41 C.F.R. §5B-2.202-70 (1977)) require general contractors to list subcontractors on all prime bids, and the Comptroller General has vigorously enforced the listing regulation by disqualifying low prime bidders who have failed to list. *See, e.g.*, 43 Comp. Gen. 206.

awarding agency's approval, and then only from the other subcontractors on the agency's approved list. Massachusetts and Connecticut have enacted so-called "bid filing" laws,[6] and other states are expected to follow.

A third and more far-reaching approach to the awarding of public contracts has been adopted in one state (North Carolina): subcontracts for the performance of designated categories of specialty work (including heating, ventilating, plumbing, electrical work and refrigeration) are awarded separately by the state awarding agency, eliminating altogether the possibility of bid shopping. Direct subcontracting is used with increasing frequency by private owners as well, although its use is limited to large prime contracts and subcontracts involving well-established specialties.[7]

In the absence of statutory protection of some kind, subcontractors will normally find it difficult to hold general contractors to the negotiated terms of a bid. Courts have been notably unsympathetic to the contractual and quasi-contractual theories on which subcontractor lawsuits are based. This is partly because courts widely refuse to construe a general contractor's use of a sub-bid in preparing his own bid on the prime contract as the kind of action constituting constructive acceptance of the subcontractor's offer,[8] and partly because negotiations between prime contractors and subcontractors are frequently conducted orally or by telephone and are therefore barred by the Statute of Frauds from being considered as evidence of an oral contract.

Complicating negotiations further, from the subcontractor's perspective, are the serious legal and economic consequences of a bidding mistake. Mistakes in calculating subcontract prices are not uncommon. Prices often depend on estimated material and labor costs that are likely to inflate rapidly; a subcontractor whose price lists are six months or even one month behind can find himself underestimating costs by several thousand dollars. If the error is so large that the general contractor is or should be aware of the probability of mistake, then courts have generally held that subcontractors could not be compelled to perform at the erroneous price. If, however, the general contractor relies on the mistaken subcontract bid and has no actual or constructive notice of the error, then courts have required subcontractor performance at the lower price.[9] This, of course, can spell financial catastrophe for a subcontractor.

From the subcontractor's perspective, negotiations with the general contractor should be pursued in accordance with two operating rules. First, office procedures should be adopted to ensure that bids are carefully checked for error before they are submitted, and periodically thereafter. As one authority has recently noted:

> [I]f the original bid was calculated by a detailed time and material take-off, then a bid check should be made by calculating the bid using unit prices based on previous cost experience. The chances of an erroneous bid being sent out are reduced the more times that a subcontractor checks the bid.[10]

---

[6]Mass.Ann.Laws ch. 149, §44A; Conn.Gen.Stat.Ann. §4-1373-f.

[7]N.C.Gen.Stat. §143-128.

[8]*See, e.g., Williams v. Favret,* 161 F.2d 822 (5th Cir. 1947).

[9]*See, e.g., Drennan v. Star Paving Co.,* 51 Cal.2d 409, 333 P.2d 767 (1958), discussed in §3.3.2, *infra.*

[10]M. Stokes, *Construction Law in Contractors' Language* (1977), at 15.

Checks should also be made after formal submission of a bid, to ensure that increased material and labor costs do not render the terms of the bid unacceptable.

Second, a subcontractor whose competitive position permits him to do so should consider submitting all bids subject to a reasonable time limitation. Bids should state on their face, "Offer good until [a date certain]," and should be revoked if unaccepted by the specified date. The longer offers are allowed to stand, the greater the risk to the offeror, who is vulnerable to bid shopping and the effects of inflation on underlying costs.

3.3. NEGOTIATING THE SUBCONTRACT: THE GENERAL CONTRACTOR'S PERSPECTIVE

From the perspective of the general contractor who frequently must negotiate dozens of subcontracts simultaneously and whose exposure to potential liability is far greater in dollar terms than that of any single subcontractor, two concerns predominate in the early stages of negotiation: the reputability of the party with whom he is subcontracting; and the degree of confidence he can place in the subcontractor's bid.

3.3.1. Selecting a Subcontractor

A general contractor must consider many factors in choosing among competing subcontractors. Price is important, but it may not be determinative. Other factors include the subcontractor's experience (particularly if the work to be undertaken involves special expertise), reputation, and financial stability. With respect to the latter two factors, much can be learned by interviewing references and performing credit checks, tasks the general contractor should always undertake before soliciting bids.

Subcontractors should also be required to show compliance with pertinent licensing requirements, particularly for those engaged in skilled crafts. Subcontractors should post payment and performance bonds.

A recurring problem is the union status of subcontractor employees. The general contractor's own union status is pertinent, as is the law of the state in which the construction project is to be performed. For an open-shop general contractor, there are decided financial advantages to employment of a non-union subcontractor; but labor problems can arise if some subcontractors on the construction site are union and others are not.

Because of differences in state law and variations in union strength, it is sometimes to a general contractor's advantage to operate open-shop and at other times to hire union employees only. A recent development is the creation of so-called "double-breasted" general contracting businesses where a union contractor forms a wholly owned subsidiary to operate open-shop in geographic areas where non-union employees are available. Two decisions of the National Labor Relations Board substantially broaden the circumstances under which general contractors can take advantage of the opportunities offered by double-breasted operation.[11]

---

[11]*Gerace Construction, Inc.*, 193 N.L.R.B. 645 (1971); *Frank N. Smith Associates, Inc.*, 194 N.L.R.B. 212 (1971).

3.3.2. Binding the Subcontractor to His Bid

General contractors must prepare prime bids on the basis of offers from subcontractors that have not been formally accepted and are therefore subject to modification or rescission after the prime contract is awarded. This can create difficult problems for a general contractor who has calculated his prime bid by relying on solicited sub-bids. Until fairly recently, general contractors who resorted to court actions to hold subcontractors to their bids met with little success, in large part because of their own reluctance to accept offers prior to the award of the prime contract and the resulting difficulty in proving the existence of a binding contract.[12]

In recent years, general contractors have prevailed with increasing frequency by suing under the quasi-contractual theory of *promissory estoppel,* a term defined in the Restatement (Second) of Contracts as follows:

> A promise which the promissor should reasonably expect to induce action or forbearance of a definite and substantial character on the part of the promissee and which does induce such action or forebearance is binding if injustice can be avoided only by enforcement of the promise. [§90.]

"Translated into layman's terms," one leading commentator has written, ". . . application of the doctrine of promissory estoppel means that when a subcontractor submits a bid, or offer, which he reasonably expects will be relied on by the prime contractor in making his own bid, and the prime does in fact utilize the bid for that purpose, the sub will be prevented from withdrawing his bid if it would be inequitable to allow him to do so."[13]

The leading case applying the doctrine of promissory estoppel is *Drennan v. Star Paving Co.,*[14] a suit by a general contractor against a subcontractor who withdrew a tendered offer after the award of the prime contract. Rejecting the plaintiff's argument that there was a binding contract between the parties, the court nevertheless held the defendant liable for damages under the doctrine of promissory estoppel:

> Defendant had reason not only to expect plaintiff to rely on its bid but to want him to. Clearly defendant had a stake in plaintiff's reliance on its bid. Given this interest and the fact that plaintiff is bound by his own bid, it is only fair that plaintiff should have at least an opportunity to accept defendant's bid after the general contract has been awarded to him.[15]

The *Drennan* holding, however, contained an important proviso. A general contractor may rely on a subcontractor's offer only if the offer is accepted without delay

---

[12]*See, e.g., James Baird Co. v. Gimbel Bros.,* 64 F.2d 344 (2d Cir. 1933).

[13]Currie, "Subcontracts," reprinted in, *Concentrated Course in Construction Contracts* (Fed. Publications, Inc. 1976), at E-ff.

[14]51 Cal.2d 409, 333 P.2d 757 (1958).

[15]333 P.2d at 760.

after award of the prime contract, and only if the general contractor refrains from reopening bargaining with that or any other subcontractor. A general contractor, in other words, may not rely on the doctrine of promissory estoppel if he engages in bid shopping at any time during the negotiating process.

The result of *Drennan* and similar cases is that a prime contractor may often be able to bind a subcontractor even though the subcontractor cannot conversely compel the prime contractor to award him a subcontract. Various methods may be employed to redress this imbalance. A subcontractor may, for example, denominate his sub-bid as simply a price quotation and not a firm bid; or he may condition his sub-bid upon the prime contractor's undertaking to enter into a subcontract with him at the specified price if the main contract is awarded. Neither approach is fully satisfactory, however, since subcontract bidding is, at best, often haphazard and, as in *Drennan*, conducted orally. On public contracts in certain states, therefore, prime contractors are required by law to list their subcontractors. Only under certain circumstances and with the permission of the awarding public agency may a prime contractor use a subcontractor other than those he has listed.

The owner also has a material stake in appropriate subcontractor selection by the prime contractor. If the owner has insisted upon the provisions contained in Article VIII of AIA Document A701, Instructions to Bidders, the proposed prime contractor will then be required to submit before the award of contract a list of subcontractors proposed for principal portions of the work. This list will enable the owner or his architect to register objections, if necessary, to any proposed subcontractor. As noted above, the proposed prime contractor may then withdraw his bid without forfeiture of bid security or may submit an acceptable substitute subcontractor. While this procedure does permit the owner to reject a subcontractor, it does not of itself permit an owner to compel a withdrawing or defaulting subcontractor to honor the terms of his sub-bid to the prime contractor. The owner must instead award the contract to the selected bidder, who, as prime contractor, must then pursue his remedies against the defaulting or withdrawing subcontractor under the principles established in *Drennan* and similar cases.

3.4. DRAFTING THE SUBCONTRACT

It is said that there are as many "standard" subcontract forms as there are general contractors and subcontractors, and generalizations concerning "standard" subcontract provisions are perilous. A starting point may be the form subcontracts promulgated by the AGC in 1966 and the American Institute of Architects (AIA Document A401) in 1972, both widely recognized as neutral forms, the terms of which favor neither the general contractor nor the subcontractor.

Neutrality is a critical consideration in drafting the subcontract. Because the relative bargaining positions of the parties are frequently disparate, with the general contractor at a considerable advantage once the prime contract is his, the subcontractor must be careful not to "sign away" substantive rights by agreeing to a contract drafted by and for the benefit of the general contractor. A subcontractor should be familiar with the terms of the AGC and AIA subcontract forms, and, if circumstances permit, should not hesitate to insist on substitution of a neutral clause from these forms for an inequitable provision suggested by the general contractor. One commentator has perceptively described the strategy subcontractors should adopt during the preliminary "battle of the forms":

> When a subcontractor is presented with an obviously loaded subcontract form, he could call the general contractor and say, "How about substituting the American Institute of Architects Standard Subcontract Form A401?" However, when orally approached, the general contractor will initially be inclined to say no because he may not be familiar with the terms of this standard subcontract form and know how to fill out the form, and he may feel that consideration of this standard subcontract form would require substantial legal review by his lawyer. So the general contractor is initially inclined to simply say no to an oral proposal to substitute a more neutral subcontract form.
>
> The wise subcontractor takes another more practical approach by filling out the terms and conditions of an AIA Standard Subcontract Form A401 and sending filled-out copies to the general contractor with a polite letter proposing to substitute the form in lieu of the original obviously loaded subcontract form. The subcontractor might sign the filled-out neutral form or await the general contractor's signature before signing and request that the general contractor sign all copies and return one copy to the subcontractor. More often than not, the subcontract form is returned in the mail signed by the general contractor without comment. The difference in using this last approach is that the general contractor can readily see that the filled-out Standard Subcontract Form A401 is more or less neutral and protects the general contractor and subcontractor equally. All the general contractor then has to do to the filled-out standard subcontract form to have a legally binding subcontract is sign his name.

However, when the general contractor responds to the subcontractor saying that he cannot accept the AIA Standard Subcontract Form A401, the subcontractor is in an excellent position to propose the AGC standard subcontract form as a compromise. More often than not, the AGC subcontract form is a very acceptable compromise with both the general contractor and the subcontractor. The AGC subcontract form is more readily accepted by general contractors than the AIA subcontract form because the AGC's form is sponsored and approved by the general contractor's own national association. In any event, either the AIA or the AGC standard subcontract form contains terms that protect both the general contractor and the subcontractor, and both forms are certainly more neutral in respect to the subcontractors than the loaded subcontract forms devised by the general contractors.

Many subcontractors also include stipulations in their bids that the subcontractor's bid be conditioned upon use of an AIA or AGC standard subcontract form between the parties if their bid is accepted. If the subcontractor's bid is accepted, the use of the stipulated standard form subcontract is then legally required to be used by the general contractor. Many subcontractors are also drafting either the AIA or the AGC subcontract form and initially sending the form to the general contractor after the general contractor has indicated that the subcontractor's bid has been accepted.

A subcontractor should not be complacent and blindly sign the general contractor's form, which is obviously loaded against the subcontractor. If a subcontractor signs a loaded subcontract form, he may need the services of a preacher rather than a lawyer to pray that nothing happens on the construction job.[16]

3.4.1. The Flow-Down Clause

Virtually all subcontracts contain "flow-down" or "conduit" clauses incorporating by reference all terms and conditions of the prime contract pertinent to the subcontracting parties. The flow-down clause contained in Article 11.1.1 of AIA Document A401 is illustrative:

> The Subcontractor shall be bound to the Contractor by the terms of this Agreement and . . . shall assume toward the Contractor all the obligations and responsibilities which the Contractor, by [the Contract] Documents, assumes toward the Owner and the Architect, and shall have the benefit of all rights, remedies and redress against the Contractor which the Contractor, by those Documents, has against the Owner, insofar as applicable to this Subcontract, provided that where any provision of the Contract Documents between the Owner and Contractor is inconsistent with any provision of this Agreement, this Agreement shall govern.

Mutuality is an important component of the flow-down clause. The subcontractor covenants to provide all services to the general contractor necessary to enable the general contractor to perform his obligations under the prime contract; in return, the general contractor agrees to provide the subcontractor with the same rights and remedies with respect to performance under the subcontract that the general contractor has against the owner.

3.4.2. Payment and Retention Clauses

Parties should devote particular attention to clauses setting forth the schedule and method of payment. General contractors normally insist on a *contingent payment clause* under which they have no obligation to compensate subcontractors until they themselves are paid by the owner. The practical effect of such a clause is to incorporate into each subcontract the payment schedule contained in the prime contract.

A contingent payment clause can operate to the substantial detriment of subcon-

---

[16]Stokes, *supra* p. 10 at 69-70.

tractors, who may find payments delayed for months or even years by the unsatisfactory work of the general contractor or other subcontractors. The harsher effects of such clauses are mitigated, however, by two factors. First, courts have construed them liberally, particularly under circumstances where payment delays are the fault of the general contractor and literal application of the contingency clause would prevent recovery by a blameless subcontractor.[17] Second, the construction industry has widely adopted the qualified contingency clauses contained in the AGC and AIA forms; these clauses make subcontractor payments contingent on payment certification by the owner or architect, but require progress payments in the event that the contractual payment schedule is not observed.

Subcontracts almost always contain *retention clauses,* pursuant to which the general contractor is permitted to withhold a portion of each scheduled payment until the subcontractor's performance is satisfactorily completed. There is substantial variation in the wording and effect of retention clauses, and subcontractors should examine suggested contract language with two considerations in mind: the duration of retention and the amount retained.

With respect to the duration of retention, subcontracts drafted by general contractors frequently permit retention until the entire construction project is completed. For subcontractors whose services are provided in the initial stages of construction, such a retention clause may mean delays of several years before retained sums are finally paid, and there is no reason why a subcontractor who has performed satisfactorily should be required to wait that long for payment. Retention clauses, therefore, should contain a savings clause requiring final payment within a specified period of time after satisfactory completion of subcontract obligations.

With respect to the amount retained, subcontractors usually prefer *line-item reduction clauses* under which the amount retained by the general contractor decreases during the lifetime of the subcontract. Subcontractors should also insist on knowing the terms of the retention clause in the prime contract and should not permit retention of a greater proportion of their payments than the corresponding proportion retained by the owner thereunder.

3.4.3. The Changes Clause

Flexibility is an important component of the relationship between subcontractor and general contractor. Unexpected delays or scheduling problems with one subcontractor can require last-minute modifications in the work assignments of other subcontractors. The purpose of the changes clause, which is a standard part of virtually every subcontract, is to permit the general contractor unilaterally to adjust subcontractual terms as circumstances on the construction site dictate. Article 11.9.1 of AIA Form A401 is a typical changes clause:

---

[17]*E.g., Thomas J. Dyer Co. v. Bishop International Engineering Co.,* 303 F.2d 655 (6th Cir. 1962); *Midland Engineering Co. v. John A. Hall Construction Co.,* 398 F.Supp. 981 (N.D.Ind. 1975); *Schuler-Hass Electric Corp. v. Aetna Casualty & Surety Co.,* 649 App.Div. 2d 260 (N.Y. 1975); *A.J. Wolfe Co. v. Baltimore Contractors, Inc.,* 355 Mass. 636, 244 N.E.2d 717 (1969); *Atlantic States Construction Co. v. Drummond & Co.,* 251 Md. 77, 246 A.2d 251 (1968).

The Subcontractor may be ordered in writing by the Contractor, without invalidating this Subcontract, to make changes in the Work within the general scope of this Subcontract consisting of additions, deletions or other revisions, the Contract Sum and the Contract Time being adjusted accordingly. The Subcontractor, prior to the commencement of such changed or revised Work, shall submit promptly to the Contractor written copies of any claim for adjustment to the Contract Sum and Contract Time for such revised Work in a manner consistent with the Contract Documents.

Changes must frequently be made quickly with little or no advance notice to subcontractors, and protracted discussion concerning the price of changes can jeopardize timely completion of the project. Changes clauses, therefore, are normally construed to require prompt performance on the subcontractor's part and expedited consideration by the general contractor of any dispute involving the terms of the change order. Subcontractors are ordinarily required by the terms of the changes clause to proceed with the work while disputes are adjudicated.

3.4.4. Scope of the Work

Subcontracts should contain a clause defining precisely the work to be performed. Precision is most effectively ensured by reference to specific drawings, specifications and clauses in the prime contract. To be avoided are "dragnet" clauses describing in boilerplate terms the work to be performed—"all work normally undertaken by those in the trade," "all work shown in the plans and specifications," "all related items," and so forth.

3.4.5. The Disputes Clauses

Most contractual disputes can be handled without recourse to formal adjudication. The primary purpose of a disputes clause is to impress that fact on the parties by providing a visible and attractive mechanism for informal resolution of any disputes that arise during construction. A comprehensive disputes clause typically establishes a two-step adjudication procedure. First, disputes are subject to negotiations between the subcontractor and general contractor, with the general contractor required to provide a written justification for his decision in any dispute not resolved by negotiation. Second, the clause may provide for arbitration of unresolved disputes by a neutral party (such as the American Arbitration Association). In that event, arbitration should be a condition precedent to the institution of judicial proceedings.

3.4.6. Other Standard Clauses

For projects involving a substantial number of subcontractors, *scheduling clauses* are often included in each subcontract to ensure that neither party will incur liability in the event that a third-party subcontractor's performance is delayed. *Safety clauses* are standard, and require subcontractors to observe basic safety requirements on the job site.

A *subcontractor default clause* is to some extent the converse of a noncontingent payment clause. It protects the innocent general contractor from prospective liability in the event of subcontractor default by allowing the general contractor to terminate the subcontract. Default clauses must spell out with considerable precision the circumstances under which a general contractor may repudiate a subcontract in anticipation of default, and such clauses are ordinarily complex. General contractors, who risk cumulative damages far in excess of the amount of any single subcontract in the event of default, ordinarily insist on default clauses in all subcontracts.

Lien waiver clauses, requiring subcontractors to waive statutory or common-law lien rights against general contractors, have largely disappeared. They are statutorily prohibited in several states.

3.5. SUBCONTRACT ADMINISTRATION

The general contractor's primary responsibility is to coordinate the work of the many subcontractors who perform the actual construction work. The general contractor must perform the intricate task of scheduling the work of subcontractors to minimize interference and wasted time and must conduct on-site inspections to ensure that work is performed satisfactorily and on schedule. Subcontract administration is the general contractor's principal concern once construction begins, and successful general contracting requires effective procedures to monitor the concurrent performance of dozens or even hundreds of subcontractors.

3.5.1. Pre-Construction Conference

A useful initial step is a pre-construction conference of subcontractors to discuss projected schedules and work assignments. Disputes over change orders can frequently be avoided by providing each subcontractor with a clear idea of his place in the subcontracting "sequence." The general contractor may also benefit from the subcontractors' experience in anticipating possible sources of delay and streamlining the flow of workers and materials at the construction site.

3.5.2. On-Site Coordination

The complex interrelationship between subcontracts requires sophisticated management techniques. Charts and schedules must be updated on a daily basis, and periodic "check dates" should be noted and used as overall schedule references. Many potential problems can be anticipated and avoided by maintaining regular contact with the separate subcontract projects.

On-site inspections should be conducted on a regular basis. A persistent problem at a large construction site is potential delay caused by duplicative inspections. A single subcontract project site may be inspected by the owner, the general contractor and other subcontractors. Inspections may lead to change orders or "constructive" change orders (usually for additional testing or reinstallation) resulting in further delay. The obligations of the parties with respect to the inspections should be indicated in the subcontract. Inspecting parties should be required to minimize potential disruption; the subcontractor in turn should have a clear idea of the frequency and scope of inspections.

3.6. ADDITIONAL SOURCE MATERIALS

General:

Bergman, B.J., "When the subcontractor fails to perform: the notice problem," 21 Prac. L. 85 (1975).

Cochrane, L. P., "Obligations of the principal's subcontractors and suppliers at default or takeover by the surety," 14 Forum 869 (1979).

Currie, O. A., "Subcontracts," reprinted in *Concentrated Course in Construction Contracts* (Fed. Publications Inc. 1976), at E-1 *ff*.

Koch, H. C., "Surety's obligation to pay subcontractor where owner fails to pay under contract," 11 Forum 1212 (1976).

Powers, J. D., "Representing the subcontractor," 8 Forum 473 (1973).

Stokes, M., *Construction Law in Contractors' Language* (McGraw-Hill, 1977), Chapter 3 ("Subcontracts"), at 67-103.

Stokes, M., J. B. Shapiro, Jr., and D. R. Hendrick, "Representing subcontractors—trying to minimize the risks," 14 Ga. S.B. J. 104 (1978).

Anno., "Building and construction contracts: right of subcontractor who has default only with primary contractor to recover against property owner in quasi-contract," 62 A.L.R. 3d 288.

Anno., "Liability of builder or subcontractor for insufficiency of building resulting from latent defects in materials used," 61 A.L.R. 3d 792.

General Contractor-Subcontractor Relationship

Petersen, Robert M., "Liability of a general contractor for negligent construction of subcontractor," 32 So.Calif.L.Rev. 203 (1959).

Schriber, Kenneth L., "Construction contracts—the problem of offer and acceptance in the general contractor-subcontractor relationship," 37 U.Cin.L. Rev. 798 (1968).

Anno., "Liability of subcontractor upon bond or other agreement indemnifying general contractor against liability for damage to person or property," 68 A.L.R. 3d 7.

Bid Shopping

Comment, "Bid shopping and peddling in the subcontract construction industry," 18 U.C.L.A. L.Rev. 389 (1970).

Promissory Estoppel Doctrine

Gaides, John B., " 'Firm Offer' problem in construction bids and the need for promissory estoppel," 10 Wm. & Mary L.Rev. 212 (1968).

Granberg, Derald E., "Promissory estoppel in California: subcontractor's bid irrevocable as result of contractor's reliance," 47 Calif.L.Rev. 405 (1959).

Griffin, Stephen K., "Promissory estoppel—the basis of a cause of action which is neither contract, tort nor quasi-contract," 40 Mo.L.Rev. 163 (1975).

Kern, James A., "Contractors: promissory estoppel," 43 Marq.L.Rev. 384 (1959–60).

Stuntebeck, Clinton, "Construction bidding—firm offer—UCC §2-205 and promissory estoppel," 18 Maine L.Rev. 297 (1966).

"Contracts: promissory estoppel applied to bind subcontractor to his sub-bid," 56 Minn.L.Rev. 493 (1972).

"Contracts—promissory estoppel and the UCC statute of frauds—subcontractor is not estopped to assert the statute of frauds despite general contractor's reliance on oral sub-bid in calculating the prime bid," 48 Miss. L.J. 883 (1977).

PART II

Substance of
Construction Contracts

CHAPTER 4

Rights and Duties Under the Construction Contract

4.1. INTRODUCTION: THE CONTRACT DOCUMENTS

Construction is an inherently complex process. It requires the coordination of many participants and is largely shaped by the contractual relationships among them. These relationships are in turn determined, to a greater extent than comparable forms of endeavor in an industrial economy, by contract documents. The most important of these is the agreement between the owner and the contractor.

To speak of a unitary contract, however, may be misleading. There are in fact several essential items that comprise the contract documents:

— The Agreement, or formal written contract;
— The Condition of the Contract (General Conditions and Supplementary Conditions);
— Drawings;
— Specifications; and
— Addenda (including amendments to the Contract Documents issued prior to execution of the Agreement).

The *Agreement* itself is usually a standard-form document (the most common of which is AIA Document A101). It identifies the parties concerned, describes the work generally, specifies the documents that comprise the formal agreement, defines time of commencement and completion, and states the contract sum. It may also include provisions for changes, termination, and method of payment. It is, nonetheless, a barebones document. It gains full meaning and definition through the incorporation by reference of the other documents mentioned above, and thereby sets forth a single, integrated contract.

Like all contracts, construction contracts use terms and phrases that must often be placed in context by reference to other, non-contractual documents—for example, information for bidders, advertisements for bids, proposals, statutes, local rules and regulations, and local building and trade codes. All of these documents, if not incorporated into the contract by specific reference, may nevertheless be used as guides to determine the respective contractual obligations of the parties.[1]

The *general conditions* (AIA Document A201) and instructions to bidders (AIA Document A701) have been described as "intricately designed, highly machined and honed boilerplates containing the principal contract provisions governing the parties involved."[2] The general conditions define the rights, responsibilities, and relationships of the parties concerned. The supplementary conditions provide a means of modifying or adapting standardized general conditions to fit the special requirements of a given project.

Drawings, commonly called working drawings or shop drawings, portray in graphic form the work to be constructed. They show dimensions, location, arrangement of components, materials, mechanical and electrical systems and wiring.

The *specifications* are usually prepared by architects or engineers. They set forth technical information concerning building materials, components, systems, and equipment indicated on the drawings. The specifications state the quality, performance characteristics, and results to be achieved by application of construction methods.

Conditions, drawings and specifications are the coin of the realm in the world of construction contracting. The contractor who takes the trouble to read and understand the fine print in these documents is miles ahead of the game. There is really no such thing as an unprecedented construction problem. Most construction problems have happened before, and contract documents are drafted with these problems in mind. It sounds simple, but bears repeating: The answer to almost any conceivable problem can be found somewhere in the documents that are signed before the project begins. The contractor who enters into an agreement without understanding its terms is asking for trouble.

4.2. GENERAL CONDITIONS

Although there is considerable range in the topics contained in the general conditions and in their arrangement, the AIA's version (AIA Document A201) may be taken as typical. The General Conditions are the rules of the game. They define the legal

---

[1]*Oxford Development Corp. v. Rausauer Builders, Inc.*, 304 N.E.2d 211 (Ind. Ct. App. 1973).

[2]Hart, "Practical Problems and Legal Trouble Spots in Construction Agreements," *Construction Contracts* 52 (PLI 1976).

relationships between the various parties and describe the many documents that are incorporated into the integrated construction contract. The very first paragraph of AIA Document A201 provides: "The Contract Documents consist of the Owner-Contractor Agreement, the Conditions of the Contract (General, Supplementary and other Conditions), the Drawings, the Specifications, and all Addenda issued prior to and all Modifications issued after execution of the Contract." A modification is then defined as a written amendment made after execution of the contract. It may take the form of a supplemental agreement between the owner and the contractor, a change order, or a written interpretation of the drawings and specifications by the architect-engineer. Article 1, ¶1.1.1 (1976 ed.).

The contract is broadly defined to include the contract documents mentioned above. It constitutes, by express provision, "the entire and integrated agreement between the parties," superseding all prior negotiations, representations, or agreements. (¶1.1.2.) The General Conditions are confined to procedures and matters arising after execution of the contract, and the words "bid" or "bidder" do not appear in any of the documents making up the contract.

This point needs to be emphasized, because it is not immediately apparent to those who lack experience with written contracts. Imagine that Owner owns a parcel of land and negotiates with Contractor to erect an apartment building on that site. Owner and Contractor negotiate orally for several weeks, and in the latter stages of negotiation the terms of a deal are written down. Contractor should be fully aware that once he signs a written contract, the terms of the written instrument are binding on him even if they do not contain (or contain in modified form) terms that were negotiated orally. (Like everything else lawyers say, this rule is subject to several exceptions. Contractor should consult §4.16 of this chapter before giving up entirely.) Particularly in this day and age, when standard-form contracts containing a myriad of obscure provisions are used to memorialize the terms of oral agreements, it is very important to read the contract documents carefully and not to rely on oral representations that are effectively erased from the slate when a written contract is executed.

Under the General Conditions, all contract documents are given the same weight and significance. AIA Document A201, for example, specifies that "[t]he Contract Documents are complementary, and what is required by any one shall be binding as if required by all." (¶1.2.3.) The contract purports to avoid any order of precedence among the documents. In this way, if there is a conflict between the specifications and the drawings (a situation that is not as uncommon as one might believe—see §4.13, *infra*), neither document will automatically prevail. Inconsistencies will be resolved on the strength of the facts in each case.

4.3. THE PARTIES

Articles 2, 3, 4, and 5 of AIA Document A201 describe the functions, rights, and obligations of the architect, owner, contractor, and subcontractor, respectively. This configuration of parties presupposes conventional construction contracting using a general contractor, a method still used on most projects but modified with increasing frequency by contractual variants such as construction management, turnkey contracting, and design-build contracting.[3] (For a fuller discussion of these alternatives to conventional contracting, see Chapter 11.)

4.3.1. The Architect

Although the architect is not a party to the contract between the owner and the general contractor, his functions and obligations are usually defined in detail in the contract documents. Especially in the early stages of construction, the architect plays an important and varied role in ensuring that on-site work proceeds smoothly.

In addition to his design work, the architect plays a fascinating role as an arbiter of disputes on the job site. The architect is deemed to be the owner's representative throughout the period of construction and until final payment. He is usually required to make regular visits to the site to familiarize himself generally with the progress and quality of the work and to determine if it is proceeding in accordance with the contract documents. However, the architect is not required to make "exhaustive or continuous on-site inspections to check the quality or quantity of the [w]ork" (¶2.2.3), and is expressly not responsible for "construction means, methods, techniques, sequences or procedures" or for the contractor's failure to carry out the work in accordance with the contract documents (¶2.2.3).

Based on his "observations" (a term of art that substitutes in the latest AIA standard forms for the more inclusive term "supervision" used in earlier versions), the architect determines amounts owing to the contractor and issues certificates for payment. (¶2.2.6.) The architect is also the principal interpreter of the contract document, and the initial arbiter of disputes between the owner and the contractor relating to execution or progress of the work or interpretation of the contract documents. If the architect's initial decision on such matters is unacceptable to either party, provision is made for arbitration.

The architect is specifically authorized to reject work that does not conform to the contract documents, to order the contractor to stop work, and to require special inspection or testing of the work.

The architect is also empowered to review shop drawings, to prepare change orders, to order minor changes in the work, to conduct inspections, to determine the dates of substantial completion and final completion, and to issue a final certificate for payment.

Notwithstanding his discretionary functions, the architect is, by almost universal practice, "not responsible for . . . the acts or omissions of the Contractor, Subcontractors, or any of their agents or employees, or any other persons performing any of the Work." (¶2.2.4.)

---

[3]The American Institute of Architects has promulgated a separate form—AIA Document A201/CM—for use on projects utilizing construction management. In most respects, the form is the same as AIA Document A201; the only significant differences relate to the legal interrelationships among the owner, the contractor; and a party not identified in AIA Document A201—the construction manager.

4.3.2. The Owner

The owner's principal responsibility is to fund the work, so that payments can be made as prescribed in the contract. He is also required to provide appropriate liability and property insurance, and to furnish all surveys describing the physical characteristics and utility locations at the site. He must secure and pay for necessary easements. He must provide information and services within his control promptly in order to avoid delay in progress of the work.

All the owner's instructions are issued to the contractor through the architect. This requirement ensures centralized administration and permits the owner to avoid assuming, even inadvertently, any of the contractor's direction and control of the means, methods, techniques, and sequences of construction—all of which are the contractor's responsibility. The owner may delegate certain responsibilities to the architect in the contract, such as approval of subcontractors, approval of change orders, and temporary suspension of the work.

4.3.3. The Contractor

The principal objective in construction contracting is, of course, to secure the services of an entity or organization skilled in the methods and techniques of construction and in the management of construction operations. AIA Document A201 provides that "[t]he Contractor shall supervise and direct the Work, using his best skill and attention. He shall be solely responsible for all construction means, methods, techniques, sequences and procedures and for coordinating all portions of the Work under the Contract." (¶4.3.1.)

The contractor is also required to provide and pay for "all labor, materials, equipment, tools, construction equipment and machinery, water, heat, utilities, transportation, and other facilities. . . ." (¶4.4.1). Exceptions, if any, will be noted if the owner is to furnish any materials or services. The contractor is liable and must pay for all applicable sales, consumer, and use taxes as part of the cost of labor and materials. Consistent with the foregoing provisions, the contractor is expressly responsible to the owner for the acts and omissions of all employees and all subcontractors, their agents and their employees, and all other persons performing any of the work under the contract.

The contractor is also responsible for scheduling the work, and on most large projects that is his most important and time-consuming responsibility. Immediately after he secures the contract, he must prepare and submit an estimated progress schedule indicating the dates for starting and completing the various stages of construction. He must also revise the schedule as required while work is in progress.

In order to facilitate effective administration of the contract, the contractor is required to keep on file at the site copies of all drawings, specifications, addenda, change orders, approved shop drawings, and field orders. These documents are available to the architect at all times and become the property of the owner upon completion of the work.

AIA Document A201 contains elaborate provisions with respect to shop drawings, inclusively defined to mean "drawings, diagrams, schedules and other data specially prepared for the Work by the Contractor or any Subcontractor, manufacturer, supplier or distributor to illustrate some portion of the Work." (Article 4.12.1). These provisions require the contractor to review, approve and submit shop drawings to the architect, noting, at the time of submission, any deviation in the shop drawings from the requirements of the contract. The architect must then review the shop drawings, "but only for conformance with the design concept of the Work and with the information given in the Contract Documents" (Article 2.2.14).

The contractor must make any corrections in the shop drawings specified by the architect. The architect's approval of shop drawings does not relieve the contractor from responsibility for any deviation from contract requirements unless the architect, having been informed of the deviation by the contractor in writing at the time of submission, has given his written approval to such deviation.

4.3.4. Subcontractors

A general contractor will usually coordinate and manage the work. At the same time, the general contractor will subcontract portions of the work to recognized trades contractors who specialize in electrical, mechanical, foundation, finishing and other discrete phases of the work. As much as 85 percent of the total value of a contract may be subcontracted in this way. Subcontractual relationships are thus of primary importance. (See Chapter 3.)

Like the architect, the subcontractor is not a party to the construction contract between the owner and the contractor. However, standard-form subcontracts often incorporate by reference all the documents comprising the general contract—a practice that is explicitly sanctioned by the General Conditions (Article 5.3.1).

Why, then, are subcontractual relationships covered in such detail in the typical construction contract? The answer lies in the control sought to be imposed by the owner and the architect over subcontracting operations. This is accomplished by requiring the contractor to follow certain procedures in selecting subcontractors and executing contracts with them.

Article 5.2 of AIA Document A201 sets forth these procedures in detail. Before award of the contract, the successful bidder must furnish the architect a written list of the subcontractors proposed for principal portions of the work. The owner and the architect are specifically granted the right to object to any subcontractor so identified by the successful bidder. In the event there is an objection, the bidder may either withdraw his bid prior to award or submit a substitute subcontractor. Should substitution increase the bid price, the owner may either accept it or disqualify the bid.

If the owner or architect refuses to accept a designated subcontractor after award of the contract, the contractor must then propose an acceptable substitute. The contract amount is then increased or decreased by the difference in cost occasioned by the substitution, followed by an appropriate change order. Article 5.2.2 confirms, in this connection, that "[t]he Contractor shall not contract with any . . . person or entity to whom the Owner or the Architect has made reasonable objection . . ."

Article 9 of AIA Document A201 defines the contractual relations required between the contractor and the subcontractors. It governs such matters as performance of the work by subcontractors, applications for payment, and submission of claims.

The most important of these matters is payments to subcontractors. Article 9.5.2 requires the contractor to pay each subcontractor, upon receipt of payment from the owner, an amount reflecting the percentage of completion allowed to the contractor on account of the subcontractor's work. This is an important provision, since contractors may otherwise delay payments to subcontractors in order to preserve cash flow. Its practical effect is tempered, however, by Article 9.5.4, which specifically states: "Neither the Owner nor the Architect shall have any obligation to pay or to see to the payment of any moneys to any Subcontractor except as may otherwise be required by law." Except for mechanics' liens, the subcontractor's legal recourse, in the event of a dispute, is solely against the contractor.

4.4. INDEMNIFICATION

Article 4.18 of AIA Document A201 contains important indemnification provisions. The contractor is required to indemnify and hold harmless the owner and the architect (and their agents and employees)

> from and against all claims, damages, losses and expenses, including but not limited to attorneys' fees, arising out of or resulting from the performance of the Work, provided that any such claim, damage, loss or expense (1) is attributable to bodily injury, sickness, disease or death, or to injury to or destruction of tangible property (other than the Work itself) including the loss of use resulting therefrom, and (2) is caused in whole or in part by any negligent act or omission of the Contractor, any Subcontractor, anyone directly or indirectly employed by any of them or anyone for whose acts any of them may be liable, regardless of whether or not it is caused in part by a party indemnified hereunder. Such obligation shall not be construed to negate, abridge, or otherwise reduce any other right or obligation of indemnity which would otherwise exist. . . . [¶4.18.1.]

Article 4.18.2 makes clear that the contractor's indemnification is not subject to limitations on amounts payable imposed by workmen's compensation or similar acts. Article 4.18.3 provides that the contractor's liability as indemnitor does not extend to liability of the architect arising out of preparation or approval of plans, drawings and the like or the architect's directions or instructions (or failure to give the same).

These indemnification provisions arise out of the contractor's presumed control of the work. If, during the construction period, an employee of the contractor or a member of the public is injured, for example, he may claim damages against the contractor. If the plaintiff can show that the injury was caused by the contractor's negligence, he has laid the legal basis for recovery. But a plaintiff may sue the owner and the architect as well as the contractor. The owner's duties as a property owner may subject him to liability. The architect's failure to detect the contractor's negligence in visits to the site may do likewise.

In either event, the negligence of the owner or architect can be deemed secondary or passive negligence. To shift the risk of such secondary liability, the parties typically provide for indemnification of the architect and owner by the contractor. This is of particular importance where an injured employee of the contractor invokes the workmen's compensation laws. Under those laws, when the contractor or his insurance carrier has paid the required statutory amounts for workmen's compensation, the contractor is ordinarily released from further liability for common-law negligence. The plaintiff may nonetheless sue the architect and the owner for common-law negligence in an amount not limited by statute. Thus, the architect and the owner may be held liable for damages far in excess of those imposed on the contractor under workmen's compensation. The contractor's indemnification protects against this risk and is thought to be equitable, given his control of the work.

The indemnification provision is not unlimited. It covers only injury or damage arising from the negligent acts or omissions of the contractor. Moreover, indemnification does not protect the architect against liability arising out of work performed by him or his giving or failure to give directions (if such giving or failure is the primary cause of the injury); nor does it extend to injury or damage to the work itself. Thus, it does not cover a claim by the owner that the contractor has failed to construct a building according to the contract documents. Finally, indemnification covers only specified claimants (employees of the contractor or a subcontractor or members of the public) and specified property damage (damage to neighboring or adjacent property caused by construction operations such as excavation).

4.5. ROYALTIES AND PATENTS

The growing use of proprietary building systems makes the possibility of patent infringement a source of concern in construction contracting. A proprietary system or process may be specified by the architect. In that event, a license fee or royalty will be noted in the specifications and reflected in the contractor's bid price. If the requirement of a fee is omitted, the owner and the contractor may become liable for claims of infringement. There is also the possibility that the contractor may use a proprietary system or process in his own operations, without the knowledge of the owner or architect.

To account for infringement liabilities, Article 4.17 of AIA Document A201 requires the contractor to pay all royalties and license fees and to defend all suits or claims for infringement of patent rights. The Article also requires the contractor to "save the owner harmless" from any loss arising from infringement, except for designs or processes specified by the owner.

4.6. MISCELLANEOUS PROVISIONS

Article 7 of AIA Document A201 assembles under one heading several unrelated provisions. Of these, the most important concern bonds (Article 7.5.1), and arbitration of disputes (Article 7.9). These subjects are described briefly below and are covered in detail elsewhere. (See Chapters 8 and 12.)

Article 7.5 gives the owner the right to require the contractor to furnish performance and payment bonds for labor and materials. The purpose of such surety bonds is to protect the owner against the contractor's default and to assure that the project will be completed in accordance with the contract documents and turned over to the owner free and clear of liens and encumbrances.

Although Article 7.5 makes the bonding requirement discretionary with the owner, most fixed-price, competitively-bid contracts routinely contemplate bonds. Indeed, where public construction is involved, the owner—a government agency, school district, or similar public body—may be subject to a statutory requirement to obtain appropriate bonding. In any event, if bonds are required, the contractor must pay the necessary premiums and must ordinarily submit evidence of bonding to the owner before commencing work or "not later than the date of execution of the contract."

Construction contracts invite disputes. These may be settled administratively by the architect; if they are not, the parties must seek resolution through litigation or arbitration. Because litigation is expensive and time-consuming, many construction contracts mandate arbitration to resolve disputes. Article 7.9 does so and incorporates by reference the Construction Industry Arbitration Rules of the American Arbitration Association. Arbitration is thought to permit persons familiar with the often technical nature of construction contract disputes to decide the issues presented more expeditiously than a court of law.

The enforceability of agreements to arbitrate varies according to applicable state law. If enforceable, however, such an agreement usually results in an arbitral award. Absent bad faith on the part of the arbitrators or failure to meet the procedural requirements of the law governing arbitration, the award is then itself enforceable, and judgment may be entered upon it in accordance with applicable law in any court of competent jurisdiction.

Not all construction-related controversies are settled by arbitration. Disputes involving personal injuries or damage to property of third persons are generally litigated, since such claimants do not have a contractual relationship with the defendant, as do the owner and the contractor, and thus are not bound by the arbitration provision in the construction contract.

4.7. TIME

The General Conditions measure the time within which the work covered by the contract must be completed, from date of commencement of the work to date of substantial completion. The date of commencement is established by the owner's notice to proceed or, absent such notice, by the date of the contract. The date of substantial completion is defined in AIA Document A201 as "the Date certified by the architect when construction is sufficiently complete, in accordance with the Contract Documents, so the Owner can occupy or utilize the Work . . . for the use for which it is intended." (Article 8.1.3.) The General Conditions characterize all time limits stated in the contract documents as "of the essence of the Contract" (Article 8.2.1), a condition not otherwise implied by operation of law.

The General Conditions also deal with delays and extensions of time. If the contractor is delayed by any act or neglect of the owner or architect, by any separate contractor employed by the owner, by changes ordered in the work, or by "labor disputes, fire, unusual delay in transportation, unavoidable casualties or other causes beyond the Contractor's control," then the contract time may be extended by an official change order. (Article 8.3.1.) A claim for extension of time must be made in writing to the architect not later than 15 days after the occurrence of delay; "otherwise it shall be waived." (Article 8.3.2.)

4.8. PAYMENT

As is to be expected, the payment provisions of the General Conditions are elaborate. Article 9 ("Payments and Completion") of AIA Document A201 is the longest of the 14 articles comprising the General Conditions. Its provisions are described in detail elsewhere. (See Chapter 7.)

Adequate financing is obviously essential to a successful construction venture. Both the owner and the general contractor need to ensure that the other party has adequate financial resources to live up to his side of the bargain. The owner can protect himself by requiring the contractor to post performance and payment bonds. The general contractor, in turn, must receive assurances that the owner has enough funding to make payments as required by the contractual payment schedule. This is achieved through the mechanism of Article 3.2, which requires the owner to provide certain financial and other information to a potential general contractor before the contract documents are executed, if the potential general contractor so requests.

4.9. SAFETY

Detailed requirements are now imposed on employers (including construction contractors) by federal legislation, most notably the Occupational Safety and Health Act of 1970. In addition, state laws prescribe minimum standards, precautions, and programs that must be implemented for the safety of workers. The general conditions place the responsibility for initiating, maintaining and supervising safety programs squarely on the contractor, who must take precautions for the safety of and prevent injury, loss or damage to (1) employees and "all other persons who may be affected thereby" (including third parties); (2) work in place and materials and equipment not yet incorporated in the work; and (3) other property at the site or adjacent to it not scheduled for removal during construction. (Article 10.2.1.) If such property suffers damage or loss caused by the contractor or any subcontractor or other person employed by him, it must be remedied by the contractor. The owner commonly protects himself against third-party liability through appropriate public liability insurance. (See Chapter 9.)

4.10. CHANGES IN THE WORK

Construction contracts commonly permit the owner to order changes in the work. If such changes are "within the general scope of the Contract," they do not have the effect of invalidating it. (Article 12.1.2.)

Such changes may consist of additions, deletions or other revisions in the work. The contractual mechanism for effecting changes is the change order, defined as "a written order to the Contractor signed by the Owner and the Architect, issued after execution of the Contract, authorizing a change in the Work or an adjustment of the Contract Sum or the Contract Time." (Article 12.1.1.)

Change orders are frequently required when excavation work reveals unanticipated problems with subsurface conditions. (*See generally* §4.15 of this chapter.) The general conditions, in fact, usually contain a specific provision on that subject. If subsurface conditions are at variance with the conditions indicated in the contract, or differ materially from those ordinarily encountered in work of the character provided for in the contract, then "the Contract Sum shall be equitably adjusted by Change Order upon claim of either party made within twenty days after the first observance of the conditions." (Article 12.2.1.)

Litigation involving unanticipated subsurface conditions is common and is often unusually complex. A good introduction to the general flavor of such litigation is *Foster Construction C.A. & Williams Brothers Co. v. United States*, 435 F.2d 873 (Ct.Cl. 1970). In that case, the Department of Commerce engaged a joint venture to construct a 56-mile stretch of the Inter-American Highway in Costa Rica. The contract called, in part, for the construction of a bridge over the Terraba River. Although the contract represented that the riverbed was firm enough to anchor standard cofferdam supports, the joint venture claimed to have discovered, once construction started, that subsurface conditions were actually too soft to support the required sheet pilings. The Court of Claims agreed with the joint venture, and ordered the Commerce Department to adjust the contract price upward to cover the extra construction costs. The Court's long decision reflects the technical complexity of subsurface claims.[4]

If the contractor wants an increase in the contract sum or an extension of time, he must give the architect notice in writing within a reasonable time after occurrence of the event giving rise to such claim and before he proceeds to execute the work, except in an emergency endangering life or property.[5] The architect may, however, order minor changes in the work, not involving a change in the contract sum or the contract time, and may issue field orders which interpret the contract documents.

For a more detailed discussion of changes, see Chapter 5.

---

[4]Other examples of unanticipated subsurface conditions are subsurface rock (*Tobin Quarries, Inc. v. United States*, 114 Ct.Cl. 286, 84 F.Supp. 1021 (1949)); water (*Virginia Engineering Co. v. United States*, 101 Ct.Cl. 516 (1944)); erroneously-drawn contour lines (*Appeal of Poblete Construction Co.*, 68-1 B.C.A ¶6860 (1968)); and underground utility lines (*Nelse Mortensen & Co. v. United States*, 301 F.Supp. 635 (E.D. Wash. 1969)).

[5]*See, e.g., Appeals of Coleman Electric Co.*, 58-2 B.C.A. ¶1928 (1958).

4.11. UNCOVERING AND CORRECTION OF THE WORK

In the ordinary course of construction, portions of the work, such as foundations, are completed and covered before subsequent portions can be commenced. The General Conditions seek to preserve the architect's right to observe each portion before it becomes inaccessible by virtue of additional work. Thus, Article 13.1.1 of AIA Document A201 provides: "If any portion of the Work should be covered contrary to the request of the Architect . . ., it must, if required in writing by the Architect, be uncovered for his observation and shall be replaced at the Contractor's expense."

However, if work has been covered in the absence of the architect's specific request to observe it beforehand, subsequent uncovering and replacement will be at the owner's expense unless the work is found to be not in accordance with the contract documents. In the latter event, the contractor bears the cost. The additional work of uncovering and replacement, if chargeable to the owner, is the subject of a change order.

The contractor is required to correct all defective work at his own expense whether the defect is observed before the date of substantial completion, within one year thereafter, or within a longer period as prescribed by applicable law or the terms of any special guarantee under the contract. The contractor is also required to remove all defective or nonconforming work from the site at his expense and to bear the cost of making good any work of separate contractors that is destroyed or damaged by such removal or correction. If the contractor fails to correct the work, the owner may do so or elect to accept the work as is. In that event, a change order is issued to reflect an appropriate reduction in the contract sum; or, if final payment has already been made, the amount of the reduction must be paid by the contractor.

4.12. TERMINATION OF THE CONTRACT

The contract usually contains reciprocal provisions for termination by the contractor or the owner. Under the AIA standard form, the contractor may unilaterally terminate if the work is stopped for a period of 30 days for reasons other than his acts or omissions. (Article 14.1.1.) Causes of work stoppage enabling the contractor to terminate include an order of a court or public authority, the failure of the architect to issue a certificate for payment, or the owner's failure to make payment in respect of a certificate previously issued.

To effect termination, the contractor must give seven days' written notice to the owner and the architect. The contractor may then recover from the owner payment for all work executed and for "any proven loss sustained upon any materials, equipment, tools, construction equipment and machinery, including reasonable profit and damage." (Article 14.1.1.)

The owner's termination rights are, in effect, much broader than the contractor's. (Article 14.2.1.) The owner may terminate if:

— The contractor is adjudged a bankrupt, the contractor makes a general assignment for the benefit of creditors, or a receiver is appointed on account of his insolvency[6];

— The contractor fails persistently to supply enough properly skilled workmen or materials;

— The contractor fails to pay subcontractors or materialmen promptly;

— The contractor disregards applicable laws or regulations; or

— The contractor is culpable to a substantial violation of the contract.

To effect termination, the owner must give seven days' written notice to the contractor and his surety, if any. The owner may then take possession of the site and all equipment, machinery and materials thereon owned by the contractor, and may finish the work himself. If the unpaid balance of the contract sum exceeds the cost of finishing the work, the excess is then paid to the contractor. If such cost exceeds the unpaid balance, the contractor must pay the difference to the owner.

4.13. DRAWINGS

Working drawings depict graphically the characteristics and extent of the work. Together with the specifications (discussed in the next section of this chapter), they enable the contractor to prepare an informed proposal by describing and locating the elements of the work. To accomplish this, the working drawings show what is involved, and what the relevant physical dimensions are. The specifications, in turn, state what the materials are, how they are to function, and from what source they can be obtained.

Drawings and specifications are the owner's responsibility. A typical contract provision, contained in Section 3 of the General Conditions of Contract for Engineering Construction published by the Association of General Contractors, thus states:

> It is agreed that the Owner will be responsible for the adequacy of the Drawings and Specifications. The Owner, through the Engineer, or the Engineer as the Owner's representative, shall furnish Drawings and Specifications which adequately represent the requirements of the work to be performed under the Contract. All such drawings and representations shall be consistent with the Contract Documents and shall be true developments thereof. Drawings and specifications which adequately represent the work to be done shall be furnished prior to the time of entering the Contract. The Engineer may, during the life of the Contract, . . . , issue additional instructions, by means of drawings or other media, necessary to illustrate changes in the work.

---

[6]But bankruptcy termination clauses may no longer be enforceable after enactment of the new federal bankruptcy code. Under the new code, 11 U.S.C. §365(e), "an executory contract . . . may not be terminated or modified . . . solely because of a provision in such contract . . . that is conditioned on . . . the insolvency or financial condition of the debtor. . . ."

Some standard-form contracts (see Article 1.2.3, AIA Document A201) purport to create parity among the contract, drawings, and specifications. Others (most notably Section 2 of AGC's General Conditions of Contract for Engineering Construction) establish priorities among the various contract documents, so that one document prevails if there is a conflict among them. Disputes may arise between the owner and the contractor over (1) whether the drawings have indeed been incorporated, or (2) whether the contract specifications, or drawings control if there is a conflict among or between them.

Incorporation is simply a matter of appropriate contract drafting. An express reference in the contract to the drawings and specifications is required. "Where the plans and specifications are by express terms made a part of the contract, the terms of the plans and specifications will control with the same force as though physically incorporated in the very contract itself." *Buchman Plumbing Co. v. Regents of the University of Minnesota*, 298 Minn. 328, 215 N.W.2d 479, 485 (1974).

More difficult to resolve are conflicts among or between the contract, specifications, and drawings. In *Oberg v. City of Los Angeles*, 132 Cal. App.2d 151, 281 P.2d 591 (1955), a contractor sought additional compensation for installing membrane waterproofing over concrete joints in connection with the construction of a subway. The city asserted that no additional compensation was due because the specifications required membrane waterproofing. The contractor contended that the contract required only the installation of rubber waterstop and that membrane waterproofing was not designated in the contract or shown in the drawings. Good construction practice did not require that both methods be applied at the same joint.

The court found, however, for the city. Since the contract and drawings omitted any mention of membrane waterproofing, but did not expressly preclude its use, the specific requirement of the specifications was deemed controlling. This was so even though that requirement was not mentioned in the contract but merely referred to in other documents incorporated by reference in the contract. ". . . [A] plan of work is subsidiary to the contract, and the latter is controlling in case of a discrepancy, and where the language thereof will permit, the specifications will be construed so as to uphold the validity of the contract."

A similar result was reached in a later California case, *Meyers v. Housing Authority of Stanislaus*, 241 Cal. App.2d 721, 50 Cal.Rptr. 856 (1966). The contractor in that case brought a declaratory judgment action to construe its obligations under a housing development construction contract. The contract in question expressly provided that "in case of difference between Drawings and Technical Specifications, the Technical Specifications shall govern." The question presented to the court was whether the contractor was required to install sewer and drainage lines and manholes beyond the project limits. Part of the lines extended beyond the project limits as shown on the architectural plot plan. The contractor contended that the drawings delimited its responsibilities under the contract. The court found, however, for the defendant housing authority. The decision was based on the technical specifications' requirement that the contractor "provided all materials and appurtenances necessary for the complete installation of each utility, whether or not all such materials and appurtenances are shown on the drawings or described in the specifications."

Although specifications may prevail over drawings inconsistent with them, they may not contravene the provisions of the contract itself. In *Jim Mahoney, Inc. v. The Galokee Corporation,* 214 Kan. 754, 522 P.2d 428 (1974), the contractor sued to recover the balance due on a nursing home construction contract. The owner counterclaimed for the cost of repairs necessary to complete the project and comply with the plans and specifications. Such costs were alleged to include the cost of asphalting the driveways and packing area. The contract incorporated the plans and specifications by reference. The specifications made no mention of asphalt, but the drawings did. The contract itself provided: "Parking and drives to be 4 [-inch] gravel base, sealed and oiled, chips applied and rolled." The court allowed, as an element of the owner's counterclaim, the cost of applying chips and oil. It disallowed the greater cost of applying an asphalt surface, finding that the positive language of the contract prevailed over the conflicting requirement of the drawing.

Reference to the specifications in the drawings may serve to enlarge the contractor's obligations where the specifications set forth requirements as to which the drawings are silent. In *Wolfe v. Warfield,* 266 Md. 621, 296 A.2d 158 (1972), the owner sued the contractor for damages arising from the contractor's failure to adhere to the specifications. The contract did not mention the specifications and simply provided that the contractor was to perform all of the work shown in the drawings prepared by the owner's architect. The drawings, however, made specific reference to the specifications. On this basis, the court found the contractor liable for failing to meet the requirements of the specifications, necessarily included in the drawings by reference. The *Wolfe* case may be reconciled with *Jim Mahoney, supra.* In *Wolfe,* the contract itself was silent; the amplification provided by the specifications did not conflict with the contract but merely added necessary detail. In *Jim Mahoney* the contract contained express language in conflict with the drawings and was therefore found to prevail.

4.14. SPECIFICATIONS

As noted in the previous section, the specifications provide technical information concerning building materials, components, systems and equipment indicated on the drawings with respect to quality, performance characteristics, and the results to be achieved by the application of construction methods. Notwithstanding any statement in the general conditions seeking to create parity among the construction documents, specifications historically have taken precedence over drawings where conflict between the two exists. As a written rather than graphic document, the specifications are most readily understood by courts and arbitral tribunals and thus carry heavier weight in litigation or arbitration.

4.14.1. Organization: The Uniform System

Until recently, the organization of specifications has been left to the individual preference of the architect or engineer preparing them. This led to a wide and confusing diversity of method. In 1963, the Construction Specifications Institute published the

"CSI Format for Building Specifications," which called for a division-section concept of specification organization and established 16 basic groupings. Each grouping is based on an interrelationship of the four fundamental factors of materials, trades, functions of work, and location of specified work.[7] The Uniform System developed by CSI, and subsequently adopted in the Uniform Construction Index published by several professional organizations, fixes in name and sequence the following divisions:

1. General requirements	9. Finishes
2. Site work	10. Specialties
3. Concrete	11. Equipment
4. Masonry	12. Furnishings
5. Metals	13. Special construction
6. Carpentry	14. Conveying systems
7. Moisture protection	15. Mechanical
8. Doors, windows, and glass	16. Electrical

Within divisions, the more commonly applicable sections are listed together under the heading "broadscope"; the less typical fall under the head of "narrowscope." Division 1 contains general provisions applicable to the work as a whole; divisions 2 through 16 contain technical provisions applicable to various types of construction, components, and equipment. Division 1 may thus serve as a modification of or addition to the general conditions.

4.14.2. General Requirements

Division 1 contains a summary of the work, incorporates the specifications as part of the contract documents, may restate the general location of the work and call attention to special site conditions, and mentions also whether the work is to be accomplished under a single contract or separate ones. Division 1 also covers project meetings, submittals, quality control, temporary facilities and controls, material and equipment, and project closeout. Submittals include, among other items, construction schedules, network analysis, progress reports, survey data, and shop drawings. Subsurface soil reports are excluded from the specifications and contract documents. Division 1, in general, amplifies certain provisions broadly treated in the general conditions, particularly those related to the contractor's operations at the site.

4.14.3. Types of Technical Specifications

The technical provisions of building specifications are of two kinds: procedure specifications and performance specifications. The former specify in detail the quality, properties, and composition of materials, as well as the procedures and construction

---

[7]*See also* Uniforms System for Construction Specifications, Data Filing & Cost Accounting (Title One—Buildings). AIA Document K103 is an example of the Uniform System.

methods to be employed; the latter prescribe performance characteristics on completion of a component or system, without stipulating the methods by which such characteristics are to be attained.

Performance specifications are most commonly used in the procurement of mechanical and electrical equipment, whose performance characteristics can be measured by satisfactory tests. With procedure specifications, by contract, the sufficiency of the architect's design must be relied upon for the ultimate intended result. Compliance with technical specifications is most often verified by testing procedures, which themselves may be set forth in the specifications. Such procedures—in reality, quality control tests—may measure the strength of concrete, water absorption of brick, absorption coefficients of acoustical materials and similar properties.

If manufactured equipment or components are involved, performance tests are required. Failure to meet such tests may permit recourse to the manufacturer through product warranties. Standard specifications covering specific materials and products may also be incorporated by reference, particularly where they describe the details, qualities, functions, and sizes of a material or product without mentioning a trade name. This is particularly true of federal specifications in connection with government construction contracts.

Technical specifications may be "closed," meaning that they specify only one proprietary product, or "open," thereby permitting the contractor to choose from among the products of several manufacturers. Open specifications are, in turn, of several kinds: (1) contractor's option specifications, where only trade names are mentioned, and unlisted products are not considered for substitution; (2) product approval specifications, which, in addition to listing trade names, permit a request for substitutions by a bidder prior to the bid date, with approval issued in the form of an addendum; (3) substitute bid specifications, which list one or more trade names but permit the bidder to attach to his bid form a proposal for substitute materials together with any related price adjustment; and (4) "or approved equal" specifications, which list one or more trade names followed by the phrase "or approved equal." (The latter deserve special note.)

4.14.4. "Or Approved Equal"

Use of this phrase in specifications opens up the widest possible competition and permits contractors to shop around for the best bargain, with resulting cost savings to the owner. Nonetheless, use of the phrase has caused much controversy and immediately raises the question of how equality can be established and who is to be the judge of it.

To meet these questions, the specifications often include a statement to this effect:

> Wherever used in these Specifications, the phrase "or approved equal" means that materials, components, and equipment proposed for use in lieu of those named will be considered acceptable only if they will, in the opinion of the architect, perform adequately the functions imposed by the general design, and if they meet the minimum standards in all respects of those of the named item.

Even a provision such as the foregoing does not fully resolve the problems presented by use of "or approved equal" language. Since the approval of the architect is required before a substitute item may be used, a bidder may include such an item in his bid only to learn after execution of the contract that the architect does not consider it equal. And if the substitute is accepted, it may be difficult to determine if the owner is entitled to a credit attributable to its reduced cost.

Notwithstanding such problems, the pro-competitive feature of an "or approved equal" provision has commended it to public authorities. State law governing public works frequently requires its incorporation into public contracts. California, for example, prohibits specification by brand or trade names ". . . unless the specification lists at least two brands or trade names of comparable quality or utility and is followed by the words 'or equal' so that bidders may furnish any equal material, product, thing, or service."[8]

4.15. SUBSURFACE CONDITIONS

Frequent sources of dispute in large-scale construction contracting are subsurface conditions at the site. Often such conditions are different from those anticipated by the contractor, making construction more difficult and costly. The question then arises whether the additional cost is compensable by the owner or whether the contractor has assumed the risk in submitting his bid and entering into the contract of construction.

Section 2.1.2 of AIA Document A701 (Instructions to Bidders) requires each bidder to represent that he "has visited the site, has familiarized himself with the local conditions under which the Work is to be performed and has correlated his observations with the requirements of the proposed Contract Documents." At the same time, Section 12.1.6 of the General Conditions (AIA Document A201) provides, as noted above, that if "concealed conditions encountered in the performance of the Work below the surface of the ground . . . be at variance with the conditions indicated by the Contract Documents, or [if] unknown physical conditions below the surface of the ground . . . , differing materially from those ordinarily encountered and generally recognized as inherent in work of the character provided for in this Contract, be encountered," then the contract sum shall be equitably adjusted by a change order.

A great variety of subsurface conditions may fall within the changes clause of the contract. Government contract cases are illustrative and include such conditions as large amounts of underground water from hidden springs; quicksand; soil different from that anticipated, making compaction more difficult; and large pieces of rock abandoned underground by a previous contractor during the construction of bridge abutments 50 years earlier.[9]

Although the facts of litigated cases vary widely, the issues upon which they turn

---

[8]Cal. Gov't. Code §4380.

[9]*See, e.g., Hall Construction Co.,* ASBCA 7627, 1962 BCA ¶3590 (1962); *Blout Brothers Construction Corp.,* ASBCA 4780, 59-2 BCA ¶2316 (1959); *Bregman Construction Corp.,* ASBCA 9000, 1963 BCA ¶4426; *Warfield Construction Co.,* IBCA 196, 1962 BCA ¶3374.

are recurrent: (1) Did the owner make any representation, express or implied, upon which the contractor relied, as to subsurface conditions? (2) Was the contractor under an obligation to investigate subsurface conditions independently? If so, did he meet that obligation?

These issues arose in *Branna Construction Corp. v. West Allegheny Joint School Authority*, 430 Pa. 214, 242 A.2d 244 (1968). In *Branna*, a contractor sued a school authority and its architect for recovery of extra costs incurred in the performance of excavation work. The contractor alleged that, immediately upon commencing excavation of a foundation for a high school building, he discovered that test borings supplied in the plans and specifications were inaccurate and materially misleading as to the subsurface conditions actually encountered. The contractor also alleged that he had relied on the test borings and did not have sufficient time within which to make his own investigation. The contractor prevailed in the trial court and obtained a jury verdict of $50,000. The defendants then appealed.

The appellate court looked first to the general conditions. These disclaimed, as to core test borings, any responsibility by the owner or the architect for subsurface conditions. The general conditions also stated: "Any data concerning subsurface conditions . . . has [sic] been obtained by the Owner for its own use only in designing this project, and bidders shall not rely on such data in estimating contract costs." Bidders were specifically required to make their own investigation of existing subsurface conditions, including evaluation of test borings. The general conditions also required the removal of "all material encountered including earth or rock formations, the cost of such excavation being included in the contract price at the time of bidding." The construction contract itself, however, did not expressly exclude from its terms the references in the general conditions to subsurface conditions. On the basis of that omission, the contractor urged that he was entitled to rely on the test borings. The appellate court rejected this argument. It found no knowing or fraudulent misrepresentation of the test borings. It also found that the contractor did not lack the necessary time in which to undertake his own investigation. "Viewing the Contract as a whole," said the court, "it is difficult to imagine in what way the [school authority] could have fashioned any stronger or clearer language indicating that [the contractor] should not rely upon the test borings, and that if different subsurface conditions were encountered, [the contractor] would be solely responsible to bear the increased financial burden." Reimbursement of the contractor's additional costs was therefore denied.

A contrary result was reached in *E.H. Morrill Co. v. State of California*, 65 Cal.2d 787, 423 P.2d 551 (1967). In *Morrill*, the contract documents contained special site conditions, which provided in relevant part:

> The site is situated on a terminal moraine. The soil is composed of granite boulders, sand, and pebbles. Boulders which may be encountered vary in size from one to four feet in diameter. It varies from six feet to twelve feet in all directions.

Once construction started, the parties realized that the boulders were substantially larger and more concentrated than represented. Although the contractor had visited the site, as required by the general conditions, to "satisfy himself as to . . . subsurface materials or obstacles to be encountered," he had relied on the state's representations in submitting his bid. The court found for the contractor despite the general conditions' requirement of site investigation. It held that the state had not merely reported the results of an investigation, but had instead made a positive assertion of fact as to subsurface conditions. The court also accorded significance to the placement of the disclaimer in the general conditions, while the representations appeared in the special conditions. It concluded that the state's responsibility for affirmative representations could not be overcome by general clauses requiring the contractor to investigate the site and assume responsibility for the work.[10]

Although contract disclaimers will generally be upheld, they will not suffice to overcome material defects in the plans or specifications or affirmative misrepresentations or non-disclosure as to subsurface conditions.[11] The contract may, of course, address the problem of subsurface conditions directly; AIA standard-form documents adopt this approach, as do federal construction contracts, which typically contain "differing site conditions" clauses. Such contracts contemplate an equitable adjustment in the contract price if unexpected subsurface conditions cause an increase in the contractor's cost. The effect of such contract provisions is to shift some or all of the risk of added cost attributable to unexpected subsurface conditions to the owner.

4.16. EXTRINSIC CONSIDERATIONS

The four corners of the contract documents will generally determine the rights and obligations of the parties. Prior or contemporaneous oral agreements are thus usually disregarded by courts in construing contract provisions. This is particularly so when the terms of the contract are unambiguous.[12] If contract terms are ambiguous, however, courts will often look at the surrounding facts and circumstances to determine the parties' true intent. In so doing, courts will apply the "parol evidence rule," which holds that verbal or parol evidence may be admitted to identify and apply the terms of the writing to the subject matter or to make definite what has been indefinitely expressed.[13]

Similarly, a party to a construction contract dispute may seek to introduce as evidence custom or usage in the industry. If the contract is clear as to the matter under contention, courts will not accept custom or usage to alter the controlling contract provision.[14] In order to have the force of law in an applicable case, custom must have notoriety, certainty, and uniformity. It must have continued over a sufficient period of time to be well-known to the parties or, in the alternative, must be so general and

---

[10]*Contra, Daniel O'Connell's Sons, Inc. v. Commonwealth*, 349 Mass. 642, 212 N.E.2d 219 (1965); *Wunderlich v. State of California*, 65 Cal.2d 777, 423 P.2d 545 (1967).

[11]*See City of Salinas v. Souza and McCue Construction Co.*, 66 Cal.2d 217, 424 P.2d 921 (1967).

[12]*See, e.g., Levco Construction Corp. v. State of New York*, 43 App.Div. 759, 350 N.Y.S.2d 219 (1973).

[13]*See, e.g., Helm v. Speith*, 298 Ky. 225, 182 S.W.2d 635 (1944).

[14]*See, e.g., Weber v. Milpitas County Water District*, 201 Cal.App.2d 666, 20 Cal.Rptr. 45 (1962).

well-established that its knowledge is presumed. Even then, evidence of a different course of dealing between the litigants may be more persuasive to a court than custom or usage.[15]

Courts may also read into construction contracts implied terms. Chief among these is the requirement that the owner furnish the contractor with the site. Thus, in *Hensler v. City of Los Angeles*, 124 Cal. App.2d 71, 268 P.2d 12 (1954), the court stated: ". . . [I]n every construction contract the law implies a covenant, where necessary, that the owner will furnish a selected site of operations to the contractor in order to enable him to adequately carry on the construction and complete the work agreed on." Another commonly implied term is the requirement that the contractor perform his obligations in a workmanlike manner. Thus, where a contractor constructed a house whose walls and ceilings cracked because of a sinking foundation, the court found an implied promise on the part of the contractor that he would construct a foundation sufficient to sustain a house of the type built.[16]

Still another implied (and often express) contract obligation is that the work be designed and constructed in accordance with local building codes, zoning ordinances, and similar laws. Compliance in design matters is primarily the responsibility of the architect employed on the work. Compliance with laws affecting the construction process itself—such as those relating to workers' safety and rights of adjacent landowners—generally rests with the contractor.

Finally, the owner is deemed to have made the implied promise that neither he nor the design professional he employs will hinder the contractor's performance—for example, by failing to pass upon the sufficiency of shop drawings in a reasonable time or failing to obtain easements or rights in the land of others necessary for the project. And if there are separate contractors, each is deemed by implication to have promised to cooperate with the others.

4.17. CONCLUSION

If the contract is unclear or ambiguous, however, extrinsic evidence outside the four corners of the contract will often supply meaning sufficient to yield resolution of a dispute.

4.18. ADDITIONAL SOURCE MATERIALS

General:

Blom-Cooper, L.J., "Building contracts—implying a 'term' or exemption clause?" 23 Sol. 147 (1956).

---

[15]*See, e.g., Korner Roofing & Sheet Metal Co. v. Smaylie Brothers, Inc.*, 118 Ohio App. 461, 188 N.E.2d 802 (1962).

[16]*Phillips v. Wick*, 288 S.W.2d 899 (Tex.Ct.Civ.App. 1956).

Laedlein, C. E., III, "Differing Site Conditions," 19 AF. L.R. 1 (1977).

Trimpi, John G., "Contracts—Changed conditions in construction contracts in North Carolina," 7 Wake Forest L.Rev. 660 (1971).

Note, "Implied terms in building agreements," 63 L.Soc.Gaz. 391 (1966).

Note, "Time for completion of building contracts," 100 Sol.J. 275 (1956).

Anno., "Building or construction contract providing for installment or 'program' payments as entire or divisible," 22 A.L.R.2d 1343.

Anno., "Cost of correction or completion, or difference in value, as measure of damages for breach of construction contract," 76 A.L.R.2d 805.

Anno., "Duty of contractor to warn owner of defects in subsurface conditions," 73 A.L.R. 3d 1213.

Anno., "Liabilities or risk of loss arising out of contract for repairs or additions to, or installations in, existing building which, without fault of either party is destroyed pending performance," 28 A.L.R.3d 788.

Anno., "Parol evidence as to limitation on cost of structure in builder's action on written cost-plus-fee construction contract," 84 A.L.R.2d 1324.

Anno., "Satisfaction of owner, construction and effect of provision in private building and construction contract that work must be done to," 44 A.L.R.2d 1114.

Parties:

Davidson, K. L., "Liability of Architects," 13 Trial 20 (1977).

Drake, N. A., "Rights and responsibilities of various parties concerned with the default of a construction contract," 3 Ill. C.L.E. 73 (1966).

Durnford, J. W., "Liability of the builder, architect and engineer for perishing and other defects in construction," 2 R.J.T. 161 (1967).

Hart, B. C., "Representing the architect in dealing with the owner and contractor," 7 Forum 197 (1972).

Hoeveler, W. M., "Building failure and the respective liabilities of the architect and the engineer," 8 Forum 481 (1973).

Kahn, R. H., "The Changing Role of the Architect," 23 St. Louis U.L.J. 222 (1979).

Kaskell, R. L., Jr., "Representing the contractor in dealing with the architect, owner and subcontractors," 7 Forum 215 (1972).

Killeen, J., "Owner liability for construction costs," 52 SB J. 526 (1977).

Maurer, C. D., Jr., "Architects, engineers and hold harmless clauses," 1976 Ins. L.J. 725 (1976).

McCormick, J. M., "Representing the owner in contracting with the architect and contractor," 8 Forum 435 (1973).

Milicevich, Mirko A., "Contracts: Liability of architect to owner for defects in plans furnished by a consultant," 48 Calif.L.Rev. 151 (1960).

Moot, R. E., "Future storm clouds for surety and contractor . . . black-white confrontation in the '70s," 6 Forum.

Murphy, G. W., "Impact of the 1976 edition of AIA Document A201 on the liability of architects and engineers to the construction surety for negligent certification of payments," 45 Ins. Counsel J. 200 (1978).

Solomon, D., "Double function of architects under R.I.B.A. contracts," 106 L.J. 55 (1956).

Sweet, J., "Owner-architect-contractor: another eternal triangle," 47 Calif. L.Rev. 645 (1959).

Note, "Finality of architect's final certificate," 22 Sol. 207 (1955).

Note, "Roles of architect and contractor in construction management," 6 U.Mich.J.L.Ref. 447 (1973).

Anno., "Applicability of res ipsa loquitur in suit by third person against contractor for injury or damage occurring after completion and acceptance of work," 84 A.L.R.2d 697.

Anno., "Architect's liability for personal injury or death from improper plans or design," 59 A.L.R.2d 1081.

Anno., "Construction contractor's liability to contractee for defects or insuffiiency of work attributable to the latter's plans and specifications," 6 A.L.R. 3d 1394.

Anno., "Effect of compensation of architect or building contractor of express provision in private building contract limiting the cost of the building," 20 A.L.R.3d 778.

Anno., "Liability of builder or subcontractor for insufficiency of building resulting from latent defects in materials used," 61 A.L.R. 3d 792.

Anno., "Negligence of building or construction contractor as ground of liability upon his part for injury or damage to third person occurring after completion and acceptance of the work," 58 A.L.R.2d 865.

Anno., "Right of architect or engineer licensed in one state to recover compensation for services rendered in another state, or in connection with construction in another state, where he was not licensed in the latter state," 32 A.L.R.3d 1151.

Anno., "Right of architect to compensation under contractual provision that fee is to be paid from construction loan funds," 92 A.L.R.3d 509.

Anno., "Tort liability of project architect for economic damages suffered by contractor," 65 A.L.R.3d 249.

Indemnity:

Anderson, Ross A., "Indemnity provisions in Wisconsin construction contracts," 60 Marguette L.Rev. 1083 (1977).

Hyde, Joe T., "Indemnity dilemma: perfectly obvious or hopelessly confused?" 24 Baylor L.Rev. 132 (1972).

McCormick, J. M., "Exculpatory and indemnity clauses binding upon sureties," 7 Forum 225 (1972).

Note, "Contracts—indemnity agreements will protect the indemnitee from his own negligence only if the obligation is expressed in unequivocal terms," 50 Tex.L.Rev. 520 (1972).

Anno., "Building contractor's liability, upon bond or other argument to indemnify owner, for injury or death of third persons resulting from owner's negligence," 27 A.L.R.3d 663.

Anno., "Duty of construction contractor to indemnify contractee held liable for injury to third person, in absence of express contract for indemnity," 97 A.L.R.2d 616.

Anno., "Fixed-price construction contract, government's right to indemnify under, for negligence of contractor," 25 L.Ed.2d 224.

Anno., "Liability of subcontractor upon bond or other agreement indemnifying general contractor against liability for damage to person or property," 68 A.L.R.3d 7.

Performance and Payment Bonds:

Greaves, T. G., Jr., "Payment and performance bonds for private construction: the AIA forms," 1963 ABA Insurance Section N&CL 272 (1963).

Milana, J. P., "Performance bond and the underlying contract: the bond obligations do not include all of the contract obligations," 12 Forum 187 (1976).

Webster, W. H., "Performance bond surety's dilemma when both principal and obligee claim the other is in default: a guide through no man's land," 12 Forum 238 (1976).

Note, "Payment and performance bonds—right of materialmen and laborers to sue as third party beneficiaries," 30 N.Y.U.L.Rev. 1447 (1955).

Arbitration:

Aksen, G., "Resolving construction contract disputes through arbitration," 23 Arb.J. 141 (1968).

Cushman, K. M., "Arbitration and state law," 23 Arb.J. 162 (1968).

Hart, B. C., "Provision in a construction contract requiring arbitration of disputes is a disadvantage both to the general contractor and his surety and to the subcontractor and his surety," 31 Ins. Counsel J. 453 (1964).

Petro, J. J., "Is arbitration compulsory in construction contracts," 4 Forum 185 (1969).

Note, "Arbitration—specific performance of construction contract," 25 Albany L.Rev. 140 (1961).

CHAPTER 5

Change Orders

5.1. INTRODUCTION

In his wonderful book *Tales of a Traveller*, Washington Irving observed:

There is a certain relief in change, even though it be from bad to worse; as I have found in travelling in a stage-coach, that it is often a comfort to shift one's position and be bruised in a new place.

The flexibility to make changes is an important part of construction contract law, albeit for a different reason. No matter how much planning precedes the beginning of actual construction, unexpected contingencies always develop. Construction projects often require last-minute additions, deletions, or changes. Most properly drafted construction contracts, therefore, contain a "changes" clause which permits the owner to order changes in the work without breaching the contract in exchange for necessary adjustments in the contract price and time for completion. A typical clause provides in part:

12.1 CHANGE ORDERS

12.1.1 A Change Order is a written order to the Contractor signed by the Owner and the Architect, issued after execution of the Contract, authorizing a change in the Work or an adjustment in the Contract Sum or the Contract Time. The Contract Sum and the Contract Time may be changed only by Change Order. A Change Order signed by the Contractor indicates his agreement therewith, including the adjustment in the Contract Sum or the Contract Time.

12.1.2 The Owner, without invalidating the Contract, may order changes in the Work within the general scope of the Contract consisting of additions, deletions or other revisions, the Contract Sum and the Contract Time being adjusted accordingly. All such changes in the Work shall be authorized by Change Order, and shall be performed under the applicable conditions of the Contract Documents.[1]

Although simple in concept, the changes clause is a frequent source of controversy between owner and contractor. It may also affect third parties such as the architect and the surety. Common questions under the changes clause include whether the changes ordered by the owner lie outside the scope of the contract; whether the authorizing change order must be in writing; whether the architect has the authority to issue a change order without the owner's knowledge or assent; whether the consent of the surety issuing performance and payment bonds for the contract is required and, if required, has been obtained; and what an appropriate adjustment in contract price or completion time should be to accommodate the change work.

5.2   FUNCTION OF A CHANGES CLAUSE

In general, the owner has no inherent *implied* right to make changes in the contract which may obligate the contractor to perform. The right to make changes is a contractual right. The fundamental purpose of a changes clause is to allow the owner unilaterally to alter the work if the alteration falls within the general scope of the contract. The clause thus confers on the owner a valuable contract right: the freedom to control the work to be done, enabling him to respond quickly to changes in plans or requirements without invalidating the contract. By judicious use of a changes clause, the owner can shape the work to current needs without having to rebid or renegotiate the entire contract.

5.3   BASIC ELEMENTS OF A CHANGES CLAUSE

Most changes clauses contain the same basic provisions. Among these, typically, are requirements that the change order be reduced to writing; that it specify the adjustment in contract price and time for completion involved; that it be signed by the owner or his agent, or both; that the contractor not stop work or refuse to execute a change order; and that the change ordered be "within the scope of the original contract," a nebulous standard that has spawned much litigation. (See §5.4.2.)

The general contract ordinarily specifies the name of the person with the authority to issue change orders. That person is usually, but not always, the architect. Contractors should not automatically assume that the architect has unlimited and automatic authority to issue change orders. Some contracts (most notably the AIA form contract)

---

[1] AIA Document A201, Art. 12 (1976 ed.).

forbid the architect from being the only person with the authority to issue change orders effecting a price increase.

The architect may not order a change in the contract or waive the requirement that a change order be reduced to writing unless the owner specifically authorizes him to do so[2] or clothes him with "apparent authority," thus making it appear to third parties, including the contractor, that the architect is authorized to order changes or to waive formal requirements such as a written change order.

To protect the owner from unauthorized changes, courts often impose an affirmative duty on contractors to determine the actual authority of the architect. In one typical case, where an architect ordered extra work without authority to do so and failed to issue a written change order, a state court held that the contractor could not recover the additional cost because the architect lacked actual authority to order the change or to waive the requirement of a written change order.[3]

The harshness of this rule is sometimes relaxed when the owner knows that the architect has ordered a change and accepts the benefits of the contractor's work.[4] Courts refer to such knowing acceptance as "ratification." However, cases in which a contractor or subcontractor prevails against the owner under the "apparent authority" or "ratification" theories of liability are fairly rare. Courts will generally give effect to changes clauses which specifically define the authority of the owner's employees or agents.[5]

5.4 CONTRACTUAL FORMALITY

Because the changes clause gives the owner such broad authority to modify the terms of his written contract with the general contractor, the contract usually imposes several formal requirements that must be observed in order to make a valid change order.

5.4.1. The Requirement of Writing; "Constructive" Change Orders

Perhaps the most important formal requirement is that the change order be in writing. This requirement serves two major purposes: it protects the owner from having to pay for unwanted work, and it constitutes physical evidence that a change in the work has actually been ordered requiring adjustment of contract price and completion time.

---

[2]Anno., "Private Construction Contracts—Extras", 2 A.L.R. 3d 620 (1965).

[3]*Kirk Reid v. Fine*, 205 Va. 778, 139 S.E. 2d 829 (1965). Paragraph 12.4.1 of AIA Document A201 gives the architect authority to order minor changes which do not affect the contract price.

Unlike private owners, the federal government is not deemed to be bound by the act of its agents when they lack actual authority, even if the government may have caused others to believe they had apparent authority. *See Federal Crop Insurance Co. v. Merrill*, 332 U.S. 380 (1947).

[4]*See* Sweet, "Owner—Architect—Contractor: Another Eternal Triangle," in *Legal Problems of Contractors, Architects and Engineers*, pp. 27–28, (1970).

As to this problem in government work, where courts sometimes strain to find either apparent authority or ratification, *see Lox Equipment Rental*, ASBCA No. 8985, 1964 BCA ¶21466; *Williams v. United States*, 130 Ct. Cl. 435, 127 F. Supp. 617 (1955).

[5]In *Barton & Sons Co.*, ASBCA 9477, 65-2 BCA ¶4874, the following clause was held to bar a contractor's claim that an agent was clothed with apparent authority to order changes: "The Civil Engineer is not authorized to increase or decrease the scope of the work nor to direct the Contractor to effect any changes. . . ."

Courts almost always give effect to a contract requirement that change orders be in writing.[6] In one case, a subcontractor was denied additional compensation for a change in the work because he had not performed pursuant to a written change order. The subcontractor sought to rely upon custom in the industry that written change orders were normally issued during or after the completion of the work. The court determined such a practice to be at variance with the terms of the written contract and found for the owner.[7]

Although a contract may specify the format for a change order, most do not. Various documents may, subject to the judge's discretion, be considered to fulfill the "written" requirement. Such writings might include letters, internal memoranda, revised plans and specifications, daily reports, field records, job minutes, notes on shop drawings, and signed time and material slips. This is another reason why contractors should keep every written note, document, and sketch they receive.

Where there is a conflict between the specifications and the contract as to the formal requirements of a writing, the terms of the contract will control, particularly where the specifications are not incorporated into the contract. In a West Virginia case, for example, the specifications required any change order to be signed by both the owner and the architect, while the contract required merely the signature of either. The change order was signed by the architect alone. The court found that, because the contract was signed after the specifications were prepared, it represented the final intent of the parties. The change order was held to be valid.[8]

Some courts have drawn a rather fine distinction between alterations on the one hand and changes or "extras" on the other. Courts paying homage to this distinction have held that authorization for an alteration may be oral, while authorization for a change must be reduced to writing. Thus, moving a partition, enlarging a rear porch, increasing the height of a wall, deepening a trench, and putting in concrete flooring in excavation work were considered by an Iowa court to be alterations rather than extras, and a written change order was not required. The same court defined an "extra" as work outside of or in addition to that required by the contract and an alteration as merely a change in the form of the structure and not its identity. Since the contract required a written change order only for extras, the contractor was permitted to recover for "alterations" ordered orally.[9] Conversely, where a construction contract required a written change order only for alterations, a New York court found the requirement inapplicable to extras.[10]

Modern contracts usually obliterate the distinction between "alterations" and

---

[6]*See, e.g., Meaux v. Southern Constr. Corp.*, 169 So. 2d 156 (La. App. 1963). A subcontractor may waive a written change order requirement, since it is there for his protection. Between a contractor and the owner, however, only the owner may waive the requirement of a writing, because the requirement exists to delimit the authority of the architect and to protect the owner against obscure claims.

See also *John W. Johnson, Inc. v. Basic Constr. Co.*, 292 F. Supp. 300 (D.D.C. 1968), *aff'd*, 429 F.2d 764 (D.C. Cir. 1970).

[7]*Johnson v. Norcross Bros.* 209 Mass. 445, 95 N.E. 833 (1911).

[8]*Caldwell v. Schmulbach*, 175 F.429 (D.W.Va), *mod. on other grounds*, 196 F. 16 (4th Cir. 1909).

[9]*Chicago Lumber & Coal Co. v. Garmer*, 132 Iowa 282, 109 N.W. 780 (1906).

[10]*Fetterolf v. S & L Constr. Co.*, 175 App. Div. 177, 161 N.Y.S. 549 (1916). Where a contract provided that if certain soil conditions were encountered, extra monies would be paid to the contractor, no change order was required because the extra work was contemplated by the contract and did not fall outside it. *Haughton Elevator Co. v. C. Rallo Contracting Co.*, 395 S.W.2d 238 (Mo. App. 1965).

"extras" by using these terms (and many others) interchangeably in the changes clause itself. The clause usually applies to "additions, deletions, and other revisions." If the changes clause is so worded, both extras and alterations are subject to its provisions.

Even though the changes clause in a construction contract expressly requires a written change order, a contractor may nonetheless be able to recover for extra work performed other than pursuant to such an order. The contractor, however, bears the burden of showing the existence of an exception and its application or the fact that a new exception is warranted. Courts agree, for example, that the requirement of a written change order does not apply to work done by direction of a public building inspector, since such work is a matter of necessity rather than choice, performed in order to comply with public building codes of which both parties are deemed to have knowledge.[11] Absence of a written change order may also be overlooked where extra work is necessitated by the owner's fault or error.[12]

Of course, even if a change order is in writing, it can still be invalid. Revised specifications approved in writing by the owner and including extra work have been upheld as a change order, thus permitting a contractor to recover for additional costs.[13] But court decisions are generally divided on this subject, and a careful contractor will not rely on revised plans or specifications to serve as a written change order.[14]

Courts also disagree with respect to the retroactive effect of a written change order issued after the commencement of extra work by the contractor. Thus, where an architect first directed extra work orally and later issued a written change order, a California court held that the change order "related back in time" and allowed the contractor to recover.[15] But a Missouri court reached the opposite conclusion on similar facts and denied the contractor's claim because the contract requirement for a written change order "contemplated that the architect's decision should be made before the articles were brought and placed in the building".[16]

The requirement of a written change order may on occasion be avoided based on the conduct of the parties.[17] A "constructive change" is one that is ordered by the owner in a manner that does not comport with the formal requirements of the changes clause. Under certain narrowly drawn circumstances, courts will enforce oral change orders—even in the face of a contractual requirement that changes be ordered in writing—when equity or the conduct of the parties suggests that a constructive change was intended. For example, a constructive change may be implied where the extra work is known to the

---

[11]*Cramp & Co. v. Central Realty Corp.*, 268 Pa. 14, 110 A.763 (1920).

[12]*Wyandotte & D. R. Co. v. King Bridge Co.*, 100 F. 197 (6th Cir. 1900) (bridge located in wrong place by owner).

[13]*Hedden Constr. Co. v. Rossiter Realty Co.*, 136 App. Div. 601, 121 N.Y.S. 64, *aff'd*, 202 N.Y. 522, 95 N.E. 1130 (1910).

[14]*See Sartoris v. Utah Constr. Co.*, 21 F.2d 1 (9th Cir. 1927), *cert. denied*, 278 U.S. 651 (plans sufficient to constitute a change order); *compare Fetterolf v. S & L Constr. Co.*, *supra* n. 10.

[15]*Bavin & Burch Co. v. Bard*, 81 Cal. App. 722, 255 P. 200 (1927).

[16]*Hunt v. Owen Bldg. & Inv. Co.*, 219 S.W. 138 (Mo. App. 1920).

[17]*Howard J. White, Inc. v. Varian Assocs.*, 178 Cal. App.2d 348, 2 Cal. Rptr. 871 (1960); *T. Lippia & Son v. Jorson*, 342 A.2d 910 (Conn. 1975).

owner and not objected to by him,[18] where the owner agrees to the additional cost of extra work,[19] or where the extra work is orally ordered by the owner or his representative.[20]

A constructive change may also be found where the parties consistently disregard the requirement for written change orders throughout the performance of the contract,[21] or when the parties' subsequent oral agreements and actions modify the prior written contract which required written change orders.[22]

Despite the various exceptions noted, a contractor receiving an oral change order performs under it at his own risk. Yet if he refuses to do so, he may be found to have breached his contract with the owner, especially if that contract requires him to continue to work under protest. Under the circumstances, the safest procedure is for the contractor to complete the work as changed only after having first filed a written protest with both the owner and architect.

5.4.2. "General Scope of the Contract"

The owner may order changes under the changes clause without invalidating or breaching the contract, but only if the changes are "within the general scope" of the contract. The changes clause thus serves the vital function of setting forth in general terms the outer limits of work that can be ordered under the existing contract. If additional work does not fall within the clause, it is deemed to be a "cardinal change" subject to competitive bidding and the negotiation of a new contract or formal amendment to the existing contract. Compelling a contractor to perform a cardinal change may be a breach of contract.[23]

Relatively little guidance exists with respect to the meaning of "the general scope of the contract." Perhaps the best formulation can be found in federal government procurement regulations which, although applicable only to government contracts, are relevant to the changes clause contained in most private construction contracts as well:

---

[18]The majority view is that such acquiescence does constitute a waiver. *See, e.g., Perry v. Levenson*, 82 App. Div. 94, 81 N.Y.S. 586, *aff'd*, 178 N.Y. 559, 70 N.E. 1104 (1903) (finding a waiver from silence); *compare Shaw v. First Baptist Church*, 44 Minn. 22, 46 N.W. 146 (1890).

Knowledge combined with a subsequent oral authorization and a failure to object constitutes a waiver. *Mayer Paving and Asphalt Co. v. Carl A. Morse, Inc.*, 365 N.E.2d 360 (Ill. 1977); *Roff v. Southern Constr. Corp.*, 163 So.2d 112 (La. App. 1964). *See also Doral Country Club, Inc. v. Curcie Bros.*, 174 So.2d 749 (Fla. App. 1965).

Knowledge by the owner that the contractor expected extra monies for orally ordered changes has also been found to be a waiver. *Harrington v. McCarthy*, 420 P.2d 790 (Idaho 1966). But where the contractor remained silent when asked by the owner if certain changes would entail extra costs, and no payment demand for the changes was made until a lien was filed, the owner did not waive the writing requirement. *Lundstrom Constr. Co. v. Dygert*, 254 Minn. 224, 94 N.W. 2d 527 (1959).

[19]*Wagner v. Graziano Constr. Co.*, 390 Pa. 445, 136 A.2d 82 (1957).

[20]*Watson Lumber Co. v. Guennewig*, 79 Ill. App. 2d 277, 266 N.E.2d 270 (1967).

[21]*Ross Engineering Co. v. Pace*, 153 F.2d 35 (4th Cir. 1946). But where the parties have consistently abided by the requirement for a writing, the conduct of the parties is such that a waiver cannot be found when one alleged change is ordered orally. *Welch-Eckman Constr. Co. v. Vancouver Plywood Co.*, 213 So.2d 134 (La. App. 1968).

[22]*Grossie v. Lafayette Constr. Co.*, 306 So.2d 453 (La. App. 1975).

[23]*Luria Bros. and Co., Inc. v. United States*, 177 Ct. Cl. 676, 369 F.2d 701 (1966).

The words "general scope of the contract" limit changes to those that do not alter the basic nature of the procurement. The change must be reasonable in amount or extent and consistent with the original intent of the parties. It does not mean the same thing as "scope of work", a phrase sometimes used for other purposes. Any change in the specifications will, of course, change the scope of the work. But a proposed change does not fall outside the "Changes" clause unless it changes the basic nature of the procurement. A borderline case might mean considering such questions as:

(A)   What is the function of the end item, is it changed or unchanged?

(B)   How does the cost of the change compare with the original contract price?

(C)   What time, facilities, and manpower will be necessary to make the change?

(D)   Do contractors in the industry have, or can they acquire the skills necessary to make the change?

(E)   Would the competitive factors have been different if the proposed change had been part of the original contract requirement?[24]

The one United States Supreme Court case on point accords with the regulations, stating that a change is within the general scope of the contract if it is "fairly and reasonably within the contemplation of the parties when the contract was entered into."[25] Other cases have similarly taken a broad view of the meaning of the phrase.[26] Thus, even a large number of changes which disrupt the normal scheduling of the work have been considered within the general scope,[27] as have changes in the quantity of earthwork required under a contract until such changes exceeded the original contract quantity by almost 50 percent.[28]

Even when changes might otherwise be deemed outside the general scope of the contract, the parties may by their actions bring them within the contract. This would be so, for example, if the contractor accepts without objection a change order embodying a fundamental or cardinal change in the work.[29]

Changes as to which the clause applies may include changed drawings or specifications, changes in the method of performing the work, alterations in the construction schedule and other similar changes, even though the finished product is substantially the same as the work originally contracted for.

---

[24]Federal Aviation Agency Procurement Manual 56–100 (1966), *quoted in* Nash & Cibinic, "The Changes Clause in Federal Construction Contracts," 35 Geo. Wash. L. Rev. 908, 910 (1967).

[25]*Freund v. United States*, 260 U.S. 60 (1922).

[26]Elimination of an entire building from a construction project was held to be a "cardinal change" and thus a breach. *General Contracting and Construction Co. v. United States*, 84 Ct. Cl. 570 (1937). *See also Luria Bros. v. United States*, 177 Ct. Cl. 676, 369 F.2d 701 (1966) (ordering contractor to place foundations on a "trial and error" basis held to be an excessive change).

[27]*Aragona Constr. Co. v. United States*, 165 Ct. Cl. 382 (1964).

[28]*Saddler v. United States*, 152 Ct. Cl. 557, 287 F.2d 411 (1961).

[29]*See Ashton-Mardian Co.*, ASBCA No. 7912, 1963 BCA 19124; *Silberblatt & Lasker, Inc. v. United States*, 210 Ct. Cl. 54 (1966).

5.5 EFFECT OF CHANGES ON PERFORMANCE BONDS

Changes in the work may radically increase the risks of default on the part of the contractor. Under well-recognized principles of the law of suretyship, such changes in the contractor's obligations, without the surety's consent, may release the surety from all obligations to the owner-obligee. Many performance bonds provide that the surety waives all notice of changes or alterations, but some performance bonds, notably bonds issued for government construction, require that the surety be notified of all changes and alterations above a certain percentage of the contract price.

A typical waiver provision reads as follows: "The Surety hereby waives notices of any alteration or extension of time made by the Owner." (See AIA Document A311 (1970 ed.).) The Department of Housing and Urban Development's performance bond (FHA Form 3452), on the other hand, provides for prior approval, as follows:

> The prior written approval of Surety shall be required with regard to any changes or alterations in the construction required by said Building Loan Agreement where the cost thereof, added to prior changes or alterations, causes the aggregate cost of all changes and alterations to exceed ten (10) percent of the face amount of this Bond. . . .

5.5.1. Changes Authorized by Bond

Even material changes in the work to be performed under the contract will not operate to release the surety where the bond authorizes such changes without the surety's prior consent. But this is only true of changes within the general scope of the contract. Changes beyond the scope—not reasonably within the contemplation of the parties—will be deemed radical or cardinal changes. If the surety's prior written consent to such changes has not been obtained, they may well result in its release under a performance or payment bond despite a waiver-of-notice provision.

As a result, courts are reluctant to characterize changes in the work as "radical." For example, a Pennsylvania court refused to find that the addition of a gasoline service station to a motel construction project would release the surety, stating that "the service station is [not] such a deviation from the original contract that the [surety] is to be released as a matter of law."[30] Similarly, when changed plans and specifications resulted in price increases equal to almost 50 percent of the original contract amount, another court failed to find a radical change in the work. "The contract," it stated, "except for the new drawings, was left intact. The work, except for the alterations made by the new drawings, was the same work, to be done for the same purpose, and upon the same premises."[31]

---

[30]*Moon Motel, Inc. v. Sun Insurance Co.*, 36 D. & C. 2d 491, 112 P.J.L. 460 (1964).

[31]*Massachusetts Bonding and Ins. Co. v. John R. Thompson Co.*, 88 F.2d 825 (8th Cir. 1937). But in *State v. Preferred Accident Ins. Co. of N.Y.*, 149 So.2d 632 (La. App. 1963), a radical change was found where the contract completion date was extended to a term twice the length of the original contract period, and where price increases totaled almost 125 percent of the original contract price.

In sum, when the surety waives its right to be notified of or to approve changes, a *material* change in the work will not release the surety, but a *radical* change will. Whether a change will be characterized as material or radical is largely a matter of fact, as to which courts have wide discretion. The safest course of action for both owner and contractor, if there is any doubt as to the nature of a change, is always to obtain the surety's prior written consent.

5.5.2 Where the Surety has Not Waived Notice of Alterations

Of course, the surety is not required to waive prior notice of changes in the work. In that event, courts will sanction release of the surety when material changes occur.

In one representative case, a construction contract provided that plans and specifications could not be modified without the surety's written consent. Without notifying the surety, the contractor installed air-conditioning units different from and inferior to those specified. When the owner sued the surety on its performance bond, the court released the surety, but only as to any claim arising from the air-conditioning units. The surety remained liable for other claims under the contract. In so holding, the court said: "[A]n unagreed change in the construction contract which results in injury to the surety will discharge the surety to the extent of the injury."[32]

In addition to requiring notification of changes, a surety may also require that changes be performed pursuant to a *written* change order. Courts have not uniformly enforced the additional requirement. While some courts have held that the failure to reduce the change order to writing releases the surety,[33] others have found that the surety cannot be prejudiced by such failure[34] or that the written change is "an immaterial formality so far as the surety on the bond is concerned. . . ."[35]

5.5.3. Waiver and Ratification by the Surety

Courts will refuse to release a surety, even in the face of material or radical changes, if the surety has ratified such changes, waived its rights to prior notice, or misled the parties as to the need for written change orders. In an illustrative case, a performance bond required the surety's consent for any changes exceeding 10 percent of the contract price. The surety's local agent knew of alterations in the work to be performed under a construction contract in excess of 10 percent and also knew that such changes had not been approved. The agent, nonetheless, permitted the parties to believe that the surety was willing to continue its obligations under the performance bond. Because the agent had affirmatively misled the other parties, the court found the surety to have waived the

---

[32]*Equitable Fire & Marine Ins. Co. v. Tiernan Building Corp.*, 190 So.2d 197 (Fla. 1966).

[33]*Burnes Estate v. Fidelity & Deposit Co. of Md.*, 96 Mo. App. 467, 70 S.W. 518 (1902).

[34]*Roberts v. Security Trust & Savings Bank*, 196 Cal. 557, 238 P. 673 (1925).

[35]*Honolulu Roofing Co. v. Felix*, 49 Haw. 578, 426 P.2d 298 (1967).

notification requirement. At the same time, the court noted that the surety's mere silence with respect to known but unauthorized changes would not constitute a waiver.[36]

5.6 PRICING THE CHANGE ORDER

Apart from formalities of notice and authorization, the absence of which may have unintended legal consequences for the contractor, the most important feature of a change order is, of course, the adjustment in contract price and time for completion resulting from the change in the work ordered by the owner. AIA Document A201 ("General Conditions of the Contract for Construction") provides that adjustment in contract price shall be determined in one of several ways:[37]

(1) by mutual acceptance of a lump sum properly itemized;

(2) by unit prices stated in the contract documents or subsequently agreed upon; or

(3) by cost plus a mutually accepted fixed or percentage fee.

Ideally, therefore, the change order will stipulate a specific adjustment in the contract price to accommodate changed work and will be accepted by the contractor. If unit pricing or cost-plus-fixed-fee methods are used, the contract should contain an appropriate schedule for additions and deletions.[38]

---

[36]*Trinity Universal Ins. Co. v. Gould,* 258 F.2d 883 (10th Cir. 1958).

[37]Paragraph 12.1.3 (1976 ed.).

[38]Set forth below are typical unit price and cost-plus-fixed-fee schedules. *See generally* Robert B. Hemphill, "Change Orders," *Architectural & Engineering News,* 1967.

TYPICAL UNIT PRICE SCHEDULE

Item	Unit	Add	Deduct
1. Rock Excavation	c.y.	——	——
2. Miscellaneous Iron Work	lb.	——	——
3. Painting	s.f.	——	——
4. Paving	s.y.	——	——
5. Ductwork	lb.	——	——
6. Concrete Masonry Walls	s.f.	——	——
7. 4" dia. Seamless Steel Pipe	l.f.	——	——
8. Reinforced Concrete Foundations	c.y.	——	——

TYPICAL COST-PLUS SCHEDULE

A.	Field Labor (straight time)	————————
B.	Field Supervisor	—— % of A
C.	Payroll Taxes	—— % of A plus B
D.	Insurance	—— % of A plus B
E.	Fringe Benefits	—— % of A
F.	Small Tools	—— % of A
G.	Overhead	—— % of A plus B
H.	Profit	—— % of A plus B
J.	Materials or Sub-contracts	—————— %
K.	Equipment Rentals	—————— %

It may happen, however, that the owner and the contractor cannot agree at the time the change order is issued on the amount of the adjustment. In that event, the standard-form AIA contract provides that the contractor "shall promptly proceed with the work involved".[39] It is then left to the architect to determine the cost of the additional work (or reduced cost if work is deleted) on the basis of the contractor's "reasonable expenditures and savings . . ., including, in the case of an increase in the Contract Sum, a reasonable allowance for overhead and profit."[40] The contractor must, however, present an itemized accounting together with appropriate supporting data.[41] The architect is then authorized, pending final determination of additional cost (or reduced cost in the event of a deletion), to make payments to the contractor on account.[42]

A change order within the general scope of the contract may therefore present the contractor with a difficult problem. Legally, the owner is entitled under the contract to issue such a change order without breaching the contract. At the same time, the contractor is obliged to proceed with the changed work even though an adjustment in price and completion time may not have been agreed to when the change order was issued.[43] In such a case, the architect is often placed in the position of an ostensibly neutral or independent arbiter between the owner and the contractor. The architect must determine the reasonable cost of the changed work in order to adjust the contract price accordingly. If the architect's determination is not acceptable to the contractor, then the latter must preserve his rights by lodging a claim for additional costs or time and using the disputes mechanism specified in the construction contract.[44] Often this will require arbitration, rather than an action at law. In most instances, however, disputes with respect to change orders are avoided by negotiated agreement between the parties since both have an interest in avoiding delay and costly litigation or arbitration proceedings.

5.7. ADDITIONAL SOURCE MATERIALS

Gold, H., "Changes, changed conditions, suspensions and delays," 2 Pub. Contract L.J. 56 (1968).

Greenberg, M. E., "Problems relating to changes and changed conditions on public contracts," 3 Pub. Contract L.J. 135 (1970).

Gutmacher, N. W., "Changes in plans and specifications furnished by the owner which violate building laws: who shall pay?", 39 U. Cin. L. Rev. 561 (1970).

Lash, R. C., " 'Changes clause' in federal construction contracts," 35 Geo. Wash. L. Rev. 908 (1967).

---

[39] AIA Document A201, ¶12.1.4 (1976 ed.).

[40] *Id.*

[41] *Id.*

[42] *Id.*

[43] *Id.*

[44] *Id.*, ¶¶7.9.1, 12.1.4, 12.3.1.

M., " 'Extras' in building contracts," 100 Sol. J. 539 (1956).

McCormick, J. M., "Contract changes and extras clauses, their validity and binding effect," 10 Forum 1 (1974).

Phelps, E. D., "Contracts: tiling of bathroom as a recoverable extra under building contract," 15 Okla. L. Rev. 42 (1962).

Reiss, J., "Understanding building contractor's claims for extras." 38 N.Y.S.B. 506 (1966).

Anno., "Extras—effect of stipulation in public building or construction contract, that alteration or extras must be ordered in writing," 2 A.L.R. 3d 620; 1 A.L.R. 3d 1273.

Anno., "Delays caused by change in plans or specifications of a public construction contract as coming within 'no damage' clause with respect to delay appearing in the contract," 10 A.L.R. 2d 810.

CHAPTER 6

Time and Delay Problems

6.1 INTRODUCTION

Although time is always of the essence in construction contracts, the law does not imply such a condition as a general rule. A delay claim is essentially a claim that the contract has been breached; and it is an elementary principle of contract law that a breach is actionable in a court of law only if the breach is material—in other words, important to the value of the contract in the eyes of the other party. Time of completion alone is not part of the basic exchange of values in a construction contract. Contractually, the owner may be said to seek construction of a structure for a given sum of money. If a contractor is delayed in completing the work and can offer no legally justifiable excuse, he may be required to compensate the owner for the costs of the delay. But he will not forfeit his right to complete the contract or to receive payment for work completed.

If, on the other hand, the owner is responsible for delay, the contractor may be entitled to an extension of time to complete the contract and to additional payment for delay costs, or both. It is rare, however, that the cause for delay can be pinpointed or assigned. Delay is often attributable to third parties or to causes beyond the control of either contractor or owner. Many construction projects are not completed on time. Someone, therefore, is usually responsible for unforeseen delays; deciding who and why can keep lawyers very busy.

Delays may be excusable but generally will not be compensable. The contractor may be granted additional time within which to complete the contract and may be relieved of liability for liquidated damages (if the parties have incorporated a liquidated damages clause in their contract), but he will not be entitled to additional payment for costs occasioned by the delay.

Inherent in most delays are disruptions, which may involve a change in the planned sequence of the contractor's work or unanticipated demobilization and remobilization of labor forces. If the owner insists on completion of the work by the original completion date, without regard to excusable delays, that may entail another form of disruption, commonly referred to as acceleration. Delay and disruption go together like the proverbial horse and carriage—or, perhaps more accurately, like cause and effect, for it is the rare owner indeed who will fume over delays without also complaining about the disruptions occasioned as a direct result.

6.2 COMMENCEMENT, SCHEDULING AND COMPLETION DATES

Construction contracts typically contain a completion date and intermediate dates for the completion of specified phases of the work. The mere inclusion of a completion date, however, does not make time an essential element of the contract. A specific statement to this effect is ordinarily required. This can be done in any one of several ways: by incorporating provisions for termination if time limitations are not met, by inserting specific progress schedule requirements in the contract, or—most directly—by including a clause in the contract making the parties liable for actual or liquidated damages in the event of delay.

The completion date is generally indicated in the contract documents or an aggregate time period is set forth, usually measured in days from the date of a notice to proceed given by the owner when various preconditions to the start of work have been met. The latter method is more common and has the advantage of protecting the owner and the contractor against delays encountered prior to issuance of the notice to proceed, for example, in obtaining permits, easements, or access to the site. Delay, then, may be defined as the time needed to complete the work beyond the originally scheduled completion date.

Occasionally, the parties fail to deal adequately with measurement of the time of performance in the contract. Such a failure can give rise to harsh results in litigation. Thus, in *Bloomfield Reorganized School Dist. No. R-14 v. Stites*, 336 S.W.2d 95 (Mo. 1960), a construction contract specified simply that a building was to be "substantially completed" in 395 days without providing for a measuring date, such as the date of a notice to proceed. The court in *Bloomfield* looked to the date of the contract for the purpose of determining when liquidated damages commenced, even though the contract was not mailed to the contractor until nine days after that date and was not fully executed and delivered until approximately six weeks after that date. The court placed weight on the contract's silence as to a "work order" or notice to proceed and its requirement that work be commenced immediately. "It is of first importance that a contract shall have definitely ascertainable dates of completion and termination," said the court. "To that end, those dates should be determinable from the recitations in the contract itself. . . ."

A contractor may avoid such problems by including in the contract a provision that "the date of commencement of the work is the date established in the notice to proceed." The contract may further obligate the owner to give notice in writing no later than a specified number of days after the date of execution and delivery of the contract. The contract should also specify a date of substantial completion, as indicated above, which may be defined as a date certified by the project architect when the structure may be occupied or used as intended. If the project is to be constructed in discrete phases or steps, the contract may also specify commencement and completion dates for designated portions of the work.

Often a contract will incorporate a schedule as part of its overall provisions. Since construction schedules must typically be revised as the work progresses, however, it is best to provide for schedule updates and to assure adherence to the project schedule, as revised, by all parties affected, including major trade subcontractors. This can be accomplished contractually by requiring the contractor to make out a progress schedule in a form approved by the project architect showing the commencement date, completion date, and the dates of completion of designated portions of the work. The contractor may also be obligated to obtain the approval of specified subcontractors and to revise the progress schedule periodically. The contractor's unexcused failure to adhere to the project schedule can then, under certain circumstances, permit the owner to terminate the contract.

6.3.   CAUSES OF DELAY

It does not unnecessarily complicate a simple subject to say that delay can be caused by four factors: the conduct of the owner; the conduct of the contractor; the mutually reinforcing conduct of both the owner and the contractor; and factors beyond the control of either party.

6.3.1.   Owner-Caused Delay

In addition to placing a contractor at risk of default under the contract's time provisions, delays also usually increase his cost of performance. When delay is caused by the owner, in the absence of a contrary contract provision, such delay may be both excusable (justifying a contractual modification) and compensable (constituting grounds for the recovery of money damages). Construction contracts often provide for both forms of relief. The AIA General Conditions state in part: "If the Contractor is delayed at any time in the progress of the work by any act or neglect of the Owner or the Architect, or by any employee of either, or by any separate contractor employed by the Owner . . ., the Contract Time shall be extended by Change Order for such reasonable time as the Architect may determine." (¶8.3.1.) The same Article also provides, however, that the foregoing does not "exclude the recovery of damages for delay by either party under any other provisions of the Contract Documents." The latter language is interpreted to mean that the contractor may be entitled to delay damages even if he has also obtained an extension of time.

Compensable owner-caused delays have been held by courts to include, among other events: (1) the owner's or architect's failure to approve shop drawings within a reasonable time; (2) the owner's failure to obtain necessary easements or building permits; (3) the owner's failure to prepare the site; (4) the owner's failure to furnish materials promised under the contract; (5) the owner's failure to obtain adequate financing; (6) the owner's failure to coordinate the work properly where multiple prime contracts are awarded; (7) the failure of the owner or architect to provide plans or specifications in a timely fashion, or the provision of defective plans or specifications; and (8) the owner's requirement of changes or additions to the work contemplated by the contract resulting in delay.[1] The owner is, on general agency principles, responsible for the acts and omissions of persons employed by him, such as architects and engineers. Finally, of course, the owner is responsible for suspensions of work he has authorized after the commencement of construction.

6.3.2 Contractor-Caused Delay

Contractor-caused delay is neither excusable nor compensable. The contractor's failure to complete the work on time may give rise to liquidated damages if the contract provides for them, or delay costs measured by the owner's actual economic loss attributable to the delay if it does not. In any event, if contractor-caused delay is material, it can be deemed a breach of contract, permitting the owner to terminate the contract and order the contractor to cease work.

A contract may provide specifically for this contingency. If the owner exercises such a right of termination legitimately, his damages are measured by the additional costs incurred in obtaining a substitute contractor and completing the work, together with other reasonably foreseeable consequential damages. If the contractor completes the work but exceeds the completion date, the owner will ordinarily seek to withhold, as damages, an amount from contract retainage.

Contractor-caused delays can stem from diverse events, including failure to order material and equipment in a timely fashion, failure to man the work properly, and delays in performance by subcontractors and others for whom the contractor is responsible.[2] Generally, in the absence of owner-caused delay or specific excusable delays (discussed below), the contractor will be accountable for the consequences of failing to complete a project within the time allotted by the contract.

6.3.3. Excusable Delays

Construction contracts typically contemplate the contractor's coordination of diverse and complex activities of many subcontractors. Contracts also often call for performance over extended periods of time. The opportunities for delay are legion.

---

[1]*Merritt-Chapman & Scott Corp. v. United States,* 439 F.2d 185 (Ct.Cl. 1971); *Appeal of Desonia Constr. Co.,* ENG BCA 3250, 73-1 BCA 9797 (1972); *Appeal of A.F. Drexler,* ASBCA 12249, 12316, 69-1 BCA 7572 (1969).

[2]*Appeal of Howard R. Dressler Co.,* GSBCA 3616-9, 73-1 BCA 9818 (1972).

Accordingly, contractors commonly seek to include exculpatory provisions to alleviate their responsibility for identifiable categories of delay. Thus, the AIA General Conditions provide:

> If the Contractor is delayed at any time in the progress of the Work by any act or neglect of the Owner or the Architect, or of any employee of either, or by any separate Contractor employed by the Owner, or by changes ordered in the Work, or by labor disputes, fire, unusual delay in transportation, adverse weather conditions not reasonably anticipatable, unavoidable casualties, or any causes beyond the Contractor's control, or by delay authorized by the Owner pending arbitration, or by any cause which the Architect determines may justify the delay, then the Contract Time shall be extended by Change Order for such reasonable time as the Architect may determine. [Article 8.3.1.][3]

Excusable delays may be the result of supervening *force majeure* events beyond the contractor's control. In order to be excused from liability for delay within the purview of clauses such as those quoted above, however, the contractor must sustain the burden of proving that the delay was attributable to the excepted causes and that it would not otherwise have occurred.[4]

The contractual significance of an excusable delay is that the owner must, in effect, grant a time extension, thereby permitting the contractor to complete the work later than the contemplated date of completion. The owner may not assess liquidated damages, may not deem the contractor in default and terminate his right to proceed, and may not demand that the contractor adhere to the original schedule of completion by accelerating the work. Excusable delays are, however, not compensable to the contractor. In other words, even if he has incurred additional costs attributable to the delay, the contractor may not recover such costs from the owner.

6.3.4. Concurrent Delays

A special category of excusable delay is concurrent delay, where delays caused by both the owner and the contractor occur at the same time. Concurrent delays are compensable to neither the owner nor the contractor, although the contractor will

---

[3]Similarly, the standard-form fixed-price construction contract issued by the United States Government provides:

> The Contractor's right to proceed shall not be so terminated nor the Contractor charged with resulting damage if:

> (1) The delay in the completion of the work arises from unforeseeable causes beyond the control and without the fault or negligence of the Contractor, including but not restricted to, acts of God, acts of the public enemy, acts of the Government in either its sovereign or contractual capacity, acts of another contractor in the performance of a contract with the Government, fires, floods, epidemics, quarantine restrictions, strikes, freight embargoes, unusually severe weather, or delays of subcontractors or suppliers arising from unforeseeable cause beyond the control and without the fault or negligence of both the Contractor and such subcontractors or suppliers.

[4]*Schweigert v. United States*, 181 Ct.Cl. 1184 (1967).

ordinarily be granted a time extension. The delay will ordinarily not be apportioned, and liquidated damages will be wholly abrogated.[5]

6.4 "NO DAMAGES" CLAUSES

Frequently, owners will seek to protect themselves from liability for delay costs by the inclusion of a "no damages" provision in the construction contract. Such a provision may exonerate the owner from damages due to delays of any sort, even delay caused by the owner. Similarly, a prime contractor may include a "no damages" provision in contracts with subcontractors. Ordinarily, courts will uphold a "no damages" provision if the particular cause of delay falls within its terms, although courts have been known to retreat behind the banner of strict construction to avoid harsh results.[6] Practical exceptions to the operation of "no damages" provisions have been carved out where the delay (1) is the result of the owner's active interference, (2) is protracted to such an unreasonable extent that the contractor may reasonably deem the contract to have been abandoned, (3) is of a kind not contemplated by the parties, or (4) is caused willfully or in bad faith.[7]

A good example is *Ippolito-Lutz, Inc. v. Cohoes Housing Authority*, 254 N.Y.S. 2d 783 (App. Div. 1968), in which a general contractor brought suit to recover withheld retainage, damages, and compensation for extra work. The owner defended on the basis of a contract provision that stated: "No payment or compensation of any kind shall be made to the Contractor for damages because of hindrance or delay from any cause in the progress of the work, whether such hindrance or delays be avoidable." The court found that the owner had failed to perform necessary acts in furtherance of the contract, denied the owner's motion for summary judgment, and stated:

> An exculpatory clause of this nature is not always absolute. It must be construed strictly against the party seeking exemption from liability because of his own fault. . . . It will not be effective against "active interference" by the contractee or where "delay is protracted to an unreasonable length."

In the absence of tortious intent, however, courts are generally reluctant to find active interference and instead attribute the owner's acts or omissions to a level of negligence or neglect that does not relieve the clause of its effect.

Unreasonable delays by the owner have also been found to avoid the effect of "no damages" provisions. The cases are, for the most part, indistinguishable from the "active interference" cases since the owner-caused delays, in addition to being unreason-

---

[5]*Commerce Int'l Co. v. United States*, 167 Ct.Cl. 529 (1964); *see United States v. United Engineering & Constr. Co.*, 234 U.S. 236 (1916).

[6]*Cunningham Bros. v. Waterloo*, 117 N.W.2d 45 (Iowa 1962).

[7]*Vanderlinde Electric Corp. v. City of Rochester*, 54 A.D.2d 155, 388 N.Y.S.2d 388 (1976); *Hawley v. Orange County Flood Control District*, 211 Cal. App. 2d 708, 27 Cal. Rptr. 478 (1963); *Housing Authority of Dallas v. Hubbell*, 325 S.W. 2d 880 (Tex. Civ. App. 1959).

able in length, usually involve the owner's failure to perform in such a way as to permit the contractor to proceed.

A special class of "no damages" cases involves claims by contractors against the United States Government. In *Severin v. United States*, 99 Ct.Cl. 435 (1943), *cert. denied*, 322 U.S. 733 (1944), and subsequent cases, the following principle has been developed: where the contractor includes a "no damages" provision in his contract with his subcontractor and the provision exonerates the contractor from the subcontractor's damages due to Government-caused delay, the contractor may not recover from the Government on behalf of and for the benefit of the subcontractor. The principle has been narrowed, however, to apply only in those cases where the contractor would not have a valid claim against the Government other than by asserting the Government's breach of contract, for example, where the contractor would have no administrative remedy permitting equitable adjustment of the contract price due to delay.

6.5   COORDINATION OF THE WORK

A particular form of delay meriting special mention is delay caused by a prime contractor who fails to protect his subcontractors from delays by other subcontractors. A similar form of delay may be attributable to an owner employing multiple prime contractors. In general, the prime contractor is by implication required to schedule the work of subcontractors so as to avoid one subcontractor's interference with the work of others. The prime contractor may therefore incur liability for a delayed subcontractor's damages if he does not take all reasonable steps to coordinate the work properly.

In *Freeman Contractors, Inc. v. Central Surety & Insurance Corp.*, 205 F.2d 607 (8th Cir. 1953), a painting subcontractor contended that the prime contractor had interfered with and delayed its work by failing to employ enough men to keep the carpentry work ahead of work performed by follow-on trade subcontractors, with the result that the painting subcontractor was unable to complete its painting in any one building or series of buildings before being ordered to move its crew to another location. The court found for the subcontractor and stated: "The contract of the subcontractor expressly provided that the work required would be performed so as not to interfere with the work of the prime contractor or with the work of other subcontractors, and, by implication, we think, that the subcontractor's work would be free from interference on the part of the general contractor and other subcontractors."

A comparable result was reached in *L.L. Hall Construction Co. v. United States*, 379 F.2d 559 (Ct.Cl. 1966), a case involving the repair and improvement of a naval air station in Florida. The Government employed several contractors for this work but failed to release two runways for the contractor's operations on time, preferring that contractors other than the plaintiff contractor complete their tasks first. The court permitted the plaintiff an equitable adjustment in the contract price under its contract with the Government, stating: "It is plain that the Government is obligated to prevent interference with orderly and reasonable progress of a contractor's work by other contractors over whom the Government has control."

6.6 MECHANISM FOR TIME EXTENSIONS

Most construction contracts contemplate the possibility of excusable delay and provide a specific means by which the contractor can obtain, or be granted, an extension of time. Under the AIA General Conditions, for example, the architect is responsible for determining whether and to what extent specified delays may warrant an extension of time under the contract. In other forms of construction contracts comparable responsibility is given to the engineer and, in public contracts, to the contracting authority.

The contractor is ordinarily required to submit a written claim for extension of time. Under the AIA General Conditions, the claim must be filed within 20 days of the occurrence of the delay. Failure to do so results in waiver of the claim for extension of time. The notice requirement is more than a mere technicality, since it serves to inform the design professional, or owner, that persons for whom they are responsible are delaying the contractor. Notice may be the only way in which the owner or design professional can discover that a delay is occurring and take timely corrective action. Contemporaneous notice also serves to discourage spurious claims of delay, lodged upon completion of the contract for the purpose of avoiding liquidated damages, and enables the owner or design professional to evaluate the causes of delay while evidence is still readily obtainable.

Courts will ordinarily honor the technical requirements imposed under the contract as to notice of delays. Notice will be deemed a condition precedent to the excusability of the contractor's delay and the consequent extension of time of his performance. This is, however, not invariably so. If the delay-causing event is so obvious that all parties can constructively foresee a delay, than the notice requirement may be disregarded.[8] Thus, the California Civil Code provides that any delay in performance of a contractor's obligation is excused when performance is delayed by the act of a creditor (even though the contract may specifically excuse the creditor). California courts have construed this statutory provision to include owners and have ruled that a contract requiring written application for a time extension may not deprive the provision of its intended effect. "Noncompliance with a provision requiring an application for an extension of time is not a proper basis for holding a contractor liable in liquidated damages for late completion caused by the owner's conduct," said the court in *Peter Kiewit Sons Co. v. Pasadena City Junior College District of Los Angeles County*, 28 Cal. Rptr. 714, 379 P.2d 18 (1963), a leading California decision. In such cases, courts view with greater concern the relief to be afforded the contractor from owner-caused delay than strict compliance with contractual notice requirements. Judicial recognition of this rationale is limited, however, to the contractor's claim for a time extension.

---

[8]*E. C. Ernst, Inc. v. General Motors Corp.*, 482 F.2d 1047 (5th Cir. 1973).

6.7. LIQUIDATED DAMAGES

In contracts for the construction of buildings or machinery, the parties often provide that a fixed sum should be paid for each day's delay in completion beyond an agreed-upon date. Since the injury caused by such delay is almost always difficult to determine, courts usually accept the estimate as reasonable and enforce contractual provisions awarding liquidated damages to the innocent party. So long as liquidated damages are not deemed to be a penalty, courts will honor the bargain of the parties.

Whether a liquidated damages provision in a contract is regarded as a penalty is a question that turns on the relationship between the amount of liquidated damages imposed and the actual damages that may reasonably be anticipated to result from a delay. If the stipulated amount is not unreasonably disproportionate to the actual damages suffered, the liquidated damages provision will not be treated as a penalty.[9]

Liquidated damage amounts are usually withheld by the owner from each progress payment until completion and acceptance of the work. Litigated cases involving liquidated damages often involve actions to recover retainage where the contractor alleges delay to have been caused by factors not within his control.

6.7.1. Delay Attributable to the Owner

A liquidated damage provision does not prevent inquiry into the cause of the delay. A contractor will not be liable, under such a provision, for failure to complete the contract within a specified time if the failure was wholly due to the owner's act or omission in delaying the work.[10] Owner-caused delay may arise from various circumstances, including failure to make the site available on time, failure of the architect or engineer to furnish plans or specifications promptly, and material additions to or alterations of the plans by the owner. (See §6.3.1.) Relief for the contractor under such facts is necessary to avoid applying a liquidated damages provision as a penalty or forfeiture.

The contractor will, however, remain responsible for diligent performance of the contract. A contractor who has been relieved of liquidated damages because of owner-caused delay will not thereafter be permitted to disregard time considerations entirely. He may still be liable for unreasonable delay on his part, and the damages assessed for such unreasonable delay may be determined at the rate specified for liquidated damages.

Similarly, the presence of a liquidated damage provision in a contract will not limit or preclude the contractor's right to an extension of time, recovery of damages, or both, against the owner for delay caused by him. The owner may not invoke the liquidated damage provision as a defense to the economic consequences of his own delay. Where the contract can be used as a basis for computing additional costs arising from the

---

[9]*Barr & Sons, Inc. v. Cherry Hill Centre, Inc.*, 217 A.2d 631 (N.J. Super. Ct. 1966).

[10]*General Insurance Co. of America v. Commerce Hyatt House*, 85 Cal. Rptr. 317 (Ct. App. 1970).

delay, the contractor may be compensated for such items as idle equipment, management and supervisory costs, interest on borrowings, increased labor costs, increased bond premiums, rehiring and retaining of employees, and similar items.

6.7.2. Delay Attributable to Both Parties

Not all cases involving liquidated damages permit an unequivocal determination of the cause of delay. What if delay is caused by both parties? Courts have differed in resolving this question. Some courts have held that any owner-caused delay completely discharges the contractor, while others have held that it merely extends proportionately the time allowed for completion. The prevailing rule adopts the former theory: where the owner has caused a substantial delay in the beginning or progress of the work, the time limit fixed in the contract, and any provision for liquidated damages based thereon, are deemed to be entirely abrogated, leaving the contractor responsible only for completion of the work within a reasonable time. The total excess time taken by the contractor will not be apportioned between the two sources of delay.

This principle is nicely illustrated by *Mosler Safe Co. v. Maiden Lane Safe Deposit Co.*, 199 N.Y. 479 (1910), an early New York case. The contractor there undertook to construct a safe and a vault. The work on each was required to be completed by a specified date. The contract contained a liquidated damages provision. The contractor, although delayed in completing the work, sued for the contract price. The owner counterclaimed for liquidated damages. There was evidence that the owner's architect had delayed progress of the work by requiring deviation from the original plans (under a clause permitting him to do so) and by omitting to pass promptly on drawings submitted by the contractor. The judge charged the jury that

> if any substantial part of the delay in completion [of the work] was caused by the wrongful acts of the defendant or its architect, or by alterations or deviation from the plans and specifications, or by failure to approve drawings within a reasonable time, or by arbitrary and capricious acts, the entire clause for liquidated damages was cancelled and abrogated, and the defendant is not entitled to recover the same.

The court then upheld a judgment in the plaintiff's favor for the entire sum retained by the owner, declaring:

> The correct rule is that where such delays are occasioned by mutual fault of the parties, the court will not attempt to apportion them, but will refuse to enforce the provision for liquidated damages.

There is authority to the contrary in several jurisdictions, which permits apportionment of damages, even where the contract does not specifically so provide. Apportionment is most feasible in cases where competent evidence exists to explain the delay chargeable to each party. Under these circumstances, the contractor is entitled to credit for the period of delay attributable to the owner in the computation of liquidated damages.[11]

6.7.3. Provision Requiring Notice for Extension

Contracts frequently require the contractor to submit a written claim in order to obtain an extension of time. (See §6.6.) Such a provision will usually be enforced by the courts as a condition precedent to the contractor's right to be excused from delay. It will be similarly enforced with respect to liquidated damages. Thus, a contractor may be subject to liquidated damages even for delays not his fault if he fails to comply with the contractual notice provision. The same result obtains where the contract empowers the architect or engineer to determine the applicable extension of time. The contractor must follow the contract procedure in seeking the decision of the architect or engineer even in respect of delays attributable to the owner.

6.8 ADDITIONAL SOURCE MATERIALS

General

> Gold, H., "Changes, changed conditions, suspension and delays," 2 Public Contract LF 56 (1968).
>
> Note, "Time for completion of building contracts," 100 Sol. J. 275 (1956).
>
> Anno., "Prime contractor's liability to subcontractor for delay in performance," 16 A.L.R.3d 1252.

Public Authority Contracts

> Vance, L. H., Jr., "Fully compensating the contractor for delay damages in Washington public works contracts," 13 Gonzaga L. Rev. 410 (1978).
>
> Note, "Government contracts—an analysis of liquidated damages, default and impossibility of performance," 16 Cath. U.L. Rev. 418 (1967).

Excusable Delays

> Anno., "Severe weather: construction contract provision excusing delay caused by 'severe weather'," 85 A.L.R.3d 1085.

---

[11]*Bedford-Carthage Stone Co. v. Ramey*, 34 S.W.2d 387 (Tex. Civ.App. 1930); *Wallis v. Wenham*, 204 Mass. 83 (1910).

Delay Damages

Braude, H. M., "Surety's liability under the Miller Act for 'delay damages,' " 36 Fed. B.J. 86 (1977).

Liquidated Damages

Anderson, N.E., "Liquidated damages in construction contracts," 1958 ABA Insurance Section N&CL 110 (1958); 5 Prac. L. 72 (1959).

Peckar, R. S., "Liquidated damages in federal construction contracts: time for a new approach," 5 Pub. Cont. L.J. 129 (1972).

Anno., "Liability of building or construction contractor for liquidated damages for breach of time limit where work is delayed by contractor or third person," 152 A.L.R. 1349.

Anno., "Liquidated damages: liability of building or construction contractor for liquidated damages for breach of time limit provision where he abandons work after time fixed for its completion," 42 A.L.R.2d 1134.

No Damage Clauses

Oles, Douglas S., " 'No damage' clauses in construction contracts: a critique," 53 Wash. L. Rev. 471 (1978).

Anno., " 'No damage' clauses," 74 A.L.R.3d 187.

Anno., "Validity, construction, and application of 'no damage' clause with respect to delay in construction contract," 10 A.L.R.2d 789.

CHAPTER 7

Payment

7.1 INTRODUCTION

Construction contract disputes usually involve money, and contract provisions governing payment go to the heart of the commercial exchange of values between the parties. Payment provisions commonly used may be of several kinds, ranging from competitively bid lump-sum fixed-price to negotiated-cost-plus-fixed-fee, with variations and alternatives in between. The different types of payment provisions are discussed below. Certain legal requirements apply to all of them, however, and frame the contractor's entitlement to receive payment and the owner's obligation to make payment.

7.2 CONDITIONS AND NONCOMPLIANCE

In simplest terms, the owner's promise to pay under a construction contract is conditioned upon the contractor's compliance with all the obligations imposed on him by the contract. A *condition* is defined as a circumstance that must occur or be excused before a promise to perform matures. Thus, if a contract calls for payment in full upon completion (an alternative seldom used on major projects, which typically provide for progress payments measured by percentage of completion), the owner may refuse to pay until the contractor has performed fully.

The legal doctrine of conditional obligation is, in theory, a powerful sanction in the owner's hands enabling him to obtain promised performance. However, strict application of the doctrine can work hardship on the contractor, particularly if the

112

condition remaining unfulfilled is minor or easily satisfied. Absolute compliance with every term of a construction contract is unusual. Contract documents are likely to be complex and detailed; a contractor must depend on the work of subcontractors and suppliers; changes in the contract may be required; interpretation of the contract documents may differ. If, under such circumstances, the owner could insist on literal fidelity to the contract conditions and enforce his insistence by nonpayment, the contractor would run the risk of suffering a loss vastly disproportionate to the economic consequences of his nonperformance.

7.3. SUBSTANTIAL PERFORMANCE

To meet this problem, courts have developed and refined the doctrine of "substantial performance." The doctrine permits the contractor to receive partial payment despite minor deviations from contract plans and specifications. The contractor's payment is determined by subtracting from the contract sum an amount equal to the damage sustained by the owner as a result of the contractor's nonperformance.[1]

The rationale for permitting partial recovery is straightforward. Even if the owner rejects the work of a contractor, the owner ordinarily receives some benefit as a result of the contractor's labor and material purchases. Were the owner to negotiate a contract with somebody else to finish the work, the owner's costs would presumably be reduced by a measurable amount corresponding to the value of the first contractor's work. Most courts have accepted the equitable notion that an owner should pay for the value of what he has received and should not reap the benefits of a windfall just because some of the work fails to meet specifications.

This does not mean, however, that contractors may always recover partial payment under the doctrine of substantial performance. Courts rely on three objective factors in deciding whether and to what extent the doctrine should be applied in a particular case.

First, the court will ordinarily examine the severity of the contractor's breach and the stage of construction at which the breach occurred. For obvious reasons, the contractor is more likely to recover some of the contract price if the breach is minor, or if the construction project is nearly completed.[2]

Second, the court will see whether the owner has accepted and occupied the project notwithstanding the contractor's failure to perform satisfactorily under the contract. If the owner derives some benefit from an almost-completed project, then the contractor's entitlement to partial recovery is substantially enhanced.[3]

---

[1]*Bullock Co. v. Allen*, 493 S.W.2d 5 (Mo. App. 1973); *Watson Lumber Co. v. Guennewig*, 79 Ill. App. 337, 226 N.E.2d 270 (1967).

[2]*Worthington Corp. v. Consolidated Aluminum Corp.*, 544 F.2d 227 (5th Cir. 1977); *Tex-Craft Builders, Inc. v. Allied Constructors of Houston, Inc.*, 465 S.W.2d 786 (Tex.Civ.App. 1971); *Edward S. Goode, Jr., General Contractor*, 66-1 B.C.A. ¶5362 (1966).

[3]*Formigli Corp. v. Fox*, 348 F.Supp. 629 (E.D. Pa. 1972).

Finally, the court will determine whether the contractor has made a good-faith effort to comply with the contract provisions. Nothing is more damaging to the contractor's case than evidence of willful departure from the terms of the contract. If, however, the contractor's breach is the result of an unintentional oversight or error, then the likelihood of partial recovery is great.[4]

A good example of these factors in action is *Plante v. Jacobs*, 103 N.W.2d 296 (Wisc. 1960). In *Plante*, a contractor sued to recover the unpaid balance of the contract price, plus extras, in connection with the construction of a house. The owners counterclaimed for damages attributable to faulty workmanship. The contractor had undertaken to construct the house for $26,765. During the course of construction the contractor was paid $20,000. The owners contended that the contractor had not performed according to the plans and specifications and, after making the initial $20,000 payment, abrogated the contract. The trial court found that the contract had been substantially performed but accorded the owners an allowance for faulty workmanship. The trial court also found that the owners had not been damaged by the contractor's misplacement of a wall between the kitchen and the living room. The amount of the allowance for faulty workmanship was deducted from the gross amount owing the contractor, and judgment was entered for the difference. The owners appealed.

The appellate court addressed the central question of substantial performance: "The test of what amounts to substantial performance seems to be whether the performance meets the essential purpose of the contract. . . . Substantial performance as applied to the construction of a house does not mean that every detail must be in strict compliance with the specifications and the plans. Something less than perfection is the test of specific performance unless all details are made the essence of the contract."

Having found that the doctrine of substantial performance should apply, the court next considered the appropriate measure of damages for the contractor's failure to comply with the contract. The court restated two rules for measuring damages: the "diminished value" rule and the "cost of repair" rule. Under the former rule, damages are measured by the difference between the value of the structure as it stands and its value had it been constructed in strict accordance with the plans and specifications. Under the latter rule, damages are measured by the reasonable cost of correcting the defects in performance. The court noted that the cost of repair could, in a given case, be greater or less than the diminution in value. "Whether a defect should fall under the cost-of-replacement rule or be considered under the diminished value rule depends upon the nature and magnitude of the defect."[5]

Applying the rules to the case before it, the court affirmed the trial court's use of the cost-of-repair rule for such items in dispute as plaster cracks in the ceilings and reconstruction of a non-load-bearing patio wall. As to misplacement of the living room wall, however, the court invoked the diminished value rule. "To tear down the wall now and rebuild it in its proper place would involve a substantial destruction of the work, if not all of it, which was put into the wall and would cause additional damage to the other parts

---

[4]*Willard S & S, Inc. v. Stevens*, 167 Pa. Super. Ct. 621 (1950).

[5]*Accord, Trader v. Grampp Builders, Inc.*, 263 A.2d 304 (Del. Super. 1970).

of the house. . . . Such economic waste is unreasonable and unjustified. . . . Expert witnesses for both parties, testifying as to the value of the house, agreed that the misplacement of the wall had no effect on the market price. The trial court properly found that "the [owners] suffered no legal damage, although [their] particular desire for specified room size was not satisfied."[6]

The diminished-value rule does not ordinarily apply where the contractor has intentionally failed to comply with the plans and specifications. In such a case, the owner is entitled to recovery of or allowance for the cost of making the work conform to the contract, not merely the difference between the value of the work as performed and the work as contemplated.[7] Thus, where a contractor substituted iron pipe for lead pipe required by the contract, he was required to pay the owner the cost of laying lead pipe, not merely the difference in value between iron and lead pipe.[8]

7.4. SEVERABILITY OF ARTICULATED CONTRACT

Construction contracts frequently contemplate several stages of work and provide for progress payments. In determining whether there has been substantial performance of such a contract, a court may characterize it as "entire" or "severable." If the contract is found to be severable, the contractor's failure to perform a discrete portion or portions of it does not prevent his recovery of payment for portions completed. If a contract is found to be entire, however, the contractor's failure to perform even one part of it could preclude partial payment or give rise to liability for the uncompleted portion. The test of severability is, in general, whether the completed portion is a complete work fit for the use intended under the contract.

This principle is well illustrated in *S & W Investment Company, Inc. v. Otis W. Sharp & Son, Inc.*, 247 La. 158, 170 So.2d 360 (1964). The owner in that case contracted to construct a swimming pool. The contract price was $4,725 and included provision of a concrete shell as a first phase, and installation of tiling, filter, ladders and trim as a second phase. The contract called for a progress payment of $3,000 upon installation of the concrete shell and payment of the balance upon completion of the pool. The contractor completed the shell and received $3,000 as a "partial payment." Thereafter heavy rains uprooted the shell. After the contractor's initial salvage attempts failed, the contractor asked for an increase in the contract price to cover the unanticipated repair work. The owner refused, and the contractor disclaimed any further obligation. The owner employed another contractor to complete the pool at a cost of $3,900 and brought suit against the initial contractor for $2,175, the difference between the remaining amount due under the original contract and the actual cost of completion.

The contractor defended on the theory that the contract was divisible into two

---

[6]*See Edgar v. Hosea*, 210 So.2d 233 (Fla. Dist. Ct. App. 1968); *Jacob & Youngs v. Kent*, 230 N.Y. 239, 129 N.E. 889 (1921).

[7]*See, e.g., Pence v. Dennie*, 41 Cal.App. 428, 182 P. 980 (1919); *Morgan v. Gamble*, 320 Pa. 165, 79 A. 410 (1911).

[8]*Morgan v. Gamble, supra.*

parts, the first including the shell and the second including the finishing work. It argued that upon its delivery and the owner's acceptance of the shell it had completed its obligation, shifting the risk of loss to the owner. The court disagreed. It deemed the contract unseverable, on the ground that it did not impose "two obligations to do two different things." The court continued:

> Clearly the contract under consideration does not admit of its being only partially executed. Neither the shell by itself nor the finishing operation alone is a complete work fit for the use intended as the object of the agreement. . . . The worth of each component part is increased by its union with the other, and absence of one renders the other virtually useless or without value. . . . Inasmuch as the defendant's obligation was not divisible, . . . it follows that the progress payment cannot form the basis of a presumptive delivery of the work as of the time it was made; and in the absence of such delivery, as well as an acceptance by the owner, the swimming pool construction remained at the risk of the contractor until its complete performance.

Cases reaching an opposite result usually involve construction of discrete units, such as housing subdivisions, where the contract price is nothing more than the sum of the unit prices. Under such circumstances, the contractor's failure to complete all the units will not bar his recovery of payment for the units completed.

7.5. QUANTUM MERUIT RECOVERY

Suppose that a contractor's work falls short of substantial performance. May he still recover the value of the benefit he has conferred on the owner? Under certain circumstances, courts have found that he may indeed do so. To prevail without reliance on the doctrine of substantial performance, the contractor generally must show that (a) the owner has in fact benefited from the work partially done and (b) the owner has accepted such work. The legal theory supporting the contractor's recovery is sometimes referred to as "quantum meruit" or "quasi-contract" recovery based on the owner's implied promise to pay for the benefit received rather than on the contract between the parties.[9]

It should be noted, however, that acceptance—and thus existence of an implied promise to pay—will not necessarily be inferred from the owner's possession and retention of a structure in the absence of some affirmative act or undertaking. The burden of proof regarding the reasonable value conferred on the owner resides with the contractor.[10]

Principles of "quantum meruit" recovery are illustrated in *Nelson v. Hazel*, 433 P.2d 120 (Sup. Ct. Idaho 1967). Nelson, the contractor, sought to foreclose a mechanic's

---

[9]*Hayeck Building & Realty Co. v. Turcotte*, 361 Mass. 785 (1972).

[10]*See, e.g., Lavelle v. DeLuca*, 48 Wis. 2d 464, 180 N.W. 2d 710 (1970).

lien for labor and materials furnished in remodeling Hazel's home. The Supreme Court of Idaho reversed a lower court judgment in favor of the contractor, finding that he was not entitled to foreclose his lien if he had not also substantially performed the contract under which the lien arose. The Supreme Court of Idaho also remanded the case to the trial court, with instructions "to assess the damages sustained . . . and to . . . take . . . additional evidence. . . ." The trial court followed the instruction by allowing the owner a set-off, in the amount of the estimated cost of repairs to restore his home to a good and workmanlike condition, from the contractor's total charges of $5,090. Since the amount of the set-off still allowed the contractor a partial recovery, the owner again appealed, contending that the contractor could not enforce collection of any amount under a contract which had not been substantially performed.

The Supreme Court then modified its earlier finding, stating that "building contracts constitute an exception to the usual contract rule that a defaulting party in a contract action cannot recover damages." The exception, said the Court, arises from the unjust enrichment that would result if the owner were to retain the value of improvements in excess of the damages caused by the contractor's breach. "Even where the contract cannot be said to be substantially performed, the weight of authority allows a negligent contractor to recover for the benefits actually conferred, in order that a forfeiture be avoided." The Court went on to note that, where defective performance is remediable, the contractor's recovery is subject to an offset in the amount of the cost of correcting the defect, measurable ordinarily by "the cost of completing the work by a third person."

The court concluded: "If the defective performance, though less than substantial, has conferred benefits on the homeowners in excess of his injury, he is under a quasi-contractual duty to pay the excess." On this theory, the Court sustained judgment in the contractor's favor for $499, the difference between the amount claimed by the contractor initially and the sum of the amount already paid by the owner and the cost of repairing defective work.

7.6 WAIVER

If a contractor has not rendered substantial performance, he may seek to excuse his nonperformance by asserting that the owner has waived precise compliance with the contract terms and conditions. Waiver is defined as the intentional relinquishment of a known right. It may be manifested by the owner's actions, words, or writings. If waiver is found, the owner will generally be required to pay the full contract price despite the contractor's deviation from the contract.

In this sense, waiver differs from the doctrine of substantial performance, which contemplates that the amount due the contractor is subject to reduction for diminution of value or cost of repair. A waiver may also constitute a change or contract modification, for example where the owner has agreed to substitution of materials different from those specified in the contract. In such a case the formal requirements for contract modification must be met. If the contractor's deviation results from an omission rather than a substitution, however, the contractor must either accept a reduction in the contract price or demonstrate that the owner has waived his right to the originally intended performance.

Waiver may be predicated upon an act or statement of the owner after the deviation from the contract obligation has occurred or during the contractor's performance. A waiver during performance presupposes the contractor's justifiable reliance and thus may be retracted or modified by the owner if reliance has not occurred. A common question in waiver cases is whether those purporting to act for the owner, such as architects and engineers, indeed have the authority to bind him by waiving elements of the contractor's performance.

Several of these principles are illustrated in *Kirk Reid Co. v. Fine*, 205 Va. 778, 139 S.E.2d 829 (1965). In that case, the contractor agreed to install air-conditioning and heating systems for a contract price of $253,700. The contract required the contractor to perform in accordance with detailed drawings and specifications prepared by the project architect, who, together with the project engineer, was to exercise general supervision over the work. As soon as work commenced, the parties discovered that air-conditioning ducts could not be installed as prescribed in the drawings because of existing electrical conduits. In addition, the room intended to house certain air-conditioning equipment was found to be less than the requisite size. The contractor contended, among other things, that the project engineer authorized certain changes in the work to accommodate these problems, with the knowledge of the project architects. The owner denied knowledge of the changes until after the work had been completed.

The contractor completed the work, as modified. By that time, the owner had paid all but $14,473 of the contract price. The architect then issued a final payment certificate evidencing the contractor's entitlement to payment of the balance due. The owner refused to pay until furnished with a compliance certificate from the architect, engineer, and materialmen indicating that the equipment installed had the capacity originally specified. When the compliance certificate was not produced, the owner refused to pay.

The contractor did not deny that significant changes in the air-conditioning equipment had been made. He asserted, however, that the architect and engineer—the owner's representatives—had authorized the changes by waiving the originally intended performance. Since the contract provided that the architect and engineer were to "have general supervision of the work," the contractor contended that their actions in approving changes were binding on the owner. The court found otherwise, noting that the architect and engineer did not, by virtue of the general supervision clause, have authority to bind the owner with respect to changes in the plans and specifications except as authorized by contract. The contract itself permitted the architect and engineer merely to make minor changes in the work, not involving extra cost, and required a written order from the owner for extra work or changes. Issuance of the final payment certificate by the architect was also found not to be dispositive of the authorization question since the contract provided that "no certificate issued or payment made to the Contractor, nor partial or entire use of occupancy of the building by the Owner, shall be an acceptance of any work or materials not in accordance with this contract."

Since the owner had not approved or ratified the changes, the court found neither waiver nor authorized change. It therefore permitted the owner to recover from the contractor an amount equal to the difference between the damages caused by the changes—calculated in accordance with the diminution-in-value rule—and the balance due under the contract.

7.7. PROGRESS PAYMENTS

Because of the size of modern construction projects and the large amount of time needed to complete them, contractors usually cannot afford to finish their work before receiving payment. They must be paid as they proceed. To meet this need, construction contracts usually provide for progress payments.[11]

7.7.1. Mechanics of Progress Payments

The General Conditions contain detailed provisions applicable to progress payments. AIA Document A201, for example, contemplates that, before the contractor's first application for payment, the contractor will submit to the architect a schedule of values of the various portions of the work, including a prorated share of overhead and profit. The total of such portions equals the contract price. The schedule of values then forms the basis for successive applications for payment by the contractor, supported by data substantiating the contractor's right to payment (less applicable retainage). The architect then issues a certificate for payment. This tells the owner that the contractor is entitled to payment in the amount certified.[12] The architect may also decline to honor an application, in whole or in part, to protect the owner against defective work, third-party claims, or similar events.

7.7.2. Valuation of Progress Payments

Progress payment amounts may be determined in several ways: (1) actual value; (2) actual cost; (3) value proportionate to the contract price; or (4) stipulated percentage of total contract price represented by completion of a given stage of the work. Since progress payments reflect the value of materials, progress payments may include materials (1) when ordered, (2) when fabricated, (3) when delivered to the site, or (4) when incorporated in the work.

Since these variables can lead to difficult determinations, the soundest approach is to look to the proportionate value of the total contract price represented by the work done for which a progress payment is requested. This is what AIA Document A201 seeks

---

[11]There is no implied right to receive progress payments in the absence of an appropriate contractual provision. *Appeal of Emsco Screen Pipe Co.*, 69-1 B.C.A. ¶7710 (1969).

[12]Whether a contractor has the right to stop work if the owner fails to make a required progress payment depends on whether the failure is substantial or not. *See Guerini Stone Co. v. P. J. Carlin Constr. Co.*, 248 U.S. 334 (1919).

to do. The contractor usually wants to receive payment at the earliest possible time, since he may be paying for materials as he receives them and may be required also to make down payments against future procurement. The owner, on the other hand, usually wants to defer payment until materials are incorporated in the work. This will tend to defeat the claims of creditors of the contractor and will avoid risk of loss if materials paid for by the owner before incorporation are lost, destroyed or stolen. Good, old-fashioned negotiation usually determines whether the contractor or the owner will prevail.

7.7.3. Retention

Just as most construction contracts provide for progress payments, so they also provide further that a percentage of each progress payment may be retained by the owner until completion of the work. Retention is ordinarily calculated by taking a fixed percentage from each progress payment. It is a security device for the owner, who can apply the retained amount to claims against the contractor before releasing the balance upon completion of the contract. Such claims may arise as the result of liquidated damages for unexcused delay, cost of repairing defective work, liability to third parties caused by the contractor's acts or omissions, or amounts due unpaid materialmen or suppliers.

Retention may present a legal problem upon completion of the contract. Suppose, for example, that a contractor has entered into a fixed-price contract to perform certain work, has furnished a surety bond to secure payment to materialmen, and has received—without having paid such materialmen—the retained amount from the owner. If the unpaid materialmen seek recovery of the amount due them from the surety on its bond in their favor, may the surety then recover the amount claimed from the owner on the theory that the prematurely released retainage is in effect a security fund intended to benefit those whom the contractor was obligated to pay, and by necessary implication, those who are subrogated to the rights of such payees? Many cases so hold. In *Hochevar v. Maryland Casualty Co.*, 114 F.2d 948 (6th Cir. 1940), retained funds were paid by a county government to a contractor without the surety's consent. The contractor failed to pay subcontractors and materialmen, who obtained judgments against the surety. The trial court awarded the surety a judgment against the county equaling the amount of the judgments against it, "on the theory that, by prematurely paying the percentages that had been retained pursuant to the contract, the County violated its duty to (the surety)."

7.7.4. Payment as a Waiver of Defects

If the owner makes a progress payment after a contract deviation, may he be deemed to have waived any contractual noncompliance on the part of the contractor? In the absence of a contract provision to the contrary, waiver can be successfully asserted. Thus, in *Swink v. Smith*, 113 N.W. 2d 515 (Neb. 1962), the plaintiff contractor sought recovery of the balance due for construction of a drainage ditch. Under the contract, the project was to be completed in 30 days—a schedule the contractor could not meet. The owner contended that the contractor had breached the contract by his failure to complete the ditch on time. The court did not accept the owner's defense, stating: ". . . the breach of the 30-day provision was waived by the subsequent actions of defendant in demanding performance as late as December 1959, and in making voluntary payments on the amount due after the 30 days had expired."

Paragraph 9.4.4 of AIA Document A201 forecloses such legal arguments of waiver by providing that progress payments shall not "constitute an acceptance of any Work not in accordance with the Contract Documents." If the construction contract contains such a provision, waiver will only be found if there is express evidence through statements or other unambiguous acts of the owner.

7.7.5. Failure to Make Progress Payments

The owner's primary obligation under a construction contract is to pay for the work performed. The owner's failure to pay goes to the heart of the contract and may permit the contractor to withhold further performance. Thus, Section 9.7.1 of AIA Document A201 allows the contractor, in the event of the owner's failure to make a scheduled payment when due, to *stop* work. The provision is silent, however, as to other legal consequences of nonpayment.

One such consequence is, of course, that the contractor may not only stop work but may also sue the owner for damages arising from the breach. Failure to pay an installment due on a construction contract is generally held to be such a material breach as to excuse further performance by the contractor and to permit a suit for damages, ordinarily equal in amount to the unpaid contract price less the reasonable cost of the work not performed.[13] Even if nonpayment falls short of a material breach, the contractor should at least be entitled to suspend work, to receive interest on the amount due, and to obtain an extension of time within which to complete the contract. He may also be entitled to consequential damages if such damages were reasonably foreseeable by the owner and unavoidably caused by nonpayment.

7.8.   COMPLETION, ACCEPTANCE, AND FINAL PAYMENT

Completion of work under a construction contract is of the utmost legal significance. It ordinarily activates final payment and liquidation of the parties' claims against each other. As a result, completion is often the subject of elaborate contract provisions.

Completion is usually a two-part process involving substantial completion and final completion. *Substantial completion* occurs when the structure contracted for is ready for occupancy or the use for which it was constructed, despite defects to be corrected or minor incomplete aspects of the work. *Final completion* contemplates final payment (including retention) and satisfaction of all contract requirements.

AIA Document A201 reflects this two-part process. The project architect is

---

[13]*See, e.g., Shapiro Engineering Corp. v. Francis O. Day Co., Inc.,* 215 Md. 373, 137 A.2d 695 (1958).

required to issue a certificate of substantial completion "which shall establish the Date of Substantial Completion, shall state the responsibilities of the Owner and the Contractor for security, maintenance, heat, utilities, damage to the Work, and insurance, and shall fix the time within which the Contractor shall complete the items listed therein." (¶9.8.1.) After final inspection and determination that the work has been fully completed, the architect then issues a final certificate for payment. This triggers payment to the contractor of remaining amounts due. Before such payment is made, however, the contractor must furnish evidence that materialmen, subcontractors, and workmen have been paid. He must also furnish a consent to the surety, if any, issuing performance or payment bonds covering the work. Failure of the owner to obtain this consent can create a liability to the surety for retainage released if bonded obligations remain outstanding.

Final payment under this procedure ordinarily amounts to a waiver of further claims by each party against the other. Under AIA Document A201, however, the waiver is subject to stated exceptions as to the owner. These include unsettled liens, faulty or defective work appearing after substantial completion, special guarantees running in the owner's favor (such as manufacturer's warranties), and failure of the work to comply with the contract documents. (¶9.9.4.)

Application of these exceptions is illustrated in *Midland v. Waller*, 430 S.W. 2d 473 (Tex. Sup. Ct. 1968). The contractor in that case had constructed a municipal swimming pool for the city of Midland, Texas. The contractor guaranteed the work for one year from the date of final acceptance. The contract contained a provision, patterned on Paragraph 9.9.4 of AIA Document A201, that final payment constituted a waiver of all claims by the owner except for, among other things, "faulty work appearing after final payment." The same provision stated, moreover, that "no certificate issued nor payment made to the contractor, nor partial or entire use or occupancy of the work by the owner, shall be an acceptance of any work or materials not in accordance with this contract."

The swimming pool was accepted by the project architect on September 15, 1963. More than a year later, various defects in the pool were discovered. The defects were attributable to the contractor's failure to construct the pool in accordance with the plans and specifications. The contractor defended on the ground that the architect's certificate of completion was a final determination that the contractor had complied with the contract. He argued that the city could not charge him with liability for defects appearing 20 months after the date of completion. The court rejected this argument:

> [C]onsidering the contract in its entirety, we hold that it means that latent defects at the time the architect issued his final certificate of payment and accepted the premises, becoming evident after the one-year warranty contained in the contract and which could not have been discovered by the exercise of ordinary care, may be made the basis of a suit for damages on account of such defects.

The case illustrates several intertwined problems arising upon completion of construction contracts. In accordance with prevailing law, it demonstrates that final acceptance does not extinguish claims arising from warranties regarding quality, work and performance furnished by the contractor or by a subcontractor, and does not extinguish claims arising from latent defects existing at the time the work was completed. The latter claims are, however, subject to the applicable statute of limitations in the jurisdiction where the work was performed.[14]

7.9. ASSIGNMENT OF RIGHT TO BE PAID

Construction contractors often finance contracts by assignment of contract proceeds to a bank or financial institution. Contractors may also obtain performance and payment bonds from a surety, thereby setting the stage for a contest between the assignee bank and the surety with respect to amounts retained by the owner in the event of the contractor's default.

This fact pattern underlies a typical case, *Framingham Trust Company v. Gould-National Batteries, Inc.*, 307 F. Supp. 1008 (D. Mass. 1969). The contractor there undertook to construct an addition to a factory for a contract price of $133,000. Before doing so, however, the contractor entered into an agreement with Framingham Trust Company assigning its accounts receivable and contract rights as security for repayment of money loaned. On the same date that it contracted with the owner to build the factory addition, the contractor also executed performance and payment bonds in favor of the owner. Several months later, before completing the work, the contractor gave notice to the owner and the surety of its inability to complete the contract and formally acknowledged its default. The contractor was later adjudicated a bankrupt.

The owner then made demand upon the surety to complete the work. The surety complied and expended $3,238 in so doing. Although it had largely completed the work at the time of its default, the contractor also owed materialmen and suppliers $53,293. The surety was thus also required to pay this amount under its payment bond. The surety then asserted a claim against the $25,692 in contract balances and retention still held by the owner and not paid to the contractor at the time of its default. The assignee bank, while conceding that the $3,238 expended by the surety to complete the work might properly be paid to it, asserted a claim for $22,454, the balance then remaining. The unpaid materialmen and suppliers took no action to create liens against the owner's property under state law.

On these facts, the court found in favor of the assignee bank. The court reasoned that the surety, by making payment to the contractor's materialmen and suppliers, obtained no rights against the owner by way of subrogation. Nor did the surety acquire a position superior to the bank's. This conclusion flowed from the court's findings (a) that, upon default, the contractor had forfeited its rights and (b) that the materialmen and suppliers enjoyed no contractual right against the owner for unpaid services and supplies. Thus, whether subrogated to the latter or the former, the surety derived no legally enforceable rights. The court placed conclusive weight on the failure of the materialmen and suppliers to obtain a statutory lien under applicable state law, a failure depriving

---

[14]*See Bickerstaff v. Frazier*, 232 So.2d 190 (Fla.App. 1970); *Ramonas v. Kerelis*, 102 Ill. App.2d 262, 243 N.W.2d 711 (1968).

them of legal rights against the owners to which the surety might have become subrogated. Accordingly, the assignee bank's claim against the owner for $22,454 was upheld.

The court's holding in *Framingham Trust Company* is not the invariable result in
such cases. There are, in fact, two distinct lines of precedent in state court decisions. In
some jurisdictions, the owner's retention of a portion of the contract price is deemed to
operate as an equitable assignment of the amount retained to meet unpaid claims for labor
and material, therefore defeating the claim of an assignee of the contractor. In other
jurisdictions, retention is regarded as protection for the owner; no equitable assignment
in favor of materialmen, laborers, or suppliers is assumed; and an assignee of the
contractor is entitled to retained sums in the first instance.[15]

7.10.   UNPAID SUPPLIERS, SUBCONTRACTORS, AND LABORERS: THE MECHANIC'S LIEN

A mechanic's lien is a statutory security device by which unpaid laborers, contractors, subcontractors, and suppliers who have improved real property may enforce payment for services and materials through the lien process. By creating a lien, these
claimants can compel a judicial sale of the subject real property if they are not paid. To
avoid this result, the owner of the property will ordinarily make payment, thereby
discharging the lien.

The law of mechanics' liens reflects the inherent financial instability of the
construction industry. The lien procedure provides legal redress to claimants who would
otherwise be subject to financial loss through prime contractors' or owners' nonpayment
or financial default. In this way, lien laws are thought to facilitate the construction process
by encouraging subcontractors and suppliers to provide goods and services without
exhaustively investigating the credit of prime contractors and owners.

Nonetheless, lien laws have been widely criticized. They are complex; they
create rights which may, depending upon state law, be subordinate to the rights of other
creditors, such as mortgagees and construction lenders; they may compel an unsophisti-
cated owner to pay twice for the same obligation, once to the prime contractor and later to
unpaid subcontractors and materialmen; they do not apply to public structures; and they
may protect only certain classes of claimants, leaving others without a statutory remedy.

7.10.1.   Who May Assert a Mechanic's Lien

Although statutory prescriptions vary, a lien claimant generally must satisfy three
tests: (a) he must show that the subject real property has been improved; (b) he must have
supplied labor or materials; and (c) the labor or materials must have been supplied for one

---

[15]The cases are collected in 13 Am.Jur.2d "Building and Construction Contracts" §90, at 90 nn. 10-11 (1964 and
1979 Cum. Supp.).

or more of the purposes specified in the controlling statute.[16] A typical statutory provision defining protected claimants states:

> Whoever performs engineering or land surveying services with respect to real estate, or contributes to the improvement of real estate by performing labor, for any of the purposes hereinafter stated, whether under contract with the owner of such real estate or at the instance of any agent, trustee, contractor or subcontractor or such owner, shall have a lien upon the improvement, and upon the land on which it is situated or to which it may be removed. . . .[17]

Among those typically protected are contractors, subcontractors, materialmen and suppliers of contractors and subcontractors, and, depending upon applicable statutes, the providers of "invisible" improvements, such as engineers, architects, and land surveyors.[18]

7.10.2. Property Subject to Lien

Mechanics' liens may be asserted only against real property. Personal property is excluded unless it becomes affixed to real property so as to qualify as a "fixture." Liens also may not be placed on public property. What is public and what is private property, however, may be a complex question. For example, public property used for private or proprietary purposes may be the subject of a lien.[19] On most public works projects, however, claimants who would otherwise be protected by lien laws may look to required payment bonds for pecuniary protection.

7.10.3. Asserting the Lien Claim

Lien laws invariably require the claimant to give notice to the owner or his agent. Such notice takes two forms: it may be a pre-lien notice furnished early in the construction process by one not in privity of contract with the owner; or it may be a claim, filed upon completion of construction with a statutorily designated office such as a county register of deeds or titles. The pre-lien notice is primarily for the benefit of the owner, who may thereby avoid double payment. The claim notice is primarily for the benefit of third parties having an interest in the property. Since the mechanic's lien is a creature of statute, a party asserting a lien must comply with statutory requirements.[20]

---

[16]*Anderson v. Breezy Point Estates*, 283 Minn. 490, 168 N.W. 2d 693 (1969).

[17]Minn. Stat. Ann. §514.01.

[18]*See generally* Anno., "Architect's Services as Within Mechanic's Lien Statute," 28 A.L.R.3d 1014 (1969), for description of state statutes.

[19]See Anno., "Right to Mechanic's Lien upon Leasehold for Supplying Labor or Material in Attaching or Installing Fixtures," 42 A.L.R.2d 685 (1955).

[20]*Zeigler Lumber & Supply Co. v. Golden Triangle Devt. Co.*, 326 A.2d 524 (Pa. Super. 1974); *Brann & Stuart Co. v. Consolidated Sun Ray, Inc.*, 433 Pa. 574, 253 A.2d 105 (1969).

The pre-lien notice must be filed at or prior to the beginning of the claimant's contribution to the improvement; the claim must be filed within a specified number of days after furnishing the last item of work or following completion or cessation of the contract.

7.10.4. Duration and Extent of the Lien

Most lien laws require that the lien claimant initiate a foreclosure action within a specified time after one of several events, including, typically, the date when the underlying debt accrued, the date when the last item of work was performed, or the date when the lien was filed. Applicable time frames and triggering events vary from state to state. A claimant must strictly comply with the controlling statutory requirements or his lien will be without effect.

Even if properly perfected, the lien is limited as to enforceable amount. For a contractor in privity of contract with the owner, the enforceable amount is generally limited by the contract price. For a subcontractor or supplier not in such privity, however, the enforceable amount is generally limited by the reasonable value of the labor performed or materials supplied.

Governing law may impose a further limitation by providing that the sum of all liens may not exceed the contract price less payments made by the owner to the contractor prior to receiving pre-lien notice. The effect of this further limitation is significant: if the owner pays the contractor all or most of the contract price before the subcontractor or supplier gives the required pre-lien notice, the owner will be liable to the claimant only for the difference between the contract price and the amount paid to the contractor. Although protecting the owner against double payment, this provision could leave nothing for the claimant. In addition to a limitation on enforceable amount, many statutes limit the size of the estate or realty subject to possible foreclosure and sale.

7.10.5. Enforcement of a Lien Claim

A lien claim is enforced through foreclosure on the property improved. The purpose of the foreclosure action is to compel the sale of the property in order to compensate the claimant or claimants. In a suit by a subcontractor or materialman, the contractor must be joined as a necessary party to the action in most states. Failure to do so may defeat the claimant's action. Other adverse claimants, such as mortgagees and construction lenders, are proper but not necessary parties.

Enforcement of a lien claim may pit the claimant against other competing interests, including subsequent purchasers, judgment creditors, and federal and state governments having tax liens. Although mechanics' liens are generally superior to all other liens or encumbrances filed after commencement of the labor or delivery of materials, intricate questions of priority may nonetheless arise where the total amount of claims exceeds the value of the property.

7.11. ADDITIONAL SOURCE MATERIALS

General

Creyke, G., Jr., "The 'Payment Gap' in federal construction contracts," 35 Geo. Wash. L.Rev. 908 (1967)

Disman, William H., Jr., "Application of the cost and value theories in measuring contractor's liability," 48 Ky. L.J. 432 (1960)

Hart, "Measurement and payment of contractor's work," *1967 Proceedings, Sec. of Ins., Neg. & Comp. Law* 51

Killeen, J., "Owner liability for construction costs," 52 Calif. S.B.J. 526 (1977)

Moss R., "Payment disputes in construction industry litigation," 53 L.A.B.J. 349 (1977)

Seidman, Herbert A., "Right of a defaulting building contractor to recover in Maryland upon the contract or in quasi-contract," 16 Md. L.Rev. 162 (1956)

Simson, P.A.L., "Deductions from payments in construction contracts," 116 Sol. J. 624 (1972)

Anno., "Liability of architect or engineer for improper issuance of certificate," 43 A.L.R.2d 1227

Anno., "Payments or advances to building contractor by obligee as affecting rights as between obligee and surety on contractor's bond," 127 A.L.R. 10

Impossibility

Scott, Terrence V., "Recovery of the costs of attempted performance in impossibility situations: an analysis of Northern Corp. v. Chugack Electric Ass'n," 6 UCLA-Alaska L.Rev. 338 (1977)

Substantial Performance

Estep, L. D., "Substantial performance—honest effort to comply with contract," 21 Mo. L. Rev. 169 (1956)

Stoljar, S. J., "Substantial performance in building and work contracts," 34 Western Aust. Ann. L.Rev. 293 (1955)

Anno., "Measure of recovery by building contractor where contract is substantially but not exactly performed," 65 A.L.R. 1297; 23 A.L.R. 1435

Mechanic's Liens

Bernstein, P., "Perfection of mechanics' liens against the lessor," 57 Ill. B.J. 996 (1969)

Mik, J. W., "Trust fund provision of the mechanics' lien act," 4 Osgoode Hall L. J. 77 (1966)

Starn, T. F.,"Compulsory arbitration and rights under the Miller Act, Mechanics lien laws, and states public improvement bond laws," 4 Forum 195 (1969)

Note, "Mechanics' liens—abandonment of construction—15 mo. suspension of construction, renegotiation of contract price, and minor changes in plans held not to prevent relation back to date of original commencement," 34 Md. L. Rev. 663 (1974)

Note, "Mechanic's liens and surety bonds in the building trades," 68 Yale L.J. 139 (1958)

PART III

Others Involved in
Ongoing Construction Contracts

CHAPTER **8**

Construction Default:
The Contractor's Bond

8.1. INTRODUCTION

Financial uncertainty is one of the hallmarks of the construction industry. The owner must be concerned about poorly managed, undercapitalized contractors; the inherent risks of the construction process itself (of which price increases, labor difficulties, and subsurface conditions are but a few); and the potentially sizable losses that can result if a project is not completed according to plans and specifications or the contractor's suppliers and materialmen are not paid.

To provide protection against such risks, the owner frequently requires the contractor to obtain surety bonds of performance and payment. In the event of the contractor's default, the owner can then look to a solvent bonding company rather than the financially distressed (or even bankrupt) contractor. Since sureties will generally provide bonds for only the most financially reliable contractors, the requirement of a bond also tends to winnow out the incompetent at the starting gate.

Contractors' bonds are thus in widespread use. They are an essential feature of the construction industry contracting process.

8.2. SURETY BONDING

The construction contract surety bond is a three-party contract between the principal (the contractor), the obligee (the owner), and the surety. Under this contract the surety is collaterally bound in the event of the principal's default. If the surety is required to pay or perform on behalf of the obligee, it may demand reimbursement from the principal for all obligations paid plus administrative costs. There are three basic kinds of surety bonds: the bid bond (an example of which is AIA Document A310), the performance bond (AIA Document A311), and the payment bond (AIA Document A311).

8.3. THE BID BOND

The bid bond assures the owner that the contractor, if selected for award of a contract, will actually proceed with it. It may also require that performance and payment bonds be furnished. If the contractor fails to do so, the bid bond becomes payable to the owner as compensation for damages sustained as a result of the contractor's refusal. The penal amount of the bond may represent a liquidation of damages, a limitation of liability, or a security device.[1]

Expressed or implied in all bid bonds, however, is a promise to pay the owner damages if the successful bidder fails to enter into the contract and to furnish the required bonds.[2] The measure of damages is either the penal amount specified in the bond or the difference between the amount of the bid submitted by the defaulting contractor and the next higher bidder (if such difference is less than the penal amount) or, in the absence of a higher bidder, the price at which the owner is ultimately forced to contract. Where the bid bond specifies a maximum penalty, that amount becomes the limit of both the contractor's and the surety's liability. This is true even though the owner may have sustained damages in excess of the bond penalty.[3]

The contractor should examine the terms of a bid bond with care. Some bid bonds are conditioned to pay the owner actual damages up to the penal amount, others to pay the penal amount as liquidated damages. The distinction can be significant. Actual damages are generally measured by the difference between the amount of the defaulting contractor's bid and the amount of the next higher bid. The fact that the next higher bidder eventually awarded the contract does not complete it is not an element of damages chargeable to the first defaulting contractor.[4] Liquidated damages need not bear any necessary relationship to the actual damages sustained by the owner. It is required only that liquidated damages constitute a reasonable expectation of the owner's actual damages resulting from refusal of the contractor to enter into a contract. If liquidated damages are reasonable when determined, they will generally be upheld by the courts even though the amount is greater than actual damages.[5]

---

[1]*See, e.g., Elsinore Union Elementary School District v. Kastorff*, 54 Cal.2d 390, 353 P.2d 713 (1960); *City of Lake Geneva v. States Improvement Co.*, 172 N.W.2d 176 (Wisc. 1969) (liquidation damages); *Board of Education v. Sever-Williams Co.*, 22 Ohio St. 2d 107, 258 N.E.2d 605 (1970) (liability restricted to damages sustained).

[2]*See, e.g., Brown v. United States*, 152 F. 964 (2d Cir. 1907).

[3]*See, e.g., Bolivar Reorganized School District No. 1 v. American Surety Company*, 307 S.W.2d 405, 70 A.L.R.2d 1361 Mo. (1957); 50 Am.Jur.2d "Suretyship" §30.

[4]*Brown v. United States*, 152 F. 964 (2d Cir. 1907).

[5]*City of Lake Geneva v. States Improvement Co.*, 45 Wis.2d 50, 172 N.W.2d 176 (1969).

Often the surety issuing a bid bond will also issue performance and payment bonds to the same contractor if he is awarded the contract. What happens if the surety then fails to issue required performance or payment bonds? As in so many other areas of construction contracting, the answer is determined by the written contract. Sureties generally disclaim in the bid bond or the bid bond application that they are under any obligation to issue required performance or payment bonds. Such a disclaimer protects the surety against liabilities for lost profits on contracts that would have been awarded but for the contractor's failure to obtain the necessary bonds. Without such a disclaimer, liability may be successfully asserted against the surety.

Furthermore, if a bid bond is conditioned upon the contractor's entering into a contract *and* furnishing performance and payment bonds, the surety may be liable on its bid bond to those who would have been protected by the required bonds had they been furnished by the contractor.[6]

Refusal of a successful bidder to enter into a contract is usually based on mistake. If the contractor can prove a mistake in his bid, both the contractor and his surety will ordinarily be relieved of liability for the contractor's refusal.[7] In some jurisdictions, however, the contractor may be required to forfeit the bid bond even though mistake can be proven.[8]

In order to rely on mistake, the contractor must offer "clear and convincing proof" of circumstances sufficient to constitute an excusable mistake. Moreover, the mistake must be one of fact, not one of law or judgment; must be of such grave consequence that enforcement of the contract would be unconscionable; must relate to a material feature of the contract; must not have come about through the contractor's culpable negligence; and must not prejudice the owner except as to loss of bargained-for performance.[9]

A subcontractor's mistake may be used as an excuse by a prime contractor if the subcontractor's mistake is such as to relieve the subcontractor of his obligation to the prime contractor.[10]

Another common reason for the principal's refusal to enter into the construction contract is that a material change in the terms or conditions of the contract occurred after the bid was submitted. If the change could not have been reasonably anticipated when the bid was submitted, the principal is entitled to withdraw his bid, thereby relieving the principal and surety from liability on the bid bond.[11] Examples of material changes include the obligee's delay in awarding the contract beyond the time for award set forth in

---

[6]*United States for the Use of Empire Plastics Corp. v. Western Casualty and Surety Company*, 429 F.2d 905 (10th Cir. 1970). In that case unpaid materialmen were permitted to recover from the surety on its bid bond, which contained an explicit promise to issue a payment bond. The bid bond was deemed to secure the contractor's statutory obligation to provide a payment bond.

[7]*M. F. Kemper Constr. Co. v. City of Los Angeles*, 37 Cal.2d 696, 235 P.2d 7 (1951).

[8]*Board of Education v. Sever-Williams Co.*, 22 Ohio St.2d 107, 258 N.E.2d 605 (1970).

[9]*Baltimore v. De Luca-Davis Constr. Co.*, 210 Md. 518, 124 A.2d 557 (1956); *Chris Berg, Inc. v. United States*, 426 F.2d 314 (Ct. Cl. 1970); Anno., "Rights and Remedies of Bidders for Public Contracts," 52 A.L.R.2d 793 (1955); Corbin, *Contracts* §616.

[10]*Kemp v. United States*, 38 F.Supp. 568 (D.Md. 1941).

[11]*People of New York v. Rouse Constr. Corp.*, 274 N.Y.S.2d 981 (1966).

the invitation to bid; the obligee's attempt to change the method of construction from that contemplated by the bid documents; or the obligee's attempt to change the use of certain materials.[12]

8.4. THE PERFORMANCE BOND

The performance bond is intended to protect the owner from the consequences of the contractor's failure to complete the contract in accordance with plans and specifications. Performance bonds are almost always referenced in the General Conditions of a major construction contract.[13]

A performance bond does not provide absolute assurance that the contract work will be completed as specified for the contract price. It does indicate that a financially responsible party stands behind the contractor, to the limit of the penal amount of the bond. Subject to that limitation, the performance bond is generally coextensive with the contractor's obligations under the contract. The person entitled to protection under the bond is usually only the named obligee—in most instances the owner. With some exceptions, mostly found in early cases, the performance bond's protection does not extend to third parties.[14]

The performance bond limits the surety's liability to a specific dollar amount. The bond agreement itself is a deceptively simple document. It typically provides:

> Whenever Contractor shall be, and declared by Owner to be in default under the Contract, the Owner having performed the Owner's obligations thereunder, the Surety may promptly remedy the default, or shall promptly
>
> 1) Complete the Contract in accordance with its terms and conditions, or
>
> 2) Obtain a bid or bids for completing the Contract in accordance with its terms and conditions, and upon determination by Surety of the lowest responsible bidder, or, if the Owner elects, upon determination by the Owner and the Surety jointly of the lowest responsible bidder, arrange for a contract between such bidder and the Owner, and make funds to pay the cost of completion less the balance of the contract price; but not exceeding, including other costs and damages for which the Surety may be liable hereunder, the amount set forth in the first paragraph hereof [the penal amount]. The term "balance of the contract price" . . . shall mean the total amount payable by the Owner to Contractor under the Contract . . ., less the amount properly paid by Owner to the Contractor. . . . [AIA Document A311.]

---

[12]*State of Connecticut v. McGraw & Co.*, 41 F.Supp. 396 (D.Conn. 1941).

[13]From AIA Document A201, The General Conditions of the Contract for Construction:

> 7.5.1. The Owner shall have the right to require the Contractor to furnish bonds covering the faithful performance of the contract and the payment of all obligations arising thereunder if and as required in the Bidding Documents or Contract Documents.

[14]*DeVries v. City of Austin*, 261 Minn. 52, 110 N.W.2d 529 (1961). *Contra, Bristol Steel and Iron Works, Inc. v. Plank*, 162 Va. 819, 178 S.E. 58 (1935).

The exact terms of the agreement may vary, depending upon whether the contract is public or private, the number of sureties involved, and the contractor's status (*i.e.*, whether the contractor is a prime contractor or a subcontractor).

Upon receiving notice from the obligee of the contractor's default, the surety has several options. It can, in the first instance, do nothing. Unless a default has in fact occurred and the bond remains valid, it will have no legal obligation to perform. In that event, the owner-obligee will ordinarily take over and complete the work, attempting thereafter to seek recovery from the surety through litigation or the threat of litigation.

If the surety believes itself to be liable on the bond, it may then (1) pay the bond penalty (the dollar amount set forth in the bond) if completion and claim payment costs are expected to exceed the penalty amount; (2) finance the contractor and complete the contract, an option that makes sense if the contract can be completed for less than the penal amount of the bond and the contractor retains the technical capacity to perform; (3) permit the owner to obtain a completing contractor and thereafter pay the cost of construction in excess of the contract funds in the owner's hands when the default occurred; or (4) take over performance of the contract by hiring a new contractor to complete the work, an option used when the substitute contractor can complete the work at less cost. Once the surety assumes control of the contract, however, it must complete it even though final completion costs exceed the penal amount. In doing so, the surety must also preserve subcontractor and supplier prices.

Validity of the performance bond can be impaired by the owner's actions. If the owner permits a cardinal change in the contract that fundamentally alters the scope of contract performance, the surety will be discharged.[15] Similarly, an owner's violation of contract terms prejudicial to the surety will provide grounds for discharge, for example, where an owner fails to carry builder's risk insurance required by the contract.[16]

8.5.   COMPLETION AND DUAL OBLIGEE BONDS

Completion bonds are special adaptations of performance bonds written to include third parties. They typically name lenders as obligees in addition to owners. Unlike a common performance bond, a completion bond naming a lender as obligee constitutes the surety's guarantee that the contract will be successfully completed, free of all liens and encumbrances. The completion bond is used most often by a developer at the request of a lending institution making a construction loan and wishing its mortgage to be the first lien upon the property improved. Under the completion bond, the surety in effect guarantees the performance of the owner and the contractor, becoming in the process an insurer of successful completion.[17] Because of the risks involved for the surety, completion bonds are infrequently written today.

---

[15]*Wunderlich Contracting Co. v. United States*, 173 Ct.Cl. 180 (1965). This is not so with respect to ordinary changes within the scope of the contract. *See, e.g., United States v. Freel*, 186 U.S. 309 (1902).

[16]*Independent School District v. Loberg Plumbing & Heating Co.*, 266 Minn. 426, 123 N.W.2d 793 (1963).

[17]*Prudence Co. v. Fidelity & Deposit Co.*, 297 U.S. 198 (1936).

The dual obligee bond typically specifies a third party, such as a lender, as an obligee in addition to the owner, while retaining the limitations on the surety's liabilities found in performance bonds generally. Thus, under a dual obligee bond, the surety merely extends its liability to an additional party. Most dual obligee bonds require, however, that the lender and the owner pay the contractor in accordance with the contract terms as a condition of the surety's liability. If the lender refuses or fails to advance funds for the project pursuant to its own commitments, the surety will be discharged.

8.6.   PAYMENT BONDS

Payment bonds, more commonly called labor and material payment bonds, assure that the contractor's obligations for labor and materials incurred under the contract will be paid. Payment bonds thus protect the owner from liens and other claims made after completion of the work and after final payment has been made to the contractor. Payment bonds, although running to the owner as obligee, also benefit subcontractors, materialmen, and laborers. In this sense, payment bonds are more complex than performance bonds.

A typical payment bond (AIA Document A311) specifies a penal amount, defines covered claimants as those having a direct contract with the contractor or a subcontractor for labor, materials, or both, used in the performance of the contract; and provides that claimants who have not been paid in full within 90 days after completion of their work may sue and execute on the bond, subject to the requirement that detailed notice of claim be given to the contractor, the owner, or the surety within 90 days of completion of work; that any suit be commenced within one year "following the date on which the Principal [*i.e.*, the contractor] ceased work on said Contract"; and that suit be brought in the state or federal court having jurisdiction over the place where the project is situated.

By their very nature, payment bonds present intricacies of coverage and procedure. As indicated above, the class of covered claimants includes anyone in privity of contract with a contractor or subcontractor, although a claimant need not perform work at the construction site to be eligible for coverage.[18] The bonded contractor must therefore police payment made through a chain of subcontractors to assure that each subcontractor in fact applies payments made by the contractor to intended suppliers, subcontractors and materialmen.

If such payments are misapplied, the bonded contractor may be required to pay twice for the same work. The problem is aggravated by the generally accepted legal principle that, in the absence of specific instructions as to application of payments, a payee may apply a payment against any debt of the payor, whether or not arising from the work in question.[19] If the payor is a subcontractor having an outstanding but unrelated

---

[18]*See, e.g., Weyerhaeuser Company v. Twin City Millwork Co.,* 291 Minn. 293, 191 N.W.2d 401 (1971).

[19]*Luksus v. United Pacific Insurance Co.,* 452 F.2d 207 (7th Cir. 1971).

debt running in favor of a second-tier subcontractor who is also a payee, the second-tier subcontractor may apply the payment to the unrelated debt and still sue the prime contractor's surety to recover payment for work done. Appropriate instructions from the prime contractor can avoid this problem.

Covered items include, among other things, (1) materials incorporated into the work, delivered to the job site, furnished pursuant to contract specifications even if not delivered to the job site (*e.g.*, items stored in a bonded warehouse), and used in the performance of the contract; (2) all labor performed at the job site and labor performed in fabricating materials off-site pursuant to the contract; (3) freight and transportation costs; (4) equipment rental and incidental repairs; (5) fuel used or consumed in connection with the work; (6) insurance premiums; (7) on federal projects, unpaid withholding taxes; (8) union pension and welfare benefits; and (9) legal interest and attorneys' fees, except, attorneys' fees in Miller Act litigation. (See §8.7, *infra*.)[20]

Items not covered include bank loans even if loan proceeds are used to pay project costs; liability or damage claims arising out of performance of the contract; and withholding taxes on state or private contracts.[21]

Applicable state law ordinarily imposes strict claim notice and suit requirements, suggested in part by the standard-form AIA document that is used for many major construction projects (AIA Document A311). Failure of an otherwise eligible claimant to comply precisely with those requirements will result in loss of claim. Requirements may vary from jurisdiction to jurisdiction. A prudent subcontractor will thus review local law in relation to the contract and be guided accordingly.

8.7 THE MILLER ACT

In a construction contract between private parties, laborers and materialmen commonly are accorded a statutory lien on the structure that is the subject of the contract to secure payment of their claims.[22] Construction contracts with the United States do not permit the assertion of such liens. As a consequence, the United States is under no legal obligation to pay persons who would otherwise be lien claimants.

To protect such persons on federal projects, federally enacted legislation requires execution of a payment bond in favor of the Government as a condition precedent to the letting of a Government Contract. This legislation is commonly known as the Miller Act. Both for its own sake and as a model for similar state statutes, the Miller Act deserves close consideration.

The Miller Act provides in relevant part (40 U.S.C. §270b):

---

[20]*See, e.g., Combs v. Jackson*, 69 Minn. 336, 72 N.W. 565 (1897); *Don's Heavy Hauling, Inc. v. Frank Malone Construction Co.*, 81 S.D. 1, 129 N.W.2d 900 (1964); *F. D. Rich Co. v. United States for the Use of Industrial Lumber Co.*, 417 U.S. 116 (1974); *United States for the Benefit of Sherman v. Carter*, 353 U.S. 210 (1957).

[21]*See, e.g., Farmers State Bank of Parkston v. Kuipers Construction Co.*, 86 S.D. 27, 190 N.W.2d 769 (1971); *Healy Plumbing & Heating Co. v. Minneapolis-St. Paul Sanitary District*, 284 Minn. 8, 169 N.W.2d 50 (1969); *Scott v. Travelers Indemnity Co.*, 215 Tenn. 173, 384 S.W.2d 38 (1964).

[22]*See* Chapter 7 and §7.7, *supra*.

(a) Every person who has furnished labor or material in the prosecution of the work provided for in such contract, in respect of which a payment bond is furnished under section 270a of this title and who has not been paid in full therefor before the expiration of a period of ninety days after the day on which the last of the labor was done or performed by him or material was furnished or supplied by him for which such claim is made, shall have the right to sue on such payment bond for the amount, or the balance thereof, unpaid at the time of institution of such suit and to prosecute said action to final execution and judgment for the sum or sums justly due him: *Provided, however,* That any person having direct contractual relationship express or implied with the contractor furnishing said payment bond shall have a right of action upon the said payment bond upon giving written notice to said contractor within ninety days from the date on which such person did or performed the last of the labor or furnished or supplied the last of the material for which such claim is made, stating with substantial accuracy the amount claimed and the name of the party to whom the material was furnished or supplied or for whom the labor was done or performed. Such notice shall be served by mailing the same by registered mail, postage prepaid, in an envelope addressed to the contractor at any place he maintains an office or conducts his business, or his residence, or in any manner in which the United States marshal of the district in which the public improvement is situated is authorized by law to serve summons.

(b) Every suit instituted under this section shall be brought in the name of the United States for the use of the person suing, in the United States District Court for any district in which the contract was to be performed and executed and not elsewhere, irrespective of the amount in controversy in such suit, but no such suit shall be commenced after the expiration of one year after the day on which the last of the labor was performed or material was supplied by him. The United States shall not be liable for the payment of any costs or expenses of any such suit.

The Miller Act protects subcontractors and those having a direct contractual relationship with subcontractors.[23] It does not, however, protect all potential claimants. Thus, in *MacEvoy v. United States for the Use of the Calvin Tomkins Co.*, 322 U.S. 102 (1944), the Supreme Court held that covered claimants are limited to (1) those materialmen, laborers and subcontractors who deal directly with the prime contractor and (2) those who have a direct contractual relationship with a subcontractor, thereby excluding remote subcontractors, the supplier of materialmen and the supplier of remote subcontractors. Recent cases suggest that covered subcontractors' status turns on the substantiality and importance of the claimant's relationship with the prime contractor.[24] In this connection, one whose obligation terminates with the delivery of the material is ordinarily a materialman; but one who delivers "customized materials" especially made for the

---

[23]*Fidelity & Deposit Co. of Maryland v. Harris*, 360 F.2d 402 (9th Cir. 1966).

[24]*F. D. Rich Co. v. United States for the Use of Industrial Lumber Co.*, 417 U.S. 116 (1974); *Aetna Casualty & Surety Co. v. United States for the Use of Gibson Steel Co.*, 382 F.2d 615 (5th Cir. 1967).

project may be considered a subcontractor, even though installation is provided by others.[25]

The distinction between subcontractor and materialman may be critical to determination of Miller Act coverage, although the Act defines neither term. In drawing the distinction, courts look to such factors as payment procedures employed by the general contractor, whether the claimant provided a subcontractor's bond, and how the parties themselves described their relationship.[26] Courts will also "telescope" tiers of subcontractors to provide Miller Act coverage where the prime contractor attempts to insert a "dummy" subcontractor between itself and the subcontractors actually performing the work.[27]

The procedural intricacies of Miller Act notice provisions must be carefully observed by prospective claimants. A claimant having a direct contractual relationship, express or implied, with the prime contractor who provided the bond need give no notice; but any person having a direct contractual relationship with a subcontractor, but no such relationship with the prime contractor, must give written notice to the prime contractor within 90 days from the date on which the claimant furnished the last of the work or material for which a claim is made.[28]

Many litigated cases concern the running of the 90-day period. Such cases have addressed the following recurrent illustrative questions:

(1) Does the 90-day period commence when supplies are shipped by a materialman or when they are received by a subcontractor? Receipt by the subcontractor was the event used in *United States for the Use of Engineering & Equipment Co. v. Wyatt*, 174 F.Supp. 260 (N.D.Fla. 1959).

(2) Must the last materials shipped be used in the performance of the work in order to commence the running of the 90-day period? *Fourt v. United States for the Use of Westinghouse Electric Supply Co.*, 235 F.2d 433 (10th Cir. 1956), held that they need not be so used, if they had been ordered for the job.

(3) If a subcontractor seeks to correct defective work or furnish replacement parts, does the 90-day period commence running from the date when the original work was completed or from the date when the defects were corrected? Several recent cases hold that corrections of defective work do not recommence the 90-day period.[29] A

---

[25]*United States for the Use of Newport News Ship-building and Dry Dock Co. v. Blount Brothers Construction Co.*, 168 F.Supp. 407 (D.Md. 1958); *F. D. Rich Co. v. United States*, 417 U.S. 116 (1974).

[26]*United States for the Use of Bryant v. Lembke Construction Co.*, 370 F.2d 293 (10th Cir. 1966); *United States for the Use of Potomac Rigging Co. v. Wright Contracting Co.*, 194 F.Supp. 444 (D.Md. 1961).

[27]*Continental Casualty Co. v. United States for the Use of Conroe Creosoting Co.*, 308 F.2d 846 (5th Cir. 1962).

[28]*United States ex rel. Material Service Division of General Dynamics Corporation v. Home Indemnity Company*, 489 F.2d 1004 (7th Cir. 1973).

[29]*United States for the Use of McGregor Architectural Iron Co. v. Merritt-Chapman & Scott Corp.*, 185 F.Supp. 381 (M.D.Pa. 1960); *United States for the Use of General Electric Co. v. H. I. Lewis Constr. Co.*, 375 F.2d 194 (2d Cir. 1967); *United States for the Use of State Electric Supply Co. v. Hesselden Construction Co.*, 404 F.2d 774 (10th Cir. 1968).

different result may obtain where supplies are originally furnished in other than usable condition, requiring replacement before the supplier can mount an enforceable claim.[30]

(4) If a supplier delivers materials in installments over a period of time in excess of 90 days, is notice timely as to all materials furnished if given within 90 days of the last delivery? The cases hold such notice to be timely, even in the absence of an installment contract, where the deliveries constitute separate transactions.[31]

Similarly, there are many cases dealing with the sufficiency of notice, which, under the Miller Act, must (1) be in writing, (2) state with substantial accuracy the amount claimed and the name of the party to whom the material was furnished or supplied or for whom the labor was done or performed, and (3) be served by registered mail, postage prepaid, in an envelope addressed to the contractor at any place he maintains an office or conducts his business, or his residence, or in any manner in which the United States Marshal of the district in which the work is situated is authorized by law to serve a summons.[32]

The Miller Act also provides that lawsuits "shall be brought . . . in the United States District Court for any district in which the contract was to be performed and executed and not elsewhere. . . ." Courts have construed this venue provision strictly. Thus, in *Southern Construction Co. v. United States for the Use of Samuel J. Pickard*, 371 U.S. 57 (1962), a subcontractor seeking recovery of amounts due on projects located in two different federal districts was required to bring a separate action in each district. Similarly, in *Pierce Contractors, Inc. v. Peerless Casualty Co.*, 81 So.2d 747 (Fla. 1955), the court held that an action on a Miller Act bond could not be maintained in a state court and that the applicable federal district court had sole jurisdiction.

The cases are in conflict as to waivability of Miller Act venue provisions. Some courts deem those provisions to be for the benefit of defendants and thus subject to waiver.[33] Other courts have found the venue provisions mandatory, non-waivable, and jurisdictional.[34] If the contract under which suit arises contains a mandatory arbitration clause, however, a Miller Act suit may be stayed until the arbitration proceedings have been completed.[35]

If a Miller Act claimant satisfies the Act's procedural requirements as to coverage,

---

[30]*United States for the Use of General Electric Co. v. Gunnar I. Johnson & Son, Inc.*, 310 F.2d 899 (8th Cir. 1962).

[31]*Noland Co. v. Allied Contractors, Inc.*, 273 F.2d 917 (4th Cir. 1969); *United States for the Use of Chemetron Corp. v. George A. Fuller Co.*, 250 F.Supp. 649 (D.Mont. 1965); *United States for the Use of J. A. Edwards & Co. v. Bregman Construction Corp.*, 172 F.Supp. 517 (E.D.N.Y. 1959).

[32]*United States for the Use of Jinks Lumber Co. v. Federal Insurance Co.*, 452 F.2d 485 (5th Cir. 1971); *United States for the Use of Turn County Transit Mix, Inc. v. McTeague Construction Co.*, 264 F. Supp. 619 (S.D.N.Y. 1967); *United States v. Peerless Casualty Co.*, 255 F.2d 137 (8th Cir. 1958). *See also Anno.*, "Sufficiency of Notice to Public Work Contractor on United States Project under Miller Act," 78 A.L.R.2d 429.

[33]*Texas Constr. Co. v. United States for the Use of Caldwell Foundry and Machine Co., Inc.*, 236 F.2d 138 (5th Cir. 1956).

[34]*United States for the Use of Vermont Maker Co. v. Roscoe-Ajax Construction Co.*, 246 F. Supp. 439 (N.D.Cal. 1965).

[35]*United States for the Use of Capolino Sons, Inc. v. Electronic & Missile Facilities, Inc.*, 364 F.2d 705 (2nd Cir.), *cert. denied*, 385 U.S. 924 (1966); *Electronic & Missile Facilities, Inc. v. United States for the Use of H. W. Moseley*, 306 F.2d 554 (5th Cir. 1962), *rev'd on other grounds*, 347 U.S. 167 (1963).

notice and venue, he must still determine whether the items for which he seeks recovery are provided for by the Miller Act payment bond. Principal litigated issues concerning recoverable damages include: (1) capital expenditures, repairs and rental; (2) incidental expenditures and attorneys' fees; (3) labor and materials furnished "in the prosecution of the work"; and (4) extra work and delay damages.

(1) The Miller Act payment bond is not intended to compensate a subcontractor for capital equipment not "substantially consumed" in its use on the project in question.[36] Thus, tools, machinery, accessories and substantial "replacement" repairs adding materially to the value of construction equipment and rendering it usable on other, unrelated projects are not "labor and materials" protected by the Miller Act bond.[37] Incidental repairs necessary to maintain equipment during the course of the work are recoverable. Also recoverable is the fair rental value of equipment leased for use on the project in question.[38]

(2) The Miller Act specifically provides coverage for taxes imposed by the United States and collected, deducted or withheld from wages paid by the contractor in performing the contract subject to bond. 40 U.S.C. §270a(d). Not included within covered "labor and materials" are insurance premiums and loans to contractors. Attorneys' fees are also not ordinarily recoverable in Miller Act litigation.[39]

(3) Although the Miller Act specifically extends liability only for labor and materials furnished in the prosecution of the work, that prescription does not require labor or materials to be incorporated in the work or even, for that matter, used at all. In *United States v. D.C. Loveys Co.*, 174 F.Supp. 44 (D.Mass. 1959), materials shipped to a subcontractor were damaged in transit and never incorporated into the work. The court, nonetheless, found the materials to have been furnished "in the prosecution of the work" since the subcontractor had assumed the risk of loss in transit. A similar result was reached where material furnished to a prime contractor was removed from the site for use elsewhere. *Glassell-Taylor Co. v. Magnolia Petroleum Co.*, 153 F.2d 527 (5th Cir. 1946).

(4) Extra work directed by the Government or a contractor is covered by the Miller Act; recovery is not dependent upon the prime contractor's ability to recover the cost of such work from the Government.[40] Delay damages, however, are ordinarily beyond the Miller Act's protection.[41]

---

[36]*United States for the Use of Chemetron Corp. v. George A. Fuller Co.*, 250 F.Supp. 649 (D. Mont. 1965).

[37]*Continental Casualty Co. v. Clarence L. Boyd Co.*, 140 F.2d 115 (10th Cir. 1944).

[38]*Massachusetts Bonding & Ins. Co. v. United States for the Use of Clarksdale Machinery Co.*, 88 F.2d 388 (5th Cir. 1937); *United States for Use of Roig v. Castro*, 71 F.Supp. 36 (D.P.R. 1947).

[39]*United States for the Use of Gibson v. Harman*, 192 F.2d 999 (4th Cir. 1951); *Bill Murphy Co. v. Elliott*, 207 F.2d 103 (5th Cir. 1953); *F.D. Rich Co. v. United States for the Use of Industrial Lumber Co.*, 417 U.S. 116 (1974).

[40]*United States for the Use of H. O. Kilsby v. George*, 243 F.2d 83 (5th Cir. 1957); *United States for the Use of Warren Painting Co. v. J. C. Boespflug Construction Co.*, 325 F.2d 54 (9th Cir. 1963).

[41]*See, e.g., L. P. Friestedt v. Fire-Proofing Co.*, 125 F.2d 1010 (10th Cir. 1942); *United States for the Use of Pittsburgh-Des Moines Steel Co. v. MacDonald Construction Co.*, 281 F.Supp. 1010 (E.D. Mo. 1968). A limited exception to this widely followed line of precedent arises where a general contractor, bonded under the Miller Act, has so deviated

8.8.   RIGHTS, LIABILITIES, AND OPTIONS OF THE PARTIES

The owner (obligee), surety, contractor (principal), and third-party beneficiaries of the bond (unpaid subcontractors, laborers and suppliers) have particular roles in and perspectives on the tangle of events precipitated by a default. This section summarizes each party's main underlying considerations.

8.8.1.   Default

A performance bond does not obligate the surety unless the contractor is, and has been declared by the owner to be, in default under the contract. The question then arises: what constitutes a default? The question is not easily answered since every breach of contract by a bonded contractor is not necessarily a default permitting the owner to call upon the contractor's surety. Thus, if a contractor is prevented from prosecuting the work because of a strike or other event beyond the control of the parties, or if he stops work because the owner fails to make payment or refuses to grant an equitable adjustment in the contract price to accommodate significant changes in the work, there will generally be no default within the contemplation of a performance bond. The events leading to the default must be those for which the contractor is responsible.

What, then, is an appropriate definition of default? Usually, the contract itself will provide guidance. Common events of default include: (1) failure to prosecute the work in timely fashion; (2) abandonment of the work; (3) permitting liens to be filed against the property on which the work is being performed; (4) failure to pay for labor or materials required in the performance of the contract; and (5) insolvency proceedings commenced against or by the contractor. A summary definition might be: the contractor's unexcused failure to perform a fundamental duty or obligation, ordinarily resulting from the contractor's inability to perform.[42]

8.8.2   The Owner

The owner's threshold problem is to demonstrate to the surety that there has in fact been a default. If the contractor has permitted an event of default to occur, as defined in the contract, the owner's task is straightforward. If contractually defined default is merely imminent, however, the owner must make a written record detailing each

---

from the contract between it and a subcontractor as to have abandoned the contract. In that event, what would otherwise be deemed unrecoverable damages are regarded as merely the increased cost of labor and materials furnished by the subcontractor and occasioned by the prime contractor's abandonment. *See, e.g., United States for the Use of Mandel Bros. Contracting Corp. v. P.J. Carlin Construction Co.,* 254 F.Supp. 637 (E.D.N.Y. 1966). The increased cost is then covered by the Miller Act. There is at least some indication that courts may extend the abandonment rationale to permit recovery of pure delay damages, even in the absence of abandonment, where delay is not attributable to the subcontractor-claimant. *See United States v. Piracci Construction Co.,* Civil Action No. 75-032 (D.D.C., Sept. 12, 1975).

[42]*See, e.g.,* AIA Document A201, Section 14.2.1, which sets forth grounds for termination of a construction contract by the owner.

instance of the contractor's failure to perform; demand corrective action; determine whether the architect must make an initial decision as to default[43]; and upon expiration of cure periods applicable to default, if no corrective action has been taken, declare the contractor in default, thereafter making a formal demand upon the surety to perform.

This process ordinarily consumes a great deal of time, during which the contractor may allege that he is not responsible for default. The contractor may cite changed conditions, changes in the work, deficient plans and specifications, the owner's nonpayment, and similar reasons excusing nonperformance. The owner must investigate and, if possible, refute the contractor's contentions contemporaneously and in writing with a view to eventual litigation. If an owner terminates a contractor for default without sufficient cause, he risks releasing the contractor and surety from all further obligations. Added to the costs of reletting for completion of the work is liability for the contractor's termination costs, lost profits, and loss of business reputation. Clearly, the owner's declaration of default is a last resort.

Once the owner has declared the contractor in default and terminated the contract, he will look principally to the surety for protection. As a general matter, the owner's rights against the surety are coextensive with his rights against the contractor, except where the surety's performance bond permits it either to complete the project *or* merely to pay excess completion costs up to the penal amount of the bond. The surety ordinarily retains this option.

If the surety elects to complete the project, the owner should obtain the surety's written agreement to do so and to pay appropriate claims under the payment bond. The owner must then be careful to fulfill its own contractual obligations, which will ordinarily include making payment of remaining contractual amounts to the completing contractor or the surety.

If the surety elects not to complete the project, the owner should seek the surety's acknowledgement of liability; mitigate damages by completing the work at the lower additional cost, if necessary by reletting a contract for the project's completion with another contractor; document all changes for which the contractor would otherwise be entitled to compensation and seek the surety's consent to such changes; insist that the surety pay appropriate claims under the payment bond, if there is one; and avoid final settlements that would by operation of law release the surety from its guaranty obligations if it has not consented to such settlements.

If the surety denies liability under its bond, the owner will ordinarily have no choice but to initiate a lawsuit. Such a suit should seek the court's declaratory judgment that the surety is obligated under the bond and liable for damages occasioned by the extra costs of completion. The owner may also wish to seek punitive damages, if the surety's refusal to honor its obligations under the bond is arbitrary or in bad faith.

The owner can ease his problems considerably in the first instance by negotiating favorable provisions in the applicable surety bonds. If possible, the owner will wish to have the surety waive the owner's notice of extensions and changes in the work.[44] The

---

[43]*See* AIA Document A201, §2.2.6.

[44]*See* AIA Document A311.

owner will also wish to avoid having to obtain the surety's consent to payments made to the contractor. As the discussion of Miller Act bonds demonstrates, the prudent owner will in addition seek a broad definition of claimants covered by the payment bond. Finally, the owner will seek maximum bond protection by resisting provisions permitting the surety either to complete the project or to pay the owner excess completion costs.

8.8.3. The Surety

The surety's considerations mirror those of the owner. Like the owner, the surety must anticipate the contractor's default and reach a reasoned judgment as to whether default has in fact occurred. If the surety undertakes to pay claims and performs the contractor's obligations before there is an admitted or declared event of default, it may lose rights to indemnification and priority rights against other creditors.[45] Nonetheless, the surety may under certain circumstances intervene before default, if by doing so it can avoid greater losses later on.

When default is contested, the surety must assess carefully the respective merits of the positions of both the owner and contractor. The surety may elect to do nothing; but in that event it runs the risk of incurring damages not limited by the penal amount of the bond.[46] For the surety to side incorrectly with the contractor subjects it to the owner's claims for breach of contract; the surety may also lose the opportunity to control and minimize completion costs. An incorrect or premature intervention on behalf of the owner, on the other hand, may cause the contractor to claim that the surety has exercised dominance, a claim which, if sustained, could vitiate the surety's rights to indemnification from the contractor. Action by the surety is clearly indicated when the default consists of the contractor's bankruptcy or other contractually defined event. In other cases, appropriate action by the surety is less certain.

Once default has occurred, the surety typically seeks to determine cost of completion and the amount of probable bond claims. This determination may require detailed review of the contractor's records, his accounts payable, and his commitments to subcontractors, materialmen and suppliers. It is, nonetheless, essential to the surety's next steps. Whether the surety looks to the penal amount of the bond or the cost of completion (by reletting or financing the default contractor) is at bottom an economic judgment. Reliance on the penal amount of the bond will be indicated where the cost of completion is likely to exceed that amount, since a surety that relets or finances the contractor receives no credit for costs advanced against the penal amount.[47]

A surety financing the defaulted contractor will typically insist upon the contractor's written admission of default, make written demands for indemnification and the posting of collateral, and seek perfected security interests in the contractor's assets in accordance with applicable law. Negotiations with payment bond claimants will em-

---

[45]*Seaboard Surety Co. v. Dale Construction Co.*, 230 F.2d 625 (1st Cir. 1956).

[46]*Continental Realty Corp. v. Andrew J. Crevolin Co.*, 380 F.Supp. 246 (S.D.W.Va. 1974).

[47]*McWaters & Bartlett v. United States for the Use of Wilson*, 272 F.2d 291 (10th Cir. 1959); *Caron v. Andrew*, 133 Cal. App. 2d 402, 284 P.2d 544 (1955).

phasize the strict procedural limitations discussed above, including those related to notice and covered claimant status. The surety will also investigate carefully whether the defaulted contractor has any setoffs or counterclaims against bond claimants; whether the contractor has already been paid by the owner for the work which is the subject of the claim; and whether the bond payment amount has been or will likely be exceeded. When the surety settles with a claimant, it typically seeks an assignment of the claim against the contractor and certification that the claimant has paid all his subcontractors, suppliers, and materialmen for work and material covered by the payment. The surety will also attempt to marshal all the available assets of the contractor, including unpaid contract balances owed by the owner; claims against the owner arising out of changes, delay and similar events; income tax and insurance premium refunds; and property of the contractor in which the surety has obtained a security interest.

It can be seen from the foregoing discussion that the surety must be concerned not only with its rights against the obligee of its bonds, but also with rights arising in relation to its principal, the contractor. These include rights of exoneration and indemnification. *Exoneration*, whether invoked as a general principle of equity or under the terms of the bond itself, permits the surety to compel the contractor to discharge his primary duty to the owner, thereby relieving the surety from having to do so. *Indemnification* may arise by implication or under the express terms of an indemnity agreement. In either case, indemnification contemplates that the contractor must reimburse the surety that has satisfied his obligations to the extent of the loss incurred plus related expenses. [48]

In assessing its legal position, the surety may rely on any legal defense available to the contractor. The surety's obligation is, in other words, no greater than that of its principal, the contractor. Similarly, if the contractor is barred from asserting a defense, so is the surety. [49] The surety should carefully consider common defenses available to the contractor. These include illegality of the construction contract; the impossibility of performance; the owner's fraud or duress in procuring the construction contract (particularly where the contractor has repudiated the contract); the owner's breach of the contract or failure to perform conditions precedent to the contractor's obligation; and underlying failure of consideration. The surety will also rely on defenses arising from or related to the bond itself, such as the owner's failure to make timely payments to the contractor, the owner's fraud or misrepresentation in inducing the surety to execute the bond, or material alteration of the contract as to scope of work or time and method of payment.

While the surety may raise defenses related to the owner's fraud or misrepresentation, it will not be relieved of its obligation as a result of fraud practiced on it by the contractor. [50] The owner's participation in the contractor's fraud will, however, constitute a defense to the surety. Where the owner actively participates, the defense—leading to the surety's disobligation—is clear enough. Where the owner merely has passive knowl-

---

[48] Subrogation differs from exoneration and indemnification. Subrogation may arise against the contractor or third parties, presupposes that the surety has paid under its bond to the obligee, and entitles the surety to whatever rights or priorities the obligee may have.

[49] *Indemnity Insurance Co. of North America v. United States*, 74 F.2d 22 (5th Cir. 1941).

[50] *Chrysler Corp. v. Hanover Insurance Co.*, 350 F.2d 652 (7th Cir. 1965).

edge of facts which if known to the surety might have deterred it from executing the bond, the defense is less certain. The prevailing rule is that the owner (a) must have reason to believe that the facts materially increase the risk beyond that which the surety intended to assume and that they are unknown to the surety, and (b) must have a reasonable opportunity to reveal those facts to the surety.[51]

A common source of dispute between the owner and the surety concerns alterations in the construction contract. If material, these may expose the surety to risk not contemplated when the construction contract was entered into. Material alterations may therefore discharge a surety either wholly or in part. Modern surety cases generally consider the surety entitled to discharge only to the extent that a material alteration caused it damage.[52] Courts also draw a distinction between alteration of construction details within the scope of the original contract, which does not discharge the surety, and alteration of concept, which may.[53] Many construction contracts and performance bonds specifically set forth the surety's consent to changes in and alterations of the contract.[54] Such provisions do not, however, apply to or permit changes in the payment provisions of the contract.[55] Thus, an owner who consistently overpays the contractor or prematurely releases retainage funds permits the surety to raise the defense of material alteration.[56]

A surety may therefore assert valid objections to enforcement of its obligations under the performance bond. These ordinarily will not, however, permit the surety to avoid liability under the payment bond to subcontractors, laborers and materialmen.[57] The surety may, nonetheless, defeat claimants who have not observed the procedural requirements of the payment bond, discussed above, as to notice, venue, and covered claimants' status. Payment bond claimants may also assert claims against the surety's performance bond when claims against the payment bond are precluded because of prior payment up to the penal amount or procedural obstacles to recovery. Courts are becoming increasingly liberal in permitting such recovery by unpaid subcontractors, laborers, and materialmen.[58] The surety must then look to whatever defenses are available under the performance bond.

A special category of claimant includes banks and financial institutions which, having taken an assignment of contract proceeds from the contractor, seek recovery of contract balances. Both the surety and the assignee bank may claim the same unpaid progress payments and retainage upon the contractor's default. In such contests, the surety generally prevails.[59]

---

[51]*Sumitomo Bank v. Iwasaki*, 70 Cal.2d 187 (1968).

[52]*See, e.g., Hochevar v. Maryland Casualty Co.*, 114 F.2d 948 (6th Cir. 1940).

[53]*See, e.g., Roberts v. Security Trust & Savings Bank*, 238 P. 673 (Cal. 1925).

[54]*See* AIA Document A311.

[55]*Airtrol Engineering Company, Inc. v. U.S. F & G*, 345 So.2d 1271 (La. 1977).

[56]*Gibbs v. Hartford Accident & Indemnity Co.*, 62 So.2d 599 (Fla. 1953).

[57]*Filippi v. McMartin*, 188 Cal.App.2d 135 (1961).

[58]*See, e.g., United States for the Use of Edward Hines Lumber Co. v. Kalady Construction Co.*, 227 F.Supp. 1017 (N.D.Ill. 1964); *Amelco Window Corp. v. Federal Insurance Co.*, 317 A.2d 398 (N.J. 1974).

[59]In *Deer Park Bank v. Aetna Insurance Company*, 86 S.D. 27, 190 N.W.2d 769 (1971), the court stated the general rule as follows:

A similar contest may arise between the surety and creditors of the contractor having perfected security interests in the contractor's assets under the Uniform Commercial Code. Again, the surety generally prevails against such creditors because it is subrogated as to the remaining contract balances to the rights of the contractor, the owner and the subcontractors it has paid. Such subrogation arises by operation of law and is not deemed to be a "security interest" within Article 9 of the Uniform Commercial Code. [60]

A claimant may obtain an arbitration award or a judgment against a bonded contractor. The surety must then determine whether it is bound to discharge the obligation so created within the penal amount of the bond. If an arbitration award is involved, the surety will ordinarily not be bound by it unless the surety has specifically consented to the arbitration. [61] The controlling document for this purpose is the surety's bond and not the construction contract. An arbitration provision in the construction contract will not bind the surety unless there is a comparable provision in the surety's bond.

A judgment obtained against a contractor, on the other hand, creates at least a rebuttable presumption of the contractor's liability to the judgment creditor in its subsequent suit against the surety. Courts are nonetheless generally willing to permit the surety to raise its own defenses to such a suit, thus depriving the previous judgment against the contractor of conclusive effect against the surety. "It is [then] open to the surety to prove if he can that judgment should have been rendered" for the contractor. [62]

8.8.4. The Contractor

The contractor's obligations run to the owner, subcontractors, and the surety. The contractor's basic undertaking is, of course, to build the project at hand in accordance with the owner's plans and specifications within the time specified. If he fails to do so, he is liable either for the cost of correcting the work or its diminution in value, plus consequential delay damages, if applicable. If he defaults and does not complete the work, he is liable to the owner for the amount by which completion costs exceed unpaid contract amounts plus consequential delay damages. To subcontractors the contractor

---

There is no definite and precise promise in the surety's bond to pay those who loan money to the contractor. Indeed, the specific agreement in the bond to pay for labor and materials negates the idea that the surety intended to obligate itself to pay any other type of claim.

See also *Fidelity and Deposit Co. of Maryland v. United States*, 132 Ct.Cl. 724, 133 F.Supp. 381, *cert. denied*, 350 U.S. 902 (1955) (surety prevails over assignee bank on both performance and payment bond because subrogation rights relate to date of execution of surety bonds). The surety's rights are superior to the assignee bank's rights where the Government continues to hold contract amounts pending judicial resolution of the contest between the bank and the surety. When payment has already been made to the assignee bank, however, the payment will be valid against the surety under the Assignment of Claims Act of 1940 unless the surety can show that the funds loaned by the assignee bank have not been used for contract performance. *See, e.g., Coconut Grove Exchange Bank v. New Amsterdam Casualty Co.*, 149 F.2d 73 (5th Cir. 1945). Similarly, the surety may be defeated in a contest with the assignee bank as to amounts earned by the contractor prior to default. *See National Union Fire Insurance Co. v. United States*, 304 F.2d 465 (Ct.Cl. 1962).

[60]*Canter v. Schlager*, 267 N.E.2d 492 (Mass. 1971); *Home Indemnity Company v. United States*, 433 F.2d 764 (Ct. Cl. 1970); *First Alabama State Bank v. Hartford Accident and Indemnity Co.*, 430 F.Supp. 907 (N.D.Ala. 1977).

[61]*Brescia Construction Co. v. Walart Construction Co.*, 190 N.E. 484 (N.Y. 1934); *Transamerica Insurance Co. v. Yonkers Contracting Co.*, 267 N.Y.S.2d 669 (1966).

[62]*Restatement of Security* §139.

owes the duty of timely payment and non-interference in their work. Finally, the contractor is ordinarily bound, by express agreement, to indemnify and hold the surety harmless against any cost or expense incurred by the surety under its bond.

The operative event triggering the surety's and the contractor's potential liabilities is, as we have seen, default under the construction contract. Once default has been declared, the contractor has essentially two options: he can cure the default or deny it. An aggressive contractor who remains in viable financial and operating condition may exercise self-help in a number of ways. He may file mechanics' liens for amounts unpaid to the date of default; continue work and demand arbitration under the construction contract; sequester his equipment to avoid the owner's seizure; and, above all, vigorously deny the existence of default. This can be coupled with an action for declaratory relief from a court in the event the surety takes over the contract or stops payment. Such an action will usually seek release of the contractor's indemnity and damages for the surety's dominance and tortious interference with the contractor's business relations. Time gained through litigation may permit the contractor to generate additional working capital.

In any event, the contractor must deal with unpaid subcontractors, who can use their statutory mechanic's lien rights to compel payment. If payment is not made, foreclosure on the subject property is the ultimate legal sanction. Nonetheless, the contractor may still have defenses. He can, for example, assess back charges for incomplete or defective work; allege the subcontractor's failure to comply with the procedural requirements of lien laws; or seek discharge of liens by giving a bond or establishing an escrow.

If the default is not cured, the contractor may avoid its legal consequences in litigation with the owner and the surety by proving the owner's fraud or misrepresentation in connection with the contract; the owner's mistake, particularly with respect to subsurface conditions; the owner's failure to make timely payment; the existence of supervening force majeure events, such as strikes, governmental interference, or frustration of purpose; or the non-occurrence of specified conditions precedent to the contractor's obligations.

Often such defenses are simply not realistic, and the contractor's self-help efforts are of little avail. The contractor may then terminate the contract and walk off the job; or, perhaps the wiser course, the contractor may choose to cooperate with the surety. Such cooperation, together with the contractor's "job memory," available equipment, and existing relationships with the owner and subcontractors, may induce the surety to make concessions to keep the contractor on the job, including financing the contractor and releasing or reducing indemnification obligations. Furthermore, cooperation may, even in the absence of such concessions, minimize the damages for which the contractor will ultimately have to respond to the surety, since the cost of reletting will often exceed the cost of continuation with the defaulted contractor.

8.8.5. The Bond Claimant

Legal protection for the bond claimant is afforded by the contractor's payment bond and statutory mechanic's lien laws. These are full of procedural pitfalls and require close scrutiny. An unpaid subcontractor or materialman must comply with rigid notice, filing and eligibility requirements. He, too, however, may exercise self-help. He can seek to repossess materials; demand direct payment from the owner, applicable state law permitting; or terminate performance and sue for the reasonable value of work performed plus consequential damages, if any.

8.8.6. Arbitration and the Surety

The surety cannot be compelled to arbitrate disputes over bond and bonding liability. Arbitration cannot be invoked unless all parties, including the surety, have expressly agreed to arbitrate.[63] On the other hand, a surety may be prevented from participating in an arbitration if not a party to the arbitration agreement.[64] Courts are split as to how an adverse arbitration decision affects the rights of the surety.[65]

8.9. OTHER TYPES OF BONDS

License or *permit bonds* are bonds required by state law, municipal ordinance, or regulation as a condition precedent to the granting of a license to engage in a specified business or the granting of a permit to exercise a certain privilege. A *lien bond* is generally given by the contractor and indemnifies the owner of realty against loss resulting from the filing of liens against his property. A "no lien bond" is a type of performance bond given in some states where, by statutory requirement, the owner-contractor agreement has been filed as a "no lien" contract, the effect of which is to deny the right to file a lien in connection with that contract.

Since the maintenance obligation contained in the contractor's agreement with the owner is usually covered by the performance bond, there are relatively few bonds written covering maintenance only. An exception is the *roofing guarantee* which may be furnished separately by a manufacturer. Although this is referred to as a "bond," it is in fact merely a warranty that binds the roofing manufacturer directly without interposition of a surety.

Subcontract bonds are performance and labor and material payment bonds required by the contractor from his subcontractors, guaranteeing that the subcontractor will faithfully perform the subcontract in accordance with its terms and pay the bills for labor and material incurred in the connection therewith. A *termite "bond"* is a form of warranty given by manufacturers or applicators of substances intended to prevent the damage caused by termites.

---

[63]*Transamerican Insurance Co. v. Yonkers Contracting Co.*, 267 N.Y.S.2d 669 (1966).

[64]*United States for the Use of Frank Trucco and Sons, Inc. v. Bregman Constr. Co.*, 256 F.2d 851 (7th Cir. 1958).

[65]*See, e.g. Transamerican Insurance Co. v. Yonkers Contracting Co.*, 267 N.Y.S. 2d 669 (1966); *contra, P.R. Post Corp. v. Maryland Casualty Co.*, 242 N.W.2d 62 (Mich. 1976).

8.10. ADDITIONAL SOURCE MATERIALS

General

Ashe, G., "New developments in statutory bond law," 74 Com.L.J. 114 (1969).

Cushman, E. H., "How to waive bond rights without really trying," 36 Ins. Counsel J. 239 (1969).

Greaves, T.G., Jr., "Payment and performance bonds for private construction," 1963 ABA Sect. Ins. N&CL 272 (1963).

McNamara, J. P. & D. Mungall, Jr., "Project update 1975: guide for the drafter of a contract bond indemnity agreement," 42 Ins. Counsel J. 291 (1975).

Merrill, M. H. & E. A. Klem, *American Casualty Co. v. Town of Shattuck*, a statutory payment bond problem and speculations engendered thereby," 20 Okla.L.Rev. 135 (1967).

Milana, J. P., "Performance bond and the underlying contract: the bond obligations do not include all of the contract obligations," 12 Forum 187 (1976).

Moss, R., "Bond practice," 44 Calif. S. B.J. 537 (1969).

R., J., "Forfeiture of construction bid bond denied because of unilateral mistake," 6 Utah L.Rev. 578 (1959).

Wiley, D. G., *Dutcher* case minority opinion and the assignment provision in construction contract bond agreements," 1963 ABA Sect. Ins. N&CL 77 (1963).

Wisner, R. S., "Liability in excess of the contract bond penalty," 43 Ins. Counsel J. 105 (1976).

Note, "Payment and performance bonds—right of materialmen and laborers to sue as third-party beneficiaries," 30 N.Y.U.L.Rev. 1447 (1955).

Note, "Performance and payment bonds," 11 Forum 600 (1976).

Seminar: "Financing, bonds, etc.," 1964 ABA Sect. Ins. N&CL 26 (1964).

Anno., "Building contractor's liability, upon bond or other agreement to indemnify owner, for injury to death of third persons resulting from owner's negligence," 27 A.L.R.3d 663.

Anno., "Employees of government project subcontractor, recovery on payment bond of prime contractor," 55 L.Ed. 2d 50.

Anno., "Labor or material furnished subcontractor for public work or improvement as within coverage of bond of principal contractor," 92 A.L.R.2d 1250.

Anno., "Liability of subcontractor upon bond or other agreement indemnifying general contractor against liability for damage to person or property," 68 A.L.R.3d 7.

Anno., "Prime contractor's liability to subcontractor's suppliers," 9 L.Ed. 2d 31.

Anno., "Public work, what constitutes, within statute relating to contractor's bond," 101 A.L.R. 565.

Anno., "Validity of statute making private property owner liable to contractor's laborers, materialmen, or subcontractors where owner fails to exact bond or employ other means of securing their payment," 59 A.L.R.2d 885.

Securities

Ashe, G., "Relative rights to funds withheld on public construction contracts: surety v. lender-assignee," 85 Banking L.J. 471 (1968).

Brady, E. F., "Bonds on federal government construction contracts: the surety's view," 46 N.Y.U.L.Rev. 262 (1971).

Braude, H. M., "Surety's liability under the Miller Act for 'delay damages'," 36 Fed.B.J. 86 (1977).

Cochrane, L. P., "Obligations of the principal's subcontractors and suppliers at default or takeover by the surety," 14 Forum 869 (1979).

Creyke, G., Jr., "Recent developments in the right of sureties in defaulted federal construction contracts," 5 B.C. Inc. & Com.L.R. 139 (1963).

Gleick, H. S., "Rights and status of sureties in bankruptcy cases of contractors," 34 Fordham L.Rev. 451 (1966).

Hollenbeck, S. M., "Surety's obligation to pay consequential damages," 11 Forum 1201 (1976).

Koch, H. C., "Surety's obligation to pay subcontractor where owner fails to pay under contract," 11 Forum 1212 (1976).

Leslie, R. E., "Deviations in relet contract do not discharge surety where right of change was reserved," 10 Forum 1 (1974).

Miller, H. E., "Problem of surety in completing contract over protest of principal," 22 Ins. Counsel J. 472 (1955).

Morris, S. C., Jr., "Federal taxes: problems of the surety as related to construction contracts," 29 Ins. Counsel J. 283 (1962).

Reinert, B. A., "Claims of contract interference by principal: right of payment bond surety to protect contract funds," 12 Forum 257 (1976).

Reynolds, H. E., "Liability of surety for tort claims against principal," 31 Ins. Counsel J. 447 (1964).

Shure, Edward Alan, "The UCC does not affect adversely the surety's priority" 11 The Forum 630 (1976).

Terrell, G. W., "How to prevent loss of a contract surety's rights by waiver and estoppel," 10 Forum 878 (1975).

Webster, W. H., "Performance bond surety's dilemma when both principal and obligee claim the other is in default: a guide through no man's land," 12 Forum 238 (1976).

Note, "Surety in federal construction contracts," 19 N.Y.U. Intra. L.Rev. 213 (1964).

Anno., "Priority between claim of surety and claim of United States against insolvent principal," 97 L.Ed. 49.

Anno., "Surety liability on bid bond for public works," 70 A.L.R.2d 1970.

Anno., "Surety relative rights, as between surety on public works contractor's bond and unpaid laborers or materialmen, in percentage retained by obligee," 61 A.L.R.2d 899.

Miller Act

Cushman, E. H., "Need for a new look in state and local legislation using the Miller Act as a model," 1963 ABA Insurance Section N&CL 279 (1963).

Dauer, "Government contracts, commercial banks & Miller Act bond sureties—a question of priorities," 14 B.C. Ind. & Comm. L.Rev. 943 (1973).

Gantt, P. H., R. D. Wallick, J. M. Proctor, "Problems of private claimants under Miller Act payment bonds," 9 W&M L.Rev. 1077 (1968).

Hume, R. R., "Contract provisions requiring arbitration of Miller Act claims," 30 Ins. Counsel J. 107 (1963).

Kirwan, F. P., "Miller Act coverage for suppliers of customized materials," 30 Ins. Counsel J. 573 (1963).

Wallick, R. D., and J. A. Stafford, "Miller Act: enforcement of the payment bond," 29 Law & Contemporary Prob. 514 (1964).

Anno., "Counterclaims required to be asserted in suits under Miller Act," 9 L.Ed. 2d 31.

Anno., "Notice under Miller Act," 78 A.L.R.2d 412.

Anno., "Protection under bond given under Miller Act (40 U.S.C. §§ 270a-270e) of one supplying labor or material to one other than the prime contractor or his immediate subcontractor," 79 A.L.R.2d 855.

Anno., "Quantum meruit recovery by subcontractor under Miller Act," 26 A.L.R. Fed. 746.

Anno., "Time limitations: construction and application of Miller Act provision limiting time for suits on payment bond," 10 A.L.R. Fed. 553.

Anno., "What constitutes supplying labor and material in the prosecution of the work provided for in the primary contract under Miller Act," 79 A.L.R.2d 843.

CHAPTER 9

Insurance in the
Construction Industry

9.1. INTRODUCTION

Construction is fraught with extraordinary risk of injury to persons and property. Contractors and others associated with the construction process are engaged typically in activities that can, and often do, subject them to substantial liabilities. This is particularly true of large-scale construction projects involving hazardous features, such as demolition, excavation, and blasting. To protect against such risks, contractors and others must obtain insurance coverage, and indeed are often required by law or contract to do so.

The extraordinary risks contractors encounter as a matter of course require extraordinary insurance protection. As those risks have escalated to reflect the impact of inflated settlements and jury verdicts, the need for comprehensive, intelligently selected insurance coverage has grown correspondingly. The result is an enormous range and complexity of possible insurance coverage.

The cost of insurance generally runs between two and four percent of total contract cost, and the average contractor pays more in insurance premiums than in taxes. Unlike other factors in the cost equation, however, insurance costs can often be controlled by selecting policies carefully to insure against only those contingencies that are likely to arise and making intelligent use of cost-saving variables and self-insurance options.

9.2. THE RUDIMENTS OF INSURANCE COVERAGE

An insurance policy may generally be described as a contract under which the insurance carrier agrees to pay the insured (or a beneficiary designated by the insured) up to an agreed amount in the event that loss from a specified risk or risks occurs while the policy is in force. For such protection, the insured pays a premium, the amount of which is a function of the duration of the policy, its face value (i.e., the amount to be paid to the insured in the event loss actually occurs), and—by far the most important factor—the probability that the risk insured against will eventuate in loss to the insured, as determined by the insurer on the basis of prior loss experience with respect to comparable risks.

The most important features of an insurance policy are the *coverage* and *exclusion clauses*. These are provisions describing particular risks and mandating either their coverage or exclusion from coverage. Typical clauses from a comprehensive property damage liability policy provide:

> [Insurer] agrees to pay on behalf of the insured all sums which the insured shall become legally liable to pay as damages because of injury to or destruction of property, including the loss of use thereof, caused by accident. Exclusion (1) . . . This policy does not apply . . . to injury to or destruction of any property arising out of . . . the collapse of or structural injury to any building or structure due . . . to excavation, including burrowing, filling or backfilling in connection therewith. . . .[1]

A fundamental principle of construction insurance (indeed, of insurance in general) is that exclusions can normally be covered, either by paying an additional premium for the deletion of an exclusion clause or by purchasing an additional insurance policy. For coverage in excess of that legally or contractually required, a contractor must balance the advantages of additional protection against the additional premium cost required, taking into account the relative risk of the particular construction work for which coverage is sought.

Carriers sell two generic types of insurance: *liability insurance*, which covers claims and lawsuits filed by third parties against the insured based on allegations of tortious or negligent conduct in connection with construction or related work, and *property insurance*, which protects against loss of or damage to property owned or used by the insured or property on which the insured is working.

9.3. LIABILITY INSURANCE: INTRODUCTION

The world of construction liability insurance is as broad as the countless risks against which contractors need protection. The kinds of liability insurance, variations in

---

[1]Quoted in *Hartford Accident & Indemnity Co. v. Kuipers Construction Co., Inc.*, 327 F.2d 333, 335 (8th Cir. 1964).

policy coverage, and exclusions from coverage are beyond enumeration. Particular kinds of construction projects may call for carefully tailored liability insurance coverage, and new forms of liability insurance are constantly developing. For example, some carriers offer insurance against nuclear catastrophe to contractors, subcontractors and design professionals who work on the construction of atomic power plants—liability coverage that did not exist a generation ago.[2]

Nonetheless, several standard types of liability insurance are offered by most major insurance carriers to those engaged in the construction process.

9.3.1. Comprehensive General Liability Insurance (CGL)

Comprehensive general liability insurance is the basic policy for construction contractors and subcontractors, although its title is something of a misnomer; it is "comprehensive" only in that it provides what might be termed a strategic outline of the contractor's general insurance needs. Most CGL policies contain significant exclusion clauses, and comprehensive coverage is rarely complete without several supplemental policies.[3]

In form, CGL policies consist of a "policy jacket" containing general declarations, premium payment schedules and provisions, definitions, and general conditions. Attached to the policy jacket are numerous "coverage parts," each containing coverage and exclusion clauses for a specified contingency or liability. A contractor generally shapes the CGL policy to the project on which he is working by selecting only those coverage parts that are appropriate to the work he is performing. A contractor's premium is calculated in large part on the basis of the coverage parts chosen. Several standard coverage parts are included in virtually all CGL policies.

Premises and operations coverage protects the contractor from liability for personal or property injury arising out of any incident occurring on the construction site or on premises owned or operated by the contractor. Protection is usually limited to the contractor's own employees; if the contractor wishes to protect himself against injuries to others, he must purchase additional coverage (*independent contractors coverage* for those working on the construction site as independent contractors, or *public liability coverage* for injuries suffered by any non-employee). In some states, premises and

---

[2]Another illustration is provided by a contractor whose construction of a controversial building on a college campus was repeatedly disrupted by student demonstrations; the contractor had to approach several insurance carriers before he could find one that would write a liability policy for loss due to student riots. *See* P.L.I., *Real Estate Construction: Current Problems* (1973), p. 207.

[3]   The extent of coverage under a typical, comprehensive general liability insurance policy leaves large areas of a contractor's business risks unprotected. Even more important, every comprehensive general liability insurance policy specifically lists areas of exclusion. It is not unusual for a policy to list well over a dozen such exclusions. Unfortunately for contractors, those exclusions often relate to precisely those high-risk perils that contractors frequently encounter. As a result, if a contractor has only a basic general liability insurance policy, he faces very real financial risks. Loss in an excluded area could result in a legal and financial catastrophe. To avoid such a catastrophe, a contractor usually must supplement his comprehensive general liability policy.

McNeil Stokes, *Construction Law in Contractors' Language* (1977), pp. 213–214.

operations coverage includes incidents involving construction-site elevators; in other states, *elevator coverage* must be purchased separately.

Premises and operations coverage is typically limited to damage caused by "accident" or "error." A substantial body of case law has arisen giving content to these terms. Generally, damage is "accidental"—hence, covered—if unexpected and unforeseen by both the insured and the injured party. Insurance companies frequently contest claims under premises and operations policies by arguing that the insured should have foreseen the likelihood of ensuing harm. Thus, in *Harleysville Mutual Casualty Co. v. Harris & Brooks, Inc.*, 248 Md. 148, 235 A.2d 556 (1967), a contractor employed to remove trees and underbrush from a construction site was sued by nearby residents whose homes and yards were coated with soot after the contractor piled shrubbery at the edge of the site and ignited it with fuel oil; the contractor's insurance carrier successfully argued that its liability policy did not cover the claims because the contractor should have anticipated the damage. Similarly, in *Kuckenberg v. Hartford Accident & Indemnity Co.*, 226 F.2d 225 (9th Cir. 1955), a contractor hired by a railroad to repair roadbed and track caused substantial damage to the railroad's rolling stock when blasting operations loosened boulders and resulted in a landslide. The contractor's insurance company argued that landslide damage was the "ordinary and expected result" of the contractor's blasting, and the court disallowed the contractor's insurance claim on the ground that damages were not caused by an "accident" within the scope of the policy.

Completed operations coverage temporarily extends liability coverage for an additional period after the contractor has completed the job-site project. Potentially the most expensive accidents are those which occur after the completion of construction work—an example being the collapse of an occupied building. Premises and operations coverage normally extends only until the completion of construction and may leave the contractor dangerously vulnerable if a project on which he has worked subsequently proves to be structurally unsound. Completed operations coverage extends the lifetime of the policy's basic liability coverage for a specified period beyond the completion date. It also covers all legal fees and costs associated with accident investigation—the latter being particularly important because of the difficult proof problems posed by structural failure months or years after completion of construction.

Contractual liability coverage (also known as *"hold harmless"* coverage) provides protection against liability incurred as the result of so-called "hold harmless" or indemnity provisions in any of the numerous contractual agreements a contractor signs during the course of a construction project. Hold harmless clauses are routinely included in such contracts, and provide in effect that the contractor will indemnify the other contracting party for damages resulting wholly or partially from the contractor's negligence.[4] Hold harmless provisions may shift otherwise legally avoidable liabilities to the general con-

---

[4]There are technically three kinds of "hold harmless" provisions, distinguished by the nature of the obligation they impose on the general contractor against whom the provisions are construed. The *limited-form hold harmless clause* indemnifies the other party for damages caused by the contractor's own negligence and serves as little more than contractual acknowledgment of common-law indemnification principles. The *intermediate-form hold harmless clause* requires indemnification for damages caused by the joint negligence of the contracting parties as well as the contractor's own negligence. The *broad-form hold harmless clause* requires indemnification for any liability due to negligence, even if

tractor and thus can have a devastating impact on contractors who are uninsured against the risks involved.

The legal consequences of one form of hold harmless clause are illustrated in *Kraft Foods v. Disheroon*, 118 Ga. App. 632, 165 S.E.2d 189 (1968), an action by a subcontractor's employee against the owner of a processing plant for personal injuries sustained in a fall from a stepladder. The employee, who was performing renovation work in the plant pursuant to a contract between the plant owner and general contractor, lost his balance when one of the plant's conveyor belt systems malfunctioned and struck the stepladder on which he was standing. The evidence showed clearly that the general contractor was not negligent and that the accident was caused by the owner's faulty maintenance of the broken conveyor belt. The plant owner was nevertheless permitted to file a third-party complaint against the general contractor on the basis of a broadly worded hold harmless clause in the contract indemnifying the owner for "damages sustained by anyone whomsoever as a result of injury to or death of any person or damage to any property howsoever caused and wheresoever occurring" (165 S.E.2d at 190). As a result the general contractor was found liable for damages he did not cause and could not have prevented.

Contractual liability coverage provides protection against a contractor's loss incurred by operation of a hold harmless clause.[5] Contractors must be careful to ensure that the scope of such coverage corresponds with potential liability exposure under the hold harmless clause or clauses to which it relates. Some carriers require separate coverage for the several separate hold harmless provisions often found in the general contract, each separate subcontract, and the architect-engineer contract.[6]

Explosion, collapse and underground coverage (commonly known as "XCU coverage") supplements a standard exclusion in the premises and operations coverage part for damage to property adjoining the construction site due to the use of explosives or

---

the other party is solely responsible therefor. For a more comprehensive discussion of the differences among the three kinds of hold harmless clauses and examples of each, *see* McNeil Stokes, *supra*, pp. 214–216.

The most widely used hold harmless provision is the one contained in Article 4, paragraph 4.18 of the American Institute of Architects' General Conditions of the Contract for Construction AIA Document A201, which provides in pertinent part:

> The Contractor shall indemnify and hold harmless the Owner and the Architect and their agents and employees from and against all claims, damages, losses and expenses including attorneys' fees arising out of or resulting from the performance of the Work, provided that any such claim, damage, loss or expense (a) is attributable to bodily injury, sickness, disease or death, or to injury to or destruction of tangible property (other than the Work itself) including the loss of use resulting therefrom, and (b) is caused in whole or in part by any negligent act or omission of the Contractor, any Subcontractor, anyone directly or indirectly employed by any of them or anyone for whose acts any of them may be liable, regardless of whether or not it is caused in part by a party indemnified hereunder.

This is an intermediate-form hold harmless clause that extends quite broadly to provide indemnification against negligent acts by contractors, design professionals, and all agents, employees, and independent contractors.

[5]Carriers offer three forms of contractual liability coverage—limited-form, intermediate-form, and broad-form coverage—corresponding to the three common kinds of hold harmless clauses. See n.4, *supra*.

[6]It should also be noted that courts are increasingly reluctant to enforce hold harmless clauses where such clauses work blatant inequities among the parties to construction contracts; the modern trend is to construe such clauses narrowly when necessary to protect innocent parties. *See Varco Pruden, Inc. v. Hampshire Construction Co., Interstate Vendaway, Inc.*, 300 A.2d 241 (Del. Super. 1972).

to subsurface excavation. "X" coverage protects against damage caused by blasting, explosive detonation, welding, and use of pressurized gases and liquids. "C" coverage protects against structural collapse due to pile driving, caisson work, underground tunneling, vibration from heavy equipment operation, quarrying, and earth movement. "U" coverage provides protection to excavators against damage to underground cables, conduits, pipe mains and sewers.

XCU coverage is essential for large-scale construction projects, particularly those in urban or heavily developed areas where the risk of damage to adjoining buildings or underground systems is substantial. XCU coverage is often one of the most expensive components of CGL insurance.

9.3.2. Insurance for Design Professionals.

The general growth in the number and size of lawsuits arising out of construction contracts has affected all participants in the construction process, including design professionals—architects and building engineers—who plan and inspect the actual construction work. Although design professionals are not generally required by law to carry liability insurance, owners are increasingly requiring comprehensive insurance coverage for architects and engineers whom they engage.[7]

Design professionals normally carry two kinds of insurance. *Public liability insurance* protects against damages incurred in the ordinary business context, for example by employees of the design professional. More important is *professional liability insurance*, often referred to as errors and omissions insurance, which covers those substantial risks that relate to an architect's or engineer's professional work product or the performance of professional services.

Professional liability insurance policies are extraordinarily complex and very expensive to maintain, particularly for small design firms. Policies contain literally dozens of exclusion clauses; and coverage is usually provided only for tasks "commonly undertaken by design professionals."[8] Policies typically feature large deductible and fairly low policy limits.

Despite their limitations, however, professional liability insurance policies are critically important for architects and engineers in the litigious contemporary world of construction contracts. An important aspect of professional liability protection lies in the insurance company's assumption of all legal and investigative costs incurred in defending against a claim or lawsuit. This, and the increasing tendency on the part of owners to

---

[7]For an excellent general introduction to potential liability problems confronting construction design professionals, *see* C. W. Dunham & R. D. Young, *Contracts, Specifications, and Law for Engineers* (McGraw-Hill Civil Engineering Series, 1971), ch. 22 ("Professional Liability of Architects and Engineers"), pp. 384–398.

[8] One policy excluded work not customarily performed by an architect. Negligence relating to boundary surveys, subsurface conditions, ground testing, tunnel and bridge activities, dams, failure to advise or require insurance for surety bonds, failure to complete contract documents on time, or to act upon shop drawings on time were also excluded in that policy, unless the loss was due to negligence in design. Also excluded were express warranties, guarantees, and estimates of probable construction cost, as well as indemnity liability assumed by the architect by contract, and liability for copyright, trademark, or patent infringements.

Justin Sweet, *Legal Aspects of Architecture, Engineering and the Construction Process* (1970), p. 772.

require professional liability coverage of architects and engineers, have made such insurance virtually mandatory for design professionals in the construction industry.

9.3.3. Workmen's Compensation and Employer Liability Insurance

CGL insurance policies normally exclude coverage of any liability incurred under state workmen's compensation laws. Under the laws of every state in the United States, employers are responsible for the payment of compensation benefits to employees who sustain job-related illnesses or injuries, and an employer normally finances such payments through the purchase of supplementary workmen's compensation insurance under which the carrier pays benefits to the injured employee at rates determined by state law.

In the construction industry, workmen's compensation insurance is often the single most expensive item in the insurance portfolio, costing as much as or more than CGL insurance and amounting in some cases to 70 percent of the total insurance premium. The tremendous cost of such insurance is a reflection of many factors: the universality of workmen's compensation programs, the large compensation payments inevitably made in an industry with as many job-related accidents as the construction industry, the long duration of such payments, the pro-employee orientation of many workmen's compensation boards, and the relative ease and modest cost of prosecuting a benefits claim.

In some states, employers must purchase workmen's compensation insurance from state-administered insurance trust funds rather than from private insurance carriers. In general, there are significant variations in the administration and benefit levels of workmen's compensation programs from state to state, and this can pose problems for contractors who do business in more than one state. Most private carriers offer an "all-states" endorsement for coverage in every state listed by the contractor in a policy supplement. The contractor must therefore maintain and update the applicable list of states.

For no other form of liability insurance is there as great a range of premium costs as there is for workmen's compensation insurance. Premiums are geared in part to the contractor's safety record. A contractor with a good record of job-site safety will pay in premiums only a fraction of the amount paid by one with a consistent loss record. The potential for cost-saving, therefore, is greater in this area than in most other liability insurance areas. For this reason it is important for the contractor to purchase his workmen's compensation insurance policy from a carrier offering comprehensive loss-prevention services in adddition to the standard range of claim-handling services.

9.3.4. Comprehensive Automobile and Vehicle Liability Insurance

The CGL insurance policy generally excludes coverage for:

Bodily injury or property damage arising out of the ownership, maintenance, operation, use, loading, or unloading of—

    1. Any automobile or aircraft owned or operated by or rented or loaned to the named insured;

    2. Any other automobile or aircraft operated by any person in the course of his employment by the named insured. . . .[9]

Automobiles, both owned and leased, are frequently driven on construction sites, and hazards, mud, and poor driving conditions on the site can contribute to accidents and resulting personal and property injury. Comprehensive automobile liability insurance provides protection against such accidents. Policies are narrowly drawn to cover only those vehicles designed for travel on public roads; coverage of mobile construction equipment such as cranes and tractors is usually excluded (although use of such equipment frequently comes within the premises and operations coverage of the CGL insurance policy).

9.3.5. Umbrella Excess Liability Insurance

    Liability under construction contracts can be enormous, in light of the staggering cost and size of construction projects, the potential loss of life and property damage resulting from structural collapse[10], and the difficulties in detecting and correcting construction errors. Raising the limits of each insurance policy to levels sufficient to cover such damages would be prohibitively expensive. A more realistic alternative is to supplement existing policy coverage through the purchase of umbrella excess liability coverage, an omnibus policy designed to provide additional insurance protection above the dollar liability limits of other policies.

    Umbrella excess liability insurance provides additional liability protection against losses in excess of the limits on the insured's CGL and automobile liability policies. A standard CGL policy may provide maximum coverage of $300,000; affordable umbrella excess liability insurance can effectively increase maximum coverage to $2 million or more, thus protecting against any insurable loss greater than the limit of the underlying policy up to the umbrella policy's own limit.

9.4 PROPERTY INSURANCE: INTRODUCTION

    If, in general terms, liability insurance can be described as protection against damage caused intentionally, unintentionally or constructively by the insured to third parties, then property insurance can be broadly described as protection against damage of which the insured is himself the victim. A general contractor commonly invests a considerable sum in equipment and materials during the course of a construction project. Much of his investment remains on the construction site, where it is subject to the elements, vandalism, theft, fire and other potential problems and dangers. Property

---

[9]Taken from McNeil Stokes, *supra* n. 3 at p. 223.

[10]The collapse of the Teton Dam in 1976 caused an estimated billion dollars of property damage; an explosion at a nuclear power plant could cause literally incalculable damage.

insurance provides protection against damage to the insured's equipment, and protection against delays caused by interruptions in the construction schedule while equipment is repaired and materials are replaced.

9.4.1. Builder's Risk Insurance

This is the most prevalent form of property insurance and protects against specific perils to property during the course of construction.

Questions likely to arise under a builder's risk policy concern the nature of the *property* covered and the particular *perils* against which the policy protects.

Generally, all property owned or leased by the insured on the construction site, all tools, equipment, machinery and materials on the site, and all completed or partially completed buildings and structures are covered. Property stored off-site and property in transit to or from the site are excluded from coverage. This exclusion can have a practical impact on the organization and administration of the construction site. For example, if prefabricated materials are to be assembled prior to being used or installed by a subcontractor, efforts are sometimes made to conduct the assembly work on-site so that business risk insurance covers any damages incurred during the assembly process. Many owners and contractors provide storage facilities on the site for the same reason. If the owner routinely prepays for materials and stores them in off-site facilities, supplementary property insurance should be procured.

Provocative problems can arise concerning the valuation of property on which an insurance claim is made. There are two widely used valuation methods. Under the *reporting form* method, the insured is required to submit monthly reports to the carrier on the actual in-place value of equipment and materials on the construction site. Less cumbersome and increasingly popular is the *completed value* method, under which the contractor estimates or predetermines the total value of equipment and materials required to complete the project and purchases insurance sufficient to cover any foreseeable loss during the lifetime of the project.

With respect to the perils or risks insured against, there are three general types of builder's risk insurance. Providing the most limited form of protection is *named-peril coverage*, which protects only against perils specifically identified in the policy. The most common form of named peril coverage is fire insurance. Other common perils for which specific policies are ordinarily provided are theft, vandalism, and floods.

All-risk coverage is designed to protect against property damage regardless of cause. Coverage is limited, however, by several important exclusion clauses. These exclude recovery for damages due to ordinary wear and tear, design or workmanship defects, and mechanical breakdown. All-risk coverage is by far the most common form of builder's risk insurance.

A relatively new development is *difference-in-conditions coverage*. Many of today's standard-form construction contracts (including the widely used Document A201 of the American Institute of Architects) require the construction-site owner to purchase and maintain property insurance for the benefit of all contractors and subcontractors whose property is stored on the site. In many instances, the owner satisfies his contractual obligation by purchasing named-peril coverage. Contractors who desire more substantial insurance protection may purchase a so-called difference-in-conditions policy, which essentially provides supplemental protection against all risks *except* those specified in the named-peril policy. In other words, the difference-in-conditions policy permits the contractor to upgrade his insurance to a level equivalent to all-risk coverage, while paying only the difference in cost between all-risk and named-peril coverage.[11]

9.4.2. Business Interruption Insurance

This covers the loss of earnings resulting from start-up delays and interruptions caused by damage to or loss of equipment and materials. Such insurance is rarely purchased, because monetary damages are difficult to estimate and because construction interruptions are so common that contractors can virtually plan for them in advance without resorting to insurance. Only when construction time is of the essence—where, for example, the owner insists on a tight construction timetable and attaches pecuniary penalties such as liquidated damages to unanticipated delays—will such insurance be practical.

9.4.3. Other Forms of Property Insurance

Contractors often purchase supplemental property insurance to provide coverage in areas excluded by clauses in the builder's risk policy or to enhance protection in high-risk areas. Two of the most common supplemental policies are *equipment floater* and *installation floater policies.* An equipment floater policy provides additional protection against damage to property stored at the construction site or used in connection with on-site work. An installation floater policy provides protection for contractors who install machinery and heavy equipment in power plants, factories and high-rise buildings. Such machinery frequently contains delicate mechanical or electrical components which are easily damaged when hoisted and fitted into place on a working construction site. An installation floater policy protects against damage to the machine being installed and the equipment (cranes, lifts, and hoists) utilized during the installation process.

Other widely-used supplemental property policies are *valuable papers coverage* for design professionals and *waiver-of-occupancy coverage* for general construction

---

[11]*See generally* P.L.I., *Real Estate Construction: Current Problems* (1973), pp. 192–193. Note also that under AIA's General Conditions, a contractor may, by means of a change order, pass on the cost of difference-of-conditions coverage to the construction-site owner if the owner elects to provide named-peril coverage instead of all-risk coverage:

> Unless otherwise provided, the Owner shall purchase . . . "all risk" insurance for physical loss or damage including, without duplication of coverage, theft, vandalism and malicious mischief. If the Owner does not intend to purchase such insurance for the full insurable value of the entire Work, he shall inform the Contractor in writing prior to commencement of the Work. The Contractor may then effect insurance which will protect the interests of himself, his Subcontractors and the Sub-subcontractors in the Work, and by appropriate Change Order the cost thereof shall be charged to the Owner.

AIA Document A201 ("General Conditions") (1976 ed.), Article 11.3.1.

work. Valuable papers coverage protects against theft, loss, or destruction of blueprints and work plans. Waiver-of-occupancy coverage is added by endorsement to the contractor's named peril or all-risk policy. The standard builder's risk policy contains a common exclusionary clause—the "occupancy" clause—which, in effect, terminates property coverage as soon as the construction site is wholly *or partially* occupied. The "occupancy" clause would work a particular hardship if, for example, a contractor were constructing two buildings on a single site, with one scheduled for completion earlier than the other. Under such circumstances, occupancy (even partial occupancy) of the first building would cancel the contractor's property policy, although construction work continued on the second building. Waiver-of-occupancy coverage provides protection by deleting the exclusionary clause.

9.5. INSURANCE PLANNING: INTRODUCTION

The large number of insurance carriers and policies from which to choose and the wide variation in premium prices make the overall cost of insurance one of the most variable factors in the cost equation. Sensible insurance planning is imperative if the contractor or design professional is to obtain needed coverage at competitive rates. Intelligent insurance planning includes two components: integrating coverage to protect against policy duplication and the use of low-cost alternatives to traditional insurance coverage.

9.5.1. Integrating Coverage

The construction industry has historically required that each party bear responsibility for his own insurance protection. This can result in expensive duplication of coverage and encourage litigation between insurance carriers to determine whose policy controls. Integrated insurance coverage can reduce an individual contractor's premium costs by eliminating certain kinds of insurance and permitting the contractor to concentrate his insurance dollars in areas where protection is not duplicated.

In addition, by shifting certain insurance costs to the party most able to afford them or the party in the best position to insure at favorable premium rates, integrated coverage can reduce the overall cost of insurance for all parties. For example, an owner may secure protection against liability claims based on acts of his contractors in two ways. He may include a "hold harmless" or indemnity clause in all prime contracts, thereby requiring each prime contractor to purchase contractual liability coverage at a substantial premium (the cost of which will in any event be passed on to the owner at a higher price for the work) or the owner, by endorsement, may include equivalent protection in his existing CGL policy. This alternative may well cost substantially less, since the owner can achieve at considerable economy through a single endorsement what all prime contractors would otherwise be required to do separately.

Policy integration is thus achieved by shifting to each participant those risks he is most capable of assuming and avoiding the uneconomic purchase of separate or redundant policies. Integrated coverage seeks to avoid the unnecessary proliferation of insurance carriers. To the extent that all parties negotiate with and purchase coverage from the same carrier or a small number of carriers, coordination is more easily achieved and overlap is minimized.

A relatively new and controversial technique for ensuring that policies are effectively integrated is the *"wrap-up" program* under which one party—usually the owner—is authorized by all other participating parties to purchase necessary coverage for every party and every aspect of the project. In theory, the owner offsets increased insurance costs through savings realized by contractors and design professionals, whose prices reflect their own insurance premium reductions.

Wrap-up programs offer significant advantages over traditional self-insurance. Overall insurance costs can be substantially reduced through elimination of overlapping policies because a single purchaser can often negotiate discounts by purchasing all coverage from a single carrier in a single transaction. Administrative costs can also be reduced. Normally, each party must present insurance certificates and proof of purchase to the owner, who must review and approve them before commencement of the project. A wrap-up program eliminates this procedure and ensures uniform handling of claims, regular premium payments, centralized records, and an effective loss prevention program under the auspices of a single insurance company.

Wrap-up insurance is not a panacea. For a contractor, the prospects of dealing with a separate wrap-up carrier on each project may be less attractive than maintaining coverage with a single established carrier. A contractor with a good safety record and correspondingly low experience rating may be penalized by wrap-up insurance, since his lower rates no longer translate into a competitive bidding advantage. There is also potential for conflict of interest. The interests of owner and contractor will frequently collide, and it is not unreasonable for the contractor to fear that the carrier will side with the owner when the owner has purchased the policies and will provide further business to the carrier in the future.

For these reasons, wrap-up programs have been limited primarily to large-scale construction projects. One authority has suggested $20 million as to the minimum cost of construction projects for which the wrap-up approach is feasible.[12]

9.5.2. Insurance in Context

Purchasing an insurance policy is only one way to protect against risk, and it is frequently not the least expensive. Intelligent insurance planning must take into account the means by which insurance premiums can be kept within reasonable limits by reducing the probability of serious financial loss because of liability for injury or property damage.

A comprehensive safety and inspection program can eliminate the causes of many on-site accidents. The most effective way to control insurance costs is to establish a low experience rating by maintaining a consistently good safety record through safety checks,

---

[12]P.L.I., *Real Estate Construction: Current Problems* (1973), p. 205.

employment of security personnel to protect property, adequate lighting, removal of dangerous obstacles from the construction site, and high standards of training and performance. Most insurance carriers provide loss prevention services as an integral part of their coverage.

Effective use of "self-insurance" can also reduce insurance costs. Self-insurance mechanisms include the judicious use of deductible and co-insurance features in policies and the decision (in certain narrow risk areas) to forego insurance altogether and budget against small but inevitable losses.

9.6. ADDITIONAL SOURCE MATERIALS

Callahan, "Completed operations exclusion in general liability policies," 1 Forum 16 (1966).

Coleman, "Insurance requirements in construction contract general conditions as an element of professional negligence," 23 St. Louis U.L.J. 222 (1979).

Hall, "Contractors' liability insurance for property damage incidental to normal operations—the standard coverage problem," 16 U.Kan.L.Rev. 181 (1968).

Morris, "Insurance problems in the construction industry," 1969 Ins.L.J. 199 (April).

Anno., "Builders' risk insurance policies," 94 A.L.R.2d 224.

Anno., "Right of owner's employee, injured by subcontractor, to recover against general contractor for breach of contract between latter and owner requiring contractor and subcontractors to carry insurance," 22 A.L.R.2d 647.

Anno., "Scope of clause excluding from contractor's or similar liability policy damage to property in care, custody or control of insured," 62 A.L.R.2d 1242.

CHAPTER **10**

Labor Relations in the Construction Industry

10.1. INTRODUCTION

A full-blown analysis of federal labor law is beyond the scope of this presentation. This chapter will nonetheless set forth the principal features of the National Labor Relations Act ("NLRA"),[1] the leading judicial and administrative decisions thereunder, and related legislation applicable to the construction industry.

The relevant legal considerations are complex, and the reach of federal law is extensive. The NLRA may affect virtually any contractor. It will apply if a "labor dispute," should one occur, would tend to burden, obstruct, or in general affect interstate or foreign commerce. In that event the National Labor Relations Board ("NLRB" or "Board") has authority to act, although as a practical matter it does not always do so.

The term "labor dispute" is broadly defined in Section 2(9) of the NLRA to mean:

Any controversy concerning terms, tenure or conditions of employment, or concerning the association or representation of persons in negotiating, fixing, maintaining, changing, or seeking to arrange terms or conditions of employment regardless of whether the disputants stand in the proximate relation of employer and employee.

---

[1]29 U.S.C. §§151 *et seq.*

"Commerce" is defined in Section 2(6) of the NLRA to include "trade, traffic, commerce, transportation, or communication among the several states. . . ." This definition is made more elastic by the NLRA's applicability to disputes *affecting* commerce, defined in Section 2(7) of the NLRA to mean "in commerce, or burdening or obstructing commerce or the free flow of commerce. . . ." The NLRB has adopted administrative standards for determining whether it will assert jurisdiction over labor disputes. The standards for non-retail businesses, which apply to the construction industry, require yearly out-of-state outflow or inflow, direct or indirect, of at least $50,000.[2] Even if a single subcontractor does not meet the jurisdictional test, the subcontractor's activities may be combined with those of the prime contractor to confer jurisdiction on the NLRB.[3]

10.2. UNFAIR LABOR PRACTICES

Any contractor, whether dealing with labor unions or on an "open shop" basis, should be aware of the unfair labor practices set forth in Section 8(a) of the NLRA. These include:

1. Interference with, restraint of, or coercion of employees in their exercise of rights of self-organization; forming, joining, or assisting labor unions; collective bargaining and pursuing other "concerted activities" (§8(a)(1));

2. Domination of or interference with the formation or administration of any labor organization (§8(a)(2));

3. Discrimination with respect to hire or tenure of employment or any terms or conditions of employment to encourage or discourage membership in any labor organization (§8(a)(3)); and

4. Refusal to bargain collectively with the employee representatives (§8(a)(5)).

The NLRA also specifies unfair labor practices of labor organizations, some of which will be discussed below as relevant to the construction industry.

10.3. THE STRUCTURE OF COLLECTIVE BARGAINING

The construction industry is fragmented and localized. Collective bargaining between contractors and unions tends to reflect this parochialism. As one commentator has noted:

Nationwide or regional collective bargaining agreements exist in some branches of the industry such as pipelines, sprinkler systems, elevator construction,

---

[2]*Spears-Dehner, Inc.*, 139 N.L.R.B. 922, 1962 CCH NLRB ¶11,768 (1962) (highway construction).

[3]*Operative Plasterers' & Cement Masons' International Association Local No. 2*, 149 N.L.R.B. 1265, 1964 CCH ¶13,607 (1964).

operating engineers on dredging work, tank work and other boilermaker operations, and electricians on transmission lines. In the main, however, bargaining is conducted separately in a small locality, a part of a state, or occasionally on a state-wide basis between each trade and one or more employer associations whose members employ members of a particular trade. It is rare for bargaining to be coordinated among trades, local unions of a single trade, or employer associations, although in some parts of the country the basic trades and general contractors tend to negotiate together. Recently, there has been some coordination of bargaining among different contractor associations, but this movement is still rare.[4]

As a consequence, negotiation and enforcement of collective bargaining agreements, and the conduct of strikes, are local affairs pursued by local unions or district councils of national unions and by local chapters of contractor associations.

10.4. MULTI-EMPLOYER OR ASSOCIATION BARGAINING

Multi-employer bargaining—an institution of long-standing in the construction industry—evolved in response to craft union pressure on individual contractors. Craft unions exerted pressure by controlling most craftsmen in a given area and withholding or threatening to withhold labor from one contractor while allowing his competitors to work. To counteract such "whipsawing," contractors resorted to multi-employer bargaining. Unions saw advantages in this as well. Multi-employer bargaining avoids separate negotiations with individual contractors and tends to establish standard wage rates and working conditions industry-wide.

Multi-employer bargaining has developed three variants: (1) association bargaining through employer-formed entities such as the Association of General Contractors; (2) informal alliances of contractors created, ad hoc, to engage in joint bargaining negotiations with unions; and (3) creation of uniform wage rates and other employment terms through standard union contracts, negotiated in the first instance with a formal association, an ad hoc bargaining group, or even a single contractor.[5]

Participation in joint negotiations takes place when the power to bargain for an employer is delegated, either formally or informally, to an employer group. The employer group or association need not have authority to bind its members; nor is it necessary that the group enter into a master contract rather than separate contracts or even that individual employers agree in advance to be bound by any contract which may be jointly negotiated. The critical determinant of participation is merely the employer's intent to be bound by group rather than individual action. To establish the necessary

---

[4]Frank S. Astroth, "Collective Bargaining in the Construction Industry," *Construction Industry Labor Relations*, 1977, p. 170 (Practising Law Institute).

[5]"The essential element in the establishment of a multi-employer union for purposes of collective bargaining is participation by the several employers, whether members or nonmembers of an association, either personally or through an authorized representative, in joint bargaining negotiations." *Kroger Co. and Allen Alsip*, 1964 CCH NLRB ¶13,365 (1964).

intent, an employer's participation for a substantial period of time in joint bargaining negotiations and the uniform adoption of the agreements resulting from such negotiations will suffice.[6] A substantial period of time may be found to exist if multi-employer bargaining has continued for at least one year.[7] However, even a substantial multi-employer bargaining history will not be deemed controlling if it has been based on contracts applicable only to members of the contracting union.[8]

Once an employer's participation in group negotiations rests on his intent to be bound by group action, he may find himself subject to a multi-employer agreement even though not having agreed in advance to be bound by it. In *Joseph McDaniel*, 226 N.L.R.B. 851, 1976 CCH NLRB ¶17,528 (1976), the NLRB held that two painting contractors who "created the appearance of having acquiesced" in multi-employer bargaining were bound by the resulting contract negotiated by the employer association. In *McDaniel* the association purported to represent and include on the negotiating committee all its members who were union contractors. Neither of the contractors signed, as requested, an assignment of bargaining rights form; nor did they sign a clause in the final agreement pursuant to which the union recognized the association as agent for its members. The NLRB found, nevertheless, that the contractors had to adhere to the final agreement:

> . . . [T]he test to be applied . . . is whether the members of the group have indicated from the outset an unequivocal intention to be bound in collective bargaining by group rather than individual action. . . . An employer who, through a course of conduct or otherwise, signifies that it has authorized the group to act in its behalf will be bound by that apparent creation of authority.

10.5. WITHDRAWAL FROM MULTI-EMPLOYER BARGAINING

In view of *McDaniel*, a contractor wishing to withdraw from multi-employer bargaining must consider the circumstances under which withdrawal will be legally effective. In general, a contractor or other employer may withdraw from a multi-employer union for any reason if the withdrawal request is (a) unequivocal, (b) made at the appropriate time, or (c) made with the implied or express consent of the union.

These rules are illustrated in *Retail Associates, Inc.*, 120 N.L.R.B. 388, 41 L.R.R.M. 1502 (1958). The NLRB there found that an employer could not withdraw from an established multi-employer bargaining group unless it gave written notice of its intention to withdraw before the date set by the prevailing contract for modification or the date agreed upon for commencement of multi-employer negotiations. After multi-employer negotiations have begun, withdrawal will not be permitted except by mutual consent under unusual circumstances. In addition, the decision to withdraw must be

---

[6]*Quality Limestone Products, Inc.*, 143 N.L.R.B. 589, 1963 CCH NLRB ¶12,445 (1963).

[7]*Consolidated Iron-Steel Mfg. Co. (Taylor & Boggis Foundry Div.)*, 98 N.L.R.B. 481 (1952).

[8]*Crucible Steel Castings Co.*, 90 N.L.R.B. 1843 (1950).

made in good faith and must contemplate abandonment of multi-employer bargaining on a relatively permanent basis.[9] Commencement of negotiations thus often has the effect of locking in members of the multi-employer group despite subsequent attempts at abandonment or disengagement; and negotiations may begin quite informally.

In *The Carvel Company,* 226 N.L.R.B. 111, 1976 CCH NLRB ¶17,421 (1976), the NLRB held that a plumbing contractor could not leave a multi-employer group of pipefitting contractors after the union had submitted its proposals. The Board reasoned that the union's disclosure of its proposals constituted commencement of negotiations, which bound the contractor to the resulting contract. To permit withdrawal, said the Board, would encourage employers to withdraw from multi-employer groups in the hope of obtaining, individually, terms more favorable than those submitted by the union to the multi-employer group.

The rules governing employer withdrawal from multi-employer bargaining also govern union withdrawals.

Withdrawal is not simply a technical consideration. It goes to the heart of multi-employer bargaining. The rules restricting withdrawal are, in fact, a matter of protection for the multi-employer group. If an employer could freely withdraw from a multi-employer group simply because he did not like the way in which negotiations were progressing or thought a strike imminent, multi-employer bargaining would be severely undermined. An employer might then enter into an interim agreement with the union. Such an agreement would typically contemplate payment by the withdrawing employer of the wage rates and other benefits ultimately negotiated on a group basis retroactive to the expiration of the previous collective bargaining agreement. If other employers were similarly induced to withdraw from the multi-employer group, its leverage would then diminish. Union members would be employed in substantial numbers under interim agreements. The union would then find it necessary to strike only a handful of remaining employer members to obtain a new agreement.

It is hardly surprising, therefore, that employer members have been required to adhere to group contracts negotiated on their behalf and that union attempts to fragment multi-employer groups have met with regulatory disapproval. If a union seeks to withdraw from the multi-employer group with respect to some employers but not others, the remaining employers may withdraw from the group.[10] Moreover, a union may not exert strike pressure against only certain members of a multi-employer group in an effort to coerce them into signing separate contracts. The NLRB has found both types of conduct to be an unlawful refusal to bargain, intended to compel employers to abandon the multi-employer bargaining group.[11]

An exception may arise if the union may legitimately withdraw and seek agreements with individual members of the group.[12] Similarly, after an impasse occurs,

---

[9]*NLRB v. Sheridan Creations, Inc.,* 357 F.2d 245 (2d Cir. 1966), *cert. denied,* 385 U.S. 1005 (1969).

[10]*Pacific Coast Ass'n of Pulp and Paper Manufacturers,* 163 N.L.R.B. 892, 1967 CCH NLRB ¶21,247 (1967).

[11]*Teamsters Union, Local 324 (Cascade Employers Ass'n, Inc.),* 127 N.L.R.B. 488, 1960 CCH NLRB ¶8803 (1960).

[12]*Cheney Lumber & Sawmill Workers, Local 264 (California Lumber Co.),* 130 N.L.R.B. 235, 1961 CCH NLRB ¶9652 (1961).

individual members of the multi-employer group may also withdraw, with or without the union's consent.[13] However, if certain members withdraw but others remain in the multi-employer group after an impasse, the union may not initiate contact with the remaining members to seek individual contracts—except with those who, having withdrawn, voluntarily request individual bargaining.[14]

10.6. MULTI-EMPLOYER COLLECTIVE BARGAINING AGREEMENTS

Multi-employer groups act, in effect, as agents for their individual members. This agency relationship may give rise to unanticipated legal consequences. In *Lewis v. Cable*, 107 F.Supp. 196 (W. D. Pa. 1952), for example, the authority of the multi-employer group was limited to negotiating the group contract with the union. A member of the group, having refused to sign or otherwise approve the group contract, was, nonetheless, still deemed to be bound by its terms since the member had accepted the benefits of the contract. Through parallel reasoning, a court in *Teamsters Local No. 839 v. Morrison-Knudsen Co.*, 270 F.2d 530 (9th Cir. 1959), found that a non-signing member on whose behalf a group contract had been negotiated could sue a union for breach of that contract. Similarly, in *George D. Auchter Co.*, 102 N.L.R.B. 881, 31 L.R.R.M. 1389 (1953), a multi-employer group that had negotiated an illegal provision in a contract with the union was held to be jointly responsible with one of its members which had denied a worker a job because of the provision.

10.7. MULTI-EMPLOYER GROUP LOCKOUTS

Although the term lockout is used in Section 8(d)(4) of the NLRA, it is nowhere defined, under either the NLRA or other federal legislation. Court and administrative usage provides the definition. In *Betts Cadillac Olds, Inc.*, 96 N.L.R.B. 268 (1961), for example, lockout is described as "cessation [by the employer] of the furnishing of work to employees in an effort to get for the employer more desirable terms." Initially held to be illegal *per se*, lockouts have gained lawful status under certain circumstances: (1) where their purpose or effect does not interfere with the statutory rights of employees; (2) where an employer faces operational difficulties created by an impending strike;[15] or (3) where, after a bargaining impasse has been reached, an employer temporarily locks out his employees solely for the purpose of bringing pressure to bear on the union in support of his legitimate bargaining position.[16] Unlawful intention cannot be inferred from the mere use of a lockout.

---

[13]*NLRB v. Hi-Way Billboards, Inc.*, 500 F.2d 181 (5th Cir. 1974).

[14]*Teamsters Union, Local 717 (Ice Cream Council, Inc.)*, 145 N.L.R.B. 865, 1964 CCH NLRB ¶12,836 (1964).

[15]*Willamette Ass'n of Plumbing and Heating Contractors, Inc.*, 125 N.L.R.B. 924 (1959).

[16]*American Ship Building Co. v. NLRB*, 380 U.S. 300 (1965).

Multi-employer groups have viewed the lockout as a means to counteract whip-saw tactics on the part of a union. Initially, the NLRB found group lockouts illegal.[17] Federal courts rejected this view, eventually prompting the NLRB to do so too. Under the *Buffalo Linen* doctrine,[18] as it came to be called, lockouts by nonstruck members of a multi-employer group are permitted as a temporary defensive measure to combat the union's strike against a member, but only to preserve the integrity of the multi-employer group.

This rationale has been adopted by the Supreme Court.[19] It has also been extended to permit members of a multi-employer group engaged in a lockout to continue to operate by using temporary replacements for locked-out employees.[20] The permissibility of group lockouts rests on the need to preserve the group as a bargaining entity. It follows, therefore, that a member who does *not* lock his employees out when the multi-employer group has issued a lockout order may be required legally to do so. Exactly this situation was presented in *Construction Industry Contractors v. Drake Co.*, 93 L.R.R.M. 2924 (1976). In that case three multi-employer associations of contractors ordered one of their members to abide by a lockout order previously issued. When the member declined to do so, the associations sought and obtained a federal court injunction. The court reviewed the members' assignment of bargaining rights to the associations as contractually binding. The associations were thus found to be "within the lawful exercise of their collective bargaining rights when they directed that bargaining unit members close down all work affected by striking crafts. . . ."

10.8. ACQUIRING REPRESENTATIONAL RIGHTS IN THE CONSTRUCTION INDUSTRY: A SUMMARY

Under Section 8(a)(3) of the NLRA, as we have seen, employers may not encourage or discourage membership in any labor organization by discriminating in hire or in tenure, terms, or conditions of employment. An employer will be deemed to have violated the NLRA if he refuses employment to an applicant because of the applicant's union activities or if he discharges, transfers, demotes, lays off, or otherwise discriminates against an employee in order to encourage or discourage union membership. The NLRA also validates certain forms of compulsory union membership that would otherwise be unlawful under its provisions. A union may thus enter into a "union security agreement" if:

— It qualifies as a "labor organization";
— It is representative of the majority of the employees in the appropriate bargaining unit to be covered by the agreement (§9(a)) (except, as to the

---

[17]*Morand Bros. Beverage Co.*, 99 N.L.R.B. 1448, 30 L.R.R.M. 1178 (1952).
[18]*Buffalo Linen Supply Co.*, 109 N.L.R.B. 447, 34 L.R.R.M. 1355 (1954).
[19]*NLRB v. Truck Drivers Local 449*, 353 U.S. 87 (1957).
[20]*NLRB v. Brown*, 380 U.S. 278 (1965).

construction industry, where pre-hire contracts, discussed below, are permitted regardless of the union's representative status pursuant to Section 8(f) of the NLRA); and

— The union's authority to enter into the agreement has not been revoked by a majority vote of the employees in the bargaining unit in a de-authorization election held within the preceding 12 months (§9(c)).

Union security agreements must meet certain statutory requirements. An applicant for employment may not be compelled, as a condition of employment, to be or become a union member before he is hired. Nor may he be required, as a condition of retaining employment, to join the union until at least 30 days after he is hired or after the effective date of the agreement, whichever is later (except for the construction industry, where union membership may be required after seven days). In states with laws prohibiting, or more strictly regulating, compulsory unionism, the agreement must conform with those laws.

The NLRB does not require that the employees' representative be selected by any given procedure, other than to require that the union be the choice of the majority of those casting votes. Selection of a representative for collective bargaining purposes is the culmination of the employees' right of self-organization. It imposes on the employer the duty to bargain collectively with the representative. Employers may freely recognize a union; or they may refuse to recognize or bargain until the union has received a certificate from the NLRB.

To obtain that certificate, the union must first win an election among the employees it purports to represent. Certification assures the union of a year's time thereafter within which to enter into an agreement with an employer. Since certification means that the union is the exclusive bargaining representative for a group of employees, it need not worry about competition from a rival union. Under Section 9(c)(1) of the NLRA, the Board provides a forum for the election procedure, which is commenced through the filing of an election petition. Such a petition is most often filed by the labor organization but may also be filed by the employer, if, having been asked by the union for recognition, he prefers to have the question of representation decided by secret-ballot election.

The union's demand for recognition may commence with notice to the employer that a majority of its employees have signed union authorization cards. The employer, faced with such a demand, may be required to bargain with the union on the basis of authorization cards, not election ballots, unless he has a "good faith doubt" as to the union's majority status.[21] Employers frequently—and unwittingly—take affirmative action, which may have the effect of undermining "good faith doubt." For example, an employer might examine the union's authorization cards and other proof of majority status and thereafter voice no objection, permit a third party to conduct an ostensibly objective examination of the authorization cards, conduct a poll of its employees to determine the extent of union support (which, of itself, could be regarded as coercive,

---

[21]*NLRB v. Gissel Packing Co.*, 395 U.S. 575 (1969).

whatever the results), or lay off known union supporters and threaten economic reprisals. These responses may achieve just the opposite of their intended effect by requiring the employer to bargain without an election.

If the union proves unable to obtain recognition on the basis of authorization cards alone, it will seek NLRB certification through an election. Contractors confronting an election sometimes try to forestall unionization by contesting the appropriateness of the bargaining unit and the timing of the election itself. The union will typically select, from the several potentially appropriate units on a construction project, that unit which it reasonably expects can elect the union. The contractor may take an opposite course. In the construction industry appropriate units may include (1) all or several of the contractor's projects and all employees employed on those projects; (2) a single project-wide unit of all construction employees; or (3) separate units within a given project according to trade or craft skills. Employer and union may not share a commonality of interest in determining which of these units is the appropriate one. As to timing, much may depend on when an election petition is filed. Toward the end of a construction project of limited duration, the petition may be dismissed if the contractor can persuade the NLRB that its operations will be completed within a short time and that there is little likelihood of additional work in the area. On the other hand, if a petition is filed before a "substantial and representative complement" of the contractor's employees has yet been hired, it may be able to dismiss the union's election petition or at least hold it in abeyance. The contractor would argue in effect that representative results can only be achieved when all its employees at peak load are included.

It should be noted, however, that the NLRB interprets the "substantial and representative complement" standard liberally and has ordered an election on a construction project where only 39 of an anticipated 190 employees were employed.[22]

10.9. PRE-HIRE AGREEMENTS

Section 8(f) of the NLRA establishes special rules applicable to the construction industry and authorizes what are known as pre-hire agreements. That section makes the union's representative status immaterial, permits union-security contracts before any employees are hired, and allows a grace period of only seven days (rather than 30 days) after hire within which employees must join the union under union-shop agreements. Section 8(f) validates practices which would otherwise be unlawful under the NLRA.

Section 8(f) is intended to address the unique labor problems of the construction industry. These are thought to arise from the prevalence of relatively short-term projects and the necessity that contractors know their labor costs before bidding. Under a pre-hire agreement, construction contractors are allowed to draw upon skilled craftsmen in the various trades without having thereafter to negotiate a contract under project time and budget constraints.

---

[22]*NLRB v. Clement-Blythe Companies,* 168 N.L.R.B. 118 (1967), *enforcement denied,* 415 F.2d 78 (4th Cir. 1969).

The statutory requirements applicable to pre-hire agreements include the following:

— The employer must be engaged in the building and construction industry;
— The employees covered must be engaged, presently or upon their employment, in the building and construction industry;
— The union must be a labor organization of which building and construction industry employees are members; and
— The union must not be established, maintained, or assisted by any employer unfair labor practices.

An agreement executed pursuant to Section 8(f) does not prevent covered employees from immediately obtaining an election to reject the union as their bargaining agent, to choose a rival union as their agent, or to rescind the union's authority to execute union-security contracts.

Critics contend that pre-hire agreements merely permit a union to require an employer, contrary to the wishes of his employees, to engage the services of union members on terms dictated by the union. This contention gains some support from *Local No. 150, International Union of Operating Engineers v. NLRB*, 480 F.2d 1186 (D.C. Cir. 1973), where the court held that a pre-hire agreement confers on the union a presumption of majority status. The employer thus has a duty to bargain collectively with the union unless the presumption is rebutted by means of a representation election. Because of their unusual nature, pre-hire agreements do not enjoy protection of the "contract bar" doctrine under which a valid union-security agreement prevents a competing union from filing an election petition and securing an election conducted by the NLRB permitting employees to select their own bargaining agent.

10.10. AGREEMENTS PERMITTED: GENERALLY

Under Section 8(a)(3) of the NLRA, compulsory union membership is permitted as a condition of employment pursuant to an agreement between the union and the employer. However, an applicant for employment may not be required, as a condition of employment, to become a union member before he is hired. Union membership may, nonetheless, be required thereafter, and, as we have seen, within seven days in the building and construction industry.

The majority status of the contracting union is essential to the validity of the union-security agreement, except in the building and construction industry.[23] Closed-shop agreements, requiring union membership as a condition of hiring and of continued employment, are prohibited by the NLRA. Union-shop agreements, requiring union membership as a condition of retaining employment, are not. Maintenance-of-member-

---

[23]NLRA, §§8(f), 9(a).

ship agreements are hybrid agreements, containing elements of union-shop and open-shop practices. They require all employees who are union members when the agreement is executed or at a specified time thereafter, and all employees who become union members thereafter, to retain union membership as a condition of employment. But maintenance-of-membership agreements do not impose any membership obligation on employees who do not join the union or who resign from the union before the agreement takes effect or during a contractual escape period.

Agency-shop agreements require all covered employees to pay the union amounts equivalent to regular dues and fees required of union members. Agency-shop agreements have been sanctioned by the Supreme Court and are deemed to be practically the equivalent of union-shop agreements.[24] Both agency- and union-shop agreements are subject to provisions of state law prohibiting union membership as a condition of employment.[25]

10.11. HIRING HALLS

As we have seen, union membership may not be required as a condition of hiring. To be lawful, therefore, a hiring agreement must be non-discriminatory. Preferential and exclusive hiring agreements, under which the union clears, dictates, or consents to the employment of union members only, have been held illegal.[26] Similarly, the NLRA is deemed to outlaw union hiring halls as a means of discriminating against non-union workers.[27] Thus, a hiring hall system under which the union refers only union members in good standing is unlawful, even in the absence of evidence that specific employees are the subject of discrimination.[28]

The existing legal rules do not prohibit use of hiring halls, only their *discriminatory* use. A contractor can therefore agree with a union to hire exclusively through a union hiring hall if the agreement provides for referral of non-union employees as well as union employees. Such an agreement gains substance if control of the hiring hall is vested in a joint employer-union committee.[29] But joint control does not insure against discriminatory union practices, which, even in the absence of such control, may be imputed to the employer, thus making him a party to the union's illegality. This may arise under an exclusive hiring hall agreement when a qualified applicant approaches the employer and is refused employment after the union has denied clearance without a valid reason.

Discrimination may also arise when employees are discharged. Under a union-

---

[24]*NLRB v. General Motors Corp.*, 373 U.S. 734 (1963).

[25]*Amalgamated Association of Street Electric Railway & Motor Coach Employees, Division 1225 v. Las Vegas-Tonopah-Reno Stage Line, Inc.*, 319 F.2d 783 (9th Cir. 1963).

[26]*Associated General Contractors (Alaska Chapter) and Local 302, IUOE*, 113 N.L.R.B. 41 (1955); *Bridge Workers, Local 792*, 128 N.L.R.B. 1259; 1960 CCH NLRB ¶9181 (1960); *Shipwrecking, Inc.*, 136 N.L.R.B. 1518, 1962 CCH NLRB ¶11,161 (1962).

[27]*NLRB v. Carpenters, Millwrights' Local 2232*, 277 F.2d 217 (5th Cir. 1960).

[28]*NLRB v. Carpenters, Local 176*, 276 F.2d 583 (1st Cir. 1960).

[29]*Chamberlin & Co.*, 94 N.L.R.B. 388 (1951).

shop agreement, an employer may not discharge an employee (1) if he has reasonable grounds for believing that union membership was not available to the employee on the same terms and conditions generally applicable to other members, or (2) if he has reasonable grounds for believing that membership was denied or terminated for reasons other than the employee's failure to pay periodic dues and initiation fees uniformly required as a condition of acquiring or retaining union membership.[30] If an employer does have "reasonable grounds" and nonetheless discharges the employee, even at the union's request, he will have committed an unfair labor practice.

10.12. STRIKES AND PICKETING IN THE CONSTRUCTION INDUSTRY

Picketing usually means the patrolling of the employer's premises to advertise a labor dispute and to influence others to support the union's position. It will be discussed here as an integral part of the strike as a labor weapon. Section 7 of the NLRA grants to employees the right to engage in "concerted activities for the purpose of collective bargaining or other mutual aid or protection." This includes the right to strike and the right to picket. Section 13 of the NLRA also protects the right to picket. These rights are of particular relevance to the construction industry, which, with four percent of the nation's work force, accounted for almost 17 percent of the nation's striking employees during a ten-year period ending in 1972. Facing such a high degree of labor unrest, contractors must give special note to the legal and illegal uses of strikes and picketing.

10.12.1. Organizational or Recognition Picketing

The NLRA imposes restrictions on organizational picketing. The restrictions arise from Congress's recognition that unions, especially in the construction industry, might otherwise picket contractors for the purpose of compelling them to sign union-security agreements, even though contrary to the wishes of a majority of the contractors' employees. The legality of pre-hire agreements in the construction industry adds a special dimension to the problem. Without the NLRA's restrictions, a union could picket a general contractor having no employees for an agreement that future employees would be covered by a union-security agreement and also that subcontractors performing work at the job site would enter into such agreements.

Section 8(b)(7) of the NLRA therefore restricts recognition of or organizational picketing by uncertified unions. It permits such picketing only when an NLRB election can be, and is, promptly requested. Specifically, Section 8(b)(7) prohibits a labor union from picketing, or threatening to picket, any employer "where an object thereof is forcing or requiring the employer to recognize or bargain with a labor organization as the representative of his employees, or forcing or requiring the employees of an employer to accept or select such labor organization as their collective bargaining representative," if:

---

[30]NLRA, §8(a)(3).

— The employer is lawfully recognizing another union, and no question of representation may appropriately be raised under the NLRA;

— A valid representational election has been conducted under Section 9(c) of the NLRA within the preceding 12 months; or

— An election petition has not been filed within 30 days after commencement of the picketing.

It is the last-mentioned condition that has occasioned the most controversy. A contractor threatened with illegal organizational picketing cannot, as a practical matter, merely await the NLRB's finding of an unfair labor practice and the issuance of a cease and desist order, inherently a time-consuming process. The statutory remedy for violation of Section 8(b)(7) is a federal district court injunction under Section 10(1), usually sought by the NLRB within two or three weeks after charges have been filed.

10.12.2. Picketing with a Secondary Objective

Section 8(b)(4) of the NLRA prohibits secondary boycotts and is of particular relevance to the construction industry. A secondary boycott occurs when a union directs pressure—whether by strike, picketing, threat, coercion, or restraint—against an employer or other person with whom it has no dispute for the purpose of persuading or coercing that person to stop dealing with a primary party with whom it does have a dispute in order to exert pressure on the primary party. To meet this and other related problems, Section 8(b)(4) proscribes certain *actions* by unions when taken to coerce specified *objectives*. Thus, a union is prohibited from (1) "engaging in, or inducing or encouraging workers to engage in, any strike or withholding of labor," or (2) "threatening, coercing, or restraining any employer or other person engaged in commerce or in an industry affecting commerce" when these actions are taken to achieve the objectives set forth in Section 8(b)(4). Those objectives are:

— Forcing an employer to join a labor organization or to enter into a "hot cargo" agreement (discussed in §10.12.3, below);

— Forcing any person to cease using, selling, handling, transporting, or otherwise dealing in the products of any other producer, processor, or manufacturer, or to cease doing business with any other person, or forcing any other employer to recognize or bargain with a labor organization as the representative of his employees unless it has been certified as the representative of those employees;

— Forcing any employer to recognize or bargain with a particular labor organization as the representative of his employees if another labor organization has been certified as the representative of such employees; and

— Forcing an employer to assign particular work to employees in a particular labor organization or in a particular trade, craft, or class rather than to employees in another labor organization or in another trade, craft, or class unless such employer fails to conform to an order or certification of the NLRB determining the bargaining representative for employees performing such work.

The second of these prohibited objectives concerns secondary boycotts. Examples of secondary boycotts commonly found in the construction industry include picketing a prime contractor to force him to cease doing business with a non-union subcontractor, and picketing a contractor to force him to use materials produced by union manufacturers.

These forms of secondary boycott are prevalent in the construction industry, in part because of common work sites. Typically, two or more contractors are engaged in work at a single job site. Unions originally contended that such contractors should be deemed allied or associated as a means of avoiding the NLRA's strictures against secondary boycotts. In *NLRB v. Denver Building and Construction Trades Council*, 341 U.S. 675 (1951), the Supreme Court ruled otherwise. It held that common-situs picketing at a construction project to protest employment of non-union labor by an electrical subcontractor violated the secondary boycott provisions of Section 8(b)(4).

The *Denver Building Trades* case led to application of the so-called *Moore Dry Dock* rules, previously developed by the NLRB, to the construction industry in order to distinguish between permitted primary activity and illegal secondary activity. These rules were first set forth in *Sailors' Union of the Pacific (Moore Dry Dock Co.)*, 92 N.L.R.B. 547, 549 (1950), and relate specifically to common situs picketing. They permit such picketing under the following circumstances:

(1) The picketing is strictly limited to times when the situs of dispute is located on the secondary employer's premises;

(2) At the time of the picketing, the primary employer is engaged in its normal business at the situs;

(3) The picketing is limited to places reasonably close to the location of the situs; and

(4) The picketing discloses clearly that the dispute is with the primary employer.

The *Moore Dry Dock* rules have been used by courts as simple evidentiary tests to aid in determining whether common-situs picketing is primary and lawful or secondary and unlawful.[31] Notwithstanding a union's compliance with the rules, picketing of a secondary employer's premises may be found illegal if the primary employer has a separate place of business elsewhere at which picketing can be conducted.[32]

The *Moore Dry Dock* rules have shaped industrial practices. To minimize the

---

[31]*See, e.g., NLRB v. Teamsters Local 968*, 225 F.2d 205 (5th Cir. 1955).

[32]*See, e.g., NLRB v. Local Union 522, Lumber Drivers*, 281 F.2d 952 (3d Cir. 1960). *But see Electrical Workers (IBEW), Local 861 (Plauche Electric, Inc.)*, 135 N.L.R.B. 250, 1962 CCH NLRB ¶10,830 (1962) (place of picketing only one factor to be considered in determining object of picketing).

impact of common-situs picketing within the rules, contractors (and other employers) developed reserved gates to be used exclusively by employees of subcontractors. Picketing against those subcontractors would then, under the rules, be confined to the reserved gates. Picketing at other gates would presumably be unlawful since those gates would be used only by subcontractors, not the prime contractor. Experience has proven the reserve gate concept to be workable, provided the general contractor takes extreme care to preserve the integrity of the respective gates. Under no circumstances may a subcontractor or a supplier to a subcontractor go through the contractor's gate. The gates must also be carefully identified so that the public is well aware of which employees are to go through which gates. If these precautions are taken, reserve gates may be established at the time picketing starts.[33]

Picketing must be limited to times when the primary employer is engaged at normal work at the site.[34] It must be limited to places reasonably close to the location of the primary employer.[35] Finally, it must clearly show that the dispute is with the primary employer.[36] These constraints do not apply where the primary and secondary employees are "allies," as evidenced by common ownership, management and control or where the secondary employer is performing "struck work."[37]

Roving-situs picketing is closely allied conceptually with common-situs picketing. It occurs when a union having a dispute with one employer pickets at the premises of another, secondary employer at times when the employees of the primary employer are temporarily present, usually for the purpose of making deliveries, installations, repairs, and the like. Roving-situs picketing is governed generally by the *Moore Dry Dock* rules. It is permissible only when the primary employer's employees are on the premises and doing their normal work. It must also be reasonably close to where they are working, must show clearly that the dispute is with the primary employer, and must not seek to induce the secondary employer's employees to stop working.[38]

Informational or area standards picketing is lawful, even when directed against a secondary employer, under the free speech guarantee of Section 8(c) of the NLRA. A union does not violate the secondary boycott provision of the NLRA when, in furtherance of a dispute with a non-union contractor, it engages in handbilling calling for a consumer

---

[33]*Building and Construction Trades Council of New Orleans (Markwell and Hartz, Inc.*, 155 N.L.R.B. 319, 1965 CCH NLRB ¶9787 (1965).

In 1977, at the urging of organized labor and with the backing of the Carter Administration, Congress almost enacted common-situs picketing legislation that would have liberalized the circumstances under which unions could organize secondary boycotts on construction sites. The legislation, described as labor's number one priority in the year immediately following President Carter's election, was defeated in the House on March 23, 1977, after ferocious lobbying by, among others, the construction industry. 123 *Cong. Rec.* H2517 (daily ed. March 23, 1977). It has never been resurrected, and common-situs picketing, once labor's most pressing concern, has subsided somewhat in importance.

[34]*Kolodziej v. Local 697, IBEW*, 535 F.2d 1257 (7th Cir. 1976).

[35]*NLRB v. Local Union No. 369, IBEW*, 528 F.2d 317 (6th Cir. 1976).

[36]*Douds for the NLRB v. Teamsters Local 976*, 139 F.Supp. 702 (S.D.N.Y. 1956).

[37]*Madden v. Teamsters, Local 810*, 222 F.Supp. 635 (N.D.Ill. 1963); *NLRB v. Business Machine & Office Appliance Mechanics Conference Board, Local 459*, 228 F.2d 553 (2d Cir. 1955).

[38]*Douds for the NLRB v. Business Machine & Office Appliance Mechanics Conference Board, Local 459*, 122 F.Supp. 43 (S.D.N.Y. 1954); *NLRB v. Teamsters, Local Union 984*, 251 F.2d 495 (6th Cir. 1958).

boycott at the premises of the company employing the non-union contractor.[39] Similarly, picketing for the purpose of advising the public that an employer, whether or not a primary employer, does not pay wages that meet standards within the locality is not unlawful.[40] The critical factor is purpose. If picketing, however characterized, is intended to induce neutrals to cease doing business with the primary employer or to induce the neutrals' employees not to cross the picket line, it is illegal.[41]

Illegal secondary activity, including secondary boycotts, is accorded expedited review by the NLRA. The NLRB will make a preliminary investigation and, in a proper case, seek an injunction in federal court under Section 10(1) of the NLRA. Even this remedy, however, entails a hearing to determine "reasonable cause" for injunctive relief. Courts require the Board to "come forward with evidence sufficient to spell out a likelihood of violation."[42]

An injunction will not be granted where the union is engaged in informational picketing; nor will it be granted where the union action falls within the "work preservation" doctrine.[43] "Work preservation" is, in effect, simply a means of characterizing a union's conduct as primary rather than secondary. It applies when the union seeks to discourage a job-site employer from using material fabricated elsewhere. Such conduct may be deemed primary if fabrication has traditionally been performed on the job site by employees of the primary employer. Picketing then will be permissible.[44] "The touchstone is whether the agreement or its maintenance is addressed to the labor relations of the contracting (struck) employer vis-a-vis his own employees."[45] An injunction will also not be granted if the primary employer and the secondary employer are deemed to be under actual common control.[46] Similarly, the secondary boycott ban will not apply to an employer who performs farmed-out "struck work" (work ordinarily performed by employees of a strike-bound firm). Such an employee is deemed to be an ally of the struck employer, rather than a neutral party.[47]

Despite its inadequacies, an injunctive proceeding under Section 10(1) of the NLRA remains the contractor's principal means of redress against illegal secondary activity. State court proceedings are precluded because of the NLRA's exclusive grant of jurisdiction over unfair labor practices to the NLRB.[48] A federally created alternative to injunctive proceedings is a suit for damages. Under Section 303 of the Labor Management Relations Act,[49] an aggrieved contractor may commence a damage suit in Federal

---

[39]*Operating Engineers, Local 139 (Oak Construction, Inc.)*, 226 N.L.R.B. 759, 1976 CCH NLRB ¶17,522 (1976).

[40]*Int'l Hod Carriers Local 41 (Calumet Constructors Association)*, 130 N.L.R.B. 78, 1961 CCH NLRB ¶9630 (1961).

[41]*Teamsters, Local 126 (Ready Mixed Concrete)*, 200 N.L.R.B. 253, 1972 CCH NLRB ¶24,809 (1972).

[42]*Danielson v. Joint Board, ILGWU*, 494 F.2d 1230 (2d Cir. 1974).

[43]*Humphrey v. Int'l Longshoremen's Ass'n, AFL-CIO*, 401 F.Supp. 1401 (E.D.Va. 1975).

[44]*See, e.g., National Woodwork Manufacturers Ass'n v. NLRB*, 386 U.S. 612 (1967).

[45]*Id.* at 644–45.

[46]*See, e.g., Los Angeles Newspaper Guild, Local 69 (Hearst Corp.) v. NLRB*, 443 F.2d 1173 (9th Cir. 1971).

[47]*Madden v. Teamsters, Local 810*, 222 F.Supp. 635 (N.D.Ill. 1963).

[48]*See, e.g., Local No. 438, Construction and General Laborer's Union v. Curry*, 371 U.S. 542 (1963).

[49]29 U.S.C. §187.

District Court against the picketing union for losses incurred as the result of an illegal strike, picketing, threat or other comparable secondary activity. Practical problems attend such damage suits, including proof of union authorization or ratification of the acts of agents in the field and participation, if factual, by the international in the local's illegal activities (since the international will almost always be a more solvent defendant than a local union).

10.12.3. Illegal Picketing: The Hot Cargo Agreement (Section 8(e) of NLRA)

Section 8(e) of the NLRA makes it an unfair labor practice:

> [F]or any labor organization and any employer to enter into any contract or agreement, express or implied, whereby such employer ceases or refrains . . . from handling, using, selling, transporting or otherwise dealing in any of the products of any other employer, or to cease doing business with any other person, and any contract or agreement . . . containing such an agreement shall be to such extent unenforceable and void. . . .

The agreements referred to in Section 8(e) are commonly called hot cargo agreements. In labor union terminology, "hot cargo" means goods produced or handled by an employer whom a union has declared to be unfair because of employment of non-union labor, non-union standard wages or working conditions, or other comparable grievances. A hot cargo agreement (usually a clause in a union contract) permits the covered employees to refuse to work on the "hot" goods of producers and shippers who have been declared unfair by the union. The quoted provision of Section 8(e) prohibits hot cargo agreements.

Section 8(e), however, also contains a limited exemption for the construction industry. Exempted from the hot cargo prohibition are agreements:

> [B]etween a labor organization and an employer in the construction industry relating to the contracting or subcontracting of work to be done at the site of the construction, alteration, painting, or repair of a building, structure, or other work. . . .

The legislative history of Section 8(e) makes it clear that the exemption applies exclusively to the contracting or subcontracting of work to be done at the site of the construction. The exemption does not apply to agreements relating to supplies or other products or materials shipped or otherwise transported and delivered to the construction site. Moreover, union pressure against an employer, by strike, inducements, threats, or other coercion, for the purpose of enforcing a hot cargo agreement is unlawful under Section 8(b)(4) of the NLRA and is not legalized by the exemption.[50]

The exemption is therefore quite narrow. Section 8(e) of the NLRA retains validity if properly invoked. Thus, in *Teamsters Local 294 (Island Dock Lumber, Inc.)*, 145 N.L.R.B. 484, 1963 CCH NLRB ¶ 12,798 (1963), the Board held that the delivery of ready-mix concrete did not fall within the scope of the exemption allowing hot cargo

---

[50]*Orange Belt District Council of Painters No. 48 v. NLRB*, 328 F.2d 538 (D.C. Cir. 1964).

agreements in the construction industry. The rationale for this decision was that supplies essentially prepared off the construction site, not requiring the immediate services of workers at the site, can be left there intact. An agreement that such supplies be handled by union employees was therefore found to be illegal.

Similar decisions have been reached by the NLRB in cases involving snaplock round pipe and rigid round pipe produced in factories or other off-site locations. Contracts between construction employers in the sheetmetal industry and sheetmetal worker local unions restricting the use of such products have been struck down as violative of Section 8(e).[51]

Section 8(e)'s exemption may best be seen as "a measure designed to allow agreements pertaining to certain secondary activities on the construction site because of the close community of interests there. . . ."[52] The exemption seeks to ensure that construction unions will not be required to have their members work in proximity to non-union employees at a construction site. The exemption is a legislative response to problems peculiar to the construction industry, "particularly those resulting from sporadic work stoppages occasioned by the traditional refusal of craft unionists to work alongside non-union men on the same project."[53]

The most significant attack to date on Section 8(e)'s exemption was mounted in *Connell Construction Company v. Plumbers & Steamfitters*, 421 U.S. 616 (1975). In *Connell*, the Supreme Court held that Section 8(e)'s exemption did not protect a hot cargo agreement between a construction industry employer and a union which did not seek to represent the employees of that employer.

The union in *Connell* was the bargaining representative for workers in the plumbing and mechanical trades in Dallas and had entered into a multi-employer bargaining agreement with the Mechanical Contractors Association of Dallas, a group of about 75 mechanical contractors. The contracts contained a "most favored nation" clause. Under that clause the union agreed that, if it granted a more favorable contract to any other employer, it would extend the same terms to all members of the Association.

Connell Construction, a general building contractor in Dallas, obtained jobs by competitive bidding. It subcontracted plumbing and mechanical work on the basis of competitive bids to both union and non-union subcontractors. Although Connell's employees were represented by various building trade unions, the defendant union (Local 100) had never sought to represent them or to bargain with Connell on their behalf. In November, 1970, Local 100 asked Connell to agree that it would subcontract mechanical work only to firms that had a current contract with Local 100. Connell refused to do so. Local 100 then stationed a picket at one of Connell's major construction sites. One hundred fifty of Connell's workers walked off the job and construction halted. Connell then filed suit in a Texas court to enjoin the picketing as a violation of state antitrust laws. Local 100 removed the case to federal court. Connell then signed the requested subcon-

---

[51]*Ohio Valley Carpenters District Council and Cardinal Industries, Inc.*, 136 N.L.R.B. 977, 1962 CCH NLRB ¶11,105 (1962).

[52]*National Woodwork Manufacturers Ass'n v. NLRB*, 386 U.S. 612, 638–39 (1967).

[53]*Essex County District Council of Carpenters v. NLRB*, 332 F.2d 636 (3d Cir. 1964).

tracting agreement under protest and amended its complaint to allege violations of the federal antitrust laws (Sections 1 and 2 of the Sherman Act). The federal district court held that the subcontracting agreement was valid under the Section 8(e) exemption and that federal law preempted the state antitrust laws.

The Supreme Court reversed. It noted that the requested subcontracting agreement did not simply prohibit a general contractor from subcontracting to any non-union firm; it prohibited instead subcontracting to any firm that did not have a contract with Local 100. Local 100 thus had complete control over subcontract work offered by general contractors which signed subcontracting agreements. In addition, the "most favored nation" clause in the multi-employer bargaining agreement meant that Local 100 would make no agreement with an unaffiliated contractor that would give it a competitive advantage over members of the Association. Local 100 could thus shelter members from competition in the portion of the market it controlled—a portion that would grow as Local 100 extracted subcontracting agreements from other contractors such as Connell.

Upon reviewing the facts, the Court concluded:

> [Local 100] does not claim to be protecting Connell's employees from having to work alongside non-union men. The agreement apparently was not designed to protect Local 100's members in that regard, since it was not limited to job sites on which they were working. . . . Nor was Local 100 trying to organize a non-union subcontractor on the building project it picketed. The union admits that it sought the agreement solely as a way of pressuring mechanical subcontractors in the Dallas area to recognize it as the representative of their employees.

> If we agreed with Local 100 that the construction-industry proviso authorizes subcontracting agreements with "stranger" contractors, not limited to any particular job site, our ruling would give construction unions an almost unlimited organizational weapon. The unions would be free to enlist any general contractor to bring economic pressure on non-union subcontractors, as long as the agreement recited that it only covered work to be performed on some job site somewhere. . . .

> We therefore hold that this agreement which is outside the context of a collective-bargaining relationship and not restricted to a particular job site, but which nonetheless obligates Connell to subcontract work only to firms that have a contract with Local 100, may be the basis of a Federal antitrust suit because it has a potential for restraining competition in the business market in ways that would not follow naturally from elimination of competition over wages and working conditions. . . .[54]

Connell makes illegal all union security agreements that are not reached within the context of an employer-employee relationship. Its impact on the exemption from the antitrust laws accorded labor unions under the Norris-La Guardia Act[55] is less clear. The

---

[54]421 U.S. at 631–32, 635.

[55]29 U.S.C. §§ 101 *et seq.*

Court did not find that an antitrust violation had occurred—merely that the basis for an antitrust suit existed.

In the aftermath of *Connell* the NLRB's General Counsel has issued guidelines for subcontracting clauses in union security agreements.

First, a subcontracting clause may be operational only at times when the employer has employees who are represented by the labor union in question.

Second, a subcontracting clause may apply only to construction sites at which the union employees are employed.

Third, although a subcontracting clause is valid if it applies after employees are hired under a previously executed pre-hire agreement under Section 8(f) of the NLRA, it is not valid if it becomes operational at a time when the employer has no employees represented by the union or if the pre-hire agreement was obtained in violation of the picketing restrictions contained in section 8(b)(7) of the NLRA.

Fourth, a subcontracting clause may not lawfully require the employer's subcontractors to maintain collective bargaining relationships with particular unions.

And fifth, the subcontracting clause must be limited to job-site work.[56]

10.12.4. Work Preservation and Right to Control

A union may, without violating Section 8(b)(4)'s prohibition of secondary boycotts, contract with an employer to preserve for the union's members work traditionally performed at the job site. "Traditional work" legitimately within the scope of a contractual work preservation clause includes work that union members have performed and are still performing at the time the clause is negotiated.[57] Work preservation is therefore a valid defense to a secondary boycott charge. In exercise of its rights under a work preservation clause, a union may refuse to handle products fabricated off-site and yet not violate Section 8(b)(4) of the NLRA.

A leading case in point is *National Woodwork Manufacturers Association v. NLRB*, 386 U.S. 612 (1967). In *National Woodwork* a carpenter's local entered into a collective bargaining agreement with a general contractor under which his employees would not be required to install precut or prefitted doors. When the general contractor precut doors and had them delivered to the job site, his employees refused to install them. In the ensuing litigation, the Supreme Court was eventually called upon to decide whether the contract clause violated Section 8(b)(4)'s ban on secondary boycotts or Section 8(e)'s ban on agreements that compel an employer to cease doing business with another employer. The Court held that neither section was intended to prohibit primary activity and then found that efforts by employees to preserve work they have traditionally performed is primary activity. The test was said by the Court to be whether

> . . . under all the surrounding circumstances, the Union's objective was the preservation of work traditionally done by [employees it represents], or whether

---

[56]NLRB General Counsel Memorandum 76–57, December 15, 1976.

[57]*American Boiler Manufacturers Ass'n v. NLRB*, 59 CCH Lab. Cases ¶13,108.

the agreement and boycott are tactically calculated to satisfy union objectives elsewhere.[58]

After the *National Woodwork* decision, the NLRB fashioned an exception to the work preservation doctrine. The exception arises when an employer, having agreed to preserve certain work for his employees, nonetheless enters into a later agreement in which he contracts away the ability to assign such work to his employees. Under these circumstances, the NLRB contended, a strike against the employer is not primary but secondary activity since the union's efforts must be directed to the entity having control over assignment of the work, in most instances the general contractor.

The NLRB's exception did not achieve judicial recognition. No fewer than five circuit courts of appeal rejected the NLRB's reasoning as inconsistent with the Supreme Court's decision in *National Woodwork*.

In *NLRB v. Enterprise Association of Steam, Hot Water, Hydraulic Sprinkler, Pneumatic Tube, Ice Machine and General Pipefitters of New York*, 429 U.S. 507 (1977), the Supreme Court upheld a narrowed interpretation of the work preservation doctrine. In *Enterprise*, the pipefitters union had a collective bargaining agreement with Hudik, Inc., a mechanical contractor. The agreement required, among other things, that the cutting and threading of internal piping be performed on the job site by Hudik's own employees. Traditionally, Hudik's employees—who were also union members—had performed such work. Hudik bid on and was awarded a subcontract by Austin, Inc., the general contractor. The subcontract required Hudik to install pre-piped climate control manufactured by unionized employees of the Slant/Fin Corporation. Hudik had, by entering into a subcontract, created a conflict with its obligations under the collective bargaining agreement. When the prefabricated units arrived at the job site to be installed by Hudik, Hudik's employees refused to do so. Austin, the general contractor, then filed secondary boycott charges with the NLRB. Although the NLRB found the charges valid,[59] the reviewing court of appeals deemed the refusal to install to be lawful primary activity.[60] But the Supreme Court, applying its own *National Woodwork* standard, found that:

> It was not error for the Board to conclude that the union's objectives were not confined to the employment relationship with Hudik but included [at least] the object of influencing Austin in a manner prohibited by Section 8(b)(4)(B).[61]

The court noted that, to make out a violation of that section, " 'it is not necessary to find that the *sole* object of the strike was secondary so long as one of the union's objectives was to influence another employer. . . .'"[62]

The Court's decision could conceivably have the unintended effect of enlarging

---

[58]386 U.S. at 644 (footnote omitted).

[59]204 N.L.R.B. 760 (1963).

[60]40 U.S.C. §§276a *et seq.* For a comprehensive explanation of the Act, *see* 2 CCH Fed. Wage-Hour Law Rptr. ¶¶26900 *ff.*

[61]429 U.S. at 530–3.

[62]*Id.* at 530 n. 17 (quoting from *NLRB v. Denver Bldg. Council*, 341 U.S. 675, 689 (1951) (emphasis in original).

the scope of labor disputes. If a union is prohibited from striking a subcontractor who has breached its agreement with the union, the union's recourse, legally, would be to strike the general contractor, *i.e.*, the entity with control over the work assignment, thereby placing an entire project in jeopardy of work stoppage and disruption.

On the other hand, should the union be precluded from striking the general contractor—on the ground that Section 8(b)(4) is intended to limit the scope of labor disputes—then it would be completely deprived of its ability to engage in primary strike activity in support of work preservation. Even under such an interpretation of the law, however, unions could still enforce work preservation provisions in collective bargaining agreements by invoking the agreements' grievance and arbitration procedures. The NLRB has found that recourse to such procedures does not itself constitute unlawful coercion and restraint under Section 8(b)(4)(B).[63]

10.13. CONSTRUCTION WAGES UNDER THE DAVIS-BACON ACT

One other federal statute of particular significance in the construction industry is the venerable Davis-Bacon Act,[64] signed into law by President Hoover half a century ago. The Act guarantees payment of administratively determined minimum wages to laborers and mechanics who are employed on federally financed construction projects costing $2,000 or more. The minimum wages are the rates found by the Secretary of Labor to be "prevailing" for discrete classifications of laborers employed in the relevant geographical area. Labor Department regulations establish detailed procedures for determining wages, and for appealing determinations to the statutorily created Wage Appeals Board in the Department's Wage and Hour Division.[65]

Prevailing wages are constantly adjusted and updated. Advertised government specifications include the applicable prevailing wages, and bidders are expected to take them into account when bids are prepared. Federal contracts almost always contain a clause requiring payment of at least the minimum Davis-Bacon Act wage; these contractual provisions are construed to require the payment of the adjusted prevailing wage even if the wage is higher than the figure in the specifications or the invitation to bid.[66]

In recent years, the wage requirements of the Davis-Bacon Act have grown increasingly unpopular with economic and political proponents of free-enterprise construction, and it would not be surprising to see the Act significantly amended by Congress.

---

[63]*Plumbers (AGC)*, 207 N.L.R.B. 698, 1973 CCH NLRB ¶25,992 (1973).

[64]40 U.S.C. §§276a *et seq.* For a comprehensive explanation of the Act, *see* 2 CCH Fed. Wage-Hour Law Rptr. ¶¶26900 *ff.*

[65]29 C.F.R. §§1.1–1.17 (1980).

[66]*United States v. Binghamton Constr. Co.*, 347 U.S. 171 (1954); *see also* Annotation, 98 L.Ed. 600 (1954); and cases collected in 91 C.J.S. "United States" §94.d. (1955 and 1980 Cum. Supp.).

10.14. ADDITIONAL SOURCE MATERIALS

Chayes, A. H., C. L. Kaufman, R. L. Wheeler, Jr., "University's role in promoting minority group employment in the construction industry," 119 U. Pa. L. Rev. 91 (1970).

Elisbury, D., "Wage protection under the Davis-Bacon Act," 28 Lab. L. J. 323 (1977).

Hain, E. B., Jr. "Black workers v. white unions: alternate strategies in the construction industry," 16 Wayne L. Rev. 37 (1969).

Leiken, E. M., "Preferential treatment in the skilled building trade: an analysis of the Philadelphia plan," 56 Cornell L. Rev. 84 (1970).

Note, "Civil rights—revised Philadelphia plan held not violative of Title VII, Civil Rights Act of 1964," 39 Fordham L. Rev. 522 (1971).

Note, "Development of judicial relief available to unions for employer violations of subcontracting clauses in the construction industry," 7 Duquesne L. Rev. 446 (1969).

Note, "Duties of a general contractor under the California labor code," 15 Hastings L. J. 604 (1964).

Note, "Philadelphia plan," 45 Notre Dame L. Rev. 678 (1970).

Note, "Philadelphia plan vs. the Chicago plan: alternative approaches for integrating the construction industry," 65 N. Y. L. U. Rev. 642 (1970).

Note, "The quota system—a new approach to a belabored problem," 4 Rutgers Camden L. J. 113 (1972).

Note, "Revised Philadelphia plan as an instrument for insuring equal employment opportunity in the construction trades: its legality and possible alternatives," 8 Houston L. Rev. 342 (1970).

Anno., "Construction and operation of 'equal opportunities clause' requiring pledge against racial discrimination in hiring under construction contract," 44 A. L. R. 3d 1283.

Anno., " 'Pre-hire' agreement with construction industry employer, legality of uncertified minority union's picketing to enforce," 54 L. Ed. 2d 586.

PART IV

Construction Management

CHAPTER **11**

The Legal Profile of the
Construction Manager

11.1 INTRODUCTION

Within the last decade, the technique known as "construction management" has reshaped the process of large-scale construction in the United States. Broadly speaking, construction management seeks to place under the owner's control the combined skills of design professionals and construction contractors while permitting application of contemporary management disciplines such as critical path management analysis (CPM) and value engineering.

Construction management came into being because owners were dissatisfied with conventional fixed-price contracting, which is thought to over-emphasize the role of the general contractor in implementing, managing, and coordinating a project. Such dissatisfaction arose in part from problems inherent in the construction industry, including:

— Extreme fragmentation of the industry, which comprises perhaps 130,000 general contractors, many of whom are small, undercapitalized, and financially unstable;

— The prevalence of subcontracting, whereby general contractors require specialized trades subcontractors to perform as much as 85 percent of the actual construction work;

193

— The primitive state of management skills and process efficiencies in the industry;

— The sharp escalation in construction costs in recent years, which places a premium on shortening the construction period through phased rather than sequential design and construction in order to keep projects within budgeted amounts; and

— The inability of architects and contractors to provide adequate management, coordination, and cost control in their conventional roles.

Fixed-price contracting often places the owner at a distinct disadvantage in handling these problems. He may have neither expertise nor control with respect to a general contractor's activities but must nonetheless pay the bills—often in excess of targeted costs. The ostensible certainty afforded by fixed-price general construction contracts has become less attractive when weighed against the inefficiencies imposed on the construction process. Construction management has emerged as an owner-induced response.

11.2 THE CONSTRUCTION MANAGER'S ROLE AS THE OWNER'S AGENT

To place the contractual role of the construction manager in proper perspective, it is necessary first to consider the nature of the conventional method of construction utilizing the general contractor as the central figure. Using that method of management, the owner contracts directly with the general contractor (who is regarded, in law, as an "independent contractor" rather than an "agent"). The general contractor then enters into subcontracts for various aspects of the work. Schematically, this form of management may be represented as a ladder, with the owner occupying the top rung, the general contractor immediately below him, and subcontractors and suppliers arranged in ranks at the bottom. (See Figure 1.)

The construction manager, on the other hand, offers professional and managerial services as the owner's agent. Typically, there is no general contractor, and the owner contracts directly with contractors representing the specialized trades. Practically and schematically, this arrangement takes on a matrix configuration. (See Figure 2.)[1]

The construction manager should be selected on the basis of an objective analysis of his professional and general contracting qualifications. Consideration should be given to his success in performing the normal general contractor's function on projects of comparable type, scope and complexity as well as his financial strength, bonding capacity, insurability and ability to assume a financial risk if the owner requires it. The owner should also take note of the construction manager's in-house staff capability and the qualifications of the personnel who will manage the project. The construction manager's

---

[1]Perkins, "A/E-CM Relations: Approaching a Modus Vivendi?", *Architectural Record* 67 (Oct. 1973).

FIGURE 1

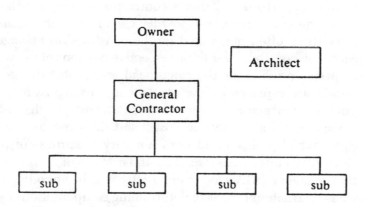

FIGURE 2

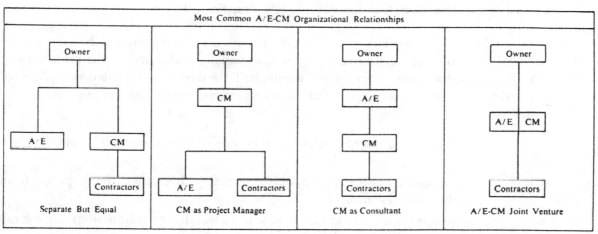

A/E = Architect Engineer
CM = Construction Manager

record for completing projects on time and within the budget should be investigated. Finally, the owner should ensure that his construction manager can work harmoniously with the owner and architect-engineer throughout the project.

11.2.1. The Construction Manager's Fee

The construction manager is a professional consultant who offers his services for a predetermined or fixed fee; a general contractor, on the other hand, seeks an entrepreneurial profit. The construction manager typically guarantees neither project cost nor completion time. Since he assumes no risk with respect to either, he expects no related profit. The construction manager may thus be thought to shift overall risk to the owner, unless he guarantees a maximum price which is possible under some forms of the construction management contract (for example, that issued by the Associated General Contractors of America). However, trades contractors—many of whom were formerly subcontractors to a general contractor—now have a direct contractual relationship with the owner (the contract often negotiated by the construction manager as the owner's agent), and assume responsibility for their respective portions of the work. Although the subcontractors' prices provide for their overhead and profit, the general contractor's overhead and profit are replaced by the construction manager's fee.

Construction management contracts are often cost-plus-fixed-fee contracts providing for recovery of (1) all allowable costs, and (2) a fee to cover profit and any unallowable costs, which is fixed and does not vary regardless of project costs. The American Institute of Architects has issued a standard form of agreement between owner and construction manager (AIA Document B801) which embodies this approach, although it provides alternate methods of determining compensation, including multiple-of-direct-personnel and percentage-of-construction-cost.[2]

11.2.2. The Construction Manager's Responsibilities

The services performed by the construction manager cover a broad range of activities and to some extent overlap those traditionally performed by the architect and the contractor; they may be performed during both the design and construction phases of a project. A comprehensive construction management contract covers five major functions:

— *Cost management*, including estimates of construction cost and development of project budget;

— *Scheduling*, often incorporating critical path method techniques, for all phases of the project;

— *Design review*, including review of formal design submissions and overall construction feasibility;

— *Bid Packaging* and contractor selection; and

— *On-site management* to provide supervision, inspection, and administration.

With regard to on-site management, the construction manager may assign personnel to the site to coordinate separate contracts; monitor the individual phases of the work to determine which crafts are on schedule; adjust the work to accommodate changed conditions and unanticipated interferences; determine whether workmanship, materials, and equipment conform to approved contract drawings and specifications; arrange for performance of field and laboratory tests where required; prepare progress reports;

---

[2]AIA Document B801 is one of a sequence of standard forms that substitute construction-management idiom for regular contracting language. *See* AIA Document A101/CM ("Standard Form of Agreement Between Owner and Contractor, Construction Management Edition") and AIA Document A201/CM ("General Conditions of the Contract for Construction, Construction Management Edition").

review change orders and change proposals; and review progress payments and recommend payments to the owner (very often as part of the construction manager's undertaking to provide administration, accounting, site communications, record-keeping, and related services).

The construction manager may also provide certain services normally performed by a general contractor, such as establishment, maintenance, and operation of temporary field construction facilities; provision for security personnel, cleanup and debris removal, and temporary utilities; and rental and operation of equipment. The costs of these "general condition" items are normally defrayed on a cost-reimbursement basis and are not part of the construction manager's fee for professional services.

The construction manager's responsibilities during the planning and design phases are extensive and varied. He reviews the architectural, civil, mechanical, electrical and structural plans and specifications as they are developed and makes recommendations as to construction feasibility, possible economies, availability of materials and labor time requirements for procurement and construction, and projected costs. Budget estimates are reviewed and revised periodically as work progresses. The construction manager also recommends the purchases and procurements of long-lead items to ensure delivery by the required dates. He will give advice on division of work for the award of trade contracts, with consideration of time of performance, availability of labor, overlapping trade jurisdictions and provisions for temporary facilities. He will also handle the receipt of competitive bids as working drawings and specifications are completed.

Again, during the construction phase, the construction manager has a wide range of duties. He maintains a supervisory staff at the project site to ensure progress of the work and to carry out inspections to make certain that work is performed according to drawings and specifications. He is responsible for the establishment of programs relating to safety, job-site records, labor relations, EEO and progress reports. He processes all payment applications as well as change orders.

11.3. CONSTRUCTION MANAGER'S LIABILITY FOR DESIGN ERRORS

The construction manager's responsibilities overlap and may even preempt those of the contractor and the architect in certain respects. What, then, are the construction manager's probable liabilities if he functions in the broad capacities outlined above? The question may best be answered in terms of liabilities associated with specific areas of responsibility.

Typically, the architect is required to prepare, for the owner's approval, both the design development documents—the drawings and other documents fixing and describing the size and character of the entire project as to structural, mechanical, and electrical systems, materials, and other appropriate essentials—and the working drawings and specifications. From this responsibility, it follows that the architect is responsible to the owner (and conceivably the contractor) for design errors. The owner will generally be upheld by the courts in his expectation that a structure will be suitable to its purpose, designed in light of applicable legal restrictions, and reasonably well-conceived in terms of the state of the art. Claims against architects may arise from breach of contract or from professional negligence, or both.

11.3.1. Breach of Owner-Architect Contract

An owner's contract claims against an architect may be based on design errors which add to construction cost, diminish the economic value of a project, or cause losses to the owner because of the claims of third parties. An architect may also be sued for breach of contract by a person who is not a party to the contract between him and the owner. For example, if the architect is obligated, expressly or impliedly, to pass upon shop drawings submitted by a contractor within a reasonable time, his failure to do so could be the basis of a claim against him by the contractor if the contractor can persuade a court that the architect's undertaking was made for his benefit.[3]

A contractor who suffers a loss because of an architect's unjustified delay may also seek to claim against the owner. In that event, if the owner's liability is based upon a breach of the contract between himself and the architect, the owner may in turn assert a claim against the architect.

11.3.2. Architect's Professional Negligence

Most claims brought against architects are based on charges of professional negligence—the architect's failure to use due care to avoid exposing others to unreasonable risks. Professional negligence can relate to any aspect of the architect's performance, including defective design, selection of inadequate or improper materials or equipment, and any other part of the design services furnished. One court, for example, has held that an architect's failure "to make any mention on its plans of the underground high-voltage line it knew was in the area" when "these plans called for excavation right where the buried electrical power line was located" amounted to negligence.[4]

11.3.3. Degree of Construction Manager's Control

If an architect undertakes to perform construction management services in addition to those normally associated with his professional role, he may enlarge his design responsibilities but he will not fundamentally change their nature. If the construction manager is not an architect, however, he may nonetheless perform design-review functions. Whether he is charged with liability for design errors will then depend on his control, if any, over ultimate design decisions.

Such control may derive from the contracts between the owner and the construc-

---

[3]*See, e.g., Peter Kiewit Sons Co. v. Iowa S. Util. Co.,* 355 F.Supp. 376, 392 (S.D. Iowa 1973).

[4]*Mallow v. Tucker, Sadler & Bennett, Inc.,* 245 Cal. App. 2d 700, 54 Cal. Rptr. 174 (1966).

tion manager and architect, respectively, or it may be impliedly negated by those contracts. The AIA construction management contract, for example, merely requires the construction manager to "review conceptual designs during development" and "provide recommendations as to relative construction feasibility." Since such an advisory function cannot reasonably be thought to encroach upon the architect's traditional responsibilities, the architect will still be obligated to assure that the construction product accords with the design, to interpret contract documents, to review shop drawings, and to act as the owner's agent in all matters relating to design quality.

11.3.4. Construction Manager's Duty to Perform Without Negligence

Nonetheless, there may be functional overlap between the construction manager and the architect in other related areas. As one commentator has noted:

> [S]ome CM's have been complaining that a lot of time-consuming administrative services otherwise provided by the A/E (though not necessarily spelled out in his agreement) are being shifted to the CM. These relate primarily to the document flow and include final checking and coordination of the documents; preliminary processing of shop drawings; preparation of bid packages and bidding documentation; on-site communications and change order analysis and processing. In addition, responsibilities for field engineering and continued on-site inspection are being assigned to the CM. Many of these tasks must be performed by the firm most involved at the job site or in the bidding process whether or not it is clearly part of that firm's contract. In most cases, this now means the CM is taking the primary responsibility.[5]

If by contract or practice a construction manager undertakes to perform specified services, including design-review services, he will create a corresponding duty to do so without negligence. What constitutes negligence is determined by reference to prevailing norms for such services.

Architects, for example, frequently assert that they have complied with customary standards of professional practice and ask that they be relieved from liability for this reason. Compliance with customary standards of conduct is taken into account in determining whether there is negligence, but it is not conclusive on the question. In a typical case,[6] injured workers instituted legal action against an architect who had participated in the design phase of a project on which they were injured, charging negligence. Through expert testimony, the architect replied that his conduct "represented good architectural and engineering practice, and was in accord with what was customarily done in the construction of other buildings." Although the court agreed that the architect had complied with local custom—a potentially exonerating standard in malpractice litigation—it did not regard compliance as conclusive on the issue of negligence:

---

[5]Perkins, *supra* n.1 at 67.

[6]*Holt v. A. L. Salzman & Sons*, 88 Ill. App. 2d 306, 232 N. E. 2d 537 (1967).

Custom is relevant in determining the standard of care because it illustrates what is feasible, it suggests a body of knowledge of which the defendant should be aware, and it warns of the possibility of far-reaching consequences if a higher standard is required.

Construction management, however, is a relatively new development; no body of custom or law has yet grown up around it. Insofar as his design-review functions are concerned, a construction manager cannot as readily rely on the defense of customary practice. Greater emphasis may therefore be placed on limitations or exculpation contained in the contract documents themselves.

11.4.   COST OVERRUNS

A construction manager customarily will guarantee neither cost nor completion time; presumably, therefore, he is not liable to the owner for costs incurred in excess of the budgeted amount. At the same time, a primary reason for an owner's use of a construction manager is to maintain control of costs. Here, then, is a sticky complication for construction managers. If cost overruns, in fact, occur, the owner may seek to impose liability on the construction manager on the basis of an express or implied cost condition in their agreement. Furthermore, cost overruns conceivably may subject a construction manager to liability notwithstanding express disclaimers written into his contract with the owner.

If there is a cost condition in the contract and project cost exceeds the project budget, the construction manager may be compelled to supervise redesign or re-engineering of the project at his own expense; even if not negligent, he may risk a reduced or lost fee. It would not appear necessary for the agreement between the owner and the construction manager to contain an express condition; the construction manager's knowledge that the owner has a specified amount of money to spend may be sufficient to establish his liability for cost overruns.

The AIA construction management contract (AIA Document B801) attempts to meet this problem by including the following provisions:

[C]ost estimates prepared by the Construction Manager represent the Construction Manager's best judgment as a professional familiar with the construction industry. It is recognized, however, that neither the Construction Manager nor the Owner has control over the cost of labor, materials or equipment, over Contractors' methods of determining bid prices or other competitive bidding or negotiating conditions . . .

No fixed limit of Construction Cost shall be established as a condition of this Agreement . . . unless such fixed limit has been agreed upon in writing and signed by the parties to this Agreement. [Articles 3.3–3.4.]

Despite such contractual protection, however, the courts may still find construction managers responsible for cost overruns. An architect who relied on the customary AIA contract disclaimer concerning the accuracy of cost estimates lost his lawsuit to recover fees for designing a project which was abandoned when the low bid substantially exceeded the contract figure. The architect claimed that he had completed his work through the receipt of bids and that his contract provided for a fee as a function of total contract price depending on state of completion. But the court concluded that "since . . . the [architect] could not perform his part of the agreement . . . he is not entitled to any compensation under the contract."[7] In view of such cases, professional societies are doing all they can in their printed forms to treat cost predictions as mere cost estimates.

If a cost condition has been created but not observed, the owner may be found to have dispensed with it. If the owner, by his actions, has abrogated the cost condition, the architect or construction manager may then be permitted to collect his fee. This result may obtain where the owner has made excessive changes during the design phase, hindered performance (for example, by not permitting bidding by contractors), or indicated that he is no longer concerned with earlier projected costs. An owner's willingness to dispense with a cost condition may be manifested by his proceeding with the project, even though bids received are higher than originally predicted.

Most lawsuits involving cost conditions are attempts by professionals to collect fees on a project the owner has abandoned because of excessive costs. Occasionally, however, the owner may institute legal action to recover interim fee payments or seek damages for breach of contract, usually where the project has been completed.

Promises must be differentiated from conditions. If a cost condition is created in the agreement, the construction manager may risk his fee, in whole or in part, upon the accuracy of his cost predictions, or he may accept responsibility for redesign without additional fee. He may not, however, be deemed to have warranted or guaranteed a maximum price and to have incurred liability for damages flowing from breach of contract. Courts have not always observed the distinction between promises and conditions and have been known to equate a fixed-cost amount with a promise that project cost will not exceed that amount. Under such an assumption, if cost incurred exceeds predicted cost, the construction manager may have breached his contract with the owner even though he used due care in making his cost prediction.

In most cases, it is difficult for the owner to recover damages if the project is completed. If he tries to recover the difference between the predicted cost and the cost incurred, he is usually met with the argument that he has a project worth what it cost him. By proceeding with the project when he knows cost incurred will exceed predicted cost, he may also be said to have brought the damages upon himself.

11.5. LETTING CONTRACTS

In order to achieve a position of least exposure to liability, the construction manager should arrange for the owner to award contracts to contractors and retain full

---

[7]*Stevens v. Fanning*, 59 Ill. App. 2d 285, 207 N.E. 2d 136 (1965).

legal responsibility for their function on the project. Both the AIA and standard-form AGC construction management contracts contemplate this procedure. The owner's contractual relationship need not preclude the construction manager from supervising the bidding process, but he will do so only as the agent of the owner. If the owner insists that the construction manager assume the contractual role of general contractor and become a party to the contract either directly or as assignee, the construction manager's fee arrangements should reflect the increased risk involved or an indemnity from liability should be obtained from the owner.

11.6.   FAULTY SCHEDULING

Under conventional contracting procedures, a general contractor is required to submit to the architect an estimated progress schedule for the work. Scheduling is thus traditionally thought to be the contractor's function. When a construction manager is used on a complex project, however, one of his primary obligations to the owner will be to coordinate the work of the project architect and multiple prime contractors, often using CPM scheduling analysis for this purpose. To the extent that he provides overall project scheduling services, the construction manager may be thought to have assumed an element of the general contractor's usual function. If there is then a delay in project completion because of the construction manager's faulty scheduling, the contractor may be able to shift liability for delay to the construction manager or the owner for whom the construction manager is acting as agent.

Ordinarily, if nothing is stated in the construction contract regarding possible disruptive events delaying the contractor's performance, the law generally requires him to assume the risks of delay. If he has agreed to perform by a specific time, he has by implication agreed to bear the risk of most events which might delay his performance. But he normally will not be held to assume the risk of delays caused by the owner. If the cause of delay can be clearly shown to reside in the construction manager, the owner's agent, the contractor may obtain a time extension; barring a "no damage" clause in the construction contract, he may claim damages attributable to the extension as well. If such a claim is based upon breach of contract, the contractor will make the claim for damages against the owner. The owner may in turn seek to hold the construction manager responsible, based on a theory of negligence or breach of contract arising from the construction manager's faulty scheduling. Alternatively, the contractor may seek to assert liability against the construction manager on a negligence theory.

11.7.   CONSTRUCTION MANAGER'S LIABILITY FOR
DELAYS AND DAMAGES

The agreement between the owner and the contractor commonly provides that if the contractor is delayed by an act or omission of the owner or the architect, or by any separate contractor employed by the owner, the period within which work under the agreement is to be completed will be extended. The agreement usually contemplates that a claim for an increase in the contract price may be asserted against the owner.

If the owner has retained a construction manager as his agent, the construction manager's negligence would be attributable legally to the owner. If the construction manager is responsible for delaying the contractor in the completion of his work, the resulting claim for an increase in contract price, if sustained against the owner, could be asserted in turn by the owner against the construction manager.

The risk of owner-caused delay increases with the complexity of the project and the number of prime contractors employed. It may also be more difficult in a complex project for an owner to recover liquidated damages from a contractor for unexcused delay. A contractor who is late in his performance often contends that he was prevented by nonperformance of another prime contractor, or that his late performance did not delay the project because other prime contractors were also late. In a single contract system, all that is important is whether there has been unexcused delay.

Delay may also occur for which the construction manager is not responsible. In that event, if the anticipated completion time is extended and the construction manager himself incurs delay costs, he may seek an increase in the fixed-fee element of his total compensation or reimbursement for standby costs.

11.8. CONSTRUCTION OPERATIONS

Each contractor is responsible to the owner for the acts and omissions of his employees and all subcontractors in the performance of the work. Indeed, the contractor usually holds the owner and architect harmless against liability arising out of performance of the work if the liability is (1) attributable to bodily injury, sickness, disease, or death, or injury to tangible property other than the work itself; and (2) is caused in whole or in part by any negligent act or omission of the contractor regardless of whether it is also caused by a party indemnified. The indemnification, however, does not extend to liability of the architect arising out of faulty preparation of drawings or instructions given or omitted by the architect. In construction management projects, the construction manager should properly be included as an indemnitee of each multiple prime contractor.

Where multiple prime contractors are under direct contract to the owner, each will presumably retain his customary obligation for operations. But the construction manager will usually be required to exercise overall supervisory responsibility. Such responsibility may exceed that of the architect, who will ordinarily not be required to make exhaustive or continuous on-site inspections to check the quantity or quality of the work. If the construction manager retains ultimate control to approve or reject all work done by the contractor (even though in conjunction with the architect), he may be deemed also to bear a corresponding obligation to exercise due care to see that the contractor performs his work properly. Failure to do so may result in imposition of liability on the construction manager by the owner, the contractor, and even third parties.

An owner who employs a competent architect and general contractor will not be subject to liability arising from the contractor's failure to follow adequate plans or the architect's failure properly to plan or supervise the work. This is so because the architect and contractor are normally not agents or servants of the owner but are independent contractors. Their negligence is not imputed to the owner. But if a construction manager, acting as the owner's agent, extends his supervisory function to control the contractor's workmen and is thought to assume direction of the work, the owner and the construction manager may be found liable for job injury to workmen or third persons. To negate this, the construction management contract may disclaim the construction manager's responsibility for construction operations. In this respect, the AIA construction management contract provides:

> The Construction Manager shall not be responsible for construction means, methods, techniques, sequences and procedures employed by Contractors in the performance of their Contracts, and shall not be responsible for the failure of any Contractor to carry out Work in accordance with the Contract Documents. [AIA Document B801, Article 1.2.7.1.]

11.9. CERTIFICATES OF PAYMENT

The construction manager may be directly or indirectly responsible for progress payments to contractors and the issuance of payment certificates. The AIA construction management contract, for example, requires the construction manager to "[m]ake recommendations to the Architect for when Work is ready for final inspection." (AIA Document B801, Article 1.2.16.) In this connection, by issuing a payment certificate, the construction manager may lead the owner to believe that the work has been performed properly. The construction manager could then be liable if the owner has either lost his claim against the contractor or the claim turns out to be uncollectable. The same may be true if the construction manager submits an incomplete list of corrections, and the owner loses his claim against the contractor because of waiver.

If the construction manager does not use due care in issuing certificates for payment, he may cause losses to the owner (or construction lender), the surety, and possibly the contractor. The owner can suffer loss through assertion of liens or premature payments. A surety, required to pay subcontractors and materialmen under the terms of a payment bond, may claim that the construction manager should be held responsible (on the theory that the latter's negligence has enabled the contractor to divert funds). The surety often looks to retainage as a fund from which to reimburse its losses. If the construction manager has reduced or liquidated retainage by premature payment to contractors and suppliers, the surety may recover against the construction manager.

11.10. POST-CONSTRUCTION LIABILITY

The owner's final payment to the contractor normally constitutes a waiver of all claims by both parties. Exceptions as to the owner are claims arising from unsettled liens, faulty or defective work appearing after substantial completion, and failure of the work to comply with the requirements of contract documents. Exceptions as to the contractor include only those previously made in writing and still unsettled.

Third parties, however, may have claims against construction managers, architects, designers, engineers, and contractors for negligence in construction arising from injury or damage incurred long after completion of construction, acceptance, and final payment (although recent legislation in many jurisdictions has limited the time during which such an action may be brought).

Early cases insulated a negligent architect or contractor from liability to third persons injured after a building had been completed and accepted by the owner. After completion and acceptance, the architect and contractor were thought to be incapable of remedying defects. Responsibility and control were deemed to have shifted to the owner, and his negligence in maintaining a defective building was considered the proximate cause of the injury.

The rule of nonliability was criticized and eventually rejected in most jurisdictions. As a result, the liability of the architect and engineer was extended to members of the general public whose presence in the building could be reasonably anticipated. The architect or contractor was thus confronted not only with an unlimited class of potential claimants but also, in many instances, with indefinite duration of liability for negligence. As to the owner, the architect's breach of duty occurs when the defective building is completed and accepted. This also measures the running of the applicable period of limitation. A third party, however, has no action against the negligent architect until injury, which may occur many years after performance of services. The statutory period would thus commence on the date of the injury.

Limitation-of-action statutes for architects and builders attack the extended duration-of-liability problem by barring actions at a given point after completion of services rather than after injury. The statutes vary in coverage from jurisdiction to jurisdiction as to persons and actions, time limitation, commencement event, and in other respects. The precise effect of such statutes may thus differ from one state to another. However, the Illinois statute, enacted in 1963, is typical:

> No action to recover damages for any injury to property, real or personal, or for injury to the person, or for bodily injury or wrongful death, arising out of the defective and unsafe condition of an improvement to real estate, nor any action for contribution or indemnity for damages sustained on account of such injury, shall be brought against any person performing or furnishing the design, planning, supervision of construction or construction of such improvement to real property, unless such cause of action shall have accrued within four years after the performance of furnishing of such services and construction. This limitation

shall not be available to any owner, tenant or person in actual possession and control of the improvement at the time such cause of action accrues.[8]

Most statutes limit actions against those persons furnishing the design, planning, supervision of construction or construction services, a category broad enough to include construction managers. Some states, however, restrict coverage to architects and professional engineers licensed by the state.

11.11. PROTECTING THE CONSTRUCTION MANAGER AGAINST LIABILITY

The construction manager may attract the liabilities of the architect and contractor, since his role embraces many of their major activities while adding new dimensions in planning, scheduling, and cost control services. In theory at least, the construction manager does not seek to supplant the functions of architect or contractor, but to guide and coordinate their activities on behalf of the owner. The construction manager may therefore be said merely to provide an additional level of responsibility—to increase total accountability rather than re-allocating it.

On a complex construction project, however, the construction manager may exercise a degree of discretion over design, scheduling, and site operations which could enable the architects and contractors employed to shift liability to him in the event of delay, design failure, injury, cost overrun, or similar occurrences. The construction manager will also be directly accountable, as a professional, to the owner for proper performance of his professional functions.

The construction manager can seek protection under the contract he enters into with the owner. The contract can, and probably should, specify that in performing his construction management services, the construction manager is expressly not assuming the obligations of architects, engineers, or contractors. Instead, those professionals will retain their full responsibility to discharge such obligations, usually under direct contract with the owner. The construction manager can also seek to broaden the indemnity commonly offered the architect and owner by the contractor to include himself as well. Such contractual protection is not foolproof by any means, but it could limit or foreclose liability in a close case.

Finally, the construction manager can obtain insurance against legal liability arising out of the performance of professional services for the owner in his capacity as a construction manager. Such insurance is available as an adaptation of standard errors-and-omission policies offered to architects. Insurance coverage will commonly exclude guarantees of project cost or completion time, however, and may exclude certain operational responsibilities as well—particularly services with respect to general condition items. The extent of coverage offered may therefore depend on the form of construction management contract employed.

---

[8]Ill. Ann. Stat., Ch. 83, §24f.

11.12. ADDITIONAL SOURCE MATERIALS

Hart, B.C., "Construction management, 'CM for Short,' the new name for an old game," 8 *Forum* 210 (1972).

Lambert, Jremiah D., "The legal profile of the construction manager," 4 *Real Estate Review* (Winter 1975).

Meyers, R. L., III, "The new contractual arrangements," in PLI, *Construction Contracts 1979* at 409–636 (1979).

Note, "Roles of architect and contractor in construction management," 6 U. Mich. J.L. Ref. 447 (1973).

Walker, N., E. N. Walker & T. K. Rohdenburg, *Legal Pitfalls in Architecture, Engineering and Building Construction*, Ch. 10 ("Legal pitfalls in the practice of construction management"), at 169–79 (2d ed. 1979).

Wickwire, J. M. & R. F. Smith, "Use of critical path method techniques in contract claims," 7 Pub-Contract L.J. 1 (1974).

PART V

Dispute Resolution

CHAPTER **12**

Construction Litigation

12.1. INTRODUCTION

The construction process by its very nature invites disputes and often involves litigation before a court or arbitral tribunal as a means of resolving those disputes. Such litigation is expensive, time-consuming, and frequently uncertain of result. On a single, complex construction project, litigation may extend to contractual relationships between and among many parties (owner, general contractor, subcontractors, architects, engineers, insurance carriers, sureties and others) and present difficult questions of law, causation, evidence and damages. At the same time, claims for damages and cost overruns are to many simply a business way of life. As a consequence, the construction industry—one of this country's largest and most diversified—is characterized by contention.

Construction is in addition a high-risk industry. Almost two-thirds of all contracting businesses fail within five years, the probable duration of many fully litigated construction contract lawsuits. A potential litigant must therefore assess not only the cost and technical complexity of a lawsuit, but also whether the defendant after years of legal action may be in such precarious financial condition that a judgment will be uncollectable. This promotes suits against multiple defendants (and the related tendency among defendants to implead insurance companies, sureties and other potentially liable third parties), with the result that construction litigation is typically more complex than litigation in many other industrial settings.

This chapter describes the different litigation forums and the actual steps a party

211

must take to prepare, try and defend against a construction claim. The next chapter tells how to minimize the likelihood of litigation and its impact if it occurs.

12.2. LITIGATION FORUMS

Until the beginning of the twentieth century, courts of law were the only forum in which parties could litigate disputes arising under construction contracts. Courts are still the most widely used forum today. However, as the expense, delay and technical complexity associated with judicial litigation have become more pronounced, arbitration has emerged as an alternative to formal courtroom proceedings.

12.2.1. Contractual Arbitration

Many construction contracts contain arbitration clauses pursuant to which disputes arising under the contract are submitted to an arbitrator or arbitration panel for resolution in accordance with the arbitration rules of the American Arbitration Association. A typical arbitration clause provides:

> All claims, disputes and other matters in question between the Contractor and the Owner arising out of, or related to, the Contract Documents or the breach thereof . . . shall be decided by arbitration in accordance with the Construction Industry Arbitration Rules of the American Arbitration Association then obtaining unless the parties mutually agree otherwise. [AIA Document A201 (1976 ed.), Article 7.9.]

Arbitration clauses usually mandate arbitration; variant clauses sometimes condition arbitration on the consent of all parties, thus preserving either party's right to resort to a court of law in the first instance. In most (but not all) states, courts will honor compulsory arbitration clauses and will not hear contract disputes if the parties have contractually agreed to arbitrate.[1]

Arbitration may offer certain advantages over judicial proceedings. First, arbitrators' expertise in construction industry matters may be more substantial than that of most judges and jurors. Second, arbitration proceedings are generally less formal. Evidentiary rules are relaxed, and arbitration panels often exercise greater discretion in

---

[1]*See, e.g., Singer Co. v. Tappan Co.,* 593 F.2d 545 (3d Cir. 1979); *Sterling Nat'l Bank & Trust Co. of New York v. Southern Scrap Export Co.,* 468 F.Supp. 1100 (S.D.N.Y. 1979); *Todd Shipyards Corp. v. Marine Vessel Leasing Corp.,* 456 F.Supp. 1384 (C.D. Cal. 1978). But there are exceptions. A party can go straight to court, notwithstanding the existence of a contractual arbitration clause, if the party contests the enforceability of the arbitration clause on the grounds of illegality or fraudulent inducement. *E.g., Hamilton Life Ins. Co. of New York v. Republic Nat'l Life Ins. Co.,* 408 F.2d 606 (2d Cir. 1969). In addition, arbitration clauses have been successfully voided in some cases as being repugnant to the public policy of the forum state. *E.g., Wickes Corp. v. Industrial Financial Corp.,* 493 F.2d 1173 (5th Cir. 1974) (Florida); *Christiansen v. Farmers Ins. Exchange,* 540 F.2d 472 (10th Cir. 1976) (Utah). Complicating matters further is a federal statute—commonly called the Federal Arbitration Act, 9 U.S.C. §§1 *ff.*—making written arbitration clauses "valid, irrevocable, and enforceable" so long as they are contained in "a contract evidencing a transaction involving commerce." 9 U.S.C. §2. The federal statute is frequently invoked, but is rarely of any significance.

deciding cases and formulating remedies. In comparison to court proceedings, arbitration is faster and therefore likely to be less costly.

One of the advantages of arbitration is also its principal shortcoming. Arbitrators are usually selected from lists maintained by the American Arbitration Association. They are full-time lawyers, contractors or engineers who are eminent in their own fields and who serve as arbitrators (sometimes without compensation) in addition to maintaining active professional lives of their own. The arbitration schedule, therefore, must be tailored to suit the convenience of busy arbitrators who, unlike judges, are frequently unable to set hearing dates weeks or months in advance. Arbitration proceedings that would ordinarily consume 50 hours of hearing time may have to be conducted in short segments over the course of many months. The process can be more disjointed than court proceedings.

No person can be compelled to arbitrate unless there is a contractual obligation to do so. An arbitration clause will often qualify or limit the circumstances under which disputes must be submitted for arbitration; within those boundaries, the decision of the arbitrator is binding on both parties and is ordinarily not subject to judicial review, except for fraud, non-arbitrability, and similar extrinsic factors.[2]

12.2.2. Court Proceedings

Most actions involving construction contracts are brought in state trial courts, although Federal District Courts have jurisdiction over two classes of cases: those seeking damages for violation of a federal statute (most commonly the Miller Act), and so-called "diversity" actions in which plaintiff and defendant are from different states and the amount sought in damages exceeds $10,000. In most state courts, the parties are entitled to a jury trial, although for tactical reasons (particularly in complex cases) the right is often waived and the case tried by a judge sitting alone.

Courts are the forum of preference when disputes are legal rather than factual. One significant difference between court proceedings and arbitration is that a court can compel the attendance of witnesses and the production of documentary evidence; an arbitrator has no subpoena power, and must depend on the voluntary cooperation of parties and witnesses.

12.2.3. Other Forums

Brief mention must be made of the forums commonly used to resolve disputes arising under public contracts. These are the administrative agencies commonly known as boards of contract appeals. There are eleven federal boards, corresponding to the various federal agencies with statutory authority to contract with private parties; the largest is the Armed Forces Board of Contract Appeals, to which all disputes involving

---

[2]*See, e.g., Storer Broadcasting Co. v. American Fed. of Television and Radio Artists, Cleveland Local*, 600 F.2d 45 (6th Cir. 1979); *Riverboat Casino, Inc. v. Local Joint Executive Bd. of Las Vegas*, 578 F.2d 250 (9th Cir. 1978).

Defense Department construction and procurement contracts are submitted. Many states have created administrative boards to serve the same function at the state and municipal levels.

12.3. PROOF PROBLEMS

Much of the expense of construction litigation is due to the complexity of factual issues which must be proved by the parties. A construction project often takes years to complete, and involves the integrated work of scores and even hundreds of workers. Proof problems can become prodigiously difficult under such circumstances, for two basic reasons.

First, proof of proximate causation and damages requires highly developed technical expertise on the part of the members of the litigating team, including counsel. Counsel must understand financial cost-accounting and bidding procedures, comparative costs and capacities of specialized equipment and materials, and the almost infinite variety of records kept by contractors, subcontractors, architects, and other construction project participants. Counsel must also make sense out of diverse documents, plans, and specifications and must work closely with their clients to do so.

Second, proof problems can be intractable, due to the interrelationships between parties and the long periods of time that may elapse between contractual breach and resulting damage. For example, a supplier may fail to honor the terms of a subcontract, forcing the subcontractor to default. The subcontractor's failure may have a ripple effect on a carefully coordinated sequence of other subcontracts. If the general contractor is later held accountable for damages due to delay, he may seek indemnification from one of his first-tier subcontractors. That subcontractor, in turn, may blame a second-tier subcontractor, who may blame a supplier, who may be out of business at the time suit is filed or whose financial records may not be accurate enough to be useful if litigation is commenced six months or a year after the fact.

12.4. DISCOVERY

Proof problems are aggravated by the fact that pre-trial discovery proceedings, the traditional method by which litigants gather proof of their claims, are of significantly less value in construction litigation than in other actions. Although the scope of permissible discovery is broad under the Federal Rules of Civil Procedure and most state-court analogs, discovery is limited or does not exist at all in non-judicial forums (such as arbitration panels or the various military and civilian Boards of Contract Appeals). Even in forums that permit discovery, the traditional discovery techniques tend to be cumbersome because of the large number of parties usually involved in construction cases and the enormous amount of paper work generated during the lifetime of a good-sized project.

We recount one example from personal experience. In a recent action under the Miller Act, we noticed the deposition of an officer of the opposing company and asked him to bring carefully identified documents from his files to the deposition, which was scheduled for the conference room at our law firm. He politely declined, on the ground that the documents described in our subpoena would fill two railroad cars and could not be transported from his office to ours without prohibitive expense and disruption.

Undaunted, we rescheduled the deposition for his office. It was, in brief, a fiasco. After literally every question, the witness excused himself from the room, searched for an hour through masses of documents in an adjoining room, then returned to give us no answer, or a highly qualified answer based on his purported inability to examine all pertinent documents. There are some cases with records so enormous that conventional discovery methods break down. Cases involving construction projects frequently come within that category.

12.5. EXPERT WITNESSES

Consider for a moment the astonishing array of matters that the members of the litigating team must master before trial, and that must then be explained in understandable and persuasive terms to the judge, jury or arbitral tribunal:

— The common terminology used to describe construction projects, materials and equipment;

— The business and financial records maintained by contractors, architects and engineers, including blueprints, shop drawings and computerized records;

— The attributes unique to specialty work;

— Commonly used bidding methods; and

— The technical problems associated with engineering and design work.

The job of an expert witness is to assist the (usually uninitiated) fact-finder in resolving matters beyond his competence or expertise. Expert witnesses frequently play a determinative role in construction litigation.

An expert witness serves three principal functions. First, the expert *explains* matters which may require elucidation by somebody with technical training or experience. Second, the expert *adds perspective* by comparing the case to other cases in which he has been involved. Third and perhaps most important, the expert *provides persuasive, objective standards* for assessing the parties' performance, standards that are often more credible in the eyes of the fact-finder than the subjective testimony of those who participated directly in events.

Two characteristics distinguish the testimony of an expert witness from that of other witnesses. First, the expert must be qualified through special training, education or experience to address authoritatively the subject on which he is prepared to testify. (It is the examining attorney's task to "qualify" an expert witness by presenting evidence of the witness's special qualifications prior to testimony; see below.) Second, the expert is free to testify on matters beyond the scope of ordinary examination. Experts may offer objective or technical assessments designed to illuminate the factual testimony of other witnesses. Experts may be asked for their opinions, based either on facts within their knowledge or on hypothetical facts suggested by the examining attorney.

Before a witness may offer expert testimony, the witness's qualifications as an expert must be established to the satisfaction of the court.[3] Whether a witness is qualified to render expert testimony is a discretionary matter for the court to determine, and precise standards for determining the prerequisites for qualification do not exist. Usually it is the task of the attorney who calls an expert witness to explain to the court the purpose for which the testimony is sought and the witness's educational or other qualifications. Opposing counsel may, through cross-examination, challenge the credentials of the witness. The decision whether to qualify a witness as an expert is entirely the court's and is rarely overturned on appeal.

The testimony of an expert witness is more persuasive if it is based on facts and observations within the witness's first-hand knowledge, rather than on hypothetical facts. The danger of testimony based on hypothetical questions is apparent; opposing counsel can effectively rebut such testimony by showing that the facts on which it is premised are untrue or disputed. As a matter of sound litigating strategy, therefore, experts should be called in as soon as contractual problems arise and should participate in the preparation and organization of evidence from the earliest possible juncture.

Expert testimony is expensive. Depending on the subject matter and the extent of participation, expert witnesses will ordinarily charge as much as $75 an hour, plus travel and incidental expenses. In complex cases, the cost of expert testimony is frequently the most expensive single litigating cost next to attorneys' fees. This factor mitigates to some extent the benefit to be derived from involving experts in the case from the earliest possible moment.

12.6. SPECIAL DEFENSES

The formal setting in which construction contracts are negotiated and executed and the prevalence of standard-form contracts mean as a practical matter that many of the standard contract defenses (such as lack of consideration or unenforceable vagueness) are unavailable to the party defending against a lawsuit for breach of a construction contract. Several standard defenses, however, are frequently invoked and have special applicability in the construction context. They are discussed briefly below.

12.6.1. Statute of Limitations

Because construction projects take years to complete and because latent structural defects are often not manifested until years or even decades after completion, the

---

[3]The term "court" is used here in a general sense to refer as well to arbitral boards and panels.

statute of limitations provides significant protection against liability. In virtually all states, the statute begins to run when the construction project is substantially completed or when contractual obligations are fully performed.

A good example of the insulation from liability provided by the statute of limitations is the recent case of *Sosnow v. Paul,*[4] a suit brought by the owner of a construction project against the architect for faulty design. The architect's plans were submitted and approved in 1965. More than five years later, cracks appeared in the building's foundation. The owner brought suit in 1971, claiming that the cracks resulted from the architect's failure to include expansion joints in the building design. The owner argued that under the state's three-year statute of limitations, his cause of action accrued when the cracks first appeared. The state's highest court unanimously ruled that the statute began to run upon completion of the architect's services in 1965. The action was deemed to be barred by the statute, and the owner's complaint was dismissed.

Most states have enacted special statutes for the construction industry establishing more realistic limitation periods (usually six to ten years) in construction contract litigation.[5]

12.6.2. Vicarious Liability

A contractor is not liable for damages caused by adhering to defective plans or specifications furnished by the owner's architect or engineer. This is true even when the contractor warrants or guarantees the results of his work; such warranties are not deemed to include defects caused by design deficiencies.

12.6.3. Contributory Negligence

A contractor or design professional is not liable if the plaintiff's own negligence is wholly or partially responsible for damages. This is a common and effective defense against delay claims. If the plaintiff's negligence has contributed to delays down the line, damages for delay are not recoverable.

12.6.4. Contractual Provisions Limiting Liability

Modern construction contracts contain a wide array of indemnification and "hold-harmless" clauses. Depending on the circumstance and the jurisdiction, such clauses are frequently given legal effect by courts. Other standard clauses also provide a degree of protection to contract parties. Limitation-of-damages clauses set a maximum limit on recoverable damages. Site investigation clauses provide protection against unanticipated soil or substratum problems. And "force majeure" clauses ensure that parties will not be liable for damages caused by floods, fires, civil commotion or other unpreventable occurrences.

---

[4]36 N.Y. 2d 780, 369 N.Y.S. 2d 693 (1975).

[5]The statutes are referenced and described in the August and September, 1977, issues of *A/E Legal Newsletter.*

12.7. PRE-TRIAL PROCEEDINGS

Four matters are ordinarily taken up during the period after discovery is completed and before trial commences. First, counsel for both sides participate in a formal pre-trial conference (or series of conferences) before the judge, the purpose of which is to dispose of ancillary issues that have been clarified or resolved during the discovery process. An effective pre-trial conference can save time for court and counsel by narrowing the issues to be submitted for trial.

Second, and usually in conjunction with a scheduled pre-trial conference, counsel obtain stipulations to facilitate the management of witnesses and evidence at trial. If facts are not in dispute, the parties can stipulate to their veracity and save themselves the time and trouble of proof. Similarly, the parties can stipulate to the authenticity and admissibility of documents to be introduced as evidence, the qualifications of expert witnesses, the use of deposition testimony for witnesses unable to testify in person, and other administrative or factual matters.

Third, pre-trial motions may be contested. Pre-trial motions are of two general types: discovery-related motions to compel the production of documents or responsive answers to interrogatories, and motions related to the substance of a party's allegations, such as motions to strike affirmative defenses and motions for summary judgment.

Finally, pre-trial conferences serve an increasingly important function as a means of encouraging settlement discussions between the parties. Parties are often required to tell the presiding judge what efforts, if any, they have made to resolve their differences without going to trial. If those efforts are not sufficient in the judge's view, then he will use a pre-trial conference as an avenue for encouraging—even, in some cases, cajoling—the parties to reach an agreement.

12.8. TRIAL

A trial (using the term in its broad sense to include proceedings in other adjudicative forums besides a court) is an adversary proceeding in which each side presents evidence to a neutral fact-finder responsible for resolving disputed contentions of fact and rendering a judgment for one party. A single trial may involve more than one claim for relief, as, for example, when a complaint contains multiple counts or related counter-claims or cross-claims are adjudicated with the original complaint.

As the preceding sections of this chapter indicate, an attorney engaged in construction contract litigation must seek to maintain a delicate balance at trial between two tactical goals. On the one hand, the attorney must master voluminous documentary and testimonial evidence; on the other, he must make the client's case comprehensible to fact-finders lacking familiarity with or expertise in the construction industry.

Construction trials involve two general issues. First, the complaining party must prove that the opposing party's conduct renders him *liable* for damages under statutory, contractual or common-law standards of liability. If liability is established, then the plaintiff must prove the existence and extent of *damages* suffered as a result of the actionable conduct.

12.8.1. Liability

The starting point is the construction contract. It establishes the duties, obligations and liabilities of the parties and suggests not only the nature of the opposing party's liability but the kind of evidence necessary to prove an actionable breach.

For example, a subcontract may call for monthly installment payments and may require that payments be tendered by certified check to a designated employee of the subcontractor. If the subcontractor subsequently alleges that installment payments were not tendered when due, the subcontract itself suggests the evidence necessary to establish liability: the testimony of the designated employee, the certified checks and any correspondence referencing the payments tendered.

Liability can be established through the testimony of witnesses, the introduction of documentary evidence, or a combination of the two. Here, as in every aspect of trial conduct, the goal is to balance comprehension with simplicity. Unnecessary documentation, particularly in the form of highly technical or legalistic contracts, can have an unintended and adverse effect if it creates the impression that a case is more complicated than it actually is. Witnesses whose testimony is disorganized or repetitive can produce the same result. Careful pre-trial preparation should result in a spare, well-organized factual presentation that neither distracts the fact-finder's attention from the essential elements of the case nor suggests that important points are being glossed over or ignored.

12.8.2. Damages

Here, of course, is where the real battle is waged. To prevail at trial, the plaintiff must prove damage as a direct result of the opposing party's breach, and must present evidence sufficient to establish an entitlement to the dollar amount sought as compensatory damages.

In many instances, particularly when damages are sought for delay or schedule disruption, damage calculations can be enormously complicated and require the assistance of expert witnesses in the fields of construction scheduling and CPM management. In general terms, an injured party is entitled to damages sufficient to place the party in the position he would have occupied had no breach occurred—a standard sufficiently speculative to encourage protracted litigation over the measure of damages. The issue can become more complicated if the opposing party alleges that the plaintiff's own conduct was partially or wholly responsible for the breach.

With the consent of both parties, trials can be bifurcated with liability issues determined first and damage issues reserved for consideration in a subsequent proceeding. Bifurcation offers several advantages: it simplifies the trial attorney's task by permitting him to focus on issues sequentially; it permits the fact-finder to concentrate on the narrower issue of liability without the distraction and possible prejudice of damage evidence; and, most important, in the event that the initial trial results in a finding of non-liability, it saves the parties from the task of preparing and presenting evidence on the superfluous damage issue. The obvious disadvantage of bifurcation is that two trials consume more time than a single trial, are inevitably more expensive, and usually result in some loss of efficiency, since witnesses may have to testify twice instead of once.

12.9. CONCLUSION

Lawyers are fond of saying that only the hard cases go to trial. The aphorism suggests that the expense and duration of modern litigation are so extraordinary that it is frequently to a litigant's practical advantage to resolve contractual disputes without seeking a court's assistance. The best strategy may be to prevent litigation before it starts. That will be the subject of the next chapter.

If litigation is commenced, then the members of the litigating team must be sure they understand the facts of the case in enough detail to present them cogently and with necessary documentation to the fact-finder. The facts must establish not only that the defendant is liable for an actionable breach, but also that the plaintiff is entitled to the damages he seeks. Always, the human element must be remembered. Juries are more likely to be persuaded by simple, comprehensible and logical truths than by the technical requirements of the contract.

12.10. ADDITIONAL SOURCE MATERIALS

Treatises

Dunham, C. W., R. D. Young & J. T. Bockrath, *Contracts, Specifications, and Law for Engineers* (3d ed. 1979).

Hohns, H. M., *Preventing and Solving Construction Contract Disputes* (1979).

O'Brien, J. J., *Construction Delay: Responsibilities, Risks, and Litigation*, at 137–204 (1976).

Simon, M. S., *Construction Contracts and Claims* (1979).

Articles and Annotations

Aksen, G., "Role of arbitration in construction contracts," *in* PLI, *Construction Contracts* at 299–309 (1976).

Anno., "Admissibility in evidence, on issue of negligence, of codes or standards of safety issued or sponsored by governmental body or by voluntary association," 58 A.L.R. 3d 148 (1974).

Currie, O.A., "Preparation and trial of construction litigation," *in* PLI, *Construction Contracts 1978* at 599–635 (1978).

Currie, O. A., "Preparation and trial of construction litigation," *in* PLI, *Construction Contracts* at 167–231, 529–61 (1976).

Grant, C. L., "An overview of the construction process—problems and claims," *in* PLI, *Construction Contracts 1979* at 859–923 (1979).

Martel, J. S., "Major recurring problems in construction litigation: bid mistakes and site investigation clauses, *in* PLI, *Construction Contracts 1976* at 101–13 (1976).

Martel, J. S., "Special defenses in construction litigation," *in* PLI, *Construction Contracts 1976* at 115–23 (1976).

Martel, J. S., R. M. Bryan, B. R. MacLeod, & S. E. Cone, "Defenses in construction litigation," *in* PLI, *Construction Contracts 1979* at 109–53 (1979).

Moss, R., "Payment disputes in construction industry litigation," 53 Los Angeles B. J. 349 (Dec. 1977).

Pemberton, J. S., Jr., "Remedies for breach of the construction or architectural contract," *in* PLI, *Construction Contracts 1978* at 327–410 (1978).

Pierce, J. D., Jr., "Special problems of multi-party litigation," *in* PLI, *Construction Contracts 1979* at 329–407 (1979).

Schechter, M., "Practical approach to construction litigation," *Trial*, Vol. 15, at 39 (June 1979).

Shepherd, J. H. & W. Lefkofsky, "Role of the technical expert as consultant to trial counsel," 56 Mich. S. B. J. 1008 (Dec. 1977).

CHAPTER 13

Minimizing the Likelihood and Impact of Construction Litigation

13.1. INTRODUCTION

The riskiness and financial fragility of the construction industry mean that it is in the interest of all parties to anticipate potential disputes and resolve them before they disrupt construction work in progress. Disputes are likely to arise on any construction project. But the experienced contractor or design professional recognizes that certain areas or phases of construction are more likely than others to generate disputes, and plans accordingly.

Intelligent litigation planning is designed to achieve three goals. First, it provides mechanisms for minimizing the likelihood of litigation before it occurs, primarily by anticipating and preventing potential problems of construction, financing and design. Second, it provides protection in the event that litigation arises. Third, and most important, it ensures that construction proceeds while disputes are litigated and resolved.

13.2. MINIMIZING THE LIKELIHOOD OF LITIGATION: PRE-CONTRACT INVESTIGATION

It goes without saying that the surest way for a contractor to avoid litigation is by dealing with reputable and well-financed owners, subcontractors and design professionals. Where possible, contractors should deal with established firms. Before contracts are signed or bids are accepted, the contractor should, at a minimum, check financial and professional references provided by potential contract signatories.

Perhaps the most common source of trouble on the construction site is the under-financed or inexperienced subcontractor who wins a contract by submitting an unrealistically low bid. Contractors must insist on enough latitude from the owner to reject bids from such subcontractors. Specifications must emphasize factors other than price, such as experience and reputation, to avoid relying on an inexperienced subcontractor. Careful selection of contract parties is, in the long run, the best insurance against costly litigation and attendant delay.

13.3. MINIMIZING THE LIKELIHOOD OF LITIGATION: CONTRACT DRAFTING

Carefully drafted documents can provide effective protection against liability. Hold-harmless and related indemnification clauses can prevent disputes by indicating which party is legally responsible for any problem that may arise. In more general terms, a contract tailored to the circumstances of a particular construction project can serve several beneficial purposes. It requires the parties to concentrate on potential problem areas before construction commences, and it permits the addition of "special-circumstance" clauses to standard-form contracts.

13.4. MINIMIZING THE LIKELIHOOD OF LITIGATION: ANTICIPATING POTENTIAL PROBLEMS

Certain aspects of the contractual relationships between owner, contractor, subcontractor and design professional pose recurring problems. Through intelligent planning, the parties can anticipate potential areas of difficulty and either minimize the likelihood of disruption or provide a mechanism for resolving disputes while construction work continues.

Some of the most common areas of potential difficulty deserve special attention.

13.4.1. Bid Mistakes

In the volatile world of construction financing, a bid that is feasible when submitted may quickly cease to be realistic as economic conditions change, particularly when weeks or even months pass between submission of the bid and acceptance by the owner. Much litigation has arisen concerning the respective rights and obligations of the parties when a bidder discovers—usually after being awarded the contract—that he cannot comply with the terms of his bid.

Problems can be avoided by carefully reviewing bids before they are submitted to catch clerical or mathematical errors. Many bids are prepared in haste and submitted under time pressure, and small errors are not detected; even modest errors can assume damaging proportions when incorporated in competitive bids that are already trimmed close to the profit margin.

Problems can also be avoided by conditioning bids to ensure that they do not remain pending beyond a reasonable period of time without appropriate modification of terms. The simplest and most widely used condition is a time limit that requires bids to be accepted by a date certain and rescinds the offer thereafter. Another condition is rarely included in bids at present, but can be expected to appear more frequently in the future, particularly on large projects: an inflation escalator that adjusts the bid by a specified percentage or amount if the acceptance date or implementation date is delayed for more than a fixed period of time.

By exercising care in the preparation of bids, limiting the lifetime of each bid and protecting the integrity of a bid from the debilitating effects of inflation, contractors can protect against a common source of litigation: arithmetic or judgmental bid mistakes that render a project unprofitable before work is even commenced.

13.4.2. Delay

This is the most common problem on the job site and a fecund source of litigation. Disruptive delay problems can be minimized in two ways. First, contracts can be carefully drafted to indicate which parties are to bear the liability for potential delays. If liability is defined with sufficient clarity, litigation can be avoided and parties will have an incentive to prevent delay. Second, any instance of potential delay should be exhaustively documented by appropriate annotations in daily log books and correspondence, and all personnel should be sensitive to the need for a comprehensive documentary "record." Delay claims are so prevalent that as a practical matter the modicum of proof required by most courts is more substantial here than in other areas of construction litigation.

13.4.3. Change Orders

Owners and contractors have varying, almost idiosyncratic, approaches to the submission and approval of change orders. Because change orders can constitute a significant proportion of the total amount expended on a project, and because contractual change order provisions are frequently drafted in technical language that poorly relates to the practical "give and take" of negotiations, parties are well advised to discuss change order procedures and to modify standard-form contract language as appropriate before the contract is executed.

13.5. MINIMIZING THE LIKELIHOOD OF LITIGATION: ON-SITE INSPECTION

Before contracts are negotiated, potential bidders should carefully inspect the proposed construction site. Most standard-form contracts contain broadly worded clauses, insulating the owner from liability for any damages caused by undetected surface or sub-surface faults. Typical is Paragraph 1.2.2 of the AIA's General Conditions (Document A201):

> By executing the Contract, the Contractor represents that he has visited the site, familiarized himself with the local conditions under which the Work is to be performed, and correlated his observations with the requirements of the Contract Documents.

It is incumbent upon a contractor to insist on modification or supplementation of this language if inspection reveals a potential problem with the condition of the site. In the leading case of *Hollerbach v. United States*, 233 U.S. 165 (1914), for example, a contractor was hired to repair a federally owned dam in Kentucky. The contract contained a standard site inspection clause requiring the contractor to "visit the site of this work, . . . ascertain the nature of the work, . . . and obtain the information necessary to enable him to make an intelligent proposal." To this general language, the Government had added a clause describing the subsurface behind the dam:

> The dam is now backed for about 50 feet with broken stone, sawdust, and sediment . . ., and it is expected that a cofferdam can be constructed with this stone. . . .

After excavation started, the contractor discovered that the dam was not backed with broken stone, as warranted in the contract. The contractor later brought suit for damages, but relief was denied by the Court of Claims on the ground that the contractor was prevented by the site inspection clause from objecting to subsurface conditions. On appeal, the Supreme Court reversed and ordered judgment for the contractor: "We think it would be going quite too far to interpret the general language of the [site inspection clause] as requiring independent investigation of facts which the specifications furnished by the Government . . . left in no doubt." 233 U.S. at 172.

Modern case law has refined and somewhat narrowed the holding in *Hollerbach*. A contractor who has signed a contract containing a site inspection clause is *not* protected against unanticipated on-site conditions unless two criteria are satisfied. First, the contract must include a positive representation concerning the condition of the site or of a specific part of the site. Second, the contractor must show that he reasonably relied on that representation when he visited the site and therefore had no cause to check the truth or falsity of the representation. If a contractor is concerned about the condition of the potential construction site, he is well advised to insist that appropriate warranties be included in the contract.

Inspection of the site is critically important before contracts are negotiated and executed. A more difficult problem is posed by inspections during the course of construction. Most contracts require design professionals to make periodic visits to the site to ensure that work is progressing according to plan. Article 1.5.4 of the AIA's standard-form owner-architect agreement (AIA Document B141), for example, provides:

> The Architect shall visit the site at intervals appropriate to the stage of construction . . . to become generally familiar with the progress and quality of

the Work and to determine in general if the Work is proceeding in accordance
with the Contract Documents. However, the Architect shall not be required to
make exhaustive or continuous on-site inspections to check the quality or quantity of the Work.

Architects are required by the terms of such an inspection clause to make
"periodic" visits. Who determines how many visits should be made and when they should
be scheduled? The question has obvious significance for the architect, who does not wish
to increase the risk of liability for design problems by being limited in his access to the
site, but at the same time does not want to waste time and manpower on unnecessary
inspections.

Contracts are now beginning to distinguish between "on-call" and "periodic
observation" clauses. An "on-call" clause generally requires architects to conduct inspections when asked to do so by the owner. A periodic observation clause—like Paragraph
1.1.14 of the AIA agreement cited above—permits the architect to schedule his own
visits, and provides greater flexibility for the design professional.

13.6. PREPARING FOR LITIGATION: MAINTAINING A FORMAL DOCUMENTATION SYSTEM

Frequently litigation's most important stage is the period before a complaint is
actually filed. Proper preparation is important in prosecuting or defending against a
lawsuit; it is also important in determining whether a potential case is strong enough to
merit the expense of litigation.

The most effective way of preparing for litigation is to maintain a formal system of
contemporaneous records and documents. The system should include, at a minimum,
the following components.

13.6.1. Files

Central files must be maintained. They should include (1) a *legal file* consisting of
the contract documents, specifications, change orders, and related materials, (2) a
chronological file for all correspondence, including internal memoranda and communications, and (3) *subject-matter files* for each subcontract, construction phase, or other
divisible unit of the project.

13.6.2. A Job-Site Log

The project superintendent should keep a daily record of work progress, either in
the form of a written log or a dictated "diary" which is transcribed at the end of each work

day. The log should record the precise date and time of arrival for all materials and subcontractors, and should explain in detail any problems that arise during the course of construction. It is important that entries be recorded at regular intervals (preferably daily) by the same person or group of people; if the log constitutes a regularly maintained business record, then it is admissible as evidence at trial under an exception to the hearsay rule.

13.6.3. Conversation Memoranda

Sometimes the most fruitful business is transacted orally. Change orders may be approved by telephone, or conversations may reveal problems. All personnel should memorialize the contents of important conversations by writing or dictating file memoranda as soon as possible after the subject conversation occurs. Oral understandings should also be memorialized by letter confirmations, particularly when modification of contractual terms is involved.

13.6.4. Accounting Records

It is often not enough for one party to show that another has breached the terms of a construction contract. The complaining party cannot recover money damages unless the breach is shown to have caused the damage and the amount of damages can be calculated with precision. Accounting records provide the important link between breach and money damages, and are often the most important and most carefully scrutinized records at trial.

13.7. MEASURE OF DAMAGES

In general, the prevailing party in an action for breach of contract may recover damages for injuries reasonably related to the breach of the contract itself. Direct damages, such as loss of profits, are usually easy to document. But the prevailing party is also entitled to recover consequential damages, defined as any damages the parties, at the time the contract was negotiated and executed, could reasonably have foreseen as resulting from the breach. Consequential damages are often the largest component in a damage claim and the most difficult to prove and to quantify. Loss of reputation, loss of efficiency, inability to bid successfully on subsequent contracts, speculative increases in the cost of labor and materials, increased insurance premiums, and interest on unpaid claims are all compensable elements of consequential damage. But damages cannot be awarded unless the prevailing party, first, establishes the causative link between breach and damage, and second, convincingly proves the actual quantum of damages incurred. Here is where accounting records play a vital role.

Appropriately annotated accounting records are in many instances the most persuasive evidence that expenditures incurred to remedy the effect of a contractual breach were proximately related to conduct by the party in breach. Accounting records also provide an accurate basis for calculating damages actually incurred; this, in turn, can be used as the starting point for estimating and explaining consequential damages.

As a general rule, damages do not have to be calculated or documented with mathematical precision, so long as estimates are reasonably accurate and are supported by adequate documentation. Convincing and comprehensible accounting records can be one of the most powerful weapons in a litigant's arsenal, and the absence of such records can be used to great advantage by an opponent intent on diverting the court's attention from more substantive issues.

13.8. PREPARING FOR LITIGATION: ASSESSING COSTS AND ALTERNATIVES

Knowing when to avoid litigation is just as important as knowing when to bring suit. Litigation is expensive, time-consuming, and disruptive. Its very substantial costs must always be kept in mind. If a case is weak or the expected recovery is small, then in all probability an action should not be commenced.

Many construction disputes can be settled amicably without going to court. Negotiated settlements have several advantages over court actions. They save all parties time and money. They avoid uncertainty by affording each party an opportunity to shape and approve the final terms of settlement. They offer greater flexibility in fashioning remedies for contract breaches than a court could ordinarily provide.

Favorable settlement terms, like favorable results in litigation, are abetted by careful preparation and recordkeeping. If damage claims can be documented and supported, then the opposing party will have a greater incentive to keep the dispute out of court.

13.9. PREVENTING DISRUPTION

Successful construction often depends on the maintenance of precise timetables. A subcontractor's work may take only a few hours or days, but its timing may be crucial and other subcontractors may not be able to commence their work until the smaller project is completed. For this reason, even a minor dispute may pose the threat of serious disruption if work is allowed to stop while the dispute is resolved.

Contractors and subcontractors are commonly required by the terms of their contracts to proceed with their work while disputes are arbitrated or litigated. Articles 7.9.1 and 7.9.3 of the AIA General Conditions (AIA Document A201) constitute a typical "disputes clause":

> All claims, disputes and other matters in question arising out of, or relating to, the Contract Documents or the breach thereof . . . shall be decided by arbitration in accordance with the Construction Industry Arbitration Rules of the

> American Arbitration Association then obtaining unless the parties mutually agree otherwise. . . . [The] Contractor shall carry on the Work and maintain its progress during any arbitration proceedings, and the Owner shall continue to make payments to the Contractor in accordance with the Contract Documents.

To some extent, the protection against disruption provided by this disputes clause is undercut by other provisions in the AIA General Conditions permitting the owner to suspend construction (Article 3.3), and allowing the contractor to recover damages for owner-caused work suspensions (Article 14.1.1). Nevertheless, it is accurate to state that construction contracts normally provide considerable protection against work stoppages. Parties are usually required to resolve contract disputes away from the construction site, and to work while arbitration procedures are invoked.

Damages for delay due to subcontractor or contractor disruption are usually severe, because the effect of even a small delay can ripple through a construction project and be magnified many times when the schedules of other subcontractors are disrupted. Contracts will sometimes specify *per diem* liquidated damages for delay. Courts are not reluctant to impose liability up to the limit of the liquidated damage clause, even when the total damages seem disproportionately large in comparison to the duration of the delay.

13.10 ADDITIONAL SOURCE MATERIALS

Treatises

Dunham, C. W., R. D. Young & J. T. Bockrath, *Contracts, Specifications, and Law for Engineers* (3d ed. 1979).

Hohns, H. M., *Preventing and Solving Construction Contract Disputes* (1979).

O'Brien, J. J., *Construction Delay: Responsibilities, Risks, and Litigation*, at 137–204 (1976).

Simon, M. S., *Construction Contracts and Claims* (1979).

Articles and Annotations

Grant, C. L., "An overview of the construction process—problems and claims," *in* PLI, *Construction Contracts 1979* at 859–923 (1979).

Hart, B. W., "Remedies for breach of construction contracts," *in* PLI, *Construction Contracts* at 147–65 (1976).

Martel, J. S., "Planning to avoid construction litigation," *in* PLI, *Construction Contracts* at 69–83 (1976).

Purcell, P. F., "Architect's viewpoint in litigation," *in* PLI, *Construction Contracts* at 233–44 (1976).

APPENDIX

Documents of The
American Institute of Architects

LIST OF DOCUMENTS

THE AMERICAN INSTITUTE OF ARCHITECTS

AIA Document A101

Standard Form of Agreement Between Owner and Contractor

where the basis of payment is a

STIPULATED SUM

1977 EDITION

THIS DOCUMENT HAS IMPORTANT LEGAL CONSEQUENCES; CONSULTATION WITH AN ATTORNEY IS ENCOURAGED WITH RESPECT TO ITS COMPLETION OR MODIFICATION

Use only with the 1976 Edition of AIA Document A201, General Conditions of the Contract for Construction.

This document has been approved and endorsed by The Associated General Contractors of America.

AGREEMENT

made as of the   day of   in the year of Nineteen
Hundred and

BETWEEN the Owner:

and the Contractor:

The Project:

The Architect: **AIA copyrighted material has been reproduced with permission of the The American Institute of Architect under permission number 81050. Further reproduction is prohibited.**

Because AIA Documents are revised from time to time, users should ascertain from the AIA the current edition(s) of the Document(s) reproduced herein.

The Owner and the Contractor agree as set forth below.

AIA DOCUMENT A101 • OWNER-CONTRACTOR AGREEMENT • ELEVENTH EDITION • JUNE 1977 • AIA®
©1977 • THE AMERICAN INSTITUTE OF ARCHITECTS, 1735 NEW YORK AVE., N.W., WASHINGTON, D. C. 20006   **A101-1977 1**

ARTICLE 1

THE CONTRACT DOCUMENTS

The Contract Documents consist of this Agreement, the Conditions of the Contract (General, Supplementary and other Conditions), the Drawings, the Specifications, all Addenda issued prior to and all Modifications issued after execution of this Agreement. These form the Contract, and all are as fully a part of the Contract as if attached to this Agreement or repeated herein. An enumeration of the Contract Documents appears in Article 7.

ARTICLE 2

THE WORK

The Contractor shall perform all the Work required by the Contract Documents for
(Here insert the caption descriptive of the Work as used on other Contract Documents.)

ARTICLE 3

TIME OF COMMENCEMENT AND SUBSTANTIAL COMPLETION

The Work to be performed under this Contract shall be commenced

and, subject to authorized adjustments, Substantial Completion shall be achieved not later than

(Here insert any special provisions for liquidated damages relating to failure to complete on time.)

ARTICLE 4

CONTRACT SUM

The Owner shall pay the Contractor in current funds for the performance of the Work, subject to additions and deductions by Change Order as provided in the Contract Documents, the Contract Sum of

The Contract Sum is determined as follows:
(State here the base bid or other lump sum amount, accepted alternates, and unit prices, as applicable.)

ARTICLE 5

PROGRESS PAYMENTS

Based upon Applications for Payment submitted to the Architect by the Contractor and Certificates for Payment issued by the Architect, the Owner shall make progress payments on account of the Contract Sum to the Contractor as provided in the Contract Documents for the period ending the   day of the month as follows:

Not later than   days following the end of the period covered by the Application for Payment   percent (%) of the portion of the Contract Sum properly allocable to labor, materials and equipment incorporated in the Work and   percent (%) of the portion of the Contract Sum properly allocable to materials and equipment suitably stored at the site or at some other location agreed upon in writing, for the period covered by the Application for Payment, less the aggregate of previous payments made by the Owner; and upon Substantial Completion of the entire Work, a sum sufficient to increase the total payments to   percent (%) of the Contract Sum, less such amounts as the Architect shall determine for all incomplete Work and unsettled claims as provided in the Contract Documents.

(If not covered elsewhere in the Contract Documents, here insert any provision for limiting or reducing the amount retained after the Work reaches a certain stage of completion.)

Payments due and unpaid under the Contract Documents shall bear interest from the date payment is due at the rate entered below, or in the absence thereof, at the legal rate prevailing at the place of the Project.
(Here insert any rate of interest agreed upon.)

(Usury laws and requirements under the Federal Truth in Lending Act, similar state and local consumer credit laws and other regulations at the Owner's and Contractor's principal places of business, the location of the Project and elsewhere may affect the validity of this provision. Specific legal advice should be obtained with respect to deletion, modification, or other requirements such as written disclosures or waivers.)

ARTICLE 6
FINAL PAYMENT

Final payment, constituting the entire unpaid balance of the Contract Sum, shall be paid by the Owner to the Contractor when the Work has been completed, the Contract fully performed, and the Architect has issued a Project Certificate for Payment which approves the final payment due the Contractor.

ARTICLE 7
MISCELLANEOUS PROVISIONS

7.1 Terms used in this Agreement which are defined in the Conditions of the Contract shall have the meanings designated in those Conditions.

7.2 The Contract Documents, which constitute the entire agreement between the Owner and the Contractor, are listed in Article 1 and, except for Modifications issued after execution of this Agreement, are enumerated as follows:

(List below the Agreement, the Conditions of the Contract [General, Supplementary and other Conditions], the Drawings, the Specifications, and any Addenda and accepted alternates, showing page or sheet numbers in all cases and dates where applicable.)

THE AMERICAN INSTITUTE OF ARCHITECTS

AIA Document A101/CM

CONSTRUCTION MANAGEMENT EDITION

Standard Form of Agreement Between Owner and Contractor

where the basis of payment is a

STIPULATED SUM

1980 EDITION

THIS DOCUMENT HAS IMPORTANT LEGAL CONSEQUENCES; CONSULTATION WITH AN ATTORNEY IS ENCOURAGED.

This document is intended to be used in conjunction with AIA Documents
A201/CM, 1980; B141/CM, 1980; and B801, 1980.

AGREEMENT

made as of the   day of   in the year of Nineteen
Hundred and

BETWEEN the Owner:

and the Contractor:

the Project:

the Construction Manager:

the Architect: AIA copyrighted material has been reproduced with permission of the The American Institute of Architect under permission number 81050. Further reproduction is prohibited.

Because AIA Documents are revised from time to time, users should ascertain from the AIA the current edition(s) of the Document(s) reproduced herein.

The Owner and the Contractor agree as set forth below.

ARTICLE 1
THE CONTRACT DOCUMENTS

The Contract Documents consist of this Agreement, the Conditions of the Contract (General, Supplementary and other Conditions), the Drawings, the Specifications, all Addenda issued prior to and all Modifications issued after execution of this Agreement. These form the Contract, and all are as fully a part of the Contract as if attached to this Agreement or repeated herein. An enumeration of the Contract Documents appears in Article 7.

ARTICLE 2
THE WORK

The Contractor shall perform all the Work required by the Contract Documents for
(Here insert the caption descriptive of the Work as used on other Contract Documents.)

ARTICLE 3
TIME OF COMMENCEMENT AND SUBSTANTIAL COMPLETION

The Work to be performed under this Contract shall be commenced

and, subject to authorized adjustments, Substantial Completion of the Work shall be achieved not later than

(Here insert any special provisions for liquidated damages relating to failure to complete on time.)

ARTICLE 4
CONTRACT SUM

The Owner shall pay the Contractor in current funds for the performance of the Work, subject to additions and deductions by Change Order as provided in the Contract Documents, the Contract Sum of

The Contract Sum is determined as follows:
(State here the base bid or other lump sum amount, accepted alternates and unit prices, as applicable.)

ARTICLE 5
PROGRESS PAYMENTS

Based upon Applications for Payment submitted to the Construction Manager by the Contractor and Project Certificates for Payment issued by the Architect, the Owner shall make progress payments on account of the Contract Sum to the Contractor as provided in the Contract Documents for the period ending the   day of each month as follows:

Not later than   days following the end of the period covered by the Application for Payment,   percent (%) of the portion of the Contract Sum properly allocable to labor, materials and equipment incorporated in the Work and   percent (%) of the portion of the Contract Sum properly allocable to materials and equipment suitably stored at the site or at some other location agreed upon in writing, for the period covered by the Application for Payment, less the aggregate of previous payments made by the Owner; and upon Substantial Completion of the Work, a sum sufficient to increase the total payments to   percent (%) of the Contract Sum, less such amounts as the Architect shall determine for all incomplete Work and unsettled claims as provided in the Contract Documents.

(If not covered elsewhere in the Contract Documents, here insert any provision for limiting or reducing the amount retained after the Work reaches a certain stage of completion.)

Payments due and unpaid under the Contract Documents shall bear interest from the date payment is due at the rate entered below, or in the absence thereof, at the legal rate prevailing at the place of the Project.
(Here insert any rate of interest agreed upon.)

(Usury laws and requirements under the Federal Truth in Lending Act, similar state and local consumer credit laws and other regulations at the Owner's and Contractor's principal places of business, the location of the Project and elsewhere may affect the validity of this provision. Specific legal advice should be obtained with respect to deletion, modification or other requirements such as written disclosures or waivers.)

ARTICLE 6

FINAL PAYMENT

Final payment, constituting the entire unpaid balance of the Contract Sum, shall be paid by the Owner to the Contractor when the Work has been completed, the Contract fully performed, and a final Certificate for Payment has been issued by the Architect.

ARTICLE 7

MISCELLANEOUS PROVISIONS

7.1   Terms used in this Agreement which are defined in the Conditions of the Contract shall have the meanings designated in those Conditions.

7.2   The Contract Documents, which constitute the entire agreement between the Owner and the Contractor, are listed in Article 1 and, except for Modifications issued after execution of this Agreement, are enumerated as follows:

(List below the Agreement, the Conditions of the Contract (General, Supplementary, and other Conditions), the Drawings, the Specifications, and any Addenda and accepted alternates, showing page or sheet numbers in all cases and dates where applicable.)

This Agreement entered into as of the day and year first written above.

OWNER   CONTRACTOR

———————————————   ———————————————

———————————————   ———————————————

———————————————   ———————————————

7.3 Temporary facilities and services:
(Here insert temporary facilities and services which are different from or in addition to those included elsewhere in the Contract Documents.)

7.4 Working Conditions:
(Here list any special conditions affecting the Contract.)

This Agreement entered into as of the day and year first written above.

OWNER

CONTRACTOR

_____

_____

_____

_____

_____

_____

THE AMERICAN INSTITUTE OF ARCHITECTS

AIA Document A201

General Conditions of the Contract for Construction

THIS DOCUMENT HAS IMPORTANT LEGAL CONSEQUENCES; CONSULTATION WITH AN ATTORNEY IS ENCOURAGED WITH RESPECT TO ITS MODIFICATION

1976 EDITION
TABLE OF ARTICLES

This document has been approved and endorsed by The Associated General Contractors of America.

INDEX

GENERAL CONDITIONS OF THE CONTRACT FOR CONSTRUCTION

ARTICLE 1

CONTRACT DOCUMENTS

1.1 DEFINITIONS

1.1.1 THE CONTRACT DOCUMENTS

The Contract Documents consist of the Owner-Contractor Agreement, the Conditions of the Contract (General, Supplementary and other Conditions), the Drawings, the Specifications, and all Addenda issued prior to and all Modifications issued after execution of the Contract. A Modification is (1) a written amendment to the Contract signed by both parties, (2) a Change Order, (3) a written interpretation issued by the Architect pursuant to Subparagraph 2.2.8, or (4) a written order for a minor change in the Work issued by the Architect pursuant to Paragraph 12.4. The Contract Documents do not include Bidding Documents such as the Advertisement or Invitation to Bid, the Instructions to Bidders, sample forms, the Contractor's Bid or portions of Addenda relating to any of these, or any other documents, unless specifically enumerated in the Owner-Contractor Agreement.

1.1.2 THE CONTRACT

The Contract Documents form the Contract for Construction. This Contract represents the entire and integrated agreement between the parties hereto and supersedes all prior negotiations, representations, or agreements, either written or oral. The Contract may be amended or modified only by a Modification as defined in Subparagraph 1.1.1. The Contract Documents shall not be construed to create any contractual relationship of any kind between the Architect and the Contractor, but the Architect shall be entitled to performance of obligations intended for his benefit, and to enforcement thereof. Nothing contained in the Contract Documents shall create any contractual relationship between the Owner or the Architect and any Subcontractor or Sub-subcontractor.

1.1.3 THE WORK

The Work comprises the completed construction required by the Contract Documents and includes all labor necessary to produce such construction, and all materials and equipment incorporated or to be incorporated in such construction.

1.1.4 THE PROJECT

The Project is the total construction of which the Work performed under the Contract Documents may be the whole or a part.

1.2 EXECUTION, CORRELATION AND INTENT

1.2.1 The Contract Documents shall be signed in not less than triplicate by the Owner and Contractor. If either the Owner or the Contractor or both do not sign the Conditions of the Contract, Drawings, Specifications, or any of the other Contract Documents, the Architect shall identify such Documents.

1.2.2 By executing the Contract, the Contractor represents that he has visited the site, familiarized himself with the local conditions under which the Work is to be performed, and correlated his observations with the requirements of the Contract Documents.

1.2.3 The intent of the Contract Documents is to include all items necessary for the proper execution and completion of the Work. The Contract Documents are complementary, and what is required by any one shall be as binding as if required by all. Work not covered in the Contract Documents will not be required unless it is consistent therewith and is reasonably inferable therefrom as being necessary to produce the intended results. Words and abbreviations which have well-known technical or trade meanings are used in the Contract Documents in accordance with such recognized meanings.

1.2.4 The organization of the Specifications into divisions, sections and articles, and the arrangement of Drawings shall not control the Contractor in dividing the Work among Subcontractors or in establishing the extent of Work to be performed by any trade.

1.3 OWNERSHIP AND USE OF DOCUMENTS

1.3.1 All Drawings, Specifications and copies thereof furnished by the Architect are and shall remain his property. They are to be used only with respect to this Project and are not to be used on any other project. With the exception of one contract set for each party to the Contract, such documents are to be returned or suitably accounted for to the Architect on request at the completion of the Work. Submission or distribution to meet official regulatory requirements or for other purposes in connection with the Project is not to be construed as publication in derogation of the Architect's common law copyright or other reserved rights.

ARTICLE 2

ARCHITECT

2.1 DEFINITION

2.1.1 The Architect is the person lawfully licensed to practice architecture, or an entity lawfully practicing architecture identified as such in the Owner-Contractor Agreement, and is referred to throughout the Contract Documents as if singular in number and masculine in gender. The term Architect means the Architect or his authorized representative.

2.2 ADMINISTRATION OF THE CONTRACT

2.2.1 The Architect will provide administration of the Contract as hereinafter described.

2.2.2 The Architect will be the Owner's representative during construction and until final payment is due. The Architect will advise and consult with the Owner. The Owner's instructions to the Contractor shall be forwarded through the Architect. The Architect will have authority to act on behalf of the Owner only to the extent provided in the Contract Documents, unless otherwise modified by written instrument in accordance with Subparagraph 2.2.18.

2.2.3 The Architect will visit the site at intervals appropriate to the stage of construction to familiarize himself generally with the progress and quality of the Work and to determine in general if the Work is proceeding in accordance with the Contract Documents. However, the Architect will not be required to make exhaustive or continuous on-site inspections to check the quality or quantity of the Work. On the basis of his on-site observations as an architect, he will keep the Owner informed of the progress of the Work, and will endeavor to guard the Owner against defects and deficiencies in the Work of the Contractor.

2.2.4 The Architect will not be responsible for and will not have control or charge of construction means, methods, techniques, sequences or procedures, or for safety precautions and programs in connection with the Work, and he will not be responsible for the Contractor's failure to carry out the Work in accordance with the Contract Documents. The Architect will not be responsible for or have control or charge over the acts or omissions of the Contractor, Subcontractors, or any of their agents or employees, or any other persons performing any of the Work.

2.2.5 The Architect shall at all times have access to the Work wherever it is in preparation and progress. The Contractor shall provide facilities for such access so the Architect may perform his functions under the Contract Documents.

2.2.6 Based on the Architect's observations and an evaluation of the Contractor's Applications for Payment, the Architect will determine the amounts owing to the Contractor and will issue Certificates for Payment in such amounts, as provided in Paragraph 9.4.

2.2.7 The Architect will be the interpreter of the requirements of the Contract Documents and the judge of the performance thereunder by both the Owner and Contractor.

2.2.8 The Architect will render interpretations necessary for the proper execution or progress of the Work, with reasonable promptness and in accordance with any time limit agreed upon. Either party to the Contract may make written request to the Architect for such interpretations.

2.2.9 Claims, disputes and other matters in question between the Contractor and the Owner relating to the execution or progress of the Work or the interpretation of the Contract Documents shall be referred initially to the Architect for decision which he will render in writing within a reasonable time.

2.2.10 All interpretations and decisions of the Architect shall be consistent with the intent of and reasonably inferable from the Contract Documents and will be in writing or in the form of drawings. In his capacity as interpreter and judge, he will endeavor to secure faithful performance by both the Owner and the Contractor, will not

show partiality to either, and will not be liable for the result of any interpretation or decision rendered in good faith in such capacity.

2.2.11 The Architect's decisions in matters relating to artistic effect will be final if consistent with the intent of the Contract Documents.

2.2.12 Any claim, dispute or other matter in question between the Contractor and the Owner referred to the Architect, except those relating to artistic effect as provided in Subparagraph 2.2.11 and except those which have been waived by the making or acceptance of final payment as provided in Subparagraphs 9.9.4 and 9.9.5, shall be subject to arbitration upon the written demand of either party. However, no demand for arbitration of any such claim, dispute or other matter may be made until the earlier of (1) the date on which the Architect has rendered a written decision, or (2) the tenth day after the parties have presented their evidence to the Architect or have been given a reasonable opportunity to do so, if the Architect has not rendered his written decision by that date. When such a written decision of the Architect states (1) that the decision is final but subject to appeal, and (2) that any demand for arbitration of a claim, dispute or other matter covered by such decision must be made within thirty days after the date on which the party making the demand receives the written decision, failure to demand arbitration within said thirty days' period will result in the Architect's decision becoming final and binding upon the Owner and the Contractor. If the Architect renders a decision after arbitration proceedings have been initiated, such decision may be entered as evidence but will not supersede any arbitration proceedings unless the decision is acceptable to all parties concerned.

2.2.13 The Architect will have authority to reject Work which does not conform to the Contract Documents. Whenever, in his opinion, he considers it necessary or advisable for the implementation of the intent of the Contract Documents, he will have authority to require special inspection or testing of the Work in accordance with Subparagraph 7.7.2 whether or not such Work be then fabricated, installed or completed. However, neither the Architect's authority to act under this Subparagraph 2.2.13, nor any decision made by him in good faith either to exercise or not to exercise such authority, shall give rise to any duty or responsibility of the Architect to the Contractor, any Subcontractor, any of their agents or employees, or any other person performing any of the Work.

2.2.14 The Architect will review and approve or take other appropriate action upon Contractor's submittals such as Shop Drawings, Product Data and Samples, but only for conformance with the design concept of the Work and with the information given in the Contract Documents. Such action shall be taken with reasonable promptness so as to cause no delay. The Architect's approval of a specific item shall not indicate approval of an assembly of which the item is a component.

2.2.15 The Architect will prepare Change Orders in accordance with Article 12, and will have authority to order minor changes in the Work as provided in Subparagraph 12.4.1.

2.2.16 The Architect will conduct inspections to determine the dates of Substantial Completion and final completion, will receive and forward to the Owner for the Owner's review written warranties and related documents required by the Contract and assembled by the Contractor, and will issue a final Certificate for Payment upon compliance with the requirements of Paragraph 9.9.

2.2.17 If the Owner and Architect agree, the Architect will provide one or more Project Representatives to assist the Architect in carrying out his responsibilities at the site. The duties, responsibilities and limitations of authority of any such Project Representative shall be as set forth in an exhibit to be incorporated in the Contract Documents.

2.2.18 The duties, responsibilities and limitations of authority of the Architect as the Owner's representative during construction as set forth in the Contract Documents will not be modified or extended without written consent of the Owner, the Contractor and the Architect.

2.2.19 In case of the termination of the employment of the Architect, the Owner shall appoint an architect against whom the Contractor makes no reasonable objection whose status under the Contract Documents shall be that of the former architect. Any dispute in connection with such appointment shall be subject to arbitration.

ARTICLE 3

OWNER

3.1 DEFINITION

3.1.1 The Owner is the person or entity identified as such in the Owner-Contractor Agreement and is referred to throughout the Contract Documents as if singular in number and masculine in gender. The term Owner means the Owner or his authorized representative.

3.2 INFORMATION AND SERVICES REQUIRED OF THE OWNER

3.2.1 The Owner shall, at the request of the Contractor, at the time of execution of the Owner-Contractor Agreement, furnish to the Contractor reasonable evidence that he has made financial arrangements to fulfill his obligations under the Contract. Unless such reasonable evidence is furnished, the Contractor is not required to execute the Owner-Contractor Agreement or to commence the Work.

3.2.2 The Owner shall furnish all surveys describing the physical characteristics, legal limitations and utility locations for the site of the Project, and a legal description of the site.

3.2.3 Except as provided in Subparagraph 4.7.1, the Owner shall secure and pay for necessary approvals, easements, assessments and charges required for the construction, use or occupancy of permanent structures or for permanent changes in existing facilities.

3.2.4 Information or services under the Owner's control shall be furnished by the Owner with reasonable promptness to avoid delay in the orderly progress of the Work.

3.2.5 Unless otherwise provided in the Contract Documents, the Contractor will be furnished, free of charge, all copies of Drawings and Specifications reasonably necessary for the execution of the Work.

3.2.6 The Owner shall forward all instructions to the Contractor through the Architect.

3.2.7 The foregoing are in addition to other duties and responsibilities of the Owner enumerated herein and especially those in respect to Work by Owner or by Separate Contractors, Payments and Completion, and Insurance in Articles 6, 9 and 11 respectively.

3.3 OWNER'S RIGHT TO STOP THE WORK

3.3.1 If the Contractor fails to correct defective Work as required by Paragraph 13.2 or persistently fails to carry out the Work in accordance with the Contract Documents, the Owner, by a written order signed personally or by an agent specifically so empowered by the Owner in writing, may order the Contractor to stop the Work, or any portion thereof, until the cause for such order has been eliminated; however, this right of the Owner to stop the Work shall not give rise to any duty on the part of the Owner to exercise this right for the benefit of the Contractor or any other person or entity, except to the extent required by Subparagraph 6.1.3.

3.4 OWNER'S RIGHT TO CARRY OUT THE WORK

3.4.1 If the Contractor defaults or neglects to carry out the Work in accordance with the Contract Documents and fails within seven days after receipt of written notice from the Owner to commence and continue correction of such default or neglect with diligence and promptness, the Owner may, after seven days following receipt by the Contractor of an additional written notice and without prejudice to any other remedy he may have, make good such deficiencies. In such case an appropriate Change Order shall be issued deducting from the payments then or thereafter due the Contractor the cost of correcting such deficiencies, including compensation for the Architect's additional services made necessary by such default, neglect or failure. Such action by the Owner and the amount charged to the Contractor are both subject to the prior approval of the Architect. If the payments then or thereafter due the Contractor are not sufficient to cover such amount, the Contractor shall pay the difference to the Owner.

ARTICLE 4

CONTRACTOR

4.1 DEFINITION

4.1.1 The Contractor is the person or entity identified as such in the Owner-Contractor Agreement and is referred to throughout the Contract Documents as if singular in number and masculine in gender. The term Contractor means the Contractor or his authorized representative.

4.2 REVIEW OF CONTRACT DOCUMENTS

4.2.1 The Contractor shall carefully study and compare the Contract Documents and shall at once report to the Architect any error, inconsistency or omission he may discover. The Contractor shall not be liable to the Owner or the Architect for any damage resulting from any such errors, inconsistencies or omissions in the Contract Documents. The Contractor shall perform no portion of the Work at any time without Contract Documents or, where required, approved Shop Drawings, Product Data or Samples for such portion of the Work.

4.3 SUPERVISION AND CONSTRUCTION PROCEDURES

4.3.1 The Contractor shall supervise and direct the Work, using his best skill and attention. He shall be solely responsible for all construction means, methods, techniques, sequences and procedures and for coordinating all portions of the Work under the Contract.

4.3.2 The Contractor shall be responsible to the Owner for the acts and omissions of his employees, Subcontractors and their agents and employees, and other persons performing any of the Work under a contract with the Contractor.

4.3.3 The Contractor shall not be relieved from his obligations to perform the Work in accordance with the Contract Documents either by the activities or duties of the Architect in his administration of the Contract, or by inspections, tests or approvals required or performed under Paragraph 7.7 by persons other than the Contractor.

4.4 LABOR AND MATERIALS

4.4.1 Unless otherwise provided in the Contract Documents, the Contractor shall provide and pay for all labor, materials, equipment, tools, construction equipment and machinery, water, heat, utilities, transportation, and other facilities and services necessary for the proper execution and completion of the Work, whether temporary or permanent and whether or not incorporated or to be incorporated in the Work.

4.4.2 The Contractor shall at all times enforce strict discipline and good order among his employees and shall not employ on the Work any unfit person or anyone not skilled in the task assigned to him.

4.5 WARRANTY

4.5.1 The Contractor warrants to the Owner and the Architect that all materials and equipment furnished under this Contract will be new unless otherwise specified, and that all Work will be of good quality, free from faults and defects and in conformance with the Contract Documents. All Work not conforming to these requirements, including substitutions not properly approved and authorized, may be considered defective. If required by the Architect, the Contractor shall furnish satisfactory evidence as to the kind and quality of materials and equipment. This warranty is not limited by the provisions of Paragraph 13.2.

4.6 TAXES

4.6.1 The Contractor shall pay all sales, consumer, use and other similar taxes for the Work or portions thereof provided by the Contractor which are legally enacted at the time bids are received, whether or not yet effective.

4.7 PERMITS, FEES AND NOTICES

4.7.1 Unless otherwise provided in the Contract Documents, the Contractor shall secure and pay for the building permit and for all other permits and governmental fees, licenses and inspections necessary for the proper execution and completion of the Work which are customarily secured after execution of the Contract and which are legally required at the time the bids are received.

4.7.2 The Contractor shall give all notices and comply with all laws, ordinances, rules, regulations and lawful orders of any public authority bearing on the performance of the Work.

4.7.3 It is not the responsibility of the Contractor to make certain that the Contract Documents are in accordance with applicable laws, statutes, building codes and regulations. If the Contractor observes that any of the Contract Documents are at variance therewith in any respect, he shall promptly notify the Architect in writing, and any necessary changes shall be accomplished by appropriate Modification.

4.7.4 If the Contractor performs any Work knowing it to be contrary to such laws, ordinances, rules and regulations, and without such notice to the Architect, he shall assume full responsibility therefor and shall bear all costs attributable thereto.

4.8 ALLOWANCES

4.8.1 The Contractor shall include in the Contract Sum all allowances stated in the Contract Documents. Items covered by these allowances shall be supplied for such amounts and by such persons as the Owner may direct, but the Contractor will not be required to employ persons against whom he makes a reasonable objection.

4.8.2 Unless otherwise provided in the Contract Documents:

.1 these allowances shall cover the cost to the Contractor, less any applicable trade discount, of the materials and equipment required by the allowance delivered at the site, and all applicable taxes;

.2 the Contractor's costs for unloading and handling on the site, labor, installation costs, overhead, profit and other expenses contemplated for the original allowance shall be included in the Contract Sum and not in the allowance;

.3 whenever the cost is more than or less than the allowance, the Contract Sum shall be adjusted accordingly by Change Order, the amount of which will recognize changes, if any, in handling costs on the site, labor, installation costs, overhead, profit and other expenses.

4.9 SUPERINTENDENT

4.9.1 The Contractor shall employ a competent superintendent and necessary assistants who shall be in attendance at the Project site during the progress of the Work. The superintendent shall represent the Contractor and all communications given to the superintendent shall be as binding as if given to the Contractor. Important communications shall be confirmed in writing. Other communications shall be so confirmed on written request in each case.

4.10 PROGRESS SCHEDULE

4.10.1 The Contractor, immediately after being awarded the Contract, shall prepare and submit for the Owner's and Architect's information an estimated progress schedule for the Work. The progress schedule shall be related to the entire Project to the extent required by the Contract Documents, and shall provide for expeditious and practicable execution of the Work.

4.11 DOCUMENTS AND SAMPLES AT THE SITE

4.11.1 The Contractor shall maintain at the site for the Owner one record copy of all Drawings, Specifications, Addenda, Change Orders and other Modifications, in good order and marked currently to record all changes made during construction, and approved Shop Drawings, Product Data and Samples. These shall be available to the Architect and shall be delivered to him for the Owner upon completion of the Work.

4.12 SHOP DRAWINGS, PRODUCT DATA AND SAMPLES

4.12.1 Shop Drawings are drawings, diagrams, schedules and other data specially prepared for the Work by the Contractor or any Subcontractor, manufacturer, supplier or distributor to illustrate some portion of the Work.

4.12.2 Product Data are illustrations, standard schedules, performance charts, instructions, brochures, diagrams and other information furnished by the Contractor to illustrate a material, product or system for some portion of the Work.

4.12.3 Samples are physical examples which illustrate materials, equipment or workmanship and establish standards by which the Work will be judged.

4.12.4 The Contractor shall review, approve and submit, with reasonable promptness and in such sequence as to cause no delay in the Work or in the work of the Owner or any separate contractor, all Shop Drawings, Product Data and Samples required by the Contract Documents.

4.12.5 By approving and submitting Shop Drawings, Product Data and Samples, the Contractor represents that he has determined and verified all materials, field measurements, and field construction criteria related thereto, or will do so, and that he has checked and coordinated the information contained within such submittals with the requirements of the Work and of the Contract Documents.

4.12.6 The Contractor shall not be relieved of responsibility for any deviation from the requirements of the Contract Documents by the Architect's approval of Shop Drawings, Product Data or Samples under Subparagraph 2.2.14 unless the Contractor has specifically informed the Architect in writing of such deviation at the time of submission and the Architect has given written approval to the specific deviation. The Contractor shall not be relieved from responsibility for errors or omissions in the Shop Drawings, Product Data or Samples by the Architect's approval thereof.

4.12.7 The Contractor shall direct specific attention, in writing or on resubmitted Shop Drawings, Product Data or Samples, to revisions other than those requested by the Architect on previous submittals.

4.12.8 No portion of the Work requiring submission of a Shop Drawing, Product Data or Sample shall be commenced until the submittal has been approved by the Architect as provided in Subparagraph 2.2.14. All such

portions of the Work shall be in accordance with approved submittals.

4.13 USE OF SITE

4.13.1 The Contractor shall confine operations at the site to areas permitted by law, ordinances, permits and the Contract Documents and shall not unreasonably encumber the site with any materials or equipment.

4.14 CUTTING AND PATCHING OF WORK

4.14.1 The Contractor shall be responsible for all cutting, fitting or patching that may be required to complete the Work or to make its several parts fit together properly.

4.14.2 The Contractor shall not damage or endanger any portion of the Work or the work of the Owner or any separate contractors by cutting, patching or otherwise altering any work, or by excavation. The Contractor shall not cut or otherwise alter the work of the Owner or any separate contractor except with the written consent of the Owner and of such separate contractor. The Contractor shall not unreasonably withhold from the Owner or any separate contractor his consent to cutting or otherwise altering the Work.

4.15 CLEANING UP

4.15.1 The Contractor at all times shall keep the premises free from accumulation of waste materials or rubbish caused by his operations. At the completion of the Work he shall remove all his waste materials and rubbish from and about the Project as well as all his tools, construction equipment, machinery and surplus materials.

4.15.2 If the Contractor fails to clean up at the completion of the Work, the Owner may do so as provided in Paragraph 3.4 and the cost thereof shall be charged to the Contractor.

4.16 COMMUNICATIONS

4.16.1 The Contractor shall forward all communications to the Owner through the Architect.

4.17 ROYALTIES AND PATENTS

4.17.1 The Contractor shall pay all royalties and license fees. He shall defend all suits or claims for infringement of any patent rights and shall save the Owner harmless from loss on account thereof, except that the Owner shall be responsible for all such loss when a particular design, process or the product of a particular manufacturer or manufacturers is specified, but if the Contractor has reason to believe that the design, process or product specified is an infringement of a patent, he shall be responsible for such loss unless he promptly gives such information to the Architect.

4.18 INDEMNIFICATION

4.18.1 To the fullest extent permitted by law, the Contractor shall indemnify and hold harmless the Owner and the Architect and their agents and employees from and against all claims, damages, losses and expenses, including but not limited to attorneys' fees, arising out of or resulting from the performance of the Work, provided that any such claim, damage, loss or expense (1) is attributable to bodily injury, sickness, disease or death, or to injury to or destruction of tangible property (other than the Work itself) including the loss of use resulting therefrom, and (2) is caused in whole or in part by any negligent act or omission of the Contractor, any Subcontractor, anyone directly or indirectly employed by any of them or anyone for whose acts any of them may be liable, regardless of whether or not it is caused in part by a party indemnified hereunder. Such obligation shall not be construed to negate, abridge, or otherwise reduce any other right or obligation of indemnity which would otherwise exist as to any party or person described in this Paragraph 4.18.

4.18.2 In any and all claims against the Owner or the Architect or any of their agents or employees by any employee of the Contractor, any Subcontractor, anyone directly or indirectly employed by any of them or anyone for whose acts any of them may be liable, the indemnification obligation under this Paragraph 4.18 shall not be limited in any way by any limitation on the amount or type of damages, compensation or benefits payable by or for the Contractor or any Subcontractor under workers' or workmen's compensation acts, disability benefit acts or other employee benefit acts.

4.18.3 The obligations of the Contractor under this Paragraph 4.18 shall not extend to the liability of the Architect, his agents or employees, arising out of (1) the preparation or approval of maps, drawings, opinions, reports, surveys, change orders, designs or specifications, or (2) the giving of or the failure to give directions or instructions by the Architect, his agents or employees provided such giving or failure to give is the primary cause of the injury or damage.

ARTICLE 5

SUBCONTRACTORS

5.1 DEFINITION

5.1.1 A Subcontractor is a person or entity who has a direct contract with the Contractor to perform any of the Work at the site. The term Subcontractor is referred to throughout the Contract Documents as if singular in number and masculine in gender and means a Subcontractor or his authorized representative. The term Subcontractor does not include any separate contractor or his subcontractors.

5.1.2 A Sub-subcontractor is a person or entity who has a direct or indirect contract with a Subcontractor to perform any of the Work at the site. The term Sub-subcontractor is referred to throughout the Contract Documents as if singular in number and masculine in gender and means a Sub-subcontractor or an authorized representative thereof.

5.2 AWARD OF SUBCONTRACTS AND OTHER CONTRACTS FOR PORTIONS OF THE WORK

5.2.1 Unless otherwise required by the Contract Documents or the Bidding Documents, the Contractor, as soon as practicable after the award of the Contract, shall furnish to the Owner and the Architect in writing the names of the persons or entities (including those who are to furnish materials or equipment fabricated to a special design) proposed for each of the principal portions of the Work. The Architect will promptly reply to the Contractor in writing stating whether or not the Owner or the Architect, after due investigation, has reasonable objection to any

such proposed person or entity. Failure of the Owner or Architect to reply promptly shall constitute notice of no reasonable objection.

5.2.2 The Contractor shall not contract with any such proposed person or entity to whom the Owner or the Architect has made reasonable objection under the provisions of Subparagraph 5.2.1. The Contractor shall not be required to contract with anyone to whom he has a reasonable objection.

5.2.3 If the Owner or the Architect has reasonable objection to any such proposed person or entity, the Contractor shall submit a substitute to whom the Owner or the Architect has no reasonable objection, and the Contract Sum shall be increased or decreased by the difference in cost occasioned by such substitution and an appropriate Change Order shall be issued; however, no increase in the Contract Sum shall be allowed for any such substitution unless the Contractor has acted promptly and responsively in submitting names as required by Subparagraph 5.2.1.

5.2.4 The Contractor shall make no substitution for any Subcontractor, person or entity previously selected if the Owner or Architect makes reasonable objection to such substitution.

5.3 SUBCONTRACTUAL RELATIONS

5.3.1 By an appropriate agreement, written where legally required for validity, the Contractor shall require each Subcontractor, to the extent of the Work to be performed by the Subcontractor, to be bound to the Contractor by the terms of the Contract Documents, and to assume toward the Contractor all the obligations and responsibilities which the Contractor, by these Documents, assumes toward the Owner and the Architect. Said agreement shall preserve and protect the rights of the Owner and the Architect under the Contract Documents with respect to the Work to be performed by the Subcontractor so that the subcontracting thereof will not prejudice such rights, and shall allow to the Subcontractor, unless specifically provided otherwise in the Contractor-Subcontractor agreement, the benefit of all rights, remedies and redress against the Contractor that the Contractor, by these Documents, has against the Owner. Where appropriate, the Contractor shall require each Subcontractor to enter into similar agreements with his Sub-subcontractors. The Contractor shall make available to each proposed Subcontractor, prior to the execution of the Subcontract, copies of the Contract Documents to which the Subcontractor will be bound by this Paragraph 5.3, and identify to the Subcontractor any terms and conditions of the proposed Subcontract which may be at variance with the Contract Documents. Each Subcontractor shall similarly make copies of such Documents available to his Sub-subcontractors.

ARTICLE 6

WORK BY OWNER OR BY SEPARATE CONTRACTORS

6.1 OWNER'S RIGHT TO PERFORM WORK AND TO AWARD SEPARATE CONTRACTS

6.1.1 The Owner reserves the right to perform work related to the Project with his own forces, and to award separate contracts in connection with other portions of the Project or other work on the site under these or similar Conditions of the Contract. If the Contractor claims that delay or additional cost is involved because of such action by the Owner, he shall make such claim as provided elsewhere in the Contract Documents.

6.1.2 When separate contracts are awarded for different portions of the Project or other work on the site, the term Contractor in the Contract Documents in each case shall mean the Contractor who executes each separate Owner-Contractor Agreement.

6.1.3 The Owner will provide for the coordination of the work of his own forces and of each separate contractor with the Work of the Contractor, who shall cooperate therewith as provided in Paragraph 6.2.

6.2   MUTUAL RESPONSIBILITY

6.2.1 The Contractor shall afford the Owner and separate contractors reasonable opportunity for the introduction and storage of their materials and equipment and the execution of their work, and shall connect and coordinate his Work with theirs as required by the Contract Documents.

6.2.2 If any part of the Contractor's Work depends for proper execution or results upon the work of the Owner or any separate contractor, the Contractor shall, prior to proceeding with the Work, promptly report to the Architect any apparent discrepancies or defects in such other work that render it unsuitable for such proper execution and results. Failure of the Contractor so to report shall constitute an acceptance of the Owner's or separate contractors' work as fit and proper to receive his Work, except as to defects which may subsequently become apparent in such work by others.

6.2.3 Any costs caused by defective or ill-timed work shall be borne by the party responsible therefor.

6.2.4 Should the Contractor wrongfully cause damage to the work or property of the Owner, or to other work on the site, the Contractor shall promptly remedy such damage as provided in Subparagraph 10.2.5.

6.2.5 Should the Contractor wrongfully cause damage to the work or property of any separate contractor, the Contractor shall upon due notice promptly attempt to settle with such other contractor by agreement, or otherwise to resolve the dispute. If such separate contractor sues or initiates an arbitration proceeding against the Owner on account of any damage alleged to have been caused by the Contractor, the Owner shall notify the Contractor who shall defend such proceedings at the Owner's expense, and if any judgment or award against the Owner arises therefrom the Contractor shall pay or satisfy it and shall reimburse the Owner for all attorneys' fees and court or arbitration costs which the Owner has incurred.

6.3   OWNER'S RIGHT TO CLEAN UP

6.3.1 If a dispute arises between the Contractor and separate contractors as to their responsibility for cleaning up as required by Paragraph 4.15, the Owner may clean up

and charge the cost thereof to the contractors responsible therefor as the Architect shall determine to be just.

ARTICLE 7

MISCELLANEOUS PROVISIONS

7.1   GOVERNING LAW

7.1.1 The Contract shall be governed by the law of the place where the Project is located.

7.2   SUCCESSORS AND ASSIGNS

7.2.1 The Owner and the Contractor each binds himself, his partners, successors, assigns and legal representatives to the other party hereto and to the partners, successors, assigns and legal representatives of such other party in respect to all covenants, agreements and obligations contained in the Contract Documents. Neither party to the Contract shall assign the Contract or sublet it as a whole without the written consent of the other, nor shall the Contractor assign any moneys due or to become due to him hereunder, without the previous written consent of the Owner.

7.3   WRITTEN NOTICE

7.3.1 Written notice shall be deemed to have been duly served if delivered in person to the individual or member of the firm or entity or to an officer of the corporation for whom it was intended, or if delivered at or sent by registered or certified mail to the last business address known to him who gives the notice.

7.4   CLAIMS FOR DAMAGES

7.4.1 Should either party to the Contract suffer injury or damage to person or property because of any act or omission of the other party or of any of his employees, agents or others for whose acts he is legally liable, claim shall be made in writing to such other party within a reasonable time after the first observance of such injury or damage.

**7.5   PERFORMANCE BOND AND LABOR AND
MATERIAL PAYMENT BOND**

7.5.1 The Owner shall have the right to require the Contractor to furnish bonds covering the faithful performance of the Contract and the payment of all obligations arising thereunder if and as required in the Bidding Documents or in the Contract Documents.

7.6   RIGHTS AND REMEDIES

7.6.1 The duties and obligations imposed by the Contract Documents and the rights and remedies available thereunder shall be in addition to and not a limitation of any duties, obligations, rights and remedies otherwise imposed or available by law.

7.6.2 No action or failure to act by the Owner, Architect or Contractor shall constitute a waiver of any right or duty afforded any of them under the Contract, nor shall any such action or failure to act constitute an approval of or acquiescence in any breach thereunder, except as may be specifically agreed in writing.

7.7 TESTS

7.7.1 If the Contract Documents, laws, ordinances, rules, regulations or orders of any public authority having jurisdiction require any portion of the Work to be inspected, tested or approved, the Contractor shall give the Architect timely notice of its readiness so the Architect may observe such inspection, testing or approval. The Contractor shall bear all costs of such inspections, tests or approvals conducted by public authorities. Unless otherwise provided, the Owner shall bear all costs of other inspections, tests or approvals.

7.7.2 If the Architect determines that any Work requires special inspection, testing, or approval which Subparagraph 7.7.1 does not include, he will, upon written authorization from the Owner, instruct the Contractor to order such special inspection, testing or approval, and the Contractor shall give notice as provided in Subparagraph 7.7.1. If such special inspection or testing reveals a failure of the Work to comply with the requirements of the Contract Documents, the Contractor shall bear all costs thereof, including compensation for the Architect's additional services made necessary by such failure; otherwise the Owner shall bear such costs, and an appropriate Change Order shall be issued.

7.7.3 Required certificates of inspection, testing or approval shall be secured by the Contractor and promptly delivered by him to the Architect.

7.7.4 If the Architect is to observe the inspections, tests or approvals required by the Contract Documents, he will do so promptly and, where practicable, at the source of supply.

7.8 INTEREST

7.8.1 Payments due and unpaid under the Contract Documents shall bear interest from the date payment is due at such rate as the parties may agree upon in writing or, in the absence thereof, at the legal rate prevailing at the place of the Project.

7.9 ARBITRATION

7.9.1 All claims, disputes and other matters in question between the Contractor and the Owner arising out of, or relating to, the Contract Documents or the breach thereof, except as provided in Subparagraph 2.2.11 with respect to the Architect's decisions on matters relating to artistic effect, and except for claims which have been waived by the making or acceptance of final payment as provided by Subparagraphs 9.9.4 and 9.9.5, shall be decided by arbitration in accordance with the Construction Industry Arbitration Rules of the American Arbitration Association then obtaining unless the parties mutually agree otherwise. No arbitration arising out of or relating to the Contract Documents shall include, by consolidation, joinder or in any other manner, the Architect, his employees or consultants except by written consent containing a specific reference to the Owner-Contractor Agreement and signed by the Architect, the Owner, the Contractor and any other person sought to be joined. No arbitration shall include by consolidation, joinder or in any other manner, parties other than the Owner, the Contractor and any other persons substantially involved in a common question of fact or law, whose presence is

required if complete relief is to be accorded in the arbitration. No person other than the Owner or Contractor shall be included as an original third party or additional third party to an arbitration whose interest or responsibility is insubstantial. Any consent to arbitration involving an additional person or persons shall not constitute consent to arbitration of any dispute not described therein or with any person not named or described therein. The foregoing agreement to arbitrate and any other agreement to arbitrate with an additional person or persons duly consented to by the parties to the Owner-Contractor Agreement shall be specifically enforceable under the prevailing arbitration law. The award rendered by the arbitrators shall be final, and judgment may be entered upon it in accordance with applicable law in any court having jurisdiction thereof.

7.9.2 Notice of the demand for arbitration shall be filed in writing with the other party to the Owner-Contractor Agreement and with the American Arbitration Association, and a copy shall be filed with the Architect. The demand for arbitration shall be made within the time limits specified in Subparagraph 2.2.12 where applicable, and in all other cases within a reasonable time after the claim, dispute or other matter in question has arisen, and in no event shall it be made after the date when institution of legal or equitable proceedings based on such claim, dispute or other matter in question would be barred by the applicable statute of limitations.

7.9.3 Unless otherwise agreed in writing, the Contractor shall carry on the Work and maintain its progress during any arbitration proceedings, and the Owner shall continue to make payments to the Contractor in accordance with the Contract Documents.

ARTICLE 8

TIME

8.1 DEFINITIONS

8.1.1 Unless otherwise provided, the Contract Time is the period of time allotted in the Contract Documents for Substantial Completion of the Work as defined in Subparagraph 8.1.3, including authorized adjustments thereto.

8.1.2 The date of commencement of the Work is the date established in a notice to proceed. If there is no notice to proceed, it shall be the date of the Owner-Contractor Agreement or such other date as may be established therein.

8.1.3 The Date of Substantial Completion of the Work or designated portion thereof is the Date certified by the Architect when construction is sufficiently complete, in accordance with the Contract Documents, so the Owner can occupy or utilize the Work or designated portion thereof for the use for which it is intended.

8.1.4 The term day as used in the Contract Documents shall mean calendar day unless otherwise specifically designated.

8.2 PROGRESS AND COMPLETION

8.2.1 All time limits stated in the Contract Documents are of the essence of the Contract.

8.2.2 The Contractor shall begin the Work on the date of commencement as defined in Subparagraph 8.1.2. He shall carry the Work forward expeditiously with adequate forces and shall achieve Substantial Completion within the Contract Time.

8.3 DELAYS AND EXTENSIONS OF TIME

8.3.1 If the Contractor is delayed at any time in the progress of the Work by any act or neglect of the Owner or the Architect, or by any employee of either, or by any separate contractor employed by the Owner, or by changes ordered in the Work, or by labor disputes, fire, unusual delay in transportation, adverse weather conditions not reasonably anticipatable, unavoidable casualties, or any causes beyond the Contractor's control, or by delay authorized by the Owner pending arbitration, or by any other cause which the Architect determines may justify the delay, then the Contract Time shall be extended by Change Order for such reasonable time as the Architect may determine.

8.3.2 Any claim for extension of time shall be made in writing to the Architect not more than twenty days after the commencement of the delay; otherwise it shall be waived. In the case of a continuing delay only one claim is necessary. The Contractor shall provide an estimate of the probable effect of such delay on the progress of the Work.

8.3.3 If no agreement is made stating the dates upon which interpretations as provided in Subparagraph 2.2.8 shall be furnished, then no claim for delay shall be allowed on account of failure to furnish such interpretations until fifteen days after written request is made for them, and not then unless such claim is reasonable.

8.3.4 This Paragraph 8.3 does not exclude the recovery of damages for delay by either party under other provisions of the Contract Documents.

ARTICLE 9

PAYMENTS AND COMPLETION

9.1 CONTRACT SUM

9.1.1 The Contract Sum is stated in the Owner-Contractor Agreement and, including authorized adjustments thereto, is the total amount payable by the Owner to the Contractor for the performance of the Work under the Contract Documents.

9.2 SCHEDULE OF VALUES

9.2.1 Before the first Application for Payment, the Contractor shall submit to the Architect a schedule of values allocated to the various portions of the Work, prepared in such form and supported by such data to substantiate its accuracy as the Architect may require. This schedule, unless objected to by the Architect, shall be used only as a basis for the Contractor's Applications for Payment.

9.3 APPLICATIONS FOR PAYMENT

9.3.1 At least ten days before the date for each progress payment established in the Owner-Contractor Agreement, the Contractor shall submit to the Architect an itemized Application for Payment, notarized if required, supported by such data substantiating the Contractor's right to payment as the Owner or the Architect may require, and reflecting retainage, if any, as provided elsewhere in the Contract Documents.

9.3.2 Unless otherwise provided in the Contract Documents, payments will be made on account of materials or equipment not incorporated in the Work but delivered and suitably stored at the site and, if approved in advance by the Owner, payments may similarly be made for materials or equipment suitably stored at some other location agreed upon in writing. Payments for materials or equipment stored on or off the site shall be conditioned upon submission by the Contractor of bills of sale or such other procedures satisfactory to the Owner to establish the Owner's title to such materials or equipment or otherwise protect the Owner's interest, including applicable insurance and transportation to the site for those materials and equipment stored off the site.

9.3.3 The Contractor warrants that title to all Work, materials and equipment covered by an Application for Payment will pass to the Owner either by incorporation in the construction or upon the receipt of payment by the Contractor, whichever occurs first, free and clear of all liens, claims, security interests or encumbrances, hereinafter referred to in this Article 9 as "liens"; and that no Work, materials or equipment covered by an Application for Payment will have been acquired by the Contractor, or by any other person performing Work at the site or furnishing materials and equipment for the Project, subject to an agreement under which an interest therein or an encumbrance thereon is retained by the seller or otherwise imposed by the Contractor or such other person.

9.4 CERTIFICATES FOR PAYMENT

9.4.1 The Architect will, within seven days after the receipt of the Contractor's Application for Payment, either issue a Certificate for Payment to the Owner, with a copy to the Contractor, for such amount as the Architect determines is properly due, or notify the Contractor in writing his reasons for withholding a Certificate as provided in Subparagraph 9.6.1.

9.4.2 The issuance of a Certificate for Payment will constitute a representation by the Architect to the Owner, based on his observations at the site as provided in Subparagraph 2.2.3 and the data comprising the Application for Payment, that the Work has progressed to the point indicated; that, to the best of his knowledge, information and belief, the quality of the Work is in accordance with the Contract Documents (subject to an evaluation of the Work for conformance with the Contract Documents upon Substantial Completion, to the results of any subsequent tests required by or performed under the Contract Documents, to minor deviations from the Contract Documents correctable prior to completion, and to any specific qualifications stated in his Certificate); and that the Contractor is entitled to payment in the amount certified. However, by issuing a Certificate for Payment, the Architect shall not thereby be deemed to represent that he has made exhaustive or continuous on-site inspections to check the quality or quantity of the Work or that he has reviewed the construction means, methods, techniques, sequences or procedures, or that he has made any examination to ascertain how or for what purpose the Contractor has used the moneys previously paid on account of the Contract Sum.

9.5 PROGRESS PAYMENTS

9.5.1 After the Architect has issued a Certificate for Payment, the Owner shall make payment in the manner and within the time provided in the Contract Documents.

9.5.2 The Contractor shall promptly pay each Subcontractor, upon receipt of payment from the Owner, out of the amount paid to the Contractor on account of such Subcontractor's Work, the amount to which said Subcontractor is entitled, reflecting the percentage actually retained, if any, from payments to the Contractor on account of such Subcontractor's Work. The Contractor shall, by an appropriate agreement with each Subcontractor, require each Subcontractor to make payments to his Subsubcontractors in similar manner.

9.5.3 The Architect may, on request and at his discretion, furnish to any Subcontractor, if practicable, information regarding the percentages of completion or the amounts applied for by the Contractor and the action taken thereon by the Architect on account of Work done by such Subcontractor.

9.5.4 Neither the Owner nor the Architect shall have any obligation to pay or to see to the payment of any moneys to any Subcontractor except as may otherwise be required by law.

9.5.5 No Certificate for a progress payment, nor any progress payment, nor any partial or entire use or occupancy of the Project by the Owner, shall constitute an acceptance of any Work not in accordance with the Contract Documents.

9.6 PAYMENTS WITHHELD

9.6.1 The Architect may decline to certify payment and may withhold his Certificate in whole or in part, to the extent necessary reasonably to protect the Owner, if in his opinion he is unable to make representations to the Owner as provided in Subparagraph 9.4.2. If the Architect is unable to make representations to the Owner as provided in Subparagraph 9.4.2 and to certify payment in the amount of the Application, he will notify the Contractor as provided in Subparagraph 9.4.1. If the Contractor and the Architect cannot agree on a revised amount, the Architect will promptly issue a Certificate for Payment for the amount for which he is able to make such representations to the Owner. The Architect may also decline to certify payment or, because of subsequently discovered evidence or subsequent observations, he may nullify the whole or any part of any Certificate for Payment previously issued, to such extent as may be necessary in his opinion to protect the Owner from loss because of:

.1 defective work not remedied,

.2 third party claims filed or reasonable evidence indicating probable filing of such claims,

.3 failure of the Contractor to make payments properly to Subcontractors or for labor, materials or equipment,

.4 reasonable evidence that the Work cannot be completed for the unpaid balance of the Contract Sum,

.5 damage to the Owner or another contractor,

.6 reasonable evidence that the Work will not be completed within the Contract Time, or

.7 persistent failure to carry out the Work in accordance with the Contract Documents.

9.6.2 When the above grounds in Subparagraph 9.6.1 are removed, payment shall be made for amounts withheld because of them.

9.7 FAILURE OF PAYMENT

9.7.1 If the Architect does not issue a Certificate for Payment, through no fault of the Contractor, within seven days after receipt of the Contractor's Application for Payment, or if the Owner does not pay the Contractor within seven days after the date established in the Contract Documents any amount certified by the Architect or awarded by arbitration, then the Contractor may, upon seven additional days' written notice to the Owner and the Architect, stop the Work until payment of the amount owing has been received. The Contract Sum shall be increased by the amount of the Contractor's reasonable costs of shut-down, delay and start-up, which shall be effected by appropriate Change Order in accordance with Paragraph 12.3.

9.8 SUBSTANTIAL COMPLETION

9.8.1 When the Contractor considers that the Work, or a designated portion thereof which is acceptable to the Owner, is substantially complete as defined in Subparagraph 8.1.3, the Contractor shall prepare for submission to the Architect a list of items to be completed or corrected. The failure to include any items on such list does not alter the responsibility of the Contractor to complete all Work in accordance with the Contract Documents. When the Architect on the basis of an inspection determines that the Work or designated portion thereof is substantially complete, he will then prepare a Certificate of Substantial Completion which shall establish the Date of Substantial Completion, shall state the responsibilities of the Owner and the Contractor for security, maintenance, heat, utilities, damage to the Work, and insurance, and shall fix the time within which the Contractor shall complete the items listed therein. Warranties required by the Contract Documents shall commence on the Date of Substantial Completion of the Work or designated portion thereof unless otherwise provided in the Certificate of Substantial Completion. The Certificate of Substantial Completion shall be submitted to the Owner and the Contractor for their written acceptance of the responsibilities assigned to them in such Certificate.

9.8.2 Upon Substantial Completion of the Work or designated portion thereof and upon application by the Contractor and certification by the Architect, the Owner shall make payment, reflecting adjustment in retainage, if any, for such Work or portion thereof, as provided in the Contract Documents.

9.9 FINAL COMPLETION AND FINAL PAYMENT

9.9.1 Upon receipt of written notice that the Work is ready for final inspection and acceptance and upon receipt of a final Application for Payment, the Architect will promptly make such inspection and, when he finds the Work acceptable under the Contract Documents and the Contract fully performed, he will promptly issue a final Certificate for Payment stating that to the best of his knowledge, information and belief, and on the basis of his observations and inspections, the Work has been completed in accordance with the terms and conditions of the Contract Documents and that the entire balance found to be due the Contractor, and noted in said final Certificate, is due and payable. The Architect's final Certificate for Payment will constitute a further representation that the conditions precedent to the Contractor's being entitled to final payment as set forth in Subparagraph 9.9.2 have been fulfilled.

9.9.2 Neither the final payment nor the remaining retained percentage shall become due until the Contractor submits to the Architect (1) an affidavit that all payrolls, bills for materials and equipment, and other indebtedness connected with the Work for which the Owner or his property might in any way be responsible, have been paid or otherwise satisfied, (2) consent of surety, if any, to final payment and (3), if required by the Owner, other data establishing payment or satisfaction of all such obligations, such as receipts, releases and waivers of liens arising out of the Contract, to the extent and in such form as may be designated by the Owner. If any Subcontractor refuses to furnish a release or waiver required by the Owner, the Contractor may furnish a bond satisfactory to the Owner to indemnify him against any such lien. If any such lien remains unsatisfied after all payments are made, the Contractor shall refund to the Owner all moneys that the latter may be compelled to pay in discharging such lien, including all costs and reasonable attorneys' fees.

9.9.3 If, after Substantial Completion of the Work, final completion thereof is materially delayed through no fault of the Contractor or by the issuance of Change Orders affecting final completion, and the Architect so confirms, the Owner shall, upon application by the Contractor and certification by the Architect, and without terminating the Contract, make payment of the balance due for that portion of the Work fully completed and accepted. If the remaining balance for Work not fully completed or corrected is less than the retainage stipulated in the Contract Documents, and if bonds have been furnished as provided in Paragraph 7.5, the written consent of the surety to the payment of the balance due for that portion of the Work fully completed and accepted shall be submitted by the Contractor to the Architect prior to certification of such payment. Such payment shall be made under the terms and conditions governing final payment, except that it shall not constitute a waiver of claims.

9.9.4 The making of final payment shall constitute a waiver of all claims by the Owner except those arising from:

.1 unsettled liens,

.2 faulty or defective Work appearing after Substantial Completion,

.3 failure of the Work to comply with the requirements of the Contract Documents, or

.4 terms of any special warranties required by the Contract Documents.

9.9.5 The acceptance of final payment shall constitute a waiver of all claims by the Contractor except those previously made in writing and identified by the Contractor as unsettled at the time of the final Application for Payment.

ARTICLE 10
PROTECTION OF PERSONS AND PROPERTY

10.1 SAFETY PRECAUTIONS AND PROGRAMS

10.1.1 The Contractor shall be responsible for initiating, maintaining and supervising all safety precautions and programs in connection with the Work.

10.2 SAFETY OF PERSONS AND PROPERTY

10.2.1 The Contractor shall take all reasonable precautions for the safety of, and shall provide all reasonable protection to prevent damage, injury or loss to:

.1 all employees on the Work and all other persons who may be affected thereby;

.2 all the Work and all materials and equipment to be incorporated therein, whether in storage on or off the site, under the care, custody or control of the Contractor or any of his Subcontractors or Sub-subcontractors; and

.3 other property at the site or adjacent thereto, including trees, shrubs, lawns, walks, pavements, roadways, structures and utilities not designated for removal, relocation or replacement in the course of construction.

10.2.2 The Contractor shall give all notices and comply with all applicable laws, ordinances, rules, regulations and lawful orders of any public authority bearing on the safety of persons or property or their protection from damage, injury or loss.

10.2.3 The Contractor shall erect and maintain, as required by existing conditions and progress of the Work, all reasonable safeguards for safety and protection, including posting danger signs and other warnings against hazards, promulgating safety regulations and notifying owners and users of adjacent utilities.

10.2.4 When the use or storage of explosives or other hazardous materials or equipment is necessary for the execution of the Work, the Contractor shall exercise the utmost care and shall carry on such activities under the supervision of properly qualified personnel.

10.2.5 The Contractor shall promptly remedy all damage or loss (other than damage or loss insured under Paragraph 11.3) to any property referred to in Clauses 10.2.1.2 and 10.2.1.3 caused in whole or in part by the Contractor, any Subcontractor, any Sub-subcontractor, or anyone directly or indirectly employed by any of them, or by anyone for whose acts any of them may be liable and for which the Contractor is responsible under Clauses 10.2.1.2 and 10.2.1.3, except damage or loss attributable to the acts or omissions of the Owner or Architect or anyone directly or indirectly employed by either of them, or by anyone for whose acts either of them may be liable, and not attributable to the fault or negligence of the Contractor. The foregoing obligations of the Contractor are in addition to his obligations under Paragraph 4.18.

10.2.6 The Contractor shall designate a responsible member of his organization at the site whose duty shall be the prevention of accidents. This person shall be the Contractor's superintendent unless otherwise designated by the Contractor in writing to the Owner and the Architect.

10.2.7 The Contractor shall not load or permit any part of the Work to be loaded so as to endanger its safety.

10.3   EMERGENCIES

10.3.1 In any emergency affecting the safety of persons or property, the Contractor shall act, at his discretion, to prevent threatened damage, injury or loss. Any additional compensation or extension of time claimed by the Contractor on account of emergency work shall be determined as provided in Article 12 for Changes in the Work.

ARTICLE 11

INSURANCE

11.1   CONTRACTOR'S LIABILITY INSURANCE

11.1.1 The Contractor shall purchase and maintain such insurance as will protect him from claims set forth below which may arise out of or result from the Contractor's operations under the Contract, whether such operations be by himself or by any Subcontractor or by anyone directly or indirectly employed by any of them, or by anyone for whose acts any of them may be liable:

.1 claims under workers' or workmen's compensation, disability benefit and other similar employee benefit acts;

.2 claims for damages because of bodily injury, occupational sickness or disease, or death of his employees;

.3 claims for damages because of bodily injury, sickness or disease, or death of any person other than his employees;

.4 claims for damages insured by usual personal injury liability coverage which are sustained (1) by any person as a result of an offense directly or indirectly related to the employment of such person by the Contractor, or (2) by any other person;

.5 claims for damages, other than to the Work itself, because of injury to or destruction of tangible property, including loss of use resulting therefrom; and

.6 claims for damages because of bodily injury or death of any person or property damage arising out of the ownership, maintenance or use of any motor vehicle.

11.1.2 The insurance required by Subparagraph 11.1.1 shall be written for not less than any limits of liability specified in the Contract Documents, or required by law, whichever is greater.

11.1.3 The insurance required by Subparagraph 11.1.1 shall include contractual liability insurance applicable to the Contractor's obligations under Paragraph 4.18.

11.1.4 Certificates of Insurance acceptable to the Owner shall be filed with the Owner prior to commencement of the Work. These Certificates shall contain a provision that coverages afforded under the policies will not be cancelled until at least thirty days' prior written notice has been given to the Owner.

11.2   OWNER'S LIABILITY INSURANCE

11.2.1 The Owner shall be responsible for purchasing and maintaining his own liability insurance and, at his option, may purchase and maintain such insurance as will protect him against claims which may arise from operations under the Contract.

11.3   PROPERTY INSURANCE

11.3.1 Unless otherwise provided, the Owner shall purchase and maintain property insurance upon the entire Work at the site to the full insurable value thereof. This insurance shall include the interests of the Owner, the Contractor, Subcontractors and Sub-subcontractors in the Work and shall insure against the perils of fire and extended coverage and shall include "all risk" insurance for physical loss or damage including, without duplication of coverage, theft, vandalism and malicious mischief. If the Owner does not intend to purchase such insurance for the full insurable value of the entire Work, he shall inform the Contractor in writing prior to commencement of the Work. The Contractor may then effect insurance which will protect the interests of himself, his Subcontractors and the Sub-subcontractors in the Work, and by appropriate Change Order the cost thereof shall be charged to the Owner. If the Contractor is damaged by failure of the Owner to purchase or maintain such insurance and to so notify the Contractor, then the Owner shall bear all reasonable costs properly attributable thereto. If not covered under the all risk insurance or otherwise provided in the Contract Documents, the Contractor shall effect and maintain similar property insurance on portions of the Work stored off the site or in transit when such portions of the Work are to be included in an Application for Payment under Subparagraph 9.3.2.

11.3.2 The Owner shall purchase and maintain such boiler and machinery insurance as may be required by the Contract Documents or by law. This insurance shall include the interests of the Owner, the Contractor, Subcontractors and Sub-subcontractors in the Work.

11.3.3 Any loss insured under Subparagraph 11.3.1 is to be adjusted with the Owner and made payable to the Owner as trustee for the insureds, as their interests may appear, subject to the requirements of any applicable mortgagee clause and of Subparagraph 11.3.8. The Contractor shall pay each Subcontractor a just share of any insurance moneys received by the Contractor, and by appropriate agreement, written where legally required for validity, shall require each Subcontractor to make payments to his Sub-subcontractors in similar manner.

11.3.4 The Owner shall file a copy of all policies with the Contractor before an exposure to loss may occur.

11.3.5 If the Contractor requests in writing that insurance for risks other than those described in Subparagraphs 11.3.1 and 11.3.2 or other special hazards be included in the property insurance policy, the Owner shall, if possible, include such insurance, and the cost thereof shall be charged to the Contractor by appropriate Change Order.

11.3.6 The Owner and Contractor waive all rights against (1) each other and the Subcontractors, Sub-subcontractors, agents and employees each of the other, and (2) the Architect and separate contractors, if any, and their subcontractors, sub-subcontractors, agents and employees, for damages caused by fire or other perils to the extent covered by insurance obtained pursuant to this Paragraph 11.3 or any other property insurance applicable to the Work, except such rights as they may have to the proceeds of such insurance held by the Owner as trustee. The foregoing waiver afforded the Architect, his agents and employees shall not extend to the liability imposed by Subparagraph 4.18.3. The Owner or the Contractor, as appropriate, shall require of the Architect, separate contractors, Subcontractors and Sub-subcontractors by appropriate agreements, written where legally required for validity, similar waivers each in favor of all other parties enumerated in this Subparagraph 11.3.6.

11.3.7 If required in writing by any party in interest, the Owner as trustee shall, upon the occurrence of an insured loss, give bond for the proper performance of his duties. He shall deposit in a separate account any money so received, and he shall distribute it in accordance with such agreement as the parties in interest may reach, or in accordance with an award by arbitration in which case the procedure shall be as provided in Paragraph 7.9. If after such loss no other special agreement is made, replacement of damaged work shall be covered by an appropriate Change Order.

11.3.8 The Owner as trustee shall have power to adjust and settle any loss with the insurers unless one of the parties in interest shall object in writing within five days after the occurrence of loss to the Owner's exercise of this power, and if such objection be made, arbitrators shall be chosen as provided in Paragraph 7.9. The Owner as trustee shall, in that case, make settlement with the insurers in accordance with the directions of such arbitrators. If distribution of the insurance proceeds by arbitration is required, the arbitrators will direct such distribution.

11.3.9 If the Owner finds it necessary to occupy or use a portion or portions of the Work prior to Substantial Completion thereof, such occupancy or use shall not commence prior to a time mutually agreed to by the Owner and Contractor and to which the insurance company or companies providing the property insurance have consented by endorsement to the policy or policies. This insurance shall not be cancelled or lapsed on account of such partial occupancy or use. Consent of the Contractor and of the insurance company or companies to such occupancy or use shall not be unreasonably withheld.

11.4   LOSS OF USE INSURANCE

11.4.1 The Owner, at his option, may purchase and maintain such insurance as will insure him against loss of use of his property due to fire or other hazards, however caused. The Owner waives all rights of action against the Contractor for loss of use of his property, including consequential losses due to fire or other hazards however caused, to the extent covered by insurance under this Paragraph 11.4.

ARTICLE 12

CHANGES IN THE WORK

12.1   CHANGE ORDERS

12.1.1 A Change Order is a written order to the Contractor signed by the Owner and the Architect, issued after execution of the Contract, authorizing a change in the Work or an adjustment in the Contract Sum or the Contract Time. The Contract Sum and the Contract Time may be changed only by Change Order. A Change Order signed by the Contractor indicates his agreement therewith, including the adjustment in the Contract Sum or the Contract Time.

12.1.2 The Owner, without invalidating the Contract, may order changes in the Work within the general scope of the Contract consisting of additions, deletions or other revisions, the Contract Sum and the Contract Time being adjusted accordingly. All such changes in the Work shall be authorized by Change Order, and shall be performed under the applicable conditions of the Contract Documents.

12.1.3 The cost or credit to the Owner resulting from a change in the Work shall be determined in one or more of the following ways:

 .1 by mutual acceptance of a lump sum properly itemized and supported by sufficient substantiating data to permit evaluation;

 .2 by unit prices stated in the Contract Documents or subsequently agreed upon;

 .3 by cost to be determined in a manner agreed upon by the parties and a mutually acceptable fixed or percentage fee; or

 .4 by the method provided in Subparagraph 12.1.4.

12.1.4 If none of the methods set forth in Clauses 12.1.3.1, 12.1.3.2 or 12.1.3.3 is agreed upon, the Contractor, provided he receives a written order signed by the Owner, shall promptly proceed with the Work involved. The cost of such Work shall then be determined by the Architect on the basis of the reasonable expenditures and savings of those performing the Work attributable to the change, including, in the case of an increase in the Contract Sum, a reasonable allowance for overhead and profit. In such case, and also under Clauses 12.1.3.3 and 12.1.3.4 above, the Contractor shall keep and present, in such form as the Architect may prescribe, an itemized accounting together with appropriate supporting data for inclusion in a Change Order. Unless otherwise provided in the Contract Documents, cost shall be limited to the following: cost of materials, including sales tax and cost of delivery; cost of labor, including social security, old age and unemployment insurance, and fringe benefits required by agreement or custom; workers' or workmen's compensation insurance; bond premiums; rental value of equipment and machinery; and the additional costs of supervision and field office personnel directly attributable to the change. Pending final determination of cost to the Owner, payments on account shall be made on the Architect's Certificate for Payment. The amount of credit to be allowed by the Contractor to the Owner for any deletion or change which results in a net decrease in the Contract Sum will be the amount of the actual net cost as confirmed by the Architect. When both additions and credits covering related Work or substitutions are involved in any one change, the allowance for overhead and profit shall be figured on the basis of the net increase, if any, with respect to that change.

12.1.5 If unit prices are stated in the Contract Documents or subsequently agreed upon, and if the quantities originally contemplated are so changed in a proposed Change Order that application of the agreed unit prices to the quantities of Work proposed will cause substantial inequity to the Owner or the Contractor, the applicable unit prices shall be equitably adjusted.

12.2 CONCEALED CONDITIONS

12.2.1 Should concealed conditions encountered in the performance of the Work below the surface of the ground or should concealed or unknown conditions in an existing structure be at variance with the conditions indicated by the Contract Documents, or should unknown physical conditions below the surface of the ground or should concealed or unknown conditions in an existing structure of an unusual nature, differing materially from those ordinarily encountered and generally recognized as inherent in work of the character provided for in this Contract, be encountered, the Contract Sum shall be equitably adjusted by Change Order upon claim by either party made within twenty days after the first observance of the conditions.

12.3 CLAIMS FOR ADDITIONAL COST

12.3.1 If the Contractor wishes to make a claim for an increase in the Contract Sum, he shall give the Architect written notice thereof within twenty days after the occurrence of the event giving rise to such claim. This notice shall be given by the Contractor before proceeding to execute the Work, except in an emergency endangering life or property in which case the Contractor shall proceed in accordance with Paragraph 10.3. No such claim shall be valid unless so made. If the Owner and the Contractor cannot agree on the amount of the adjustment in the Contract Sum, it shall be determined by the Architect. Any change in the Contract Sum resulting from such claim shall be authorized by Change Order.

12.3.2 If the Contractor claims that additional cost is involved because of, but not limited to, (1) any written interpretation pursuant to Subparagraph 2.2.8, (2) any order by the Owner to stop the Work pursuant to Paragraph 3.3 where the Contractor was not at fault, (3) any written order for a minor change in the Work issued pursuant to Paragraph 12.4, or (4) failure of payment by the Owner pursuant to Paragraph 9.7, the Contractor shall make such claim as provided in Subparagraph 12.3.1.

12.4 MINOR CHANGES IN THE WORK

12.4.1 The Architect will have authority to order minor changes in the Work not involving an adjustment in the Contract Sum or an extension of the Contract Time and not inconsistent with the intent of the Contract Documents. Such changes shall be effected by written order, and shall be binding on the Owner and the Contractor.

The Contractor shall carry out such written orders promptly.

ARTICLE 13

UNCOVERING AND CORRECTION OF WORK

13.1 UNCOVERING OF WORK

13.1.1 If any portion of the Work should be covered contrary to the request of the Architect or to requirements specifically expressed in the Contract Documents, it must, if required in writing by the Architect, be uncovered for his observation and shall be replaced at the Contractor's expense.

13.1.2 If any other portion of the Work has been covered which the Architect has not specifically requested to observe prior to being covered, the Architect may request to see such Work and it shall be uncovered by the Contractor. If such Work be found in accordance with the Contract Documents, the cost of uncovering and replacement shall, by appropriate Change Order, be charged to the Owner. If such Work be found not in accordance with the Contract Documents, the Contractor shall pay such costs unless it be found that this condition was caused by the Owner or a separate contractor as provided in Article 6, in which event the Owner shall be responsible for the payment of such costs.

13.2 CORRECTION OF WORK

13.2.1 The Contractor shall promptly correct all Work rejected by the Architect as defective or as failing to conform to the Contract Documents whether observed before or after Substantial Completion and whether or not fabricated, installed or completed. The Contractor shall bear all costs of correcting such rejected Work, including compensation for the Architect's additional services made necessary thereby.

13.2.2 If, within one year after the Date of Substantial Completion of the Work or designated portion thereof or within one year after acceptance by the Owner of designated equipment or within such longer period of time as may be prescribed by law or by the terms of any applicable special warranty required by the Contract Documents, any of the Work is found to be defective or not in accordance with the Contract Documents, the Contractor shall correct it promptly after receipt of a written notice from the Owner to do so unless the Owner has previously given the Contractor a written acceptance of such condition. This obligation shall survive termination of the Contract. The Owner shall give such notice promptly after discovery of the condition.

13.2.3 The Contractor shall remove from the site all portions of the Work which are defective or non-conforming and which have not been corrected under Subparagraphs 4.5.1, 13.2.1 and 13.2.2, unless removal is waived by the Owner.

13.2.4 If the Contractor fails to correct defective or nonconforming Work as provided in Subparagraphs 4.5.1, 13.2.1 and 13.2.2, the Owner may correct it in accordance with Paragraph 3.4.

13.2.5 If the Contractor does not proceed with the correction of such defective or non-conforming Work within a reasonable time fixed by written notice from the Architect, the Owner may remove it and may store the materials or equipment at the expense of the Contractor. If the Contractor does not pay the cost of such removal and storage within ten days thereafter, the Owner may upon ten additional days' written notice sell such Work at auction or at private sale and shall account for the net proceeds thereof, after deducting all the costs that should have been borne by the Contractor, including compensation for the Architect's additional services made necessary thereby. If such proceeds of sale do not cover all costs which the Contractor should have borne, the difference shall be charged to the Contractor and an appropriate Change Order shall be issued. If the payments then or thereafter due the Contractor are not sufficient to cover such amount, the Contractor shall pay the difference to the Owner.

13.2.6 The Contractor shall bear the cost of making good all work of the Owner or separate contractors destroyed or damaged by such correction or removal.

13.2.7 Nothing contained in this Paragraph 13.2 shall be construed to establish a period of limitation with respect to any other obligation which the Contractor might have under the Contract Documents, including Paragraph 4.5 hereof. The establishment of the time period of one year after the Date of Substantial Completion or such longer period of time as may be prescribed by law or by the terms of any warranty required by the Contract Documents relates only to the specific obligation of the Contractor to correct the Work, and has no relationship to the time within which his obligation to comply with the Contract Documents may be sought to be enforced, nor to the time within which proceedings may be commenced to establish the Contractor's liability with respect to his obligations other than specifically to correct the Work.

13.3 ACCEPTANCE OF DEFECTIVE OR NON-CONFORMING WORK

13.3.1 If the Owner prefers to accept defective or non-conforming Work, he may do so instead of requiring its removal and correction, in which case a Change Order will be issued to reflect a reduction in the Contract Sum where appropriate and equitable. Such adjustment shall be effected whether or not final payment has been made.

ARTICLE 14

TERMINATION OF THE CONTRACT

14.1 TERMINATION BY THE CONTRACTOR

14.1.1 If the Work is stopped for a period of thirty days under an order of any court or other public authority having jurisdiction, or as a result of an act of government, such as a declaration of a national emergency making materials unavailable, through no act or fault of the Contractor or a Subcontractor or their agents or employees or any other persons performing any of the Work under a contract with the Contractor, or if the Work should be stopped for a period of thirty days by the Contractor because the Architect has not issued a Certificate for Payment as provided in Paragraph 9.7 or because the Owner has not made payment thereon as provided in Paragraph 9.7, then the Contractor may, upon seven additional days' written notice to the Owner and the Architect, terminate the Contract and recover from the Owner payment for all Work executed and for any proven loss sustained upon any materials, equipment, tools, construction equipment and machinery, including reasonable profit and damages.

14.2 TERMINATION BY THE OWNER

14.2.1 If the Contractor is adjudged a bankrupt, or if he makes a general assignment for the benefit of his creditors, or if a receiver is appointed on account of his insolvency, or if he persistently or repeatedly refuses or fails, except in cases for which extension of time is provided, to supply enough properly skilled workmen or proper materials, or if he fails to make prompt payment to Subcontractors or for materials or labor, or persistently disregards laws, ordinances, rules, regulations or orders of any public authority having jurisdiction, or otherwise is guilty of a substantial violation of a provision of the Contract Documents, then the Owner, upon certification by the Architect that sufficient cause exists to justify such action, may without prejudice to any right or remedy and after giving the Contractor and his surety, if any, seven days' written notice, terminate the employment of the Contractor and take possession of the site and of all materials, equipment, tools, construction equipment and machinery thereon owned by the Contractor and may finish the Work by whatever method he may deem expedient. In such case the Contractor shall not be entitled to receive any further payment until the Work is finished.

14.2.2 If the unpaid balance of the Contract Sum exceeds the costs of finishing the Work, including compensation for the Architect's additional services made necessary thereby, such excess shall be paid to the Contractor. If such costs exceed the unpaid balance, the Contractor shall pay the difference to the Owner. The amount to be paid to the Contractor or to the Owner, as the case may be, shall be certified by the Architect, upon application, in the manner provided in Paragraph 9.4, and this obligation for payment shall survive the termination of the Contract.

THE AMERICAN INSTITUTE OF ARCHITECTS

AIA Document A201/CM

CONSTRUCTION MANAGEMENT EDITION

General Conditions of the Contract for Construction

THIS DOCUMENT HAS IMPORTANT LEGAL CONSEQUENCES; CONSULTATION WITH AN ATTORNEY IS ENCOURAGED.

1980 EDITION
TABLE OF ARTICLES

AIA DOCUMENT A201/CM • GENERAL CONDITIONS OF THE CONTRACT FOR CONSTRUCTION
CONSTRUCTION MANAGEMENT EDITION • JUNE 1980 EDITION • AIA® • © 1980 • THE
AMERICAN INSTITUTE OF ARCHITECTS, 1735 NEW YORK AVE., N.W., WASHINGTON, D.C. 20006

A201/CM — 1980   1

INDEX

AIA DOCUMENT A201/CM • GENERAL CONDITIONS OF THE CONTRACT FOR CONSTRUCTION
CONSTRUCTION MANAGEMENT EDITION • JUNE 1980 EDITION • AIA® • © 1980 • THE
AMERICAN INSTITUTE OF ARCHITECTS, 1735 NEW YORK AVE., N.W., WASHINGTON, D.C. 20006

GENERAL CONDITIONS OF THE CONTRACT FOR CONSTRUCTION

ARTICLE 1
CONTRACT DOCUMENTS

1.1 DEFINITIONS

1.1.1 THE CONTRACT DOCUMENTS

The Contract Documents consist of the Owner-Contractor Agreement, the Conditions of the Contract (General, Supplementary and other Conditions), the Drawings, the Specifications, and all Addenda issued prior to and all Modifications issued after execution of the Contract. A Modification is (1) a written amendment to the Contract signed by both parties, (2) a Change Order, (3) a written interpretation issued by the Architect pursuant to Subparagraph 2.3.11, or (4) a written order for a minor change in the Work issued by the Architect pursuant to Paragraph 12.4. The Contract Documents do not include Bidding Documents such as the Advertisement or Invitation to Bid, the Instructions to Bidders, sample forms, the Contractor's Bid or portions of Addenda relating to any of these, or any other documents unless specifically enumerated in the Owner-Contractor Agreement.

1.1.2 THE CONTRACT

The Contract Documents form the Contract for Construction. This Contract represents the entire and integrated agreement between the parties hereto and supersedes all prior negotiations, representations or agreements, either written or oral. The Contract may be amended or modified only by a Modification as defined in Subparagraph 1.1.1. The Contract Documents shall not be construed to create any contractual relationship of any kind between the Architect and the Contractor, between the Construction Manager and the Contractor or between the Architect and the Construction Manager, but the Architect and the Construction Manager shall be entitled to performance of the obligations of the Contractor intended for their benefit and to enforcement thereof. Nothing contained in the Contract Documents shall create any contractual relationship between the Owner, the Construction Manager or the Architect and any Subcontractor or Sub-subcontractor.

1.1.3 THE WORK

The Work comprises the completed construction required of the Contractor by the Contract Documents, and includes all labor necessary to produce such construction, and all materials and equipment incorporated or to be incorporated in such construction.

1.1.4 THE PROJECT

The Project, as defined in the Owner-Contractor Agreement, is the total construction of which the Work performed under the Contract Documents is a part.

1.2 EXECUTION, CORRELATION AND INTENT

1.2.1 The Contract Documents shall be signed in not less than quadruplicate by the Owner and the Contractor. If either the Owner or the Contractor or both do not sign the Conditions of the Contract, Drawings, Specifications or any of the other Contract Documents, the Architect shall identify such Documents.

1.2.2 Execution of the Contract by the Contractor is a representation that the Contractor has visited the site, become familiar with the local conditions under which the Work is to be performed, and has correlated personal observations with the requirements of the Contract Documents.

1.2.3 The intent of the Contract Documents is to include all items necessary for the proper execution and completion of the Work. The Contract Documents are complementary, and what is required by any one shall be as binding as if required by all. Work not covered in the Contract Documents will not be required unless it is consistent therewith and is reasonably inferable therefrom as being necessary to produce the intended results. Words and abbreviations which have well-known technical or trade meanings are used in the Contract Documents in accordance with such recognized meanings.

1.2.4 The organization of the Specifications into divisions, sections and articles, and the arrangement of Drawings shall not control the Contractor in dividing the Work among Subcontractors or in establishing the extent of Work to be performed by any trade.

1.3 OWNERSHIP AND USE OF DOCUMENTS

1.3.1 All Drawings, Specifications and copies thereof furnished by the Architect are and shall remain the property of the Architect. They are to be used only with respect to this Project and are not to be used on any other Project. With the exception of one contract set for each party to the Contract, such documents are to be returned or suitably accounted for to the Architect on request at the completion of the Work. Submission or distribution to meet official regulatory requirements or for other purposes in connection with the Project is not to be construed as publication in derogation of the Architect's common law copyright or other reserved rights.

ARTICLE 2
ADMINISTRATION OF THE CONTRACT

2.1 THE ARCHITECT

2.1.1 The Architect is the person lawfully licensed to practice architecture, or an entity lawfully practicing architecture, identified as such in the Owner-Contractor Agreement. The term Architect means the Architect or the Architect's authorized representative.

2.2 THE CONSTRUCTION MANAGER

2.2.1 The Construction Manager is the person or entity identified as such in the Owner-Contractor Agreement. The term Construction Manager means the Construction Manager or the Construction Manager's authorized representative.

2.3 ADMINISTRATION OF THE CONTRACT

2.3.1 The Architect and the Construction Manager will

provide administration of the Contract as hereinafter described.

2.3.2 The Architect and the Construction Manager will be the Owner's representatives during construction and until final payment to all contractors is due. The Architect and the Construction Manager will advise and consult with the Owner. All instructions to the Contractor shall be forwarded through the Construction Manager. The Architect and the Construction Manager will have authority to act on behalf of the Owner only to the extent provided in the Contract Documents, unless otherwise modified by written instrument in accordance with Subparagraph 2.3.22.

2.3.3 The Construction Manager will determine in general that the Work of the Contractor is being performed in accordance with the Contract Documents, and will endeavor to guard the Owner against defects and deficiencies in the Work of the Contractor.

2.3.4 The Architect will visit the site at intervals appropriate to the stage of construction to become generally familiar with the progress and quality of the Work and to determine in general if the Work is proceeding in accordance with the Contract Documents. However, the Architect will not be required to make exhaustive or continuous on-site inspections to check the quality or quantity of the Work. On the basis of on-site observations as an architect, the Architect will keep the Owner informed of the progress of the Work, and will endeavor to guard the Owner against defects and deficiencies in the Work of the Contractor.

2.3.5 Neither the Architect nor the Construction Manager will be responsible for or have control or charge of construction means, methods, techniques, sequences or procedures, or for safety precautions and programs in connection with the Work, and neither will be responsible for the Contractor's failure to carry out the Work in accordance with the Contract Documents. Neither the Architect nor the Construction Manager will be responsible for or have control or charge over the acts or omissions of the Contractor, Subcontractors, or any of their agents or employees, or any other persons performing any of the Work.

2.3.6 The Architect and the Construction Manager shall at all times have access to the Work wherever it is in preparation and progress. The Contractor shall provide facilities for such access so that the Architect and the Construction Manager may perform their functions under the Contract Documents.

2.3.7 The Construction Manager will schedule and coordinate the Work of all contractors on the Project including their use of the site. The Construction Manager will keep the Contractor informed of the Project Construction Schedule to enable the Contractor to plan and perform the Work properly.

2.3.8 The Construction Manager will review all Applications for Payment by the Contractor, including final payment, and will assemble them with similar applications from other contractors on the Project into a combined Project Application for Payment. The Construction Manager will then make recommendations to the Architect for certification for payment.

2.3.9 Based on the Architect's observations, the recommendations of the Construction Manager and an evaluation of the Project Application for Payment, the Architect will determine the amount owing to the Contractor and will issue a Project Certificate for Payment incorporating such amount, as provided in Paragraph 9.4.

2.3.10 The Architect will be the interpreter of the requirements of the Contract Documents and the judge of the performance thereunder by both the Owner and the Contractor.

2.3.11 The Architect will render interpretations necessary for the proper execution or progress of the Work, with reasonable promptness and in accordance with agreed upon time limits. Either party to the Contract may make written request to the Architect for such interpretations.

2.3.12 Claims, disputes and other matters in question between the Contractor and the Owner relating to the execution or progress of the Work or the interpretation of the Contract Documents shall be referred initially to the Architect for decision. After consultation with the Construction Manager, the Architect will render a decision in writing within a reasonable time.

2.3.13 All interpretations and decisions of the Architect shall be consistent with the intent of and reasonably inferable from the Contract Documents and will be in writing or in graphic form. In this capacity as interpreter and judge, the Architect will endeavor to secure faithful performance by both the Owner and the Contractor, will not show partiality to either, and will not be liable for the result of any interpretation or decision rendered in good faith in such capacity.

2.3.14 The Architect's decisions in matters relating to artistic effect will be final if consistent with the intent of the Contract Documents.

2.3.15 Any claim, dispute or other matter in question between the Contractor and the Owner referred to the Architect through the Construction Manager, except those relating to artistic effect as provided in Subparagraph 2.3.14 and those which have been waived by the making or acceptance of final payment as provided in Subparagraphs 9.9.4 through 9.9.6, inclusive, shall be subject to arbitration upon the written demand of either party. However, no demand for arbitration of any such claim, dispute or other matter may be made until the earlier of (1) the date on which the Architect has rendered a written decision, or (2) the tenth day after the parties have presented their evidence to the Architect or have been given a reasonable opportunity to do so, if the Architect has not rendered a written decision by that date. When such a written decision of the Architect states (1) that the decision is final but subject to appeal, and (2) that any demand for arbitration of a claim, dispute or other matter covered by such decision must be made within thirty days after the date on which the party making the demand receives the written decision, failure to demand arbitration within said thirty day period will result in the Architect's decision becoming final and binding upon the Owner and the Contractor. If the Architect renders a decision after arbitration proceedings have been initiated, such decision may be entered as evidence but will not supersede any arbitration proceedings unless the decision is acceptable to all parties concerned.

AIA DOCUMENT A201/CM • GENERAL CONDITIONS OF THE CONTRACT FOR CONSTRUCTION
CONSTRUCTION MANAGEMENT EDITION • JUNE 1980 EDITION • AIA® • © 1980 • THE
AMERICAN INSTITUTE OF ARCHITECTS, 1735 NEW YORK AVE., N.W., WASHINGTON, D.C. 20006

2.3.16 The Architect will have authority to reject Work which does not conform to the Contract Documents, and to require special inspection or testing, but will take such action only after consultation with the Construction Manager. Subject to review by the Architect, the Construction Manager will have the authority to reject Work which does not conform to the Contract Documents. Whenever, in the Construction Manager's opinion, it is considered necessary or advisable for the implementation of the intent of the Contract Documents, the Construction Manager will have authority to require special inspection or testing of the Work in accordance with Subparagraph 7.7.2 whether or not such Work be then fabricated, installed or completed. The foregoing authority of the Construction Manager will be subject to the provisions of Subparagraphs 2.3.10 through 2.3.16, inclusive, with respect to interpretations and decisions of the Architect. However, neither the Architect's nor the Construction Manager's authority to act under this Subparagraph 2.3.16, nor any decision made by them in good faith either to exercise or not to exercise such authority shall give rise to any duty or responsibility of the Architect or the Construction Manager to the Contractor, any Subcontractor, any of their agents or employees, or any other person performing any of the Work.

2.3.17 The Construction Manager will receive from the Contractor and review all Shop Drawings, Product Data and Samples, coordinate them with information contained in related documents, and transmit to the Architect those recommended for approval.

2.3.18 The Architect will review and approve or take other appropriate action upon the Contractor's submittals such as Shop Drawings, Product Data and Samples, but only for conformance with the design concept of the Work and the information given in the Contract Documents. Such action shall be taken with reasonable promptness so as to cause no delay. The Architect's approval of a specific item shall not indicate approval of an assembly of which the item is a component.

2.3.19 Following consultation with the Construction Manager, the Architect will take appropriate action on Change Orders in accordance with Article 12, and will have authority to order minor changes in the Work as provided in Subparagraph 12.4.1.

2.3.20 The Construction Manager will maintain at the Project site one record copy of all Contracts, Drawings, Specifications, Addenda, Change Orders and other Modifications pertaining to the Project, in good order and marked currently to record all changes made during construction, and approved Shop Drawings, Product Data and Samples. These shall be available to the Architect and the Contractor, and shall be delivered to the Architect for the Owner upon completion of the Project.

2.3.21 The Construction Manager will assist the Architect in conducting inspections to determine the dates of Substantial Completion and final completion, and will receive and forward to the Owner for the Owner's review written warranties and related documents required by the Contract and assembled by the Contractor. The Architect will issue a final Project Certificate for Payment upon compliance with the requirements of Paragraph 9.9.

2.3.22 The duties, responsibilities and limitations of authority of the Architect and the Construction Manager as the Owner's representatives during construction as set forth in the Contract Documents, will not be modified or extended without written consent of the Owner, the Contractor, the Architect and the Construction Manager which consent shall not be unreasonably withheld. Failure of the Contractor to respond within ten days to a written request shall constitute consent by the Contractor.

2.3.23 In case of the termination of the employment of the Architect or the Construction Manager, the Owner shall appoint an architect or a construction manager against whom the Contractor makes no reasonable objection and whose status under the Contract Documents shall be that of the former architect or construction manager, respectively. Any dispute in connection with such appointments shall be subject to arbitration.

ARTICLE 3
OWNER

3.1 DEFINITION

3.1.1 The Owner is the person or entity identified as such in the Owner-Contractor Agreement. The term Owner means the Owner or the Owner's authorized representative.

3.2 INFORMATION AND SERVICES REQUIRED OF THE OWNER

3.2.1 The Owner shall, at the request of the Contractor, at the time of execution of the Owner-Contractor Agreement, furnish to the Contractor reasonable evidence that the Owner has made financial arrangements to fulfill the Owner's obligations under the Contract. Unless such reasonable evidence is furnished, the Contractor is not required to execute the Owner-Contractor Agreement or to commence the Work.

3.2.2 The Owner shall furnish all surveys describing the physical characteristics, legal limitations and utility locations for the site of the Project, and a legal description of the site.

3.2.3 Except as provided in Subparagraph 4.7.1, the Owner shall secure and pay for necessary approvals, easements, assessments and charges required for the construction, use or occupancy of permanent structures or for permanent changes in existing facilities.

3.2.4 Information or services under the Owner's control shall be furnished by the Owner with reasonable promptness to avoid delay in the orderly progress of the Work.

3.2.5 Unless otherwise provided in the Contract Documents, the Contractor will be furnished, free of charge, all copies of Drawings and Specifications reasonably necessary for the execution of the Work.

3.2.6 The Owner shall forward all instructions to the Contractor through the Construction Manager, with simultaneous notification to the Architect.

3.2.7 The foregoing are in addition to other duties and responsibilities of the Owner enumerated herein and especially those in respect to Work By Owner or By Separate Contractors, Payments and Completion, and Insurance in Articles 6, 9 and 11, respectively.

3.3 OWNER'S RIGHT TO STOP THE WORK

3.3.1 If the Contractor fails to correct defective Work as required by Paragraph 13.2, or persistently fails to carry out the Work in accordance with the Contract Documents, the Owner, by a written order signed personally or by an agent specifically so empowered by the Owner in writing, may order the Contractor to stop the Work, or any portion thereof, until the cause for such order has been eliminated; however, this right of the Owner to stop the Work shall not give rise to any duty on the part of the Owner to exercise this right for the benefit of the Contractor or any other person or entity, except to the extent required by Subparagraph 6.1.3.

3.4 OWNER'S RIGHT TO CARRY OUT THE WORK

3.4.1. If the Contractor defaults or neglects to carry out the Work in accordance with the Contract Documents, and fails within seven days after receipt of written notice from the Owner to commence and continue correction of such default or neglect with diligence and promptness, the Owner may, after seven days following receipt by the Contractor of an additional written notice and without prejudice to any other remedy the Owner may have, make good such deficiencies. In such case an appropriate Change Order shall be issued deducting from the payments then or thereafter due the Contractor the cost of correcting such deficiencies, including compensation for the Architect's and the Construction Manager's additional services made necessary by such default, neglect or failure. Such action by the Owner and the amount charged to the Contractor are both subject to the prior approval of the Architect, after consultation with the Construction Manager. If the payments then or thereafter due the Contractor are not sufficient to cover such amount, the Contractor shall pay the difference to the Owner.

ARTICLE 4
CONTRACTOR

4.1 DEFINITION

4.1.1 The Contractor is the person or entity identified as such in the Owner-Contractor Agreement. The term Contractor means the Contractor or the Contractor's authorized representative.

4.2 REVIEW OF CONTRACT DOCUMENTS

4.2.1 The Contractor shall carefully study and compare the Contract Documents and shall at once report to the Architect and the Construction Manager any error, inconsistency or omission that may be discovered. The Contractor shall not be liable to the Owner, the Architect or the Construction Manager for any damage resulting from any such errors, inconsistencies or omissions in the Contract Documents. The Contractor shall perform no portion of the Work at any time without Contract Documents or, where required, approved Shop Drawings, Product Data or Samples for such portion of the Work.

4.3 SUPERVISION AND CONSTRUCTION PROCEDURES

4.3.1 The Contractor shall supervise and direct the Work, using the Contractor's best skill and attention. The Contractor shall be solely responsible for all construction means, methods, techniques, sequences and procedures;

and shall coordinate all portions of the Work under the Contract, subject to the overall coordination of the Construction Manager.

4.3.2 The Contractor shall be responsible to the Owner for the acts and omissions of the Contractor's employees, Subcontractors and their agents and employees, and any other persons performing any of the Work under a contract with the Contractor.

4.3.3 The Contractor shall not be relieved from the Contractor's obligations to perform the Work in accordance with the Contract Documents either by the activities or duties of the Construction Manager or the Architect in their administration of the Contract, or by inspections, tests or approvals required or performed under Paragraph 7.7 by persons other than the Contractor.

4.4 LABOR AND MATERIALS

4.4.1 Unless otherwise provided in the Contract Documents, the Contractor shall provide and pay for all labor, materials, equipment, tools, construction equipment and machinery, water, heat, utilities, transportation, and other facilities and services necessary for the proper execution and completion of the Work, whether temporary or permanent and whether or not incorporated or to be incorporated in the Work.

4.4.2 The Contractor shall at all times enforce strict discipline and good order among the Contractor's employees and shall not employ on the Work any unfit person or anyone not skilled in the task assigned them.

4.5 WARRANTY

4.5.1 The Contractor warrants to the Owner, the Architect and the Construction Manager that all materials and equipment furnished under this Contract will be new unless otherwise specified, and that all Work will be of good quality, free from faults and defects and in conformance with the Contract Documents. All Work not conforming to these requirements, including substitutions not properly approved and authorized, may be considered defective. If required by the Architect or the Construction Manager, the Contractor shall furnish satisfactory evidence as to the kind and quality of materials and equipment. This warranty is not limited by the provisions of Paragraph 13.2.

4.6 TAXES

4.6.1 The Contractor shall pay all sales, consumer, use and other similar taxes for the Work or portions thereof provided by the Contractor which are legally enacted at the time bids are received, whether or not yet effective.

4.7 PERMITS, FEES AND NOTICES

4.7.1 Unless otherwise provided in the Contract Documents, the Owner shall secure and pay for the building permit and the Contractor shall secure and pay for all other permits and governmental fees, licenses and inspections necessary for the proper execution and completion of the Work which are customarily secured after execution of the Contract and which are legally required at the time bids are received.

4.7.2 The Contractor shall give all notices and comply with all laws, ordinances, rules, regulations and lawful orders of any public authority bearing on the performance of the Work.

AIA DOCUMENT A201/CM • GENERAL CONDITIONS OF THE CONTRACT FOR CONSTRUCTION
CONSTRUCTION MANAGEMENT EDITION • JUNE 1980 EDITION • AIA® • © 1980 • THE
AMERICAN INSTITUTE OF ARCHITECTS, 1735 NEW YORK AVE., N.W., WASHINGTON, D.C. 20006

4.7.3 It is not the responsibility of the Contractor to make certain that the Contract Documents are in accordance with applicable laws, statutes, building codes and regulations. If the Contractor observes that any of the Contract Documents are at variance therewith in any respect, the Contractor shall promptly notify the Architect and the Construction Manager in writing, and any necessary changes shall be accomplished by appropriate Modification.

4.7.4 If the Contractor performs any Work knowing it to be contrary to such laws, ordinances, rules and regulations, and without such notice to the Architect and the Construction Manager, the Contractor shall assume full responsibility therefor and shall bear all costs attributable thereto.

4.8 ALLOWANCES

4.8.1 The Contractor shall include in the Contract Sum all allowances stated in the Contract Documents. Items covered by these allowances shall be supplied for such amounts and by such persons as the Construction Manager may direct, but the Contractor will not be required to employ persons against whom the Contractor makes a reasonable objection.

4.8.2 Unless otherwise provided in the Contract Documents:

.1 these allowances shall cover the cost to the Contractor, less any applicable trade discount, of the materials and equipment required by the allowance, delivered at the site, and all applicable taxes;

.2 the Contractor's costs for unloading and handling on the site, labor, installation costs, overhead, profit and other expenses contemplated for the original allowance shall be included in the Contract Sum and not in the allowance;

.3 whenever the cost is more or less than the allowance, the Contract Sum shall be adjusted accordingly by Change Order, the amount of which will recognize changes, if any, in handling costs on the site, labor, installation costs, overhead, profit and other expenses.

4.9 SUPERINTENDENT

4.9.1 The Contractor shall employ a competent superintendent and necessary assistants who shall be in attendance at the Project site during the progress of the Work. The superintendent shall represent the Contractor and all communications given to the superintendent shall be as binding as if given to the Contractor. Important communications shall be confirmed in writing. Other communications shall be so confirmed on written request in each case.

4.10 CONTRACTOR'S CONSTRUCTION SCHEDULE

4.10.1 The Contractor, immediately after being awarded the Contract, shall prepare and submit for the Construction Manager's approval a Contractor's Construction Schedule for the Work which shall provide for expeditious and practicable execution of the Work. This schedule shall be coordinated by the Construction Manager with the Project Construction Schedule. The Contractor's Construction Schedule shall be revised as required by the conditions of the Work and the Project, subject to the Construction Manager's approval.

4.11 DOCUMENTS AND SAMPLES AT THE SITE

4.11.1 The Contractor shall maintain at the Project site, on a current basis, one record copy of all Drawings, Specifications, Addenda, Change Orders and other Modifications, in good order and marked currently to record all changes made during construction, and approved Shop Drawings, Product Data and Samples. These shall be available to the Architect and the Construction Manager. The Contractor shall advise the Construction Manager on a current basis of all changes in the Work made during construction.

4.12 SHOP DRAWINGS, PRODUCT DATA AND SAMPLES

4.12.1 Shop Drawings are drawings, diagrams, schedules and other data specially prepared for the Work by the Contractor or any Subcontractor, manufacturer, supplier or distributor to illustrate some portion of the Work.

4.12.2 Product Data are illustrations, standard schedules, performance charts, instructions, brochures, diagrams and other information furnished by the Contractor to illustrate a material, product or system for some portion of the Work.

4.12.3 Samples are physical examples which illustrate materials, equipment or workmanship, and establish standards by which the Work will be judged.

4.12.4 The Contractor shall prepare, review, approve and submit through the Construction Manager, with reasonable promptness and in such sequence as to cause no delay in the Work or in the work of the Owner or any separate contractor, all Shop Drawings, Product Data and Samples required by the Contract Documents. The Contractor shall cooperate with the Construction Manager in the Construction Manager's coordination of the Contractor's Shop Drawings, Product Data and Samples with those of other separate contractors.

4.12.5 By preparing, approving and submitting Shop Drawings, Product Data and Samples, the Contractor represents that the Contractor has determined and verified all materials, field measurements and field construction criteria related thereto, or will do so with reasonable promptness, and has checked and coordinated the information contained within such submittals with the requirements of the Work, the Project and the Contract Documents.

4.12.6 The Contractor shall not be relieved of responsibility for any deviation from the requirements of the Contract Documents by the Architect's approval of Shop Drawings, Product Data or Samples under Subparagraph 2.3.18, unless the Contractor has specifically informed the Architect and the Construction Manager in writing of such deviation at the time of submission and the Architect has given written approval to the specific deviation. The Contractor shall not be relieved from responsibility for errors or omissions in the Shop Drawings, Product Data or Samples by the Architect's approval of them.

4.12.7 The Contractor shall direct specific attention, in writing or on resubmitted Shop Drawings, Product Data or Samples, to revisions other than those requested by the Architect on previous submittals.

4.12.8 No portion of the Work requiring submission of a Shop Drawing, Product Data or Sample shall be commenced until the submittal has been approved by the Architect as provided in Subparagraph 2.3.18. All such portions of the Work shall be in accordance with approved submittals.

4.13 USE OF SITE

4.13.1 The Contractor shall confine operations at the site to areas permitted by law, ordinances, permits and the Contract Documents, and shall not unreasonably encumber the site with any materials or equipment.

4.13.2 The Contractor shall coordinate all of the Contractor's operations with, and secure approval from, the Construction Manager before using any portion of the site.

4.14 CUTTING AND PATCHING OF WORK

4.14.1 The Contractor shall be responsible for all cutting, fitting or patching that may be required to complete the Work or to make its several parts fit together properly.

4.14.2 The Contractor shall not damage or endanger any portion of the Work or the work of the Owner or any separate contractors by cutting, patching or otherwise altering any work, or by excavation. The Contractor shall not cut or otherwise alter the work of the Owner or any separate contractor except with the written consent of the Owner and of such separate contractor. The Contractor shall not unreasonably withhold from the Owner or any separate contractor consent to cutting or otherwise altering the Work.

4.15 CLEANING UP

4.15.1 The Contractor shall at all times keep the premises free from accumulation of waste materials or rubbish caused by the Contractor's operations. At the completion of the Work, the Contractor shall remove all the Contractor's waste materials and rubbish from and about the Project as well as all the Contractor's tools, construction equipment, machinery and surplus materials.

4.15.2 If the Contractor fails to clean up at the completion of the Work, the Owner may do so as provided in Paragraph 3.4 and the cost thereof shall be charged to the Contractor.

4.16 COMMUNICATIONS

4.16.1 The Contractor shall forward all communications to the Owner and the Architect through the Construction Manager.

4.17 ROYALTIES AND PATENTS

4.17.1 The Contractor shall pay all royalties and license fees, shall defend all suits or claims for infringement of any patent rights and shall save the Owner and the Construction Manager harmless from loss on account thereof, except that the Owner, or the Construction Manager as the case may be, shall be responsible for all such loss when a particular design, process or the product of a particular manufacturer or manufacturers is selected by such person or such person's agent. If the Contractor, or the Construction Manager as the case may be, has reason to believe that the design, process or product selected is an infringement of a patent, that party shall be responsible for such loss unless such information is promptly given to the others and also to the Architect.

4.18 INDEMNIFICATION

4.18.1 To the fullest extent permitted by law, the Contractor shall indemnify and hold harmless the Owner, the Architect, the Construction Manager, and their agents and employees from and against all claims, damages, losses and expenses, including, but not limited to, attorneys' fees arising out of or resulting from the performance of the Work, provided that any such claim, damage, loss or expense (1) is attributable to bodily injury, sickness, disease or death, or to injury to or destruction of tangible property (other than the Work itself) including the loss of use resulting therefrom, and (2) is caused in whole or in part by any negligent act or omission of the Contractor, any Subcontractor, anyone directly or indirectly employed by any of them or anyone for whose acts any of them may be liable, regardless of whether or not it is caused in part by a party indemnified hereunder. Such obligation shall not be construed to negate, abridge or otherwise reduce any other right or obligation of indemnity which would otherwise exist as to any party or person described in this Paragraph 4.18.

4.18.2 In any and all claims against the Owner, the Architect, the Construction Manager or any of their agents or employees by any employee of the Contractor, any Subcontractor, anyone directly or indirectly employed by any of them or anyone for whose acts any of them may be liable, the indemnification obligation under this Paragraph 4.18 shall not be limited in any way by any limitation on the amount or type of damages, compensation or benefits payable by or for the Contractor or any Subcontractor under workers' or workmen's compensation acts, disability benefit acts or other employee benefit acts.

4.18.3 The obligations of the Contractor under this Paragraph 4.18 shall not extend to the liability of the Architect or the Construction Manager, their agents or employees, arising out of (1) the preparation or approval of maps, drawings, opinions, reports, surveys, Change Orders, designs or specifications, or (2) the giving of or the failure to give directions or instructions by the Architect or the Construction Manager, their agents or employees, provided such giving or failure to give is the primary cause of the injury or damage.

ARTICLE 5
SUBCONTRACTORS

5.1 DEFINITION

5.1.1 A Subcontractor is a person or entity who has a direct contract with the Contractor to perform any of the Work at the site. The term Subcontractor means a Subcontractor or a Subcontractor's authorized representative. The term Subcontractor does not include any separate contractor or any separate contractor's subcontractors.

5.1.2 A Sub-subcontractor is a person or entity who has a direct or indirect contract with a Subcontractor to perform any of the Work at the site. The term Sub-subcontractor means a Sub-subcontractor or an authorized representative thereof.

5.2 AWARDS OF SUBCONTRACTS AND OTHER CONTRACTS FOR PORTIONS OF THE WORK

5.2.1 Unless otherwise required by the Contract Documents or the Bidding Documents, the Contractor, as soon as practicable after the award of the Contract, shall furnish to the Construction Manager in writing for review by the Owner, the Architect and the Construction Manager, the names of the persons or entities (including those who are to furnish materials or equipment fabricated to a special design) proposed for each of the principal portions of the Work. The Construction Manager will promptly reply to the Contractor in writing stating whether or not the Owner, the Architect or the Construction Manager, after due investigation, has reasonable objection to any such proposed person or entity. Failure of the Construction Manager to reply promptly shall constitute notice of no reasonable objection.

5.2.2 The Contractor shall not contract with any such proposed person or entity to whom the Owner, the Architect or the Construction Manager has made reasonable objection under the provisions of Subparagraph 5.2.1. The Contractor shall not be required to contract with anyone to whom the Contractor has a reasonable objection.

5.2.3 If the Owner, the Architect or the Construction Manager has reasonable objection to any such proposed person or entity, the Contractor shall submit a substitute to whom the Owner, the Architect and the Construction Manager have no reasonable objection, and the Contract Sum shall be increased or decreased by the difference in cost occasioned by such substitution and an appropriate Change Order shall be issued; however, no increase in the Contract Sum shall be allowed for any such substitution unless the Contractor has acted promptly and responsively in submitting names as required by Subparagraph 5.2.1.

5.2.4 The Contractor shall make no substitution for any Subcontractor, person or entity previously selected if the Owner, the Architect or the Construction Manager makes reasonable objection to such substitution.

5.3 SUBCONTRACTUAL RELATIONS

5.3.1 By an appropriate agreement, written where legally required for validity, the Contractor shall require each Subcontractor, to the extent of the Work to be performed by the Subcontractor, to be bound to the Contractor by the terms of the Contract Documents, and to assume toward the Contractor all the obligations and responsibilities which the Contractor, by these Documents, assumes toward the Owner, the Architect and the Construction Manager. Said agreement shall preserve and protect the rights of the Owner, the Architect and the Construction Manager under the Contract Documents with respect to the Work to be performed by the Subcontractor so that the subcontracting thereof will not prejudice such rights, and shall allow to the Subcontractor, unless specifically provided otherwise in the Contractor-Subcontractor Agreement, the benefit of all rights, remedies and redress against the Contractor that the Contractor, by these Documents, has against the Owner. Where appropriate, the Contractor shall require each Subcontractor to enter into similar agreements with their Sub-subcontractors. The Contractor shall make available to each proposed Subcontractor, prior to the execution of the Subcontract, copies of the Contract Documents to which the Subcontractor will be bound by this Paragraph 5.3, and identify to the Subcontractor any terms and conditions of the proposed Subcontract which may be at variance with the Contract Documents. Each Subcontractor shall similarly make copies of such Documents available to their Sub-subcontractors.

ARTICLE 6
WORK BY OWNER OR BY SEPARATE CONTRACTORS

6.1 OWNER'S RIGHT TO PERFORM WORK AND TO AWARD SEPARATE CONTRACTS

6.1.1 The Owner reserves the right to perform work related to the Project with the Owner's own forces, and to award separate contracts in connection with other portions of the Project or other work on the site under these or similar Conditions of the Contract. If the Contractor claims that delay, damage or additional cost is involved because of such action by the Owner, the Contractor shall make such claim as provided elsewhere in the Contract Documents.

6.1.2 When separate contracts are awarded for different portions of the Project or other work on the site, the term Contractor in the Contract Documents in each case shall mean the Contractor who executes each separate Owner-Contractor Agreement.

6.1.3 The Owner will provide for the coordination of the work of the Owner's own forces and of each separate contractor with the Work of the Contractor, who shall cooperate therewith as provided in Paragraph 6.2.

6.2 MUTUAL RESPONSIBILITY

6.2.1 The Contractor shall afford the Owner, the Construction Manager and separate contractors reasonable opportunity for the introduction and storage of their materials and equipment and the execution of their work, and shall connect and coordinate the Work with theirs as required by the Contract Documents.

6.2.2 If any part of the Contractor's Work depends for proper execution or results upon the work of the Owner or any separate contractor, the Contractor shall, prior to proceeding with the Work, promptly report to the Construction Manager any apparent discrepancies or defects in such other work that render it unsuitable for such proper execution and results. Failure of the Contractor so to report shall constitute an acceptance of the Owner's or separate contractor's work as fit and proper to receive the Work, except as to defects which may subsequently become apparent in such work by others.

6.2.3 Any costs caused by defective or ill-timed work shall be borne by the party responsible therefor.

6.2.4 Should the Contractor wrongfully cause damage to the work or property of the Owner, or to other work or property on the site, the Contractor shall promptly remedy such damage as provided in Subparagraph 10.2.5.

6.2.5 Should the Contractor wrongfully delay or cause damage to the work or property of any separate contractor, the Contractor shall, upon due notice, promptly attempt to settle with such other contractor by agreement, or otherwise to resolve the dispute. If such separate contractor sues or initiates an arbitration proceeding against the Owner on account of any delay or damage alleged to have been caused by the Contractor, the Owner shall notify the Contractor who shall defend such proceedings at the Owner's expense, and if any judgment or award against the Owner arises therefrom, the Contractor shall pay or satisfy it and shall reimburse the Owner for all attorneys' fees and court or arbitration costs which the Owner has incurred.

6.3 OWNER'S RIGHT TO CLEAN UP

6.3.1 If a dispute arises between the Contractor and separate contractors as to their responsibility for cleaning up as required by Paragraph 4.15, the Owner may clean up and charge the cost thereof to the contractors responsible therefor as the Construction Manager shall determine to be just.

ARTICLE 7
MISCELLANEOUS PROVISIONS

7.1 GOVERNING LAW

7.1.1 The Contract shall be governed by the law of the place where the Project is located.

7.2 SUCCESSORS AND ASSIGNS

7.2.1 The Owner and the Contractor, respectively, bind themselves, their partners, successors, assigns and legal representatives to the other party hereto and to the partners, successors, assigns and legal representatives of such other party with respect to all covenants, agreements and obligations contained in the Contract Documents. Neither party to the Contract shall assign the Contract or sublet it as a whole without the written consent of the other.

7.3 WRITTEN NOTICE

7.3.1 Written notice shall be deemed to have been duly served if delivered in person to the individual or member of the firm or entity or to an officer of the corporation for whom it was intended, or if delivered at or sent by registered or certified mail to the last business address known to the party giving the notice.

7.4 CLAIMS FOR DAMAGES

7.4.1 Should either party to the Contract suffer injury or damage to person or property because of any act or omission of the other party or of any of the other party's employees, agents or others for whose acts such party is legally liable, claim shall be made in writing to such other party within a reasonable time after the first observance of such injury or damage.

7.5 PERFORMANCE BOND AND LABOR AND MATERIAL PAYMENT BOND

7.5.1 The Owner shall have the right to require the Contractor to furnish bonds covering the faithful performance of the Contract and the payment of all obligations arising thereunder if and as required in the Bidding Documents or the Contract Documents.

7.6 RIGHTS AND REMEDIES

7.6.1 The duties and obligations imposed by the Contract Documents and the rights and remedies available thereunder shall be in addition to, and not a limitation of, any duties, obligations, rights and remedies otherwise imposed or available by law.

7.6.2 No action or failure to act by the Owner, the Architect, the Construction Manager or the Contractor shall constitute a waiver of any right or duty afforded any of them under the Contract, nor shall any such action or failure to act constitute an approval of or acquiescence in any breach thereunder, except as may be specifically agreed in writing.

7.7 TESTS

7.7.1 If the Contract Documents, laws, ordinances, rules, regulations or orders of any public authority having jurisdiction require any portion of the Work to be inspected, tested or approved, the Contractor shall give the Architect and the Construction Manager timely notice of its readiness so the Architect and the Construction Manager may observe such inspection, testing or approval. The Contractor shall bear all costs of such inspections, tests or approvals conducted by public authorities. Unless otherwise provided, the Owner shall bear all costs of other inspections, tests or approvals.

7.7.2 If the Architect or the Construction Manager determines that any Work requires special inspection, testing or approval which Subparagraph 7.7.1 does not include, the Construction Manager will, upon written authorization from the Owner, instruct the Contractor to order such special inspection, testing or approval, and the Contractor shall give notice as provided in Subparagraph 7.7.1. If such special inspection or testing reveals a failure of the Work to comply with the requirements of the Contract Documents, the Contractor shall bear all costs thereof, including compensation for the Architect's and the Construction Manager's additional services made necessary by such failure; otherwise the Owner shall bear such costs, and an appropriate Change Order shall be issued.

7.7.3 Required certificates of inspection, testing or approval shall be secured by the Contractor and the Contractor shall promptly deliver them to the Construction Manager for transmittal to the Architect.

7.7.4 If the Architect or the Construction Manager wishes to observe the inspections, tests or approvals required by the Contract Documents, they will do so promptly and, where practicable, at the source of supply.

7.8 INTEREST

7.8.1 Payments due and unpaid under the Contract Documents shall bear interest from the date payment is due at such rate as the parties may agree upon in writing or, in the absence thereof, at the legal rate prevailing at the place of the Project.

7.9 ARBITRATION

7.9.1 All claims, disputes and other matters in question between the Contractor and the Owner arising out of or relating to the Contract Documents or the breach thereof, except as provided in Subparagraph 2.3.14 with respect to the Architect's decisions on matters relating to artistic effect, and except for claims which have been waived by the making or acceptance of final payment as provided by Subparagraphs 9.9.4 through 9.9.6, inclusive, shall be decided by arbitration in accordance with the Construction Industry Arbitration Rules of the American Arbitration Association then obtaining unless the parties mutually agree otherwise. No arbitration arising out of or relating to the Contract Documents shall include, by consolidation, joinder or in any other manner, the Architect, the Construction Manager, their employees or consultants except by written consent containing a specific reference to the Owner-Contractor Agreement and signed by the Architect, the Construction Manager, the Owner, the Contractor and any other person sought to be joined. No arbitration shall include by consolidation, joinder or in any other manner, parties other than the Owner, the Contractor and any other persons substantially involved in a common question of fact or law, whose presence is required if complete relief is to be accorded in the arbitration. No person other than the Owner or the Contractor shall be included as an original third party or additional third party to an arbitration whose interest or responsibility is insubstantial. Any consent to arbitration involving an additional person or persons shall not constitute consent to arbitration of any dispute not described therein or with any person not named or described therein. The foregoing agreement to arbitrate and any other agreement to arbitrate with an additional person or persons duly consented to by the parties to the Owner-Contractor Agreement shall be specifically enforceable under the prevailing arbitration law. The award rendered by the arbitrators shall be final, and judgment may be entered upon it in accordance with applicable law in any court having jurisdiction thereof.

7.9.2 Notice of the demand for arbitration shall be filed in writing with the other party to the Owner-Contractor Agreement and with the American Arbitration Association, and a copy shall be filed with the Architect and the Construction Manager. The demand for arbitration shall be made within the time limits specified in Subparagraph 2.3.15 where applicable, and in all other cases within a reasonable time after the claim, dispute or other matter in question has arisen; and in no event shall it be made after the date when institution of legal or equitable proceedings based on such claim, dispute or other matter in question would be barred by the applicable statute of limitations.

7.9.3 Unless otherwise agreed in writing, the Contractor shall carry on the Work and maintain its progress during any arbitration proceedings, and the Owner shall continue to make payments to the Contractor in accordance with the Contract Documents.

ARTICLE 8
TIME

8.1 DEFINITIONS

8.1.1 Unless otherwise provided, the Contract Time is the period of time allotted in the Contract Documents for Substantial Completion of the Work as defined in Subparagraph 8.1.3, including authorized adjustments thereto.

8.1.2 The date of commencement of the Work is the date established in a notice to proceed. If there is no notice to proceed, it shall be such other date as may be established in the Owner-Contractor Agreement or elsewhere in the Contract Documents.

8.1.3 The Date of Substantial Completion of the Work or designated portion thereof is the Date certified by the Architect when construction is sufficiently complete, in

accordance with the Contract Documents, so that the Owner or separate contractors can occupy or utilize the Work or a designated portion thereof for the use for which it is intended.

8.1.4 The Date of Substantial Completion of the Project or designated portion thereof is the Date certified by the Architect when construction is sufficiently complete so the Owner can occupy or utilize the Project or designated portion thereof for the use for which it was intended.

8.1.5 The term day as used in the Contract Documents shall mean calendar day unless specifically designated otherwise.

8.2 PROGRESS AND COMPLETION

8.2.1 All time limits stated in the Contract Documents are of the essence of the Contract.

8.2.2 The Contractor shall begin the Work on the date of commencement as defined in Subparagraph 8.1.2. The Contractor shall carry the Work forward expeditiously with adequate forces and shall achieve Substantial Completion of the Work within the Contract Time.

8.3 DELAYS AND EXTENSIONS OF TIME

8.3.1 If the Contractor is delayed at any time in the progress of the Work by any act or neglect of the Owner, the Architect, the Construction Manager, any of their employees, any separate contractor employed by the Owner, or by changes ordered in the Work, labor disputes, fire, unusual delay in transportation, adverse weather conditions not reasonably anticipatable, unavoidable casualties, any causes beyond the Contractor's control, delay authorized by the Owner pending arbitration, or by any other cause which the Construction Manager determines may justify the delay, then the Contract Time shall be extended by Change Order for such reasonable time as the Construction Manager may determine.

8.3.2 Any claim for extension of time shall be made in writing to the Construction Manager not more than twenty days after the commencement of the delay; otherwise it shall be waived. In the case of a continuing delay only one claim is necessary. The Contractor shall provide an estimate of the probable effect of such delay on the progress of the Work.

8.3.3 If no agreement is made stating the dates upon which interpretations as provided in Subparagraph 2.3.11 shall be furnished, then no claim for delay shall be allowed on account of failure to furnish such interpretations until fifteen days after written request is made for them, and not then unless such claim is reasonable.

8.3.4 This Paragraph 8.3 does not exclude the recovery of damages for delay by either party under other provisions of the Contract Documents.

ARTICLE 9
PAYMENTS AND COMPLETION

9.1 CONTRACT SUM

9.1.1 The Contract Sum is stated in the Owner-Contractor Agreement and, including authorized adjustments thereto, is the total amount payable by the Owner to the Contractor for the performance of the Work under the Contract Documents.

9.2   SCHEDULE OF VALUES

9.2.1 Before the first Application for Payment, the Contractor shall submit to the Construction Manager a schedule of values allocated to the various portions of the Work, prepared in such form and supported by such data to substantiate its accuracy as the Architect and the Construction Manager may require. This schedule, unless objected to by the Construction Manager or the Architect, shall be used only as a basis for the Contractor's Applications for Payment.

9.3   APPLICATIONS FOR PAYMENT

9.3.1 At least fifteen days before the date for each progress payment established in the Owner-Contractor Agreement, the Contractor shall submit to the Construction Manager an itemized Application for Payment, notarized if required, supported by such data substantiating the Contractor's right to payment as the Owner, the Architect or the Construction Manager may require, and reflecting retainage, if any, as provided elsewhere in the Contract Documents. The Construction Manager will assemble the Application with similar applications from other contractors on the Project into a combined Project Application for Payment and forward it with recommendations to the Architect within seven days.

9.3.2 Unless otherwise provided in the Contract Documents, payments will be made on account of materials or equipment not incorporated in the Work but delivered and suitably stored at the site and, if approved in advance by the Owner, payments may similarly be made for materials or equipment suitably stored at some other location agreed upon in writing. Payments for materials or equipment stored on or off the site shall be conditioned upon submission by the Contractor of bills of sale or such other procedures satisfactory to the Owner to establish the Owner's title to such materials or equipment or otherwise protect the Owner's interest, including applicable insurance and transportation to the site for those materials and equipment stored off the site.

9.3.3 The Contractor warrants that title to all Work, materials and equipment covered by an Application for Payment will pass to the Owner either by incorporation in the construction or upon receipt of payment by the Contractor, whichever occurs first, free and clear of all liens, claims, security interests or encumbrances, hereinafter referred to in this Article 9 as "liens"; and that no Work, materials or equipment covered by an Application for Payment will have been acquired by the Contractor, or by any other person performing Work at the site or furnishing materials and equipment for the Project, subject to an agreement under which an interest therein or an encumbrance thereon is retained by the seller or otherwise imposed by the Contractor or such other person.

9.4   CERTIFICATES FOR PAYMENT

9.4.1 The Architect will, within seven days after the receipt of the Project Application for Payment with the recommendations of the Construction Manager, review the Project Application for Payment and either issue a Project Certificate for Payment to the Owner with a copy to the Construction Manager for distribution to the Contractor for such amounts as the Architect determines are properly due, or notify the Construction Manager in writing of

the reasons for withholding a Certificate as provided in Subparagraph 9.6.1. Such notification will be forwarded to the Contractor by the Construction Manager.

9.4.2 The issuance of a Project Certificate for Payment will constitute a representation by the Architect to the Owner that, based on the Architect's observations at the site as provided in Subparagraph 2.3.4 and the data comprising the Project Application for Payment, the Work has progressed to the point indicated; that, to the best of the Architect's knowledge, information and belief, the quality of the Work is in accordance with the Contract Documents (subject to an evaluation of the Work for conformance with the Contract Documents upon Substantial Completion of the Work, to the results of any subsequent tests required by or performed under the Contract Documents, to minor deviations from the Contract Documents correctable prior to completion, and to any specific qualifications stated in the Certificate); and that the Contractor is entitled to payment in the amount certified. However, by issuing a Project Certificate for Payment, the Architect shall not thereby be deemed to represent that the Architect has made exhaustive or continuous on-site inspections to check the quality or quantity of the Work, has reviewed the construction means, methods, techniques, sequences or procedures, or has made any examination to ascertain how or for what purpose the Contractor has used the monies previously paid on account of the Contract Sum.

9.5   PROGRESS PAYMENTS

9.5.1 After the Architect has issued a Project Certificate for Payment, the Owner shall make payment in the manner and within the time provided in the Contract Documents.

9.5.2 The Contractor shall promptly pay each Subcontractor upon receipt of payment from the Owner, out of the amount paid to the Contractor on account of such Subcontractor's Work, the amount to which said Subcontractor is entitled, reflecting the percentage actually retained, if any, from payments to the Contractor on account of such Subcontractor's Work. The Contractor shall, by an appropriate agreement with each Subcontractor, require each Subcontractor to make payments to their Sub-subcontractors in similar manner.

9.5.3 The Architect may, on request and at the Architect's discretion, furnish to any Subcontractor, if practicable, information regarding the percentages of completion or the amounts applied for by the Contractor and the action taken thereon by the Architect on account of Work done by such Subcontractor.

9.5.4 Neither the Owner, the Architect nor the Construction Manager shall have any obligation to pay or to see to the payment of any monies to any Subcontractor except as may otherwise be required by law.

9.5.5 No certification of a progress payment, any progress payment, or any partial or entire use or occupancy of the Project by the Owner, shall constitute an acceptance of any Work not in accordance with the Contract Documents.

9.6   PAYMENTS WITHHELD

9.6.1 The Architect, following consultation with the Construction Manager, may decline to certify payment

AIA DOCUMENT A201/CM • GENERAL CONDITIONS OF THE CONTRACT FOR CONSTRUCTION
CONSTRUCTION MANAGEMENT EDITION • JUNE 1980 EDITION • AIA® • © 1980 • THE
AMERICAN INSTITUTE OF ARCHITECTS, 1735 NEW YORK AVE., N.W., WASHINGTON, D.C. 20006

and may withhold the Certificate in whole or in part to the extent necessary to reasonably protect the Owner, if, in the Architect's opinion, the Architect is unable to make representations to the Owner as provided in Subparagraph 9.4.2. If the Architect is unable to make representations to the Owner as provided in Subparagraph 9.4.2, and to certify payment in the amount of the Project Application, the Architect will notify the Construction Manager as provided in Subparagraph 9.4.1. If the Contractor and the Architect cannot agree on a revised amount, the Architect will promptly issue a Project Certificate for Payment for the amount for which the Architect is able to make such representations to the Owner. The Architect may also decline to certify payment or, because of subsequently discovered evidence or subsequent observations, the Architect may nullify the whole or any part of any Project Certificate for Payment previously issued to such extent as may be necessary, in the Architect's opinion, to protect the Owner from loss because of:

.1 defective Work not remedied;

.2 third party claims filed or reasonable evidence indicating probable filing of such claims;

.3 failure of the Contractor to make payments properly to Subcontractors, or for labor, materials or equipment;

.4 reasonable evidence that the Work cannot be completed for the unpaid balance of the Contract Sum;

.5 damage to the Owner or another contractor;

.6 reasonable evidence that the Work will not be completed within the Contract Time; or

.7 persistent failure to carry out the Work in accordance with the Contract Documents.

9.6.2 When the grounds in Subparagraph 9.6.1 above are removed, payment shall be made for amounts withheld because of them.

9.7 FAILURE OF PAYMENT

9.7.1 If the Construction Manager should fail to issue recommendations within seven days of receipt of the Contractor's Application for Payment, or if, through no fault of the Contractor, the Architect does not issue a Project Certificate for Payment within seven days after the Architect's receipt of the Project Application for Payment, or if the Owner does not pay the Contractor within seven days after the date established in the Contract Documents any amount certified by the Architect or awarded by arbitration, then the Contractor may, upon seven additional days' written notice to the Owner, the Architect and the Construction Manager, stop the Work until payment of the amount owing has been received. The Contract Sum shall be increased by the amount of the Contractor's reasonable costs of shut-down, delay and start-up, which shall be effected by appropriate Change Order in accordance with Paragraph 12.3.

9.8 SUBSTANTIAL COMPLETION

9.8.1 When the Contractor considers that the Work, or a designated portion thereof which is acceptable to the Owner, is substantially complete as defined in Subparagraph 8.1.3, the Contractor shall prepare for the Construction Manager a list of items to be completed or corrected. The failure to include any items on such list does not alter the responsibility of the Contractor to complete all Work in accordance with the Contract Documents. When the Architect, on the basis of inspection and consultation with the Construction Manager, determines that the Work or designated portion thereof is substantially complete, the Architect will then prepare a Certificate of Substantial Completion of the Work which shall establish the Date of Substantial Completion of the Work, shall state the responsibilities of the Owner and the Contractor for security, maintenance, heat, utilities, damage to the Work and insurance, and shall fix the time within which the Contractor shall complete the items listed therein. The Certificate of Substantial Completion of the Work shall be submitted to the Owner and the Contractor for their written acceptance of the responsibilities assigned to them in such Certificate.

9.8.2 Upon Substantial Completion of the Work or designated portion thereof, and upon application by the Contractor and certification by the Architect, the Owner shall make payment, reflecting adjustment in retainage, if any, for such Work or portion thereof as provided in the Contract Documents.

9.8.3 When the Architect, on the basis of inspections, determines that the Project or designated portion thereof is substantially complete, the Architect will then prepare a Certificate of Substantial Completion of the Project which shall establish the Date of Substantial Completion of the Project and fix the time within which the Contractor shall complete any uncompleted items on the Certificate of Substantial Completion of the Work.

9.8.4 Warranties required by the Contract Documents shall commence on the Date of Substantial Completion of the Project or designated portion thereof unless otherwise provided in the Certificate of Substantial Completion of the Work or designated portion thereof.

9.9 FINAL COMPLETION AND FINAL PAYMENT

9.9.1 Following the Architect's issuance of the Certificate of Substantial Completion of the Work or designated portion thereof, and the Contractor's completion of the Work, the Contractor shall forward to the Construction Manager a written notice that the Work is ready for final inspection and acceptance, and shall also forward to the Construction Manager a final Application for Payment. Upon receipt, the Construction Manager will make the necessary evaluations and forward recommendations to the Architect who will promptly make such inspection. When the Architect finds the Work acceptable under the Contract Documents and the Contract fully performed, the Architect will issue a Project Certificate for Payment which will approve the final payment due the Contractor. This approval will constitute a representation that, to the best of the Architect's knowledge, information and belief, and on the basis of observations and inspections, the Work has been completed in accordance with the Terms and Conditions of the Contract Documents and that the entire balance found to be due the Contractor, and noted in said Certificate, is due and payable. The Architect's approval of said Project Certificate for Payment will constitute a further representation that the conditions precedent to the Contractor's being entitled to final payment as set forth in Subparagraph 9.9.2 have been fulfilled.

9.9.2 Neither the final payment nor the remaining retainage shall become due until the Contractor submits to the Architect, through the Construction Manager, (1) an affidavit that all payrolls, bills for materials and equipment, and other indebtedness connected with the Work for which the Owner or the Owner's property might in any way be responsible, have been paid or otherwise satisfied, (2) consent of surety, if any, to final payment, and (3) if required by the Owner, other data establishing payment or satisfaction of all such obligations, such as receipts, releases and waivers of liens arising out of the Contract, to the extent and in such form as may be designated by the Owner. If any Subcontractor refuses to furnish a release or waiver required by the Owner, the Contractor may furnish a bond satisfactory to the Owner to indemnify the Owner against any such lien. If any such lien remains unsatisfied after all payments are made, the Contractor shall refund to the Owner all monies that the latter may be compelled to pay in discharging such lien, including all costs and reasonable attorneys' fees.

9.9.3 If, after Substantial Completion of the Work, final completion thereof is materially delayed through no fault of the Contractor or by the issuance of Change Orders affecting final completion, and the Construction Manager so confirms, the Owner shall, upon application by the Contractor and certification by the Architect and without terminating the Contract, make payment of the balance due for that portion of the Work fully completed and accepted. If the remaining balance for Work not fully completed or corrected is less than the retainage stipulated in the Contract Documents, and if bonds have been furnished as provided in Paragraph 7.5, the written consent of the surety to the payment of the balance due for that portion of the Work fully completed and accepted shall be submitted by the Contractor to the Construction Manager prior to certification of such payment. Such payment shall be made under the Terms and Conditions governing final payments, except that it shall not constitute a waiver of claims.

9.9.4 The making of final payment shall, after the Date of Substantial Completion of the Project, constitute a waiver of all claims by the Owner except those arising from:

.1 unsettled liens;

.2 faulty or defective Work appearing after Substantial Completion of the Work;

.3 failure of the Work to comply with the requirements of the Contract Documents; or

.4 terms of any special warranties required by the Contract Documents.

9.9.5 The acceptance of final payment shall, after the Date of Substantial Completion of the Project, constitute a waiver of all claims by the Contractor except those previously made in writing and identified by the Contractor as unsettled at the time of the final Application for Payment.

9.9.6 All provisions of this Agreement, including without limitation those establishing obligations and procedures, shall remain in full force and effect notwithstanding the making or acceptance of final payment prior to the Date of Substantial Completion of the Project.

ARTICLE 10
PROTECTION OF PERSONS AND PROPERTY

10.1 SAFETY PRECAUTIONS AND PROGRAMS

10.1.1 The Contractor shall be responsible for initiating, maintaining and supervising all safety precautions and programs in connection with the Work.

10.2 SAFETY OF PERSONS AND PROPERTY

10.2.1 The Contractor shall take all reasonable precautions for the safety of, and shall provide all reasonable protection to prevent damage, injury or loss to:

.1 all employees on the Work and all other persons who may be affected thereby;

.2 all the Work and all materials and equipment to be incorporated therein, whether in storage on or off the site, under the care, custody or control of the Contractor or any of the Contractor's Subcontractors or Sub-subcontractors;

.3 other property at the site or adjacent thereto, including trees, shrubs, lawns, walks, pavements, roadways, structures and utilities not designated for removal, relocation or replacement in the course of construction; and

.4 the work of the Owner or other separate contractors.

10.2.2 The Contractor shall give all notices and comply with all applicable laws, ordinances, rules, regulations and lawful orders of any public authority bearing on the safety of persons or property or their protection from damage, injury or loss.

10.2.3 The Contractor shall erect and maintain, as required by existing conditions and the progress of the Work, all reasonable safeguards for safety and protection, including posting danger signs and other warnings against hazards, promulgating safety regulations and notifying owners and users of adjacent utilities.

10.2.4 When the use or storage of explosives or other hazardous materials or equipment is necessary for the execution of the Work, the Contractor shall exercise the utmost care and shall carry on such activities under the supervision of properly qualified personnel.

10.2.5 The Contractor shall promptly remedy all damage or loss (other than damage or loss insured under Paragraph 11.3) to any property referred to in Clauses 10.2.1.2 and 10.2.1.3 caused in whole or in part by the Contractor, any Subcontractor, any Sub-subcontractor, anyone directly or indirectly employed by any of them, or by anyone for whose acts any of them may be liable, and for which the Contractor is responsible under Clauses 10.2.1.2 and 10.2.1.3, except damage or loss attributable to the acts or omissions of the Owner, the Architect, the Construction Manager or anyone directly or indirectly employed by any of them, or by anyone for whose acts any of them may be liable, and not attributable to the fault or negligence of the Contractor. The foregoing obligations of the Contractor are in addition to the Contractor's obligations under Paragraph 4.18.

10.2.6 The Contractor shall designate a responsible member of the Contractor's organization at the site whose duty shall be the prevention of accidents. This person shall be the Contractor's superintendent unless

AIA DOCUMENT A201/CM • GENERAL CONDITIONS OF THE CONTRACT FOR CONSTRUCTION
CONSTRUCTION MANAGEMENT EDITION • JUNE 1980 EDITION • AIA® • © 1980 • THE
AMERICAN INSTITUTE OF ARCHITECTS, 1735 NEW YORK AVE., N.W., WASHINGTON, D.C. 20006

otherwise designated by the Contractor in writing to the Owner and the Construction Manager.

10.2.7 The Contractor shall not load or permit any part of the Work to be loaded so as to endanger its safety.

10.3 EMERGENCIES

10.3.1 In any emergency affecting the safety of persons or property the Contractor shall act, at the Contractor's discretion, to prevent threatened damage, injury or loss. Any additional compensation or extension of time claimed by the Contractor on account of emergency work shall be determined as provided in Article 12 for Changes in the Work.

ARTICLE 11
INSURANCE

11.1 CONTRACTOR'S LIABILITY INSURANCE

11.1.1 The Contractor shall purchase and maintain insurance for protection from the claims set forth below which may arise out of or result from the Contractor's operations under the Contract, whether such operations be by the Contractor or by any Subcontractor, or by anyone directly or indirectly employed by any of them, or by anyone for whose acts any of them may be liable:

.1 claims under workers' or workmen's compensation, disability benefit and other similar employee benefit acts;

.2 claims for damages because of bodily injury, occupational sickness or disease, or death of the Contractor's employees;

.3 claims for damages because of bodily injury, sickness or disease, or death of any person other than the Contractor's employees;

.4 claims for damages insured by usual personal injury liability coverage which are sustained (1) by any person as a result of an offense directly or indirectly related to the employment of such person by the Contractor, or (2) by any other person;

.5 claims for damages, other than to the Work itself, because of injury to or destruction of tangible property, including loss of use resulting therefrom; and

.6 claims for damages because of bodily injury or death of any person or property damage arising out of the ownership, maintenance or use of any motor vehicle.

11.1.2 The insurance required by Subparagraph 11.1.1 shall be written for not less than any limits of liability specified in the Contract Documents or required by law, whichever is greater.

11.1.3 The insurance required by Subparagraph 11.1.1 shall include contractual liability insurance applicable to the Contractor's obligations under Paragraph 4.18.

11.1.4 Certificates of Insurance acceptable to the Owner shall be submitted to the Construction Manager for transmittal to the Owner prior to commencement of the Work. These Certificates shall contain a provision that coverages afforded under the policies will not be canceled until at least thirty days' prior written notice has been given to the Owner.

11.2 OWNER'S LIABILITY INSURANCE

11.2.1 The Owner shall be responsible for purchasing and maintaining Owner's liability insurance and, at the Owner's option, may purchase and maintain insurance for protection against claims which may arise from operations under the Contract.

11.3 PROPERTY INSURANCE

11.3.1 Unless otherwise provided, the Owner shall purchase and maintain property insurance upon the entire Work at the site to the full insurable value thereof. This insurance shall include the interests of the Owner, the Construction Manager, the Contractor, Subcontractors and Sub-subcontractors in the Work, and shall insure against the perils of fire and extended coverage and shall include "all risk" insurance for physical loss or damage including, without duplication of coverage, theft, vandalism and malicious mischief. If the Owner does not intend to purchase such insurance for the full insurable value of the entire Work, the Owner shall inform the Contractor in writing prior to commencement of the Work. The Contractor may then effect insurance which will protect the interests of the Contractor, the Contractor's Subcontractors and the Sub-subcontractors in the Work, and by appropriate Change Order the cost thereof shall be charged to the Owner. If the Contractor is damaged by failure of the Owner to purchase or maintain such insurance and to so notify the Contractor, then the Owner shall bear all reasonable costs properly attributable thereto. If not covered under the all risk insurance or otherwise provided in the Contract Documents, the Contractor shall effect and maintain similar property insurance on portions of the Work stored off the site or in transit when such portions of the Work are to be included in an Application for Payment under Subparagraph 9.3.2.

11.3.2 The Owner shall purchase and maintain such boiler and machinery insurance as may be required by the Contract Documents or by law. This insurance shall include the interests of the Owner, the Construction Manager, the Contractor, Subcontractors and Sub-subcontractors in the Work.

11.3.3 Any loss insured under Subparagraph 11.3.1 is to be adjusted with the Owner and made payable to the Owner as trustee for the insureds, as their interests may appear, subject to the requirements of any applicable mortgagee clause and of Subparagraph 11.3.8. The Contractor shall pay each Subcontractor a just share of any insurance monies received by the Contractor, and by appropriate agreement, written where legally required for validity, shall require each Subcontractor to make payments to their Sub-subcontractors in similar manner.

11.3.4 The Owner shall file a copy of all policies with the Contractor before an exposure to loss may occur.

11.3.5 If the Contractor requests in writing that insurance for risks other than those described in Subparagraphs 11.3.1 and 11.3.2, or other special hazards, be included in the property insurance policy, the Owner shall, if possible, include such insurance, and the cost thereof shall be charged to the Contractor by appropriate Change Order.

11.3.6 The Owner and the Contractor waive all rights against (1) each other and the Subcontractors, Sub-sub-contractors, agents and employees of each other, and (2) the Architect, the Construction Manager and separate contractors, if any, and their subcontractors, sub-subcontractors, agents and employees, for damages caused by fire or other perils to the extent covered by insurance obtained pursuant to this Paragraph 11.3 or any other property insurance applicable to the Work, except such rights as they may have to the proceeds of such insurance held by the Owner as trustee. The foregoing waiver afforded the Architect, the Construction Manager, their agents and employees shall not extend to the liability imposed by Subparagraph 4.18.3. The Owner or the Contractor, as appropriate, shall require of the Architect, the Construction Manager, separate contractors, Subcontractors and Sub-subcontractors by appropriate agreements, written where legally required for validity, similar waivers each in favor of all other parties enumerated in this Subparagraph 11.3.6.

11.3.7 If required in writing by any party in interest, the Owner as trustee shall, upon the occurrence of an insured loss, give bond for the proper performance of the Owner's duties. The Owner shall deposit in a separate account any money so received, and shall distribute it in accordance with such agreement as the parties in interest may reach, or in accordance with an award by arbitration in which case the procedure shall be as provided in Paragraph 7.9. If after such loss no other special agreement is made, replacement of damaged Work shall be covered by an appropriate Change Order.

11.3.8 The Owner, as trustee, shall have power to adjust and settle any loss with the insurers unless one of the parties in interest shall object, in writing within five days after the occurrence of loss, to the Owner's exercise of this power, and if such objection be made, arbitrators shall be chosen as provided in Paragraph 7.9. The Owner as trustee shall, in that case, make settlement with the insurers in accordance with the directions of such arbitrators. If distribution of the insurance proceeds by arbitration is required, the arbitrators will direct such distribution.

11.3.9 If the Owner finds it necessary to occupy or use a portion or portions of the Work prior to Substantial Completion thereof, such occupancy shall not commence prior to a time mutually agreed to by the Owner and the Contractor and to which the insurance company or companies providing the property insurance have consented by endorsement to the policy or policies. This insurance shall not be canceled or lapsed on account of such partial occupancy. Consent of the Contractor and of the insurance company or companies to such occupancy or use shall not be unreasonably withheld.

11.4   LOSS OF USE INSURANCE

11.4.1 The Owner, at the Owner's option, may purchase and maintain insurance for protection against loss of use of the Owner's property due to fire or other hazards, however caused. The Owner waives all rights of action against the Contractor for loss of use of the Owner's property, including consequential losses due to fire or other hazards however caused, to the extent covered by insurance under this Paragraph 11.4.

ARTICLE 12
CHANGES IN THE WORK

12.1   CHANGE ORDERS

12.1.1 A Change Order is a written order to the Contractor signed to show the recommendation of the Construction Manager, the approval of the Architect and the authorization of the Owner, issued after execution of the Contract, authorizing a change in the Work or an adjustment in the Contract Sum or the Contract Time. The Contract Sum and the Contract Time may be changed only by Change Order. A Change Order signed by the Contractor indicates the Contractor's agreement therewith, including the adjustment in the Contract Sum or the Contract Time.

12.1.2 The Owner, without invalidating the Contract, may order changes in the Work within the general scope of the Contract consisting of additions, deletions or other revisions, the Contract Sum and the Contract Time being adjusted accordingly. All such changes in the Work shall be authorized by Change Order, and shall be performed under the applicable conditions of the Contract Documents.

12.1.3 The cost or credit to the Owner resulting from a change in the Work shall be determined in one or more of the following ways:

.1   by mutual acceptance of a lump sum properly itemized and supported by sufficient substantiating data to permit evaluation;

.2   by unit prices stated in the Contract Documents or subsequently agreed upon;

.3   by cost to be determined in a manner agreed upon by the parties and a mutually acceptable fixed or percentage fee; or

.4   by the method provided in Subparagraph 12.1.4.

12.1.4 If none of the methods set forth in Clauses 12.1.3.1, 12.1.3.2 or 12.1.3.3 is agreed upon, the Contractor, provided a written order signed by the Owner is received, shall promptly proceed with the Work involved. The cost of such Work shall then be determined by the Architect, after consultation with the Construction Manager, on the basis of the reasonable expenditures and savings of those performing the Work attributable to the change, including, in the case of an increase in the Contract Sum, a reasonable allowance for overhead and profit. In such case, and also under Clauses 12.1.3.3 and 12.1.3.4 above, the Contractor shall keep and present, in such form as the Owner, the Architect or the Construction Manager may prescribe, an itemized accounting together with appropriate supporting data for inclusion in a Change Order. Unless otherwise provided in the Contract Documents, cost shall be limited to the following: cost of materials, including sales tax and cost of delivery; cost of labor, including social security, old age and unemployment insurance, and fringe benefits required by agreement or custom; workers' or workmen's compensation insurance; bond premiums; rental value of equipment and machinery; and the additional costs of supervision and field office personnel directly attributable to the change. Pending final determination of cost to the Owner, payments on account shall be made on the Architect's approval of a Project Certificate for Payment.

AIA DOCUMENT A201/CM • GENERAL CONDITIONS OF THE CONTRACT FOR CONSTRUCTION CONSTRUCTION MANAGEMENT EDITION • JUNE 1980 EDITION • AIA® • © 1980 • THE AMERICAN INSTITUTE OF ARCHITECTS, 1735 NEW YORK AVE., N.W., WASHINGTON, D.C. 20006

The amount of credit to be allowed by the Contractor to the Owner for any deletion or change which results in a net decrease in the Contract Sum will be the amount of the actual net cost as confirmed by the Architect after consultation with the Construction Manager. When both additions and credits covering related Work or substitutions are involved in any one change, the allowance for overhead and profit shall be figured on the basis of the net increase, if any, with respect to that change.

12.1.5 If unit prices are stated in the Contract Documents or subsequently agreed upon, and if the quantities originally contemplated are so changed in a proposed Change Order that application of the agreed unit prices to the quantities of Work proposed will cause substantial inequity to the Owner or the Contractor, the applicable unit prices shall be equitably adjusted.

12.2 CONCEALED CONDITIONS

12.2.1 Should concealed conditions encountered in the performance of the Work below the surface of the ground or should concealed or unknown conditions in an existing structure be at variance with the conditions indicated by the Contract Documents, or should unknown physical conditions below the surface of the ground or should concealed or unknown conditions in an existing structure of an unusual nature, differing materially from those ordinarily encountered and generally recognized as inherent in work of the character provided for in this Contract, be encountered, the Contract Sum shall be equitably adjusted by Change Order upon claim by either party made within twenty days after the first observance of the conditions.

12.3 CLAIMS FOR ADDITIONAL COST

12.3.1 If the Contractor wishes to make a claim for an increase in the Contract Sum, the Contractor shall give the Architect and the Construction Manager written notice thereof within twenty days after the occurrence of the event giving rise to such claim. This notice shall be given by the Contractor before proceeding to execute the Work, except in an emergency endangering life or property in which case the Contractor shall proceed in accordance with Paragraph 10.3. No such claim shall be valid unless so made. If the Owner and the Contractor cannot agree on the amount of the adjustment in the Contract Sum, it shall be determined by the Architect after consultation with the Construction Manager. Any change in the Contract Sum resulting from such claim shall be authorized by Change Order.

12.3.2 If the Contractor claims that additional cost is involved because of, but not limited to, (1) any written interpretation pursuant to Subparagraph 2.3.11, (2) any order by the Owner to stop the Work pursuant to Paragraph 3.3 where the Contractor was not at fault, or any such order by the Construction Manager as the Owner's agent, (3) any written order for a minor change in the Work issued pursuant to Paragraph 12.4, or (4) failure of payment by the Owner pursuant to Paragraph 9.7, the Contractor shall make such claim as provided in Subparagraph 12.3.1.

12.4 MINOR CHANGES IN THE WORK

12.4.1 The Architect will have authority to order minor changes in the Work not involving an adjustment in the

Contract Sum or extension of the Contract Time and not inconsistent with the intent of the Contract Documents. Such changes shall be effected by written order issued through the Construction Manager, and shall be binding on the Owner and the Contractor. The Contractor shall carry out such written orders promptly.

ARTICLE 13
UNCOVERING AND CORRECTION OF WORK

13.1 UNCOVERING OF WORK

13.1.1 If any portion of the Work should be covered contrary to the request of the Architect or the Construction Manager, or to requirements specifically expressed in the Contract Documents, it must, if required in writing by either, be uncovered for their observation and shall be replaced at the Contractor's expense.

13.1.2 If any other portion of the Work has been covered which the Architect or the Construction Manager has not specifically requested to observe prior to its being covered, either may request to see such Work and it shall be uncovered by the Contractor. If such Work be found in accordance with the Contract Documents, the cost of uncovering and replacement shall, by appropriate Change Order, be charged to the Owner. If such Work be found not in accordance with the Contract Documents, the Contractor shall pay such costs unless it be found that this condition was caused by the Owner or a separate contractor as provided in Article 6, in which event the Owner shall be responsible for the payment of such costs.

13.2 CORRECTION OF WORK

13.2.1 The Contractor shall promptly correct all Work rejected by the Architect or the Construction Manager as defective or as failing to conform to the Contract Documents whether observed before or after Substantial Completion of the Project and whether or not fabricated, installed or completed. The Contractor shall bear all costs of correcting such rejected Work, including compensation for the Architect's and the Construction Manager's additional services made necessary thereby.

13.2.2 If, within one year after the Date of Substantial Completion of the Project or designated portion thereof, or within one year after acceptance by the Owner of designated equipment, or within such longer period of time as may be prescribed by the terms of any applicable special warranty required by the Contract Documents, any of the Work is found to be defective or not in accordance with the Contract Documents, the Contractor shall correct it promptly after receipt of a written notice from the Owner to do so unless the Owner has previously given the Contractor a written acceptance of such condition. This obligation shall survive both final payment for the Work or designated portion thereof and termination of the Contract. The Owner shall give such notice promptly after discovery of the condition.

13.2.3 The Contractor shall remove from the site all portions of the Work which are defective or nonconforming and which have not been corrected under Subparagraphs 4.5.1, 13.2.1 and 13.2.2, unless removal is waived by the Owner.

13.2.4 If the Contractor fails to correct defective or nonconforming Work as provided in Subparagraphs 4.5.1,

13.2.1 and 13.2.2, the Owner may correct it in accordance with Paragraph 3.4.

13.2.5 If the Contractor does not proceed with the correction of such defective or nonconforming Work within a reasonable time fixed by written notice from the Architect issued through the Construction Manager, the Owner may remove it and may store the materials or equipment at the expense of the Contractor. If the Contractor does not pay the cost of such removal and storage within ten days thereafter, the Owner may, upon ten additional days' written notice, sell such Work at auction or at private sale and shall account for the net proceeds thereof, after deducting all the costs that should have been borne by the Contractor, including compensation for the Architect's and the Construction Manager's additional services made necessary thereby. If such proceeds of sale do not cover all costs which the Contractor should have borne, the difference shall be charged to the Contractor and an appropriate Change Order shall be issued. If the payments then or thereafter due the Contractor are not sufficient to cover such amount, the Contractor shall pay the difference to the Owner.

13.2.6 The Contractor shall bear the cost of making good all work of the Owner or separate contractors destroyed or damaged by such correction or removal.

13.2.7 Nothing contained in this Paragraph 13.2 shall be construed to establish a period of limitation with respect to any other obligation which the Contractor might have under the Contract Documents, including Paragraph 4.5 hereof. The establishment of the time periods noted in Subparagraph 13.2.2, or such longer period of time as may be prescribed by law or by the terms of any warranty required by the Contract Documents, relates only to the specific obligation of the Contractor to correct the Work, and has no relationship to the time within which the Contractor's obligation to comply with the Contract Documents may be sought to be enforced, nor to the time within which proceedings may be commenced to establish the Contractor's liability with respect to the Contractor's obligations other than specifically to correct the Work.

13.3 ACCEPTANCE OF DEFECTIVE OR NONCONFORMING WORK

13.3.1 If the Owner prefers to accept defective or nonconforming Work, the Owner may do so instead of requiring its removal and correction, in which case a Change Order will be issued to reflect a reduction in the Contract Sum where appropriate and equitable. Such adjustment shall be effected whether or not final payment has been made.

ARTICLE 14
TERMINATION OF THE CONTRACT

14.1 TERMINATION BY THE CONTRACTOR

14.1.1 If the Work is stopped for a period of thirty days under an order of any court or other public authority having jurisdiction, or as a result of an act of government such as a declaration of a national emergency making materials unavailable, through no act or fault of the Contractor or a Subcontractor or their agents or employees or any other persons performing any of the Work under a contract with the Contractor, or if the Work should be stopped for a period of thirty days by the Contractor because of the Construction Manager's failure to recommend or the Architect's failure to issue a Project Certificate for Payment as provided in Paragraph 9.7 or because the Owner has not made payment thereon as provided in Paragraph 9.7, then the Contractor may, upon seven additional days' written notice to the Owner, the Architect and the Construction Manager, terminate the Contract and recover from the Owner payment for all Work executed and for any proven loss sustained upon any materials, equipment, tools, construction equipment and machinery, including reasonable profit and damages.

14.2 TERMINATION BY THE OWNER

14.2.1 If the Contractor is adjudged a bankrupt, or makes a general assignment for the benefit of creditors, or if a receiver is appointed on account of the Contractor's insolvency, or if the Contractor persistently or repeatedly refuses or fails, except in cases for which extension of time is provided, to supply enough properly skilled workers or proper materials, or fails to make prompt payment to Subcontractors or for materials or labor, or persistently disregards laws, ordinances, rules, regulations or orders of any public authority having jurisdiction, or otherwise is guilty of a substantial violation of a provision of the Contract Documents, and fails within seven days after receipt of written notice to commence and continue correction of such default, neglect or violation with diligence and promptness, the Owner, upon certification by the Architect after consultation with the Construction Manager that sufficient cause exists to justify such action, may, after seven days following receipt by the Contractor of an additional written notice and without prejudice to any other remedy the Owner may have, terminate the employment of the Contractor and take possession of the site and of all materials, equipment, tools, construction equipment and machinery thereon owned by the Contractor and may finish the Work by whatever methods the Owner may deem expedient. In such case the Contractor shall not be entitled to receive any further payment until the Work is finished.

14.2.2 If the unpaid balance of the Contract Sum exceeds the costs of finishing the Work, including compensation for the Architect's and the Construction Manager's additional services made necessary thereby, such excess shall be paid to the Contractor. If such costs exceed the unpaid balance, the Contractor shall pay the difference to the Owner. The amount to be paid to the Contractor or to the Owner, as the case may be, shall be certified by the Architect, upon application, in the manner provided in Paragraph 9.4, and this obligation for payment shall survive the termination of the Contract.

AIA DOCUMENT A201/CM • GENERAL CONDITIONS OF THE CONTRACT FOR CONSTRUCTION
CONSTRUCTION MANAGEMENT EDITION • JUNE 1980 EDITION • AIA® • © 1980 • THE
AMERICAN INSTITUTE OF ARCHITECTS, 1735 NEW YORK AVE., N.W., WASHINGTON, D.C. 20006

THE AMERICAN INSTITUTE OF ARCHITECTS

AIA Document A305

Contractor's Qualification Statement
1979 EDITION

Required in advance of consideration of application to bid or as a qualification statement in advance of award of contract. Approved and recommended by The American Institute of Architects and The Associated General Contractors of America.

The Undersigned certifies under oath the truth and correctness of all statements and of all answers to questions made hereinafter.

SUBMITTED TO:

ADDRESS:

SUBMITTED BY: Corporation ☐
NAME: Partnership ☐
ADDRESS: Individual ☐
PRINCIPAL OFFICE: Joint Venture ☐
                                                           Other ☐

1.0 How many years has your organization been in business as a General Contractor?

2.0 How many years has your organization been in business under its present business name?
   2.1 Under what other or former names has your organization operated?

AIA DOCUMENT A305 • CONTRACTOR'S QUALIFICATION STATEMENT • MARCH 1979 EDITION • AIA®
©1979 • THE AMERICAN INSTITUTE OF ARCHITECTS, 1735 NEW YORK AVENUE, N.W., WASHINGTON, D.C. 20006   A305-1979 1

3.0 If a corporation answer the following:
    3.1 Date of incorporation:
    3.2 State of incorporation:
    3.3 President's name:
    3.4 Vice-president's name(s):

    3.5 Secretary's name:
    3.6 Treasurer's name:

4.0 If an individual or a partnership answer the following:
    4.1 Date of organization:
    4.2 Name and address of all partners (State whether general or limited partnership):

5.0 If other than a corporation or partnership, describe organization and name principals:

6.0 List states and categories in which your organization is legally qualified to do business. Indicate registration or license numbers, if applicable. List states in which partnership or trade name is filed.

7.0 We normally perform the following work with our own forces:

8.0 Have you ever failed to complete any work awarded to you? If so, note when, where, and why:

9.0 Within the last five years, has any officer or partner of your organization ever been an officer or partner of another organization when it failed to complete a construction contract? If so, attach a separate sheet of explanation.

10.0 On a separate sheet, list major construction projects your organization has in process, giving the name of project, owner, architect, contract amount, percent complete, and scheduled completion date.

11.0 On a separate sheet, list the major projects your organization has completed in the past five years, giving the name of project, owner, architect, contract amount, date of completion, and percentage of the cost of the work performed with your own forces.

12.0 On a separate sheet, list the construction experience of the key individuals of your organization.

13.0 Trade References:

14.0 Bank References:

15.0 Name of Bonding Company and name and address of agent:

16.0 Attach a financial statement, audited if available, including Contractor's latest balance sheet and income statement showing the following items:

A. Current Assets (e.g., cash, joint venture accounts, accounts receivable, notes receivable, accrued income, deposits, materials inventory and prepaid expenses):

B. Net Fixed Assets:

C. Other Assets:

D. Current Liabilities (e.g., accounts payable, notes payable, accrued expenses, provision for income taxes, advances, accrued salaries, and accrued payroll taxes):

E. Other Liabilities (e.g., capital, capital stock, authorized and outstanding shares par values, earned surplus, and retained earnings):

Name of firm preparing financial statement and date thereof:

Is this financial statement for the identical organization named on page one?

If not, explain the relationship and financial responsibility of the organization whose financial statement is provided (e.g., parent-subsidiary).

Will this organization act as guarantor of the contract for construction?

17.0 Dated at

this   day of   19

Name of Organization:

      By:
      Title:

18.0

M   being duly sworn deposes and says
that he/she is the   of

Contractor(s), and that answers to the foregoing questions and all statements therein contained are
true and correct.

Subscribed and sworn before me this   day of   19

Notary Public:

My Commission Expires:

THE AMERICAN INSTITUTE OF ARCHITECTS

AIA Document A310

Bid Bond

KNOW ALL MEN BY THESE PRESENTS, that we
(Here insert full name and address or legal title of Contractor)

as Principal, hereinafter called the Principal, and
(Here insert full name and address or legal title of Surety)

a corporation duly organized under the laws of the State of
as Surety, hereinafter called the Surety, are held and firmly bound unto
(Here insert full name and address or legal title of Owner)

as Obligee, hereinafter called the Obligee, in the sum of

Dollars ($),

for the payment of which sum well and truly to be made, the said Principal and the said Surety, bind ourselves, our heirs, executors, administrators, successors and assigns, jointly and severally, firmly by these presents.

WHEREAS, the Principal has submitted a bid for
(Here insert full name, address and description of project)

NOW, THEREFORE, if the Obligee shall accept the bid of the Principal and the Principal shall enter into a Contract with the Obligee in accordance with the terms of such bid, and give such bond or bonds as may be specified in the bidding or Contract Documents with good and sufficient surety for the faithful performance of such Contract and for the prompt payment of labor and material furnished in the prosecution thereof, or in the event of the failure of the Principal to enter such Contract and give such bond or bonds, if the Principal shall pay to the Obligee the difference not to exceed the penalty hereof between the amount specified in said bid and such larger amount for which the Obligee may in good faith contract with another party to perform the Work covered by said bid, then this obligation shall be null and void, otherwise to remain in full force and effect.

Signed and sealed this   day of   19

_____
(Witness)

{
_____ _____
(Principal)   (Seal)
_____
(Title)

_____
(Witness)

{
_____ _____
(Surety)   (Seal)
_____
(Title)

AIA DOCUMENT A310 · BID BOND · AIA ® · FEBRUARY 1970 ED · THE AMERICAN
INSTITUTE OF ARCHITECTS, 1735 N.Y. AVE., N.W., WASHINGTON, D. C. 20006

1

THE AMERICAN INSTITUTE OF ARCHITECTS

AIA Document A311

Performance Bond

KNOW ALL MEN BY THESE PRESENTS: that

(Here insert full name and address or legal title of Contractor)

as Principal, hereinafter called Contractor, and,

(Here insert full name and address or legal title of Surety)

as Surety, hereinafter called Surety, are held and firmly bound unto

(Here insert full name and address or legal title of Owner)

as Obligee, hereinafter called Owner, in the amount of

Dollars ($),

for the payment whereof Contractor and Surety bind themselves, their heirs, executors, administrators, successors and assigns, jointly and severally, firmly by these presents.

WHEREAS,

Contractor has by written agreement dated   19   , entered into a contract with Owner for
(Here insert full name, address and description of project)

in accordance with Drawings and Specifications prepared by

(Here insert full name and address or legal title of Architect)

which contract is by reference made a part hereof, and is hereinafter referred to as the Contract.

AIA DOCUMENT A311 · PERFORMANCE BOND AND LABOR AND MATERIAL PAYMENT BOND · AIA ®
FEBRUARY 1970 ED. · THE AMERICAN INSTITUTE OF ARCHITECTS, 1735 N.Y. AVE., N.W., WASHINGTON, D. C. 20006   1

288

PERFORMANCE BOND

NOW, THEREFORE, THE CONDITION OF THIS OBLIGATION is such that, if Contractor shall promptly and faithfully perform said Contract, then this obligation shall be null and void; otherwise it shall remain in full force and effect.

The Surety hereby waives notice of any alteration or extension of time made by the Owner.

Whenever Contractor shall be, and declared by Owner to be in default under the Contract, the Owner having performed Owner's obligations thereunder, the Surety may promptly remedy the default, or shall promptly

1) Complete the Contract in accordance with its terms and conditions, or

2) Obtain a bid or bids for completing the Contract in accordance with its terms and conditions, and upon determination by Surety of the lowest responsible bidder, or, if the Owner elects, upon determination by the Owner and the Surety jointly of the lowest responsible bidder, arrange for a contract between such bidder and Owner, and make available as Work progresses (even though there should be a default or a succession of defaults under the contract or contracts of completion arranged under this paragraph) sufficient funds to pay the cost of completion less the balance of the contract price; but not exceeding, including other costs and damages for which the Surety may be liable hereunder, the amount set forth in the first paragraph hereof. The term "balance of the contract price," as used in this paragraph, shall mean the total amount payable by Owner to Contractor under the Contract and any amendments thereto, less the amount properly paid by Owner to Contractor.

Any suit under this bond must be instituted before the expiration of two (2) years from the date on which final payment under the Contract falls due.

No right of action shall accrue on this bond to or for the use of any person or corporation other than the Owner named herein or the heirs, executors, administrators or successors of the Owner.

Signed and sealed this   day of   19

_____
(Witness)

_____ (Principal)   (Seal)

_____ (Title)

_____
(Witness)

_____ (Surety)   (Seal)

_____ (Title)

THE AMERICAN INSTITUTE OF ARCHITECTS

AIA Document A311

Labor and Material Payment Bond

THIS BOND IS ISSUED SIMULTANEOUSLY WITH PERFORMANCE BOND IN FAVOR OF THE
OWNER CONDITIONED ON THE FULL AND FAITHFUL PERFORMANCE OF THE CONTRACT

KNOW ALL MEN BY THESE PRESENTS: that

(Here insert full name and address or legal title of Contractor)

as Principal, hereinafter called Principal, and

(Here insert full name and address or legal title of Surety)

as Surety, hereinafter called Surety, are held and firmly bound unto

(Here insert full name and address or legal title of Owner)

as Obligee, hereinafter called Owner, for the use and benefit of claimants as hereinbelow defined, in the

amount of

(Here insert a sum equal to at least one-half of the contract price)   Dollars ($),

for the payment whereof Principal and Surety bind themselves, their heirs, executors, administrators,
successors and assigns, jointly and severally, firmly by these presents.

WHEREAS,

Principal has by written agreement dated   19   , entered into a contract with Owner for
(Here insert full name, address and description of project)

in accordance with Drawings and Specifications prepared by

(Here insert full name and address or legal title of Architect)

which contract is by reference made a part hereof, and is hereinafter referred to as the Contract.

AIA DOCUMENT A311 • PERFORMANCE BOND AND LABOR AND MATERIAL PAYMENT BOND • AIA ®
FEBRUARY 1970 ED. • THE AMERICAN INSTITUTE OF ARCHITECTS, 1735 N.Y. AVE., N.W., WASHINGTON, D. C. 20006   **3**

LABOR AND MATERIAL PAYMENT BOND

NOW, THEREFORE, THE CONDITION OF THIS OBLIGATION is such that, if Principal shall promptly make payment to all claimants as hereinafter defined, for all labor and material used or reasonably required for use in the performance of the Contract, then this obligation shall be void; otherwise it shall remain in full force and effect, subject, however, to the following conditions:

1. A claimant is defined as one having a direct contract with the Principal or with a Subcontractor of the Principal for labor, material, or both, used or reasonably required for use in the performance of the Contract, labor and material being construed to include that part of water, gas, power, light, heat, oil, gasoline, telephone service or rental of equipment directly applicable to the Contract.

2. The above named Principal and Surety hereby jointly and severally agree with the Owner that every claimant as herein defined, who has not been paid in full before the expiration of a period of ninety (90) days after the date on which the last of such claimant's work or labor was done or performed, or materials were furnished by such claimant, may sue on this bond for the use of such claimant, prosecute the suit to final judgment for such sum or sums as may be justly due claimant, and have execution thereon. The Owner shall not be liable for the payment of any costs or expenses of any such suit.

3. No suit or action shall be commenced hereunder by any claimant:

a) Unless claimant, other than one having a direct contract with the Principal, shall have given written notice to any two of the following: the Principal, the Owner, or the Surety above named, within ninety (90) days after such claimant did or performed the last of the work or labor, or furnished the last of the materials for which said claim is made, stating with substantial

accuracy the amount claimed and the name of the party to whom the materials were furnished, or for whom the work or labor was done or performed. Such notice shall be served by mailing the same by registered mail or certified mail, postage prepaid, in an envelope addressed to the Principal, Owner or Surety, at any place where an office is regularly maintained for the transaction of business, or served in any manner in which legal process may be served in the state in which the aforesaid project is located, save that such service need not be made by a public officer.

b) After the expiration of one (1) year following the date on which Principal ceased Work on said Contract, it being understood, however, that if any limitation embodied in this bond is prohibited by any law controlling the construction hereof such limitation shall be deemed to be amended so as to be equal to the minimum period of limitation permitted by such law.

c) Other than in a state court of competent jurisdiction in and for the county or other political subdivision of the state in which the Project, or any part thereof, is situated, or in the United States District Court for the district in which the Project, or any part thereof, is situated, and not elsewhere.

4. The amount of this bond shall be reduced by and to the extent of any payment or payments made in good faith hereunder, inclusive of the payment by Surety of mechanics' liens which may be filed of record against said improvement, whether or not claim for the amount of such lien be presented under and against this bond.

Signed and sealed this   day of   19

_____ (Witness)	{ _____ (Principal) (Seal)
	_____ (Title)
_____ (Witness)	{ _____ (Surety) (Seal)
	_____ (Title)

THE AMERICAN INSTITUTE OF ARCHITECTS

AIA Document A401

SUBCONTRACT
Standard Form of Agreement Between Contractor and Subcontractor

1978 EDITION

Use with the latest edition of the appropriate AIA Documents as follows:

A101, Owner-Contractor Agreement — Stipulated Sum
A107, Abbreviated Owner-Contractor Agreement with General Conditions
A111, Owner-Contractor Agreement — Cost plus Fee
A201, General Conditions of the Contract for Construction.

*THIS DOCUMENT HAS IMPORTANT LEGAL CONSEQUENCES: CONSULTATION WITH
AN ATTORNEY IS ENCOURAGED WITH RESPECT TO ITS COMPLETION OR MODIFICATION*

This document has been approved and endorsed by the American Subcontractors Association
and the Associated Specialty Contractors, Inc.

AGREEMENT

made as of the   day of   in the year Nineteen
Hundred and

BETWEEN the Contractor:

and the Subcontractor:

The Project:

The Owner:

The Architect:

The Contractor and Subcontractor agree as set forth below.

AIA DOCUMENT A401 • CONTRACTOR-SUBCONTRACTOR AGREEMENT • ELEVENTH EDITION • APRIL 1978 • AIA®
©1978 • THE AMERICAN INSTITUTE OF ARCHITECTS, 1735 NEW YORK AVE., N.W., WASHINGTON, D.C. 20006

A401-1978 1

ARTICLE 1
THE CONTRACT DOCUMENTS

1.1 The Contract Documents for this Subcontract consist of this Agreement and any Exhibits attached hereto, the Agreement between the Owner and Contractor dated as of   , the Conditions of the Contract between the Owner and Contractor (General, Supplementary and other Conditions), the Drawings, the Specifications, all Addenda issued prior to and all Modifications issued after execution of the Agreement between the Owner and Contractor and agreed upon by the parties to this Subcontract. These form the Subcontract, and are as fully a part of the Subcontract as if attached to this Agreement or repeated herein.

1.2 Copies of the above documents which are applicable to the Work under this Subcontract shall be furnished to the Subcontractor upon his request. An enumeration of the applicable Contract Documents appears in Article 15.

ARTICLE 2
THE WORK

2.1 The Subcontractor shall perform all the Work required by the Contract Documents for

(Here insert a precise description of the Work covered by this Subcontract and refer to numbers of Drawings and pages of Specifications including Addenda, Modifications and accepted Alternates.)

ARTICLE 3
TIME OF COMMENCEMENT AND SUBSTANTIAL COMPLETION

3.1 The Work to be performed under this Subcontract shall be commenced
and, subject to authorized adjustments, shall be substantially completed not later than

(Here insert the specific provisions that are applicable to this Subcontract including any information pertaining to notice to proceed or other method of modification for commencement of Work, starting and completion dates, or duration, and any provisions for liquidated damages relating to failure to complete on time.)

3.2 Time is of the essence of this Subcontract.

3.3 No extension of time will be valid without the Contractor's written consent after claim made by the Subcontractor in accordance with Paragraph 11.10.

ARTICLE 4
THE CONTRACT SUM

4.1 The Contractor shall pay the Subcontractor in current funds for the performance of the Work, subject to additions and deductions authorized pursuant to Paragraph 11.9, the Contract Sum of
dollars ($).

The Contract Sum is determined as follows:

(State here the base bid or other lump sum amount, accepted alternates, and unit prices, as applicable.)

ARTICLE 5
PROGRESS PAYMENTS

5.1 The Contractor shall pay the Subcontractor monthly progress payments in accordance with Paragraph 12.4 of this Subcontract.

5.2 Applications for monthly progress payments shall be in writing and in accordance with Paragraph 11.8, shall state the estimated percentage of the Work in this Subcontract that has been satisfactorily completed and shall be submitted to the Conractor on or before the   day of each month.

(Here insert details on (1) payment procedures and date of monthly applications, or other procedure if on other than a monthly basis, (2) the basis on which payment will be made on account of materials and equipment suitably stored at the site or other location agreed upon in writing, and (3) any provisions consistent with the Contract Documents for limiting or reducing the amount retained after the Work reaches a certain stage of completion.)

5.3 When the Subcontractor's Work or a designated portion thereof is substantially complete and in accordance with the Contract Documents, the Contractor shall, upon application by the Subcontractor, make prompt application for payment of such Work. Within thirty days following issuance by the Architect of the Certificate for Payment covering such substantially completed Work, the Contractor shall, to the full extent provided in the Contract Documents, make payment to the Subcontractor of the entire unpaid balance of the Contract Sum or of that portion of the Contract Sum attributable to the substantially completed Work, less any portion of the funds for the Subcontractor's Work withheld in accordance with the Certificate to cover costs of items to be completed or corrected by the Subcontractor.

(Delete the above Paragraph if the Contract Documents do not provide for, and the Subcontractor agrees to forego, release of retainage for the Subcontractor's Work prior to completion of the entire Project.)

5.4 Progress payments or final payment due and unpaid under this Subcontract shall bear interest from the date payment is due at the rate entered below or, in the absence thereof, at the legal rate prevailing at the place of the Project.

(Here insert any rate of interest agreed upon.)

(Usury laws and requirements under the Federal Truth in Lending Act, similar state and local consumer credit laws and other regulations at the Owner's, Contractor's and Subcontractor's principal places of business, the location of the Project and elsewhere may affect the validity of this provision. Specific legal advice should be obtained with respect to deletion, modification, or other requirements such as written disclosures or waivers.)

ARTICLE 6
FINAL PAYMENT

6.1 Final payment, constituting the entire unpaid balance of the Contract Sum, shall be due when the Work described in this Subcontract is fully completed and performed in accordance with the Contract Documents and is satisfactory to the Architect, and shall be payable as follows, in accordance with Article 5 and with Paragraph 12.4 of this Subcontract:

(Here insert the relevant conditions under which or time in which final payment will become payable.)

6.2 Before issuance of the final payment, the Subcontractor, if required, shall submit evidence satisfactory to the Contractor that all payrolls, bills for materials and equipment, and all known indebtedness connected with the Subcontractor's Work have been satisfied.

ARTICLE 7
PERFORMANCE BOND AND LABOR AND MATERIAL PAYMENT BOND

(Here insert any requirement for the furnishing of bonds by the Subcontractor.)

ARTICLE 8
TEMPORARY FACILITIES AND SERVICES

8.1   Unless otherwise provided in this Subcontract, the Contractor shall furnish and make available at no cost to the Subcontractor the following temporary facilities and services:

ARTICLE 9
INSURANCE

9.1   Prior to starting work, the Subcontractor shall obtain the required insurance from a responsible insurer, and shall furnish satisfactory evidence to the Contractor that the Subcontractor has complied with the requirements of this Article 9. Similarly, the Contractor shall furnish to the Subcontractor satisfactory evidence of insurance required of the Contractor by the Contract Documents.

9.2   The Contractor and Subcontractor waive all rights against each other and against the Owner, the Architect, separate contractors and all other subcontractors for damages caused by fire or other perils to the extent covered by property insurance provided under the General Conditions, except such rights as they may have to the proceeds of such insurance.

(Here insert any insurance requirements and Subcontractor's responsibility for obtaining, maintaining and paying for necessary insurance with limits equalling or exceeding those specified in the Contract Documents and inserted below, or required by law. If applicable, this shall include fire insurance and extended coverage, public liability, property damage, employer's liability, and workers' or workmen's compensation insurance for the Subcontractor and his employees. The insertion should cover provisions for notice of cancellation, allocation of insurance proceeds, and other aspects of insurance.)

ARTICLE 10
WORKING CONDITIONS

(Here insert any applicable arrangements concerning working conditions and labor matters for the Project.)

GENERAL CONDITIONS

ARTICLE 11
SUBCONTRACTOR

11.1 RIGHTS AND RESPONSIBILITIES

11.1.1 The Subcontractor shall be bound to the Contractor by the terms of this Agreement and, to the extent that provisions of the Contract Documents between the Owner and Contractor apply to the Work of the Subcontractor as defined in this Agreement, the Subcontractor shall assume toward the Contractor all the obligations and responsibilities which the Contractor, by those Documents, assumes toward the Owner and the Architect, and shall have the benefit of all rights, remedies and redress against the Contractor which the Contractor, by those Documents, has against the Owner, insofar as applicable to this Subcontract, provided that where any provision of the Contract Documents between the Owner and Contractor is inconsistent with any provision of this Agreement, this Agreement shall govern.

11.1.2 The Subcontractor shall not assign this subcontract without the written consent of the Contractor, nor subcontract the whole of this Subcontract without the written consent of the Contractor, nor further subcontract portions of this Subcontract without written notification to the Contractor when such notification is requested by the Contractor. The Subcontractor shall not assign any amounts due or to become due under this Subcontract without written notice to the Contractor.

11.2 EXECUTION AND PROGRESS OF THE WORK

11.2.1 The Subcontractor agrees that the Contractor's equipment will be available to the Subcontractor only at the Contractor's discretion and on mutually satisfactory terms.

11.2.2 The Subcontractor shall cooperate with the Contractor in scheduling and performing his Work to avoid conflict or interference with the work of others.

11.2.3 The Subcontractor shall promptly submit shop drawings and samples required in order to perform his Work efficiently, expeditiously and in a manner that will not cause delay in the progress of the Work of the Contractor or other subcontractors.

11.2.4 The Subcontractor shall furnish periodic progress reports on the Work as mutually agreed, including information on the status of materials and equipment under this Subcontract which may be in the course of preparation or manufacture.

11.2.5 The Subcontractor agrees that all Work shall be done subject to the final approval of the Architect. The Architect's decisions in matters relating to artistic effect shall be final if consistent with the intent of the Contract Documents.

11.2.6 The Subcontractor shall pay for all materials, equipment and labor used in, or in connection with, the performance of this Subcontract through the period covered by previous payments received from the Contractor, and shall furnish satisfactory evidence, when requested by the Contractor, to verify compliance with the above requirements.

11.3 LAWS, PERMITS, FEES AND NOTICES

11.3.1 The Subcontractor shall give all notices and comply with all laws, ordinances, rules, regulations and orders of any public authority bearing on the performance of the Work under this Subcontract. The Subcontractor shall secure and pay for all permits and governmental fees, licenses and inspections necessary for the proper execution and completion of the Subcontractor's Work, the furnishing of which is required of the Contractor by the Contract Documents.

11.3.2 The Subcontractor shall comply with Federal, State and local tax laws, social security acts, unemployment compensation acts and workers' or workmen's compensation acts insofar as applicable to the performance of this Subcontract.

11.4 WORK OF OTHERS

11.4.1 In carrying out his Work, the Subcontractor shall take necessary precautions to protect properly the finished work of other trades from damage caused by his operations.

11.4.2 The Subcontractor shall cooperate with the Contractor and other subcontractors whose work might interfere with the Subcontractor's Work, and shall participate in the preparation of coordinated drawings in areas of congestion as required by the Contract Documents, specifically noting and advising the Contractor of any such interference.

11.5 SAFETY PRECAUTIONS AND PROCEDURES

11.5.1 The Subcontractor shall take all reasonable safety precautions with respect to his Work, shall comply with all safety measures initiated by the Contractor and with all applicable laws, ordinances, rules, regulations and orders of any public authority for the safety of persons or property in accordance with the requirements of the Contract Documents. The Subcontractor shall report within three days to the Contractor any injury to any of the Subcontractor's employees at the site.

11.6 CLEANING UP

11.6.1 The Subcontractor shall at all times keep the premises free from accumulation of waste materials or rubbish arising out of the operations of this Subcontract. Unless otherwise provided, the Subcontractor shall not be held responsible for unclean conditions caused by other contractors or subcontractors.

11.7 WARRANTY

11.7.1 The Subcontractor warrants to the Owner, the Architect and the Contractor that all materials and equipment furnished shall be new unless otherwise specified, and that all Work under this Subcontract shall be of good quality, free from faults and defects and in conformance with the Contract Documents. All Work not conforming to these requirements, including substitutions not properly approved and authorized, may be considered defective. The warranty provided in this Paragraph 11.7 shall be in addition to and not in limitation of any other warranty or remedy required by law or by the Contract Documents.

11.8 APPLICATIONS FOR PAYMENT

11.8.1 The Subcontractor shall submit to the Contractor applications for payment at such times as stipulated in Article 5 to enable the Contractor to apply for payment.

11.8.2 If payments are made on the valuation of Work done, the Subcontractor shall, before the first application, submit to the Contractor a schedule of values of the various parts of the Work aggregating the total sum of this Subcontract, made out in such detail as the Subcontractor and Contractor may agree upon or as required by the Owner, and supported by such evidence as to its correctness as the Contractor may direct. This schedule, when approved by the Contractor, shall be used only as a basis for Applications for Payment, unless it be found to be in error. In applying for payment, the Subcontractor shall submit a statement based upon this schedule.

11.8.3 If payments are made on account of materials or equipment not incorporated in the Work but delivered and suitably stored at the site or at some other location agreed upon in writing, such payments shall be in accordance with the terms and conditions of the Contract Documents.

11.9 CHANGES IN THE WORK

11.9.1 The Subcontractor may be ordered in writing by the Contractor, without invalidating this Subcontract, to make changes in the Work within the general scope of this Subcontract consisting of additions, deletions or other revisions, the Contract Sum and the Contract Time being adjusted accordingly. The Subcontractor, prior to the commencement of such changed or revised Work, shall submit promptly to the Contractor written copies of any claim for adjustment to the Contract Sum and Contract Time for such revised Work in a manner consistent with the Contract Documents.

11.10 CLAIMS OF THE SUBCONTRACTOR

11.10.1 The Subcontractor shall make all claims promptly to the Contractor for additional cost, extensions of time, and damages for delays or other causes in accordance with the Contract Documents. Any such claim which will affect or become part of a claim which the Contractor is required to make under the Contract Documents within a specified time period or in a specified manner shall be made in sufficient time to permit the Contractor to satisfy the requirements of the Contract Documents. Such claims shall be received by the Contractor not less than two working days preceding the time by which the Contractor's claim must be made. Failure of the Subcontractor to make such a timely claim shall bind the Subcontractor to the same consequences as those to which the Contractor is bound.

11.11 INDEMNIFICATION

11.11.1 To the fullest extent permitted by law, the Subcontractor shall indemnify and hold harmless the Owner the Architect and the Contractor and all of their agents and employees from and against all claims, damages, losses and expenses, including but not limited to attor-

ney's fees, arising out of or resulting from the performance of the Subcontractor's Work under this Subcontract, provided that any such claim, damage, loss, or expense is attributable to bodily injury, sickness, disease, or death, or to injury to or destruction of tangible property (other than the Work itself) including the loss of use resulting therefrom, to the extent caused in whole or in part by any negligent act or omission of the Subcontractor or anyone directly or indirectly employed by him or anyone for whose acts he may be liable, regardless of whether it is caused in part by a party indemnified hereunder. Such obligation shall not be construed to negate, or abridge, or otherwise reduce any other right or obligation of indemnity which would otherwise exist as to any party or person described in this Paragraph 11.11.

11.11.2 In any and all claims against the Owner, the Architect, or the Contractor or any of their agents or employees by any employee of the Subcontractor, anyone directly or indirectly employed by him or anyone for whose acts he may be liable, the indemnification obligation under this Paragraph 11.11 shall not be limited in any way by any limitation on the amount or type of damages, compensation or benefits payable by or for the Subcontractor under workers' or workmen's compensation acts, disability benefit acts or other employee benefit acts.

11.11.3 The obligations of the Subcontractor under this Paragraph 11.11 shall not extend to the liability of the Architect, his agents or employees arising out of (1) the preparation or approval of maps, drawings, opinions, reports, surveys, Change Orders, designs or specifications, or (2) the giving of or the failure to give directions or instructions by the Architect, his agents or employees provided such giving or failure to give is the primary cause of the injury or damage.

11.12 SUBCONTRACTOR'S REMEDIES

11.12.1 If the Contractor does not pay the Subcontractor through no fault of the Subcontractor, within seven days from the time payment should be made as provided in Paragraph 12.4, the Subcontractor may, without prejudice to any other remedy he may have, upon seven additional days' written notice to the Contractor, stop his Work until payment of the amount owing has been received. The Contract Sum shall, by appropriate adjustment, be increased by the amount of the Subcontractor's reasonable costs of shutdown, delay and start-up.

ARTICLE 12
CONTRACTOR

12.1 RIGHTS AND RESPONSIBILITIES

12.1.1 The Contractor shall be bound to the Subcontractor by the terms of this Agreement, and to the extent that provisions of the Contract Documents between the Owner and the Contractor apply to the Work of the Subcontractor as defined in this Agreement, the Contractor shall assume toward the Subcontractor all the obligations and responsibilities that the Owner, by those Documents, assumes toward the Contractor, and shall have the benefit of all rights, remedies and redress against the Subcontractor which the Owner, by those Documents, has against the Contractor. Where any provision of the

AIA DOCUMENT A401 • CONTRACTOR-SUBCONTRACTOR AGREEMENT • ELEVENTH EDITION • APRIL 1978 • AIA®
©1978 • THE AMERICAN INSTITUTE OF ARCHITECTS, 1735 NEW YORK AVE., N.W., WASHINGTON, D.C. 20006

Contract Documents between the Owner and the Contractor is inconsistent with any provisions of this Agreement, this Agreement shall govern.

12.2   SERVICES PROVIDED BY THE CONTRACTOR

12.2.1   The Contractor shall cooperate with the Subcontractor in scheduling and performing his Work to avoid conflicts or interference in the Subcontractor's Work, and shall expedite written responses to submittals made by the Subcontractor in accordance with Paragraphs 11.2, 11.9 and 11.10. As soon as practicable after execution of this Agreement, the Contractor shall provide the Subcontractor a copy of the estimated progress schedule of the Contractor's entire Work which the Contractor has prepared and submitted for the Owner's and the Architect's information, together with such additional scheduling details as will enable the Subcontractor to plan and perform his Work properly. The Subcontractor shall be notified promptly of any subsequent changes in the progress schedule and the additional scheduling details.

12.2.2   The Contractor shall provide suitable areas for storage of the Subcontractor's materials and equipment during the course of the Work. Any additional costs to the Subcontractor resulting from the relocation of such facilities at the direction of the Contractor shall be reimbursed by the Contractor.

12.3   COMMUNICATIONS

12.3.1   The Contractor shall promptly notify the Subcontractor of all modifications to the Contract between the Owner and the Contractor which affect this Subcontract and which were issued or entered into subsequent to the execution of this Subcontract.

12.3.2   The Contractor shall not give instructions or orders directly to employees or workmen of the Subcontractor except to persons designated as authorized representatives of the Subcontractor.

12.4   PAYMENTS TO THE SUBCONTRACTOR

12.4.1   Unless otherwise provided in the Contract Documents, the Contractor shall pay the Subcontractor each progress payment and the final payment under this Subcontract within three working days after he receives payment from the Owner, except as provided in Subparagraph 12.4.3. The amount of each progress payment to the Subcontractor shall be the amount to which the Subcontractor is entitled, reflecting the percentage of completion allowed to the Contractor for the Work of this Subcontractor applied to the Contract Sum of this Subcontract, and the percentage actually retained, if any, from payments to the Contractor on account of such Subcontractor's Work, plus, to the extent permitted by the Contract Documents, the amount allowed for materials and equipment suitably stored by the Subcontractor, less the aggregate of previous payments to the Subcontractor.

12.4.2   The Contractor shall permit the Subcontractor to request directly from the Architect information regarding the percentages of completion or the amount certified on account of Work done by the Subcontractor.

12.4.3   If the Architect does not issue a Certificate for Payment or the Contractor does not receive payment for any cause which is not the fault of the Subcontractor, the Contractor shall pay the Subcontractor, on demand, a progress payment computed as provided in Subparagraph 12.4.1 or the final payment as provided in Article 6.

12.5   CLAIMS BY THE CONTRACTOR

12.5.1   The Contractor shall make no demand for liquidated damages for delay in any sum in excess of such amount as may be specifically named in this Subcontract, and liquidated damages shall be assessed against this Subcontractor only for his negligent acts and his failure to act in accordance with the terms of this Agreement, and in no case for delays or causes arising outside the scope of this Subcontract, or for which other subcontractors are responsible.

12.5.2   Except as may be indicated in this Agreement, the Contractor agrees that no claim for payment for services rendered or materials and equipment furnished by the Contractor to the Subcontractor shall be valid without prior notice to the Subcontractor and unless written notice thereof is given by the Contractor to the Subcontractor not later than the tenth day of the calendar month following that in which the claim originated.

12.6   CONTRACTORS' REMEDIES

12.6.1   If the Subcontractor defaults or neglects to carry out the Work in accordance with this Agreement and fails within three working days after receipt of written notice from the Contractor to commence and continue correction of such default or neglect with diligence and promptness, the Contractor may, after three days following receipt by the Subcontractor of an additional written notice, and without prejudice to any other remedy he may have, make good such deficiencies and may deduct the cost thereof from the payments then or thereafter due the Subcontractor, provided, however, that if such action is based upon faulty workmanship or materials and equipment, the Architect shall first have determined that the workmanship or materials and equipment are not in accordance with the Contract Documents.

ARTICLE 13
ARBITRATION

13.1   All claims, disputes and other matters in question arising out of, or relating to, this Subcontract, or the breach thereof, shall be decided by arbitration, which shall be conducted in the same manner and under the same procedure as provided in the Contract Documents with respect to disputes between the Owner and the Contractor, except that a decision by the Architect shall not be a condition precedent to arbitration. If the Contract Documents do not provide for arbitration or fail to specify the manner and procedure for arbitration, it shall be conducted in accordance with the Construction Industry Arbitration Rules of the American Arbitration Association then obtaining unless the parties mutually agree otherwise.

13.2   Except by written consent of the person or entity sought to be joined, no arbitration arising out of or relating to the Contract Documents shall include, by consolidation, joinder or in any other manner, any person or entity not a party to the Agreement under which such arbitration arises, unless it is shown at the time the demand for arbitration is filed that (1) such person or entity is substantially involved in a common question of fact or law,

(2) the presence of such person or entity is required if complete relief is to be accorded in the arbitration, (3) the interest or responsibility of such person or entity in the matter is not insubstantial, and (4) such person or entity is not the Architect, his employee or his consultant. This agreement to arbitrate and any other written agreement to arbitrate with an additional person or persons referred to herein shall be specifically enforceable under the prevailing arbitration law.

13.3 The Contractor shall permit the Subcontractor to be present and to submit evidence in any arbitration proceeding involving his rights.

13.4 The Contractor shall permit the Subcontractor to exercise whatever rights the Contractor may have under the Contract Documents in the choice of arbitrators in any dispute, if the sole cause of the dispute is the Work, materials, equipment, rights or responsibilities of the Subcontractor; or if the dispute involves the Subcontractor and any other subcontractor or subcontractors jointly, the Contractor shall permit them to exercise such rights jointly.

13.5 The award rendered by the arbitrators shall be final, and judgment may be entered upon it in accordance with applicable law in any court having jurisdiction thereof.

13.6 This Article shall not be deemed a limitation of any rights or remedies which the Subcontractor may have under any Federal or State mechanics' lien laws or under any applicable labor and material payment bonds unless such rights or remedies are expressly waived by him.

ARTICLE 14
TERMINATION

14.1 TERMINATION BY THE SUBCONTRACTOR

14.1.1 If the Work is stopped for a period of thirty days through no fault of the Subcontractor because the Contractor has not made payments thereon as provided in this Agreement, then the Subcontractor may without prejudice to any other remedy he may have, upon seven additional days' written notice to the Contractor, terminate this Subcontract and recover from the Contractor payment for all Work executed and for any proven loss resulting from the stoppage of the Work, including reasonable overhead, profit and damages.

14.2 TERMINATION BY THE CONTRACTOR

14.2.1 If the Subcontractor persistently or repeatedly fails or neglects to carry out the Work in accordance with the Contract Documents or otherwise to perform in accordance with this Agreement and fails within seven days after receipt of written notice to commence and continue correction of such default or neglect with diligence and promptness, the Contractor may, after seven days following receipt by the Subcontractor of an additional written notice and without prejudice to any other remedy he may have, terminate the Subcontract and finish the Work by whatever method he may deem expedient. If the unpaid balance of the Contract Sum exceeds the expense of finishing the Work, such excess shall be paid to the Subcontractor, but if such expense exceeds such unpaid balance, the Subcontractor shall pay the difference to the Contractor.

ARTICLE 15
MISCELLANEOUS PROVISIONS

15.1 Terms used in this Agreement which are defined in the Conditions of the Contract shall have the meanings designated in those Conditions.

15.2 The Contract Documents, which constitute the entire Agreement between the Owner and the Contractor, are listed in Article 1, and the documents which are applicable to this Subcontract, except for Addenda and Modifications issued after execution of this Subcontract, are enumerated as follows:

(List below the Agreement, the Conditions of the Contract [General, Supplementary, and other Conditions], the Drawings, the Specifications, and any Addenda and accepted Alternates, showing page or sheet numbers in all cases and dates where applicable. Continue on succeeding pages as required.)

This Agreement entered into as of the day and year first written above.

CONTRACTOR

_____

_____

_____

SUBCONTRACTOR

_____

_____

_____

AIA DOCUMENT A401 • CONTRACTOR-SUBCONTRACTOR AGREEMENT • ELEVENTH EDITION • APRIL 1978 • AIA®
©1978 • THE AMERICAN INSTITUTE OF ARCHITECTS, 1735 NEW YORK AVE., N.W., WASHINGTON, D.C. 20006

RECOMMENDED GUIDE FOR

Bidding Procedures
&
Contract Awards

For use when competitive lump sum bids are requested in connection with building and related construction.

The American Institute of Architects
The Associated General Contractors of America

FOREWORD

The practice of awarding contracts for construction on the basis of competitive proposals is one of long standing.

Competitive features of this procedure require the Contractor to be constantly on the alert for new and more efficient methods of operation.

This Guide is intended to establish a spirit of understanding and cooperation between the contracting parties and the Architect essential to the elimination of wasteful effort and the attainment of desirable objectives in the bidding procedure and the award of contracts.

It is believed the best interests of the architectural profession will be furthered if architects adhere to this procedure, and in supporting this procedure contractors and subcontractors will further their own interests as well as the interests of architects and the building public.

1 THE OWNER HAS A RIGHT TO EXPECT

Accurate Drawings The Owner has a right to expect that the Architect has exercised due diligence, skill, and good judgment in the preparation of the Contract Documents to the end that the accepted Contractor will deliver, in full compliance with the Contract Documents, without misunderstanding or unexpected cost, a building adequate for its intended purpose.

2 THE CONTRACTOR HAS A RIGHT TO EXPECT

Contract Documents The Contractor has a right to expect that the information shown and described in the Contract Documents is sufficient to enable him to prepare complete and accurate estimates and that he will not be penalized for any deficiencies in these documents.

Local Ordinances The Contractor is entitled to assume the Architect is familiar with local ordinances pertaining to the design and construction of buildings and has described in the Specifications any unusual stipulations which would affect cost. The Contractor accepts responsibility for compliance with local administrative requirements concerning building operations. (See Paragraphs 4.6 and 4.7 of AIA Document A201, the General Conditions of the Contract for Construction.)

Permits The Architect where applicable should file as early as possible required sets of documents with the appropriate local authorities to start processing for a general building permit.

3 THE ARCHITECT HAS A RIGHT TO EXPECT

Selection of Bidders The Architect is entitled to full confidence from the Owner during the selection of the bidders and the taking of bids. The Owner should not attempt to dictate either the bidders to receive invitations to bid or the bidding procedures.

Instructions to Bidders Instructions to bidders explain the procedures to be followed in preparing and submitting bids and are used in conjunction with the proposed Contract Documents. Instructions to Bidders, AIA Document A701, should be used for this purpose.

Contractors' Responsibility Each contractor invited to bid has the responsibility to the Architect and the Owner to ascertain, prior to accepting the invitation, if he will be able to properly prepare a bid and submit same at the time and place requested. He is expected to utilize every effort to obtain the lowest possible prices within the limits of ethical construction practices and in complete conformance with the requirements of the Contract Documents. In the event a contractor cannot meet the above requirements, he should immediately notify the Architect and withdraw from the bidding. The Architect also has the right to expect that every contractor invited to bid is in every respect a general contractor who utilizes his own directly engaged employees for as much of the construction as is practicable, and maintains qualified and sufficient supervisory personnel to properly coordinate all phases of the Work.

4 CONTRACT DOCUMENTS

Contract Documents
The Contract Documents for every building construction contract should consist of the AIA Standard Forms of Agreement Between Owner and Contractor (AIA Documents A101, A107 or A111) and the General Conditions of the Contract for Construction (AIA Document A201), current editions, the Supplementary Conditions or other Conditions, the Drawings, the Specifications, the Addenda and all Modifications.

Forms of Agreement
These Standard Forms of Agreement and the General Conditions are drafted with careful regard to the rights and responsibilities of both Owner and Contractor, and outline the duties and functions of the Architect.

General Conditions
The General Conditions of the Contract for Construction (AIA Document A201), current edition, should be used without change.

The formulation and adoption of standard General Conditions has been one of the most important contributions to modern construction practice. But the whole purpose of standardizing general conditions is lost when architects and engineers alter or change portions of the standard documents to suit individual convenience. Any additional articles, if required, should be added in properly numbered sequences under a general heading, "Supplementary Conditions", so that contractors will instantly recognize particular requirements of the Project and will not be required to recheck the basic General Conditions for changes or alterations in the standard provisions.

Supplementary Conditions
The aim of the documents referred to above is the establishment of a national standard. The Supplementary Conditions should include such modifications of the standard provisions only as may be required by local physical, legal, climatic or other conditions.

Special Conditions
Under this heading the Contractor should be informed of conditions not covered elsewhere which are applicable to the specific Project. These may be covered in Division 1 of the Uniform System also.

Special Form of Contract
If a special form of contract is to be used, a copy should be included in the document furnished to the bidders.

AIA DOCUMENT A501 • AGC DOCUMENT 23 • RECOMMENDED GUIDE FOR BIDDING PROCEDURES AND CONTRACT AWARDS • NOVEMBER 1969 EDITION • WASHINGTON, D.C. 20006

5 DRAWINGS

Working Drawings The Drawings must be clear, complete, accurate, and adequately dimensioned and should be of sufficient scale for estimating purposes.

Plot plan-Survey A plot plan should be furnished bidders from information furnished by the Owner showing locations of site, property lines, survey of site, base angles, bench marks, existing conditions, existing utilities, structures, trees, et cetera. Existing topographical conditions should be shown. Soil Borings should be taken to determine sub-surface conditions, their location should be indicated on the Drawings, and a copy of the laboratory report furnished. Intended new structures should be shown in place together with intended finished grades.

Standardization In indicating materials and their use, nationally accepted standard symbols and abbreviations should be employed.

Large Scale Details Construction sections and large scale details sufficient for intelligent bidding and for the purpose of correlating all parts of the Work should be a part of the Working Drawings. This is particularly important when the size of the project makes necessary the preparation of the Working Drawings at a scale less than $\frac{1}{8}'' = 1'.0$

Structural-Mechanical-Electrical For clear indication, structural, mechanical and electrical Work should be shown on separate drawings with special attention to the more intricate details.

6 SPECIFICATIONS

Specifications This document should be complete, clear and concise with adequate description of the various classes of Work segregated under the proper Divisions, Sections and Articles. The Divisions should follow those established in the "Uniform System for Construction Specifications, Data Filing and Cost Accounting", as developed and endorsed by The AIA (AIA Document K103), American Society of Landscape Architects (ASLA Document 3D), The AGC (AGC Document 19), Construction Specifications Institute (CSI Document #001a), Council of Mechanical Specialty Contracting Industries, Inc., National Society of Professional Engineers (NSPE Document 1924) and the Producers' Council, Inc. Each Section and Article should be identified for easy reference.

Allowances All Allowances should be grouped in a separate section titled "Allowances". Allowances which are intended to be included in subcontracts should be clearly cross referenced in the Sections of the Specifications pertaining to the Work covered by such Allowances. Requirements should be clearly set forth establishing precisely what the Allowances include and what they do not include.

Trade Terms Standard trade terms for materials, equipment and processes should be used.

"Or Approved Equal" The use of the term "or approved equal", without prior determination of materials that can be approved as equal, frequently results in differences of opinion and misunderstandings and should be eliminated. This may be done in the following ways:

(1) Closed Specifications list only one trade name for each product. No substitutions are allowed. This type of specification should be used when there is only one product which will properly serve.

(2) Contractor's Option Specifications list all trade names which will be accepted for each product.

(3) Product Approval Specifications list one or more trade names for each product. However, the Contractor may request substitutions prior to a specified time before the bids are due and, if the request is granted, he may bid using the approved substitute.

(4) Substitute Bid Specifications list one or more trade names for each product. The Contractor's base bid must be compiled on the use of the listed products. However, the Contractor may attach to his bid form a proposal for a substitute material and show the amount to be added to or to be deducted from the base bid if the proposed substitute is approved.

Guaranteed Result Specifying both the method and a result for any particular phase of the Work should be avoided.

7 TIME OF COMPLETION

Substantial Completion Substantial Completion is defined in the current edition of AIA Document A201, Subparagraph 8.1.3 as follows: "The Date of Substantial Completion of the Work or designated portion thereof is the Date certified by the Architect when construction is sufficiently complete, in accordance with the Contract Documents, so the Owner may occupy the Work or designated portion thereof for the use for which it is intended."

Time Since time of completion is of the essence of the Contract, the Architect should set a completion date and each bidder should provide in his bid

AIA DOCUMENT A501 • **AGC DOCUMENT 23** • RECOMMENDED GUIDE FOR BIDDING PROCEDURES AND CONTRACT AWARDS • NOVEMBER 1969 EDITION • WASHINGTON, D.C. 20006

all costs necessary to complete the Project on or before the time stated. However, the Owner should be advised that strikes, "acts of God", and other situations beyond the control of the Contractor and Architect may extend the time of completion and that the Contractor and Architect cannot be held responsible for such delay.

Liquidated Damage Clause   If sufficiently important, a liquidated damage clause may be included. If more than one contract is involved, the mutual responsibilities of separate contractors for delays and damages must be made clear.

8 INSURANCE AND BONDS

Insurance   Article 11 of AIA Document A201 provides general insurance requirements for the Project. The Architect should receive written instructions from the Owner in regard to modifications to Article 11, including special insurance requirements, if any. Bidders also should include the cost of any other insurance protection they may require which is not covered in Article 11. Note should be made of the requirement in Paragraph 4.18 of AIA Document A201 relative to indemnification. The Owner should be advised to seek legal and insurance counsel on his insurance requirements and on any insurance to be carried by the Contractor for the protection of the Owner's interest in the Project. In all cases the minimum amounts of coverage should be determined by the Owner and stated in the Contract Documents, and the Contractor should be required to furnish to the Owner certificates of coverage in sufficient number.

Choice of Sureties   No action should be taken which would bring about a departure from the traditional practice of permitting the Contractor to secure surety bonds or insurance from reputable companies of their choosing acceptable to the Owner and Architect. Depriving the Contractor of this traditional prerogative is contrary to the best interests of the Owner.

Insurance Guides   Chapter 7, "Insurance and Bonds of Suretyship", from The Architect's Handbook of Professional Practice, Insurance and Bond Check List (AGC Document No. 29) and Insurance for Contractors by Walter T. Derk (available from Fred S. James and Co., 1 N. LaSalle St., Chicago, Ill.), are recommended as guides to insurance information.

9 ROYALTIES AND PATENTS

The Contractor shall give consideration to costs that may be involved for royalties and patents for which he will be responsible, as provided in Paragraph 7.7 of AIA Document A201, General Conditions of the Contract for Construction.

10 BIDDING

Qualifications of Bidders

Except where otherwise prohibited by legal requirements, bidders should be limited to contractors of established skill, integrity and responsibility, and of proved competence for work of the character and size involved. They should be selected by the Architect with the concurrence of the Owner.

Number of Bidders

A sufficient number of bidders should be invited to bid to insure adequate price competition. Normally, this can be accomplished with approximately six bidders.

A selected bidder should promptly advise the Architect if he is not interested in submitting a bid.

Issuance of Drawings and Specifications

Each contractor who is invited to bid on the Work should be furnished, free of charge, Drawings and Specifications covering all branches of the Work which his bid is to include and, upon request, at least one set of the Drawings and Specifications for all branches of the Work for which separate bids may be taken by the Owner.

For typical projects, the following is submitted as a guide:

(1) For small projects $300,000 and under — two sets.
(2) For larger projects $300,000 to $1,000,000 — three sets.
(3) For projects in excess of $1,000,000 — three or more sets.

When bidding time is limited, or the Work is complicated, or there is a multiplicity of subtrades involved, it will be in the Owner's interest to increase the number of the above recommended sets of documents commensurate with the type of Work to be done and the time within which the general bids are to be submitted. It should be noted that the Owner reimburses the Architect for the cost of providing bidding documents to the contractors unless another arrangement is made between the Owner and Architect.

Each bidder should be allowed to retain these sets until the Contract has been awarded, or until he is definitely out of the competition, whereupon the documents should be returned to the Architect. It is advisable to require a deposit from each bidder for the documents furnished, such deposit to be refunded to him upon timely return of the documents in good condition.

If a bidder requires additional sets of Drawings for the preparation of his bid, the Architect should provide them to him at cost.

Such additional sets should be returned promptly also since it is customary that all Drawings and Specifications remain the property of the Architect whether or not reproduction charges have been paid by the Contractor.

Plan Rooms   Sets of documents for use by sub-bidders should be provided in adequate number at central trade offices or plan rooms established in the area in which the building is located and made available at the Architect's office for the purpose of facilitating and expediting the preparation of sub-bids.

It is recommended that the location of plan rooms be listed in the bidding documents.

Standard Bid Blank   A blank bid form should be prepared by the Architect for each project with copies bound into each volume of the Project Manual. Extra copies shall be furnished to each bidder with the documents for use in preparing his bid.

Non-Standard Proposals   Bids which are not submitted on the standard form of proposal or by the bidding time specified should be rejected.

Use of Alternates   An Alternate is defined as any specified change in the Drawings and Specifications. Alternates should be requested only where they are believed to be of special importance to the Owner, either as a means of (1) insuring a proposal within a limited appropriation, or (2) providing an opportunity to make an important determination in the selection of materials or processes. If Alternates are requested, they should be limited to no more than necessary.

Selection of Alternates should be made by the Owner, acting upon the Architect's recommendations, for the best interest of the Project in line with available funds. The selection of Alternates should not be manipulated to favor any one bidder over another.

The Alternates selected should be included in determining the low bid.

Unit Prices   Unit prices should be specified only when they are necessary and can be accurately described and estimated. When used, separate unit prices should be requested in the form of "additions to" and "deductions from" the Work as indicated.

Time for Preparing Bids

Adequate time in which to prepare estimates is essential to sound and effective price competition, and therefore a reasonable time should be allowed for preparing bids. In general, this should not be less than two weeks. In large or complicated work three weeks or longer may be desirable. If, for the best interest of the Project, extension of the time for bidding becomes necessary, bidders should be so notified at least three working days prior to the originally scheduled opening date. Bidders should take full advantage of the bidding time allowed. It is recommended that a prebid conference be held to resolve questions bidders may have.

Addenda

No Addenda should be issued later than four working days before time for receipt of bids. Answers to questions from bidders should be in writing, in the form of Addenda, with a copy sent to each bidder. Contractors should submit questions to the Architect in advance to allow sufficient time for the Architect to respond. Architects should also allow for sufficient time to prepare and distribute Addenda. Contractors should be allowed sufficient time to review the Addenda in order to prepare a responsible bid.

Submission of Bids

Architects should cooperate to avoid conflicts in bidding dates for important projects.

Bids should be delivered at a designated place and not later than a designated time, preferably on a Tuesday, Wednesday, Thursday, or Friday afternoon, but not on a legal holiday or the day following. If bids are not opened in the presence of the bidders, a tabulation of all bids received should be furnished each bidder.

Bid guarantees should be optional with the Owner. On private projects it is not recommended that a bid guarantee be required from invited bidders.

11 AWARD OF CONTRACT

Low Bidder

If bids are received only from prequalified and invited bidders, the Contract should be awarded to the lowest bidder. Except in very special cases and for good cause, action should be taken within ten days of receipt of bids.

Error in Bid

If, after bids are opened, the low bidder claims he has made an appreciable error in the preparation of his bid and can support such claim with evidence satisfactory to the Owner and the Architect, he should be

AIA DOCUMENT A501 • AGC DOCUMENT 23 • RECOMMENDED GUIDE FOR BIDDING PROCEDURES AND CONTRACT AWARDS • NOVEMBER 1969 EDITION • WASHINGTON, D.C. 20006 permitted to withdraw his bid. His bid guarantee should be returned and he should be disqualified from again bidding on the Project in the event additional bids are requested.

In such event, action on the remaining bids should be considered as though the withdrawn bid had not been received.

Under no circumstances should a bidder be permitted to alter his bid after bids have been opened except in accordance with the first sentence of the following paragraph.

Changes

Minor changes required before signing of the Contract should be negotiated only with the selected bidder. If major changes are necessary, they may be negotiated with the low bidder or the original bids can be rejected and new bids secured from the original list of bidders on the basis of revised Drawings and Specifications.

Rejection of Bids

The Owner has the right to reject all bids for good and sufficient cause. However, this should not be done as a subterfuge (1) to accept a bidder who did not submit a bid before the prices of the others were made public, or (2) to obtain an estimate of the cost of the Work and proceed to award it in segregated or separate contracts or to a bidder definitely selected in advance.

12 CONTRACTS

Single Contracts

It is recommended that a complete project be included under a single contract. The General Contractor under this system assumes full responsibility for the supervision and completion of the Project at a guaranteed cost to the Owner.

With the general concurrence of the Owner and Architect, it is important that final selection of each Subcontractor be left in the hands of the General Contractor. This insures that the General Contractor is fully responsible for the proper execution of all Subcontracts consistent with the provisions of Article 5, Subcontractors, AIA Document A201.

Separate Contracts

When portions of the Work are let by the Owner separately, as provided in AIA Document A201, Article 6, Separate Contracts, it is important that the Contract Documents make clear beyond doubt the elements of the Work and the party responsible for coordinating the Work of the several prime contractors.

Whether it is to be the Architect or Owner, under these circumstances, he should have a suitable administrative staff to coordinate, administer and complete the Project.

If improperly coordinated and administered, separate contracts can result in confusion, delay and loss to the Owner.

13 SUBCONTRACTS AND SUBCONTRACTORS

Basis of Sub-Bids

Every sub-bid should be based on identified Sections in the Specifications and the related Drawings.

Unsolicited Sub-Bids

A general contractor has no responsibility to accept any unsolicited sub-bid.

Misuse of Sub-Bids

It is unethical, unwise and detrimental to the best interests of the construction industry for a general contractor, prior to the award of the Contract, to disclose to the Architect, Owner or others the amounts of sub-bids or quotations obtained in confidence for the purpose of preparing his bid.

Receipt of Sub-Bids

It is imperative that general contractors receive sub-bids sufficiently in advance of the time for submitting their bids to permit adequate analysis and compilation.

AIA DOCUMENT A501 • **AGC DOCUMENT 23** • RECOMMENDED GUIDE FOR BIDDING PROCEDURES AND CONTRACT AWARDS • NOVEMBER 1969 EDITION • WASHINGTON, D.C. 20006

THE AMERICAN INSTITUTE OF ARCHITECTS

AIA Document A701

Instructions to Bidders

1978 EDITION

Use only with the 1976 Edition of AIA Document A201, General Conditions of the Contract for Construction

TABLE OF ARTICLES

AIA DOCUMENT A701 • INSTRUCTIONS TO BIDDERS • THIRD EDITION • MAY 1978 • AIA® • ©1978
THE AMERICAN INSTITUTE OF ARCHITECTS, 1735 NEW YORK AVE., N.W., WASHINGTON, D. C. 20006   **A701-1978 1**

INSTRUCTIONS TO BIDDERS

ARTICLE 1
DEFINITIONS

1.1 Bidding Documents include the Advertisement or Invitation to Bid, Instructions to Bidders, the bid form, other sample bidding and contract forms and the proposed Contract Documents including any Addenda issued prior to receipt of bids. The Contract Documents proposed for the Work consist of the Owner-Contractor Agreement, the Conditions of the Contract (General, Supplementary and other Conditions), the Drawings, the Specifications and all Addenda issued prior to and all Modifications issued after execution of the Contract.

1.2 All definitions set forth in the General Conditions of the Contract for Construction, AIA Document A201, or in other Contract Documents are applicable to the Bidding Documents.

1.3 Addenda are written or graphic instruments issued by the Architect prior to the execution of the Contract which modify or interpret the Bidding Documents by addition, deletions, clarifications or corrections.

1.4 A Bid is a complete and properly signed proposal to do the Work or designated portion thereof for the sums stipulated therein, submitted in accordance with the Bidding Documents.

1.5 The Base Bid is the sum stated in the Bid for which the Bidder offers to perform the Work described in the Bidding Documents as the base, to which work may be added or from which work may be deleted for sums stated in Alternate Bids.

1.6 An Alternate Bid (or Alternate) is an amount stated in the Bid to be added to or deducted from the amount of the Base Bid if the corresponding change in the Work, as described in the Bidding Documents, is accepted.

1.7 A Unit Price is an amount stated in the Bid as a price per unit of measurement for materials or services as described in the Bidding Documents or in the proposed Contract Documents.

1.8 A Bidder is a person or entity who submits a Bid.

1.9 A Sub-bidder is a person or entity who submits a bid to a Bidder for materials or labor for a portion of the Work.

ARTICLE 2
BIDDER'S REPRESENTATIONS

2.1 Each Bidder by making his Bid represents that:

2.1.1 He has read and understands the Bidding Documents and his Bid is made in accordance therewith.

2.1.2 He has visited the site, has familiarized himself with the local conditions under which the Work is to be performed and has correlated his observations with the requirements of the proposed Contract Documents.

2.1.3 His Bid is based upon the materials, systems and equipment required by the Bidding Documents without exception.

ARTICLE 3
BIDDING DOCUMENTS

3.1   COPIES

3.1.1 Bidders may obtain complete sets of the Bidding Documents from the issuing office designated in the Advertisement or Invitation to Bid in the number and for the deposit sum, if any, stated therein. The deposit will be refunded to Bidders who submit a bona fide Bid and return the Bidding Documents in good condition within ten days after receipt of Bids. The cost of replacement of any missing or damaged documents will be deducted from the deposit. A Bidder receiving a Contract award may retain the Bidding Documents and his deposit will be refunded.

3.1.2 Bidding Documents will not be issued directly to Sub-bidders or others unless specifically offered in the Advertisement or Invitation to Bid.

3.1.3 Bidders shall use complete sets of Bidding Documents in preparing Bids; neither the Owner nor the Architect assume any responsibility for errors or misinterpretations resulting from the use of incomplete sets of Bidding Documents.

3.1.4 The Owner or the Architect in making copies of the Bidding Documents available on the above terms do so only for the purpose of obtaining Bids on the Work and do not confer a license or grant for any other use.

3.2   INTERPRETATION OR CORRECTION OF BIDDING DOCUMENTS

3.2.1 Bidders and Sub-bidders shall promptly notify the Architect of any ambiguity, inconsistency or error which they may discover upon examination of the Bidding Documents or of the site and local conditions.

3.2.2 Bidders and Sub-bidders requiring clarification or interpretation of the Bidding Documents shall make a written request which shall reach the Architect at least seven days prior to the date for receipt of Bids.

3.2.3 Any interpretation, correction or change of the Bidding Documents will be made by Addendum. Interpretations, corrections or changes of the Bidding Documents made in any other manner will not be binding, and Bidders shall not rely upon such interpretations, corrections and changes.

3.3   SUBSTITUTIONS

3.3.1 The materials, products and equipment described in the Bidding Documents establish a standard of required function, dimension, appearance and quality to be met by any proposed substitution.

3.3.2 No substitution will be considered prior to receipt of Bids unless written request for approval has been received by the Architect at least ten days prior to the date for receipt of Bids. Each such request shall include the name of the material or equipment for which it is to be substituted and a complete description of the proposed substitute including drawings, cuts, performance and test data and any other information necessary for an evaluation. A statement setting forth any changes in other materials, equipment or other Work that incorporation of the substitute would require shall be included. The burden of proof of the merit of the proposed substitute is upon the proposer. The Architect's decision of approval or disapproval of a proposed substitution shall be final.

3.3.3 If the Architect approves any proposed substitution prior to receipt of Bids, such approval will be set forth in an Addendum. Bidders shall not rely upon approvals made in any other manner.

3.3.4 No substitutions will be considered after the Contract award unless specifically provided in the Contract Documents.

3.4 ADDENDA

3.4.1 Addenda will be mailed or delivered to all who are known by the Architect to have received a complete set of Bidding Documents.

3.4.2 Copies of Addenda will be made available for inspection wherever Bidding Documents are on file for that purpose.

3.4.3 No Addenda will be issued later than four days prior to the date for receipt of Bids except an Addendum withdrawing the request for Bids or one which includes postponement of the date for receipt of Bids.

3.4.4 Each Bidder shall ascertain prior to submitting his bid that he has received all Addenda issued, and he shall acknowledge their receipt in his Bid.

ARTICLE 4
BIDDING PROCEDURE

4.1 FORM AND STYLE OF BIDS

4.1.1 Bids shall be submitted on forms identical to the form included with the Bidding Documents, in the quantity required by Article 9.

4.1.2 All blanks on the bid form shall be filled in by typewriter or manually in ink.

4.1.3 Where so indicated by the makeup of the bid form, sums shall be expressed in both words and figures, and in case of discrepancy between the two, the amount written in words shall govern.

4.1.4 Any interlineation, alteration or erasure must be initialed by the signer of the Bid.

4.1.5 All requested Alternates shall be bid. If no change in the Base Bid is required, enter "No Change."

4.1.6 Where two or more Bids for designated portions of the Work have been requested, the Bidder may, without forfeiture of his bid security, state his refusal to accept award of less than the combination of Bids he so stipulates. The Bidder shall make no additional stipulations on the bid form nor qualify his Bid in any other manner.

4.1.7 Each copy of the Bid shall include the legal name of the Bidder and a statement that the Bidder is a sole proprietor, a partnership, a corporation, or some other legal entity. Each copy shall be signed by the person or persons legally authorized to bind the Bidder to a contract. A Bid by a corporation shall further give the state of incorporation and have the corporate seal affixed. A Bid submitted by an agent shall have a current power of attorney attached certifying the agent's authority to bind the Bidder.

4.2 BID SECURITY

4.2.1 If so stipulated in the Advertisement or Invitation to Bid, each Bid shall be accompanied by a bid security in the form and amount required by Article 9 pledging that the Bidder will enter into a contract with the Owner on the terms stated in his Bid and will, if required, furnish bonds as described hereunder in Article 7 covering the faithful performance of the Contract and the payment of all obligations arising thereunder. Should the Bidder refuse to enter into such Contract or fail to furnish such bonds if required, the amount of the bid security shall be forfeited to the Owner as liquidated damages, not as a penalty. The amount of the bid security shall not be forfeited to the Owner in the event the Owner fails to comply with Subparagraph 6.2.1.

4.2.2 If a surety bond is required it shall be written on AIA Document A310, Bid Bond, and the attorney-in-fact who executes the bond on behalf of the surety shall affix to the bond a certified and current copy of his power of attorney.

4.2.3 The Owner will have the right to retain the bid security of Bidders to whom an award is being considered until either (a) the Contract has been executed and bonds, if required, have been furnished, or (b) the specified time has elapsed so that Bids may be withdrawn, or (c) all Bids have been rejected.

4.3 SUBMISSION OF BIDS

4.3.1 All copies of the Bid, the bid security, if any, and any other documents required to be submitted with the Bid shall be enclosed in a sealed opaque envelope. The envelope shall be addressed to the party receiving the Bids and shall be identified with the Project name, the Bidder's name and address and, if applicable, the designated portion of the Work for which the Bid is submitted. If the Bid is sent by mail the sealed envelope shall be enclosed in a separate mailing envelope with the notation "SEALED BID ENCLOSED" on the face thereof.

4.3.2 Bids shall be deposited at the designated location prior to the time and date for receipt of Bids indicated in the Advertisement or Invitation to Bid, or any extension thereof made by Addendum. Bids received after the time and date for receipt of Bids will be returned unopened.

4.3.3 The Bidder shall assume full responsibility for timely delivery at the location designated for receipt of Bids.

4.3.4 Oral, telephonic or telegraphic Bids are invalid and will not receive consideration.

4.4 MODIFICATION OR WITHDRAWAL OF BID

4.4.1 A Bid may not be modified, withdrawn or canceled by the Bidder during the stipulated time period following the time and date designated for the receipt of Bids, and each Bidder so agrees in submitting his Bid.

4.4.2 Prior to the time and date designated for receipt of Bids, any Bid submitted may be modified or withdrawn by notice to the party receiving Bids at the place designated for receipt of Bids. Such notice shall be in writing over the signature of the Bidder or by telegram; if by telegram, written confirmation over the signature of the Bidder shall be mailed and postmarked on or before the date and time set for receipt of Bids, and it shall be so worded as not to reveal the amount of the original Bid.

4.4.3 Withdrawn Bids may be resubmitted up to the time designated for the receipt of Bids provided that they are then fully in conformance with these Instructions to Bidders.

4.4.4 Bid security, if any is required, shall be in an amount sufficient for the Bid as modified or resubmitted.

ARTICLE 5
CONSIDERATION OF BIDS

5.1 OPENING OF BIDS

5.1.1 Unless stated otherwise in the Advertisement or Invitation to Bid, the properly identified Bids received on time will be opened publicly and will be read aloud. An abstract of the Base Bids and Alternate Bids, if any, will be made available to Bidders. When it has been stated that Bids will be opened privately, an abstract of the same information may, at the discretion of the Owner, be made available to the Bidders within a reasonable time.

5.2 REJECTION OF BIDS

5.2.1 The Owner shall have the right to reject any or all Bids and to reject a Bid not accompanied by any required bid security or by other data required by the Bidding Documents, or to reject a Bid which is in any way incomplete or irregular.

5.3 ACCEPTANCE OF BID (AWARD)

5.3.1 It is the intent of the Owner to award a Contract to the lowest responsible Bidder provided the Bid has been submitted in accordance with the requirements of the Bidding Documents and does not exceed the funds available. The Owner shall have the right to waive any informality or irregularity in any Bid or Bids received and to accept the Bid or Bids which, in his judgment, is in his own best interests.

5.3.2 The Owner shall have the right to accept Alternates in any order or combination, unless otherwise specifically provided in Article 9, and to determine the low Bidder on the basis of the sum of the Base Bid and the Alternates accepted.

ARTICLE 6
POST BID INFORMATION

6.1 CONTRACTOR'S QUALIFICATION STATEMENT

6.1.1 Bidders to whom award of a Contract is under consideration shall submit to the Architect, upon request, a properly executed AIA Document A305, Contractor's Qualification Statement, unless such a Statement has been previously required and submitted as a prerequisite to the issuance of Bidding Documents.

6.2 OWNER'S FINANCIAL CAPABILITY

6.2.1 The Owner shall, at the request of the Bidder to whom award of a Contract is under consideration and no later than seven days prior to the expiration of the time for withdrawal of Bids, furnish to the Bidder reasonable evidence that the Owner has made financial arrangements to fulfill the Contract obligations. Unless such reasonable evidence is furnished, the Bidder will not be required to execute the Owner-Contractor Agreement.

6.3 SUBMITTALS

6.3.1 The Bidder shall, within seven days of notification of selection for the award of a Contract for the Work, submit the following information to the Architect:

    .1 a designation of the Work to be performed by the Bidder with his own forces;

    .2 the proprietary names and the suppliers of principal items or systems of materials and equipment proposed for the Work;

    .3 a list of names of the Subcontractors or other persons or entities (including those who are to furnish materials or equipment fabricated to a special design) proposed for the principal portions of the Work.

6.3.2 The Bidder will be required to establish to the satisfaction of the Architect and the Owner the reliability and responsibility of the persons or entities proposed to furnish and perform the Work described in the Bidding Documents.

6.3.3 Prior to the award of the Contract, the Architect will notify the Bidder in writing if either the Owner or the Architect, after due investigation, has reasonable objection to any such proposed person or entity. If the Owner or Architect has reasonable objection to any such proposed person or entity, the Bidder may, at his option, (1) withdraw his Bid, or (2) submit an acceptable substitute person or entity with an adjustment in his bid price to cover the difference in cost occasioned by such substitution. The Owner may, at his discretion, accept the adjusted bid price or he may disqualify the Bidder. In the event of either withdrawal or disqualification under this Subparagraph, bid security will not be forfeited, notwithstanding the provisions of Paragraph 4.4.1.

6.3.4 Persons and entities proposed by the Bidder and to whom the Owner and the Architect have made no reasonable objection under the provisions of Subparagraph 6.3.3 must be used on the Work for which they were proposed and shall not be changed except with the written consent of the Owner and the Architect.

ARTICLE 7
PERFORMANCE BOND AND LABOR AND MATERIAL PAYMENT BOND

7.1 BOND REQUIREMENTS

7.1.1 Prior to execution of the Contract, if required in Article 9 hereinafter, the Bidder shall furnish bonds covering the faithful performance of the Contract and the payment of all obligations arising thereunder in such form and amount as the Owner may prescribe. Bonds may be secured through the Bidder's usual sources. If the furnishing of such bonds is stipulated hereinafter in Article 9, the cost shall be included in the Bid.

7.1.2 If the Owner has reserved the right to require that bonds be furnished subsequent to the execution of the Contract, the cost shall be adjusted as provided in the Contract Documents.

7.1.3 If the Owner requires that bonds be obtained from other than the Bidder's usual source, any change in cost will be adjusted as provided in the Contract Documents.

7.2   TIME OF DELIVERY AND FORM OF BONDS

7.2.1 The Bidder shall deliver the required bonds to the Owner not later than the date of execution of the Contract, or if the Work is to be commenced prior thereto in response to a letter of intent, the Bidder shall, prior to commencement of the Work, submit evidence satisfactory to the Owner that such bonds will be furnished.

7.2.2 Unless otherwise required in Article 9, the bonds shall be written on AIA Document A311, Performance Bond and Labor and Material Payment Bond.

7.2.3 The Bidder shall require the attorney-in-fact who executes the required bonds on behalf of the surety to affix thereto a certified and current copy of his power of attorney.

ARTICLE 8
FORM OF AGREEMENT BETWEEN OWNER AND CONTRACTOR

8.1   FORM TO BE USED

8.1.1 Unless otherwise required in the Bidding Documents, the Agreement for the Work will be written on AIA Document A101, Standard Form of Agreement Between Owner and Contractor, where the basis of payment is a Stipulated Sum.

ARTICLE 9
SUPPLEMENTARY INSTRUCTIONS

AIA DOCUMENT A701 • INSTRUCTIONS TO BIDDERS • THIRD EDITION • MAY 1978 • AIA® • ©1978
THE AMERICAN INSTITUTE OF ARCHITECTS, 1735 NEW YORK AVE., N.W., WASHINGTON, D. C. 20006

THE AMERICAN INSTITUTE OF ARCHITECTS

AIA Document B141

Standard Form of Agreement Between Owner and Architect

1977 EDITION

*THIS DOCUMENT HAS IMPORTANT LEGAL CONSEQUENCES; CONSULTATION WITH
AN ATTORNEY IS ENCOURAGED WITH RESPECT TO ITS COMPLETION OR MODIFICATION*

AGREEMENT

made as of the   day of   in the year of Nineteen
Hundred and

BETWEEN the Owner:

and the Architect:

For the following Project:
(Include detailed description of Project location and scope.)

The Owner and the Architect agree as set forth below.

AIA DOCUMENT B141 • OWNER-ARCHITECT AGREEMENT • THIRTEENTH EDITION • JULY 1977 • AIA® • © 1977
THE AMERICAN INSTITUTE OF ARCHITECTS, 1735 NEW YORK AVENUE, N.W., WASHINGTON, D.C. 20006   **B141-1977 1**

TERMS AND CONDITIONS OF AGREEMENT BETWEEN OWNER AND ARCHITECT

ARTICLE 1

ARCHITECT'S SERVICES AND RESPONSIBILITIES

BASIC SERVICES

The Architect's Basic Services consist of the five phases described in Paragraphs 1.1 through 1.5 and include normal structural, mechanical and electrical engineering services and any other services included in Article 15 as part of Basic Services.

1.1 SCHEMATIC DESIGN PHASE

1.1.1 The Architect shall review the program furnished by the Owner to ascertain the requirements of the Project and shall review the understanding of such requirements with the Owner.

1.1.2 The Architect shall provide a preliminary evaluation of the program and the Project budget requirements, each in terms of the other, subject to the limitations set forth in Subparagraph 3.2.1.

1.1.3 The Architect shall review with the Owner alternative approaches to design and construction of the Project.

1.1.4 Based on the mutually agreed upon program and Project budget requirements, the Architect shall prepare, for approval by the Owner, Schematic Design Documents consisting of drawings and other documents illustrating the scale and relationship of Project components.

1.1.5 The Architect shall submit to the Owner a Statement of Probable Construction Cost based on current area, volume or other unit costs.

1.2 DESIGN DEVELOPMENT PHASE

1.2.1 Based on the approved Schematic Design Documents and any adjustments authorized by the Owner in the program or Project budget, the Architect shall prepare, for approval by the Owner, Design Development Documents consisting of drawings and other documents to fix and describe the size and character of the entire Project as to architectural, structural, mechanical and electrical systems, materials and such other elements as may be appropriate.

1.2.2 The Architect shall submit to the Owner a further Statement of Probable Construction Cost.

1.3 CONSTRUCTION DOCUMENTS PHASE

1.3.1 Based on the approved Design Development Documents and any further adjustments in the scope or quality of the Project or in the Project budget authorized by the Owner, the Architect shall prepare, for approval by the Owner, Construction Documents consisting of Drawings and Specifications setting forth in detail the requirements for the construction of the Project.

1.3.2 The Architect shall assist the Owner in the preparation of the necessary bidding information, bidding forms, the Conditions of the Contract, and the form of Agreement between the Owner and the Contractor.

1.3.3 The Architect shall advise the Owner of any adjustments to previous Statements of Probable Construction Cost indicated by changes in requirements or general market conditions.

1.3.4 The Architect shall assist the Owner in connection with the Owner's responsibility for filing documents required for the approval of governmental authorities having jurisdiction over the Project.

1.4 BIDDING OR NEGOTIATION PHASE

1.4.1 The Architect, following the Owner's approval of the Construction Documents and of the latest Statement of Probable Construction Cost, shall assist the Owner in obtaining bids or negotiated proposals, and assist in awarding and preparing contracts for construction.

1.5 CONSTRUCTION PHASE—ADMINISTRATION OF THE CONSTRUCTION CONTRACT

1.5.1 The Construction Phase will commence with the award of the Contract for Construction and, together with the Architect's obligation to provide Basic Services under this Agreement, will terminate when final payment to the Contractor is due, or in the absence of a final Certificate for Payment or of such due date, sixty days after the Date of Substantial Completion of the Work, whichever occurs first.

1.5.2 Unless otherwise provided in this Agreement and incorporated in the Contract Documents, the Architect shall provide administration of the Contract for Construction as set forth below and in the edition of AIA Document A201, General Conditions of the Contract for Construction, current as of the date of this Agreement.

1.5.3 The Architect shall be a representative of the Owner during the Construction Phase, and shall advise and consult with the Owner. Instructions to the Contractor shall be forwarded through the Architect. The Architect shall have authority to act on behalf of the Owner only to the extent provided in the Contract Documents unless otherwise modified by written instrument in accordance with Subparagraph 1.5.16.

1.5.4 The Architect shall visit the site at intervals appropriate to the stage of construction or as otherwise agreed by the Architect in writing to become generally familiar with the progress and quality of the Work and to determine in general if the Work is proceeding in accordance with the Contract Documents. However, the Architect shall not be required to make exhaustive or continuous on-site inspections to check the quality or quantity of the Work. On the basis of such on-site observations as an architect, the Architect shall keep the Owner informed of the progress and quality of the Work, and shall endeavor to guard the Owner against defects and deficiencies in the Work of the Contractor.

1.5.5 The Architect shall not have control or charge of and shall not be responsible for construction means, methods, techniques, sequences or procedures, or for safety precautions and programs in connection with the Work, for the acts or omissions of the Contractor, Subcontractors or any other persons performing any of the Work, or for the failure of any of them to carry out the Work in accordance with the Contract Documents.

1.5.6 The Architect shall at all times have access to the Work wherever it is in preparation or progress.

1.5.7 The Architect shall determine the amounts owing to the Contractor based on observations at the site and on evaluations of the Contractor's Applications for Payment, and shall issue Certificates for Payment in such amounts, as provided in the Contract Documents.

1.5.8 The issuance of a Certificate for Payment shall constitute a representation by the Architect to the Owner, based on the Architect's observations at the site as provided in Subparagraph 1.5.4 and on the data comprising the Contractor's Application for Payment, that the Work has progressed to the point indicated; that, to the best of the Architect's knowledge, information and belief, the quality of the Work is in accordance with the Contract Documents (subject to an evaluation of the Work for conformance with the Contract Documents upon Substantial Completion, to the results of any subsequent tests required by or performed under the Contract Documents, to minor deviations from the Contract Documents correctable prior to completion, and to any specific qualifications stated in the Certificate for Payment); and that the Contractor is entitled to payment in the amount certified. However, the issuance of a Certificate for Payment shall not be a representation that the Architect has made any examination to ascertain how and for what purpose the Contractor has used the moneys paid on account of the Contract Sum.

1.5.9 The Architect shall be the interpreter of the requirements of the Contract Documents and the judge of the performance thereunder by both the Owner and Contractor. The Architect shall render interpretations necessary for the proper execution or progress of the Work with reasonable promptness on written request of either the Owner or the Contractor, and shall render written decisions, within a reasonable time, on all claims, disputes and other matters in question between the Owner and the Contractor relating to the execution or progress of the Work or the interpretation of the Contract Documents.

1.5.10 Interpretations and decisions of the Architect shall be consistent with the intent of and reasonably inferable from the Contract Documents and shall be in written or graphic form. In the capacity of interpreter and judge, the Architect shall endeavor to secure faithful performance by both the Owner and the Contractor, shall not show partiality to either, and shall not be liable for the result of any interpretation or decision rendered in good faith in such capacity.

1.5.11 The Architect's decisions in matters relating to artistic effect shall be final if consistent with the intent of the Contract Documents. The Architect's decisions on any other claims, disputes or other matters, including those in question between the Owner and the Contractor, shall be subject to arbitration as provided in this Agreement and in the Contract Documents.

1.5.12 The Architect shall have authority to reject Work which does not conform to the Contract Documents. Whenever, in the Architect's reasonable opinion, it is necessary or advisable for the implementation of the intent of the Contract Documents, the Architect will have authority to require special inspection or testing of the Work in accordance with the provisions of the Contract Documents, whether or not such Work be then fabricated, installed or completed.

1.5.13 The Architect shall review and approve or take other appropriate action upon the Contractor's submittals such as Shop Drawings, Product Data and Samples, but only for conformance with the design concept of the Work and with the information given in the Contract Documents. Such action shall be taken with reasonable promptness so as to cause no delay. The Architect's approval of a specific item shall not indicate approval of an assembly of which the item is a component.

1.5.14 The Architect shall prepare Change Orders for the Owner's approval and execution in accordance with the Contract Documents, and shall have authority to order minor changes in the Work not involving an adjustment in the Contract Sum or an extension of the Contract Time which are not inconsistent with the intent of the Contract Documents.

1.5.15 The Architect shall conduct inspections to determine the Dates of Substantial Completion and final completion, shall receive and forward to the Owner for the Owner's review written warranties and related documents required by the Contract Documents and assembled by the Contractor, and shall issue a final Certificate for Payment.

1.5.16 The extent of the duties, responsibilities and limitations of authority of the Architect as the Owner's representative during construction shall not be modified or extended without written consent of the Owner, the Contractor and the Architect.

1.6 PROJECT REPRESENTATION BEYOND BASIC SERVICES

1.6.1 If the Owner and Architect agree that more extensive representation at the site than is described in Paragraph 1.5 shall be provided, the Architect shall provide one or more Project Representatives to assist the Architect in carrying out such responsibilities at the site.

1.6.2 Such Project Representatives shall be selected, employed and directed by the Architect, and the Architect shall be compensated therefor as mutually agreed between the Owner and the Architect as set forth in an exhibit appended to this Agreement, which shall describe the duties, responsibilities and limitations of authority of such Project Representatives.

1.6.3 Through the observations by such Project Representatives, the Architect shall endeavor to provide further protection for the Owner against defects and deficiencies in the Work, but the furnishing of such project representation shall not modify the rights, responsibilities or obligations of the Architect as described in Paragraph 1.5.

1.7 ADDITIONAL SERVICES

The following Services are not included in Basic Services unless so identified in Article 15. They shall be provided if authorized or confirmed in writing by the Owner, and they shall be paid for by the Owner as provided in this Agreement, in addition to the compensation for Basic Services.

1.7.1 Providing analyses of the Owner's needs, and programming the requirements of the Project.

1.7.2 Providing financial feasibility or other special studies.

1.7.3 Providing planning surveys, site evaluations, environmental studies or comparative studies of prospective sites, and preparing special surveys, studies and submissions required for approvals of governmental authorities or others having jurisdiction over the Project.

1.7.4 Providing services relative to future facilities, systems and equipment which are not intended to be constructed during the Construction Phase.

1.7.5 Providing services to investigate existing conditions or facilities or to make measured drawings thereof, or to verify the accuracy of drawings or other information furnished by the Owner.

1.7.6 Preparing documents of alternate, separate or sequential bids or providing extra services in connection with bidding, negotiation or construction prior to the completion of the Construction Documents Phase, when requested by the Owner.

1.7.7 Providing coordination of Work performed by separate contractors or by the Owner's own forces.

1.7.8 Providing services in connection with the work of a construction manager or separate consultants retained by the Owner.

1.7.9 Providing Detailed Estimates of Construction Cost, analyses of owning and operating costs, or detailed quantity surveys or inventories of material, equipment and labor.

1.7.10 Providing interior design and other similar services required for or in connection with the selection, procurement or installation of furniture, furnishings and related equipment.

1.7.11 Providing services for planning tenant or rental spaces.

1.7.12 Making revisions in Drawings, Specifications or other documents when such revisions are inconsistent with written approvals or instructions previously given, are required by the enactment or revision of codes, laws or regulations subsequent to the preparation of such documents or are due to other causes not solely within the control of the Architect.

1.7.13 Preparing Drawings, Specifications and supporting data and providing other services in connection with Change Orders to the extent that the adjustment in the Basic Compensation resulting from the adjusted Construction Cost is not commensurate with the services required of the Architect, provided such Change Orders are required by causes not solely within the control of the Architect.

1.7.14 Making investigations, surveys, valuations, inventories or detailed appraisals of existing facilities, and services required in connection with construction performed by the Owner.

1.7.15 Providing consultation concerning replacement of any Work damaged by fire or other cause during con-

struction, and furnishing services as may be required in connection with the replacement of such Work.

1.7.16 Providing services made necessary by the default of the Contractor, or by major defects or deficiencies in the Work of the Contractor, or by failure of performance of either the Owner or Contractor under the Contract for Construction.

1.7.17 Preparing a set of reproducible record drawings showing significant changes in the Work made during construction based on marked-up prints, drawings and other data furnished by the Contractor to the Architect.

1.7.18 Providing extensive assistance in the utilization of any equipment or system such as initial start-up or testing, adjusting and balancing, preparation of operation and maintenance manuals, training personnel for operation and maintenance, and consultation during operation.

1.7.19 Providing services after issuance to the Owner of the final Certificate for Payment, or in the absence of a final Certificate for Payment, more than sixty days after the Date of Substantial Completion of the Work.

1.7.20 Preparing to serve or serving as an expert witness in connection with any public hearing, arbitration proceeding or legal proceeding.

1.7.21 Providing services of consultants for other than the normal architectural, structural, mechanical and electrical engineering services for the Project.

1.7.22 Providing any other services not otherwise included in this Agreement or not customarily furnished in accordance with generally accepted architectural practice.

1.8 TIME

1.8.1 The Architect shall perform Basic and Additional Services as expeditiously as is consistent with professional skill and care and the orderly progress of the Work. Upon request of the Owner, the Architect shall submit for the Owner's approval a schedule for the performance of the Architect's services which shall be adjusted as required as the Project proceeds, and shall include allowances for periods of time required for the Owner's review and approval of submissions and for approvals of authorities having jurisdiction over the Project. This schedule, when approved by the Owner, shall not, except for reasonable cause, be exceeded by the Architect.

ARTICLE 2

THE OWNER'S RESPONSIBILITIES

2.1 The Owner shall provide full information regarding requirements for the Project including a program, which shall set forth the Owner's design objectives, constraints and criteria, including space requirements and relationships, flexibility and expandability, special equipment and systems and site requirements.

2.2 If the Owner provides a budget for the Project it shall include contingencies for bidding, changes in the Work during construction, and other costs which are the responsibility of the Owner, including those described in this Article 2 and in Subparagraph 3.1.2. The Owner shall, at the request of the Architect, provide a statement of funds available for the Project, and their source.

2.3 The Owner shall designate, when necessary, a representative authorized to act in the Owner's behalf with respect to the Project. The Owner or such authorized representative shall examine the documents submitted by the Architect and shall render decisions pertaining thereto promptly, to avoid unreasonable delay in the progress of the Architect's services.

2.4 The Owner shall furnish a legal description and a certified land survey of the site, giving, as applicable, grades and lines of streets, alleys, pavements and adjoining property; rights-of-way, restrictions, easements, encroachments, zoning, deed restrictions, boundaries and contours of the site; locations, dimensions and complete data pertaining to existing buildings, other improvements and trees; and full information concerning available service and utility lines both public and private, above and below grade, including inverts and depths.

2.5 The Owner shall furnish the services of soil engineers or other consultants when such services are deemed necessary by the Architect. Such services shall include test borings, test pits, soil bearing values, percolation tests, air and water pollution tests, ground corrosion and resistivity tests, including necessary operations for determining subsoil, air and water conditions, with reports and appropriate professional recommendations.

2.6 The Owner shall furnish structural, mechanical, chemical and other laboratory tests, inspections and reports as required by law or the Contract Documents.

2.7 The Owner shall furnish all legal, accounting and insurance counseling services as may be necessary at any time for the Project, including such auditing services as the Owner may require to verify the Contractor's Applications for Payment or to ascertain how or for what purposes the Contractor uses the moneys paid by or on behalf of the Owner.

2.8 The services, information, surveys and reports required by Paragraphs 2.4 through 2.7 inclusive shall be furnished at the Owner's expense, and the Architect shall be entitled to rely upon the accuracy and completeness thereof.

2.9 If the Owner observes or otherwise becomes aware of any fault or defect in the Project or nonconformance with the Contract Documents, prompt written notice thereof shall be given by the Owner to the Architect.

2.10 The Owner shall furnish required information and services and shall render approvals and decisions as expeditiously as necessary for the orderly progress of the Architect's services and of the Work.

ARTICLE 3
CONSTRUCTION COST

3.1 DEFINITION

3.1.1 The Construction Cost shall be the total cost or estimated cost to the Owner of all elements of the Project designed or specified by the Architect.

3.1.2 The Construction Cost shall include at current market rates, including a reasonable allowance for overhead and profit, the cost of labor and materials furnished by the Owner and any equipment which has been de-signed, specified, selected or specially provided for by the Architect.

3.1.3 Construction Cost does not include the compensation of the Architect and the Architect's consultants, the cost of the land, rights-of-way, or other costs which are the responsibility of the Owner as provided in Article 2.

3.2 RESPONSIBILITY FOR CONSTRUCTION COST

3.2.1 Evaluations of the Owner's Project budget, Statements of Probable Construction Cost and Detailed Estimates of Construction Cost, if any, prepared by the Architect, represent the Architect's best judgment as a design professional familiar with the construction industry. It is recognized, however, that neither the Architect nor the Owner has control over the cost of labor, materials or equipment, over the Contractor's methods of determining bid prices, or over competitive bidding, market or negotiating conditions. Accordingly, the Architect cannot and does not warrant or represent that bids or negotiated prices will not vary from the Project budget proposed, established or approved by the Owner, if any, or from any Statement of Probable Construction Cost or other cost estimate or evaluation prepared by the Architect.

3.2.2 No fixed limit of Construction Cost shall be established as a condition of this Agreement by the furnishing, proposal or establishment of a Project budget under Subparagraph 1.1.2 or Paragraph 2.2 or otherwise, unless such fixed limit has been agreed upon in writing and signed by the parties hereto. If such a fixed limit has been established, the Architect shall be permitted to include contingencies for design, bidding and price escalation, to determine what materials, equipment, component systems and types of construction are to be included in the Contract Documents, to make reasonable adjustments in the scope of the Project and to include in the Contract Documents alternate bids to adjust the Construction Cost to the fixed limit. Any such fixed limit shall be increased in the amount of any increase in the Contract Sum occurring after execution of the Contract for Construction.

3.2.3 If the Bidding or Negotiation Phase has not commenced within three months after the Architect submits the Construction Documents to the Owner, any Project budget or fixed limit of Construction Cost shall be adjusted to reflect any change in the general level of prices in the construction industry between the date of submission of the Construction Documents to the Owner and the date on which proposals are sought.

3.2.4 If a Project budget or fixed limit of Construction Cost (adjusted as provided in Subparagraph 3.2.3) is exceeded by the lowest bona fide bid or negotiated proposal, the Owner shall (1) give written approval of an increase in such fixed limit, (2) authorize rebidding or renegotiating of the Project within a reasonable time, (3) if the Project is abandoned, terminate in accordance with Paragraph 10.2, or (4) cooperate in revising the Project scope and quality as required to reduce the Construction Cost. In the case of (4), provided a fixed limit of Construction Cost has been established as a condition of this Agreement, the Architect, without additional charge, shall modify the Drawings and Specifications as necessary to comply

AIA DOCUMENT B141 • OWNER-ARCHITECT AGREEMENT • THIRTEENTH EDITION • JULY 1977 • AIA® • © 1977
THE AMERICAN INSTITUTE OF ARCHITECTS, 1735 NEW YORK AVENUE, N.W., WASHINGTON, D.C. 20006

with the fixed limit. The providing of such service shall be the limit of the Architect's responsibility arising from the establishment of such fixed limit, and having done so, the Architect shall be entitled to compensation for all services performed, in accordance with this Agreement, whether or not the Construction Phase is commenced.

ARTICLE 4

DIRECT PERSONNEL EXPENSE

4.1 Direct Personnel Expense is defined as the direct salaries of all the Architect's personnel engaged on the Project, and the portion of the cost of their mandatory and customary contributions and benefits related thereto, such as employment taxes and other statutory employee benefits, insurance, sick leave, holidays, vacations, pensions and similar contributions and benefits.

ARTICLE 5

REIMBURSABLE EXPENSES

5.1 Reimbursable Expenses are in addition to the Compensation for Basic and Additional Services and include actual expenditures made by the Architect and the Architect's employees and consultants in the interest of the Project for the expenses listed in the following Subparagraphs:

5.1.1 Expense of transportation in connection with the Project; living expenses in connection with out-of-town travel; long distance communications, and fees paid for securing approval of authorities having jurisdiction over the Project.

5.1.2 Expense of reproductions, postage and handling of Drawings, Specifications and other documents, excluding reproductions for the office use of the Architect and the Architect's consultants.

5.1.3 Expense of data processing and photographic production techniques when used in connection with Additional Services.

5.1.4 If authorized in advance by the Owner, expense of overtime work requiring higher than regular rates.

5.1.5 Expense of renderings, models and mock-ups requested by the Owner.

5.1.6 Expense of any additional insurance coverage or limits, including professional liability insurance, requested by the Owner in excess of that normally carried by the Architect and the Architect's consultants.

ARTICLE 6

PAYMENTS TO THE ARCHITECT

6.1 PAYMENTS ON ACCOUNT OF BASIC SERVICES

6.1.1 An initial payment as set forth in Paragraph 14.1 is the minimum payment under this Agreement.

6.1.2 Subsequent payments for Basic Services shall be made monthly and shall be in proportion to services performed within each Phase of services, on the basis set forth in Article 14.

6.1.3 If and to the extent that the Contract Time initially established in the Contract for Construction is exceeded or extended through no fault of the Architect, compensation for any Basic Services required for such extended period of Administration of the Construction Contract shall be computed as set forth in Paragraph 14.4 for Additional Services.

6.1.4 When compensation is based on a percentage of Construction Cost, and any portions of the Project are deleted or otherwise not constructed, compensation for such portions of the Project shall be payable to the extent services are performed on such portions, in accordance with the schedule set forth in Subparagraph 14.2.2, based on (1) the lowest bona fide bid or negotiated proposal or, (2) if no such bid or proposal is received, the most recent Statement of Probable Construction Cost or Detailed Estimate of Construction Cost for such portions of the Project.

**6.2 PAYMENTS ON ACCOUNT OF
ADDITIONAL SERVICES**

6.2.1 Payments on account of the Architect's Additional Services as defined in Paragraph 1.7 and for Reimbursable Expenses as defined in Article 5 shall be made monthly upon presentation of the Architect's statement of services rendered or expenses incurred.

6.3 PAYMENTS WITHHELD

6.3.1 No deductions shall be made from the Architect's compensation on account of penalty, liquidated damages or other sums withheld from payments to contractors, or on account of the cost of changes in the Work other than those for which the Architect is held legally liable.

6.4 PROJECT SUSPENSION OR TERMINATION

6.4.1 If the Project is suspended or abandoned in whole or in part for more than three months, the Architect shall be compensated for all services performed prior to receipt of written notice from the Owner of such suspension or abandonment, together with Reimbursable Expenses then due and all Termination Expenses as defined in Paragraph 10.4. If the Project is resumed after being suspended for more than three months, the Architect's compensation shall be equitably adjusted.

ARTICLE 7

ARCHITECT'S ACCOUNTING RECORDS

7.1 Records of Reimbursable Expenses and expenses pertaining to Additional Services and services performed on the basis of a Multiple of Direct Personnel Expense shall be kept on the basis of generally accepted accounting principles and shall be available to the Owner or the Owner's authorized representative at mutually convenient times.

ARTICLE 8

OWNERSHIP AND USE OF DOCUMENTS

8.1 Drawings and Specifications as instruments of service are and shall remain the property of the Architect whether the Project for which they are made is executed or not. The Owner shall be permitted to retain copies, including reproducible copies, of Drawings and Specifications for information and reference in connection with the Owner's use and occupancy of the Project. The Drawings and Specifications shall not be used by the Owner on other projects, for additions to this Project, or for completion of this Project by others provided the Architect is not in default under this Agreement, except by agreement in writing and with appropriate compensation to the Architect.

8.2 Submission or distribution to meet official regulatory requirements or for other purposes in connection with the Project is not to be construed as publication in derogation of the Architect's rights.

ARTICLE 9

ARBITRATION

9.1 All claims, disputes and other matters in question between the parties to this Agreement, arising out of or relating to this Agreement or the breach thereof, shall be decided by arbitration in accordance with the Construction Industry Arbitration Rules of the American Arbitration Association then obtaining unless the parties mutually agree otherwise. No arbitration, arising out of or relating to this Agreement, shall include, by consolidation, joinder or in any other manner, any additional person not a party to this Agreement except by written consent containing a specific reference to this Agreement and signed by the Architect, the Owner, and any other person sought to be joined. Any consent to arbitration involving an additional person or persons shall not constitute consent to arbitration of any dispute not described therein or with any person not named or described therein. This Agreement to arbitrate and any agreement to arbitrate with an additional person or persons duly consented to by the parties to this Agreement shall be specifically enforceable under the prevailing arbitration law.

9.2 Notice of the demand for arbitration shall be filed in writing with the other party to this Agreement and with the American Arbitration Association. The demand shall be made within a reasonable time after the claim, dispute or other matter in question has arisen. In no event shall the demand for arbitration be made after the date when institution of legal or equitable proceedings based on such claim, dispute or other matter in question would be barred by the applicable statute of limitations.

9.3 The award rendered by the arbitrators shall be final, and judgment may be entered upon it in accordance with applicable law in any court having jurisdiction thereof.

ARTICLE 10

TERMINATION OF AGREEMENT

10.1 This Agreement may be terminated by either party upon seven days' written notice should the other party fail substantially to perform in accordance with its terms through no fault of the party initiating the termination.

10.2 This Agreement may be terminated by the Owner upon at least seven days' written notice to the Architect in the event that the Project is permanently abandoned.

10.3 In the event of termination not the fault of the Architect, the Architect shall be compensated for all services performed to termination date, together with Reimbursable Expenses then due and all Termination Expenses as defined in Paragraph 10.4.

10.4 Termination Expenses include expenses directly attributable to termination for which the Architect is not otherwise compensated, plus an amount computed as a percentage of the total Basic and Additional Compensation earned to the time of termination, as follows:

  .1 20 percent if termination occurs during the Schematic Design Phase; or

  .2 10 percent if termination occurs during the Design Development Phase; or

  .3 5 percent if termination occurs during any subsequent phase.

ARTICLE 11

MISCELLANEOUS PROVISIONS

11.1 Unless otherwise specified, this Agreement shall be governed by the law of the principal place of business of the Architect.

11.2 Terms in this Agreement shall have the same meaning as those in AIA Document A201, General Conditions of the Contract for Construction, current as of the date of this Agreement.

11.3 As between the parties to this Agreement: as to all acts or failures to act by either party to this Agreement, any applicable statute of limitations shall commence to run and any alleged cause of action shall be deemed to have accrued in any and all events not later than the relevant Date of Substantial Completion of the Work, and as to any acts or failures to act occurring after the relevant Date of Substantial Completion, not later than the date of issuance of the final Certificate for Payment.

11.4 The Owner and the Architect waive all rights against each other and against the contractors, consultants, agents and employees of the other for damages covered by any property insurance during construction as set forth in the edition of AIA Document A201, General Conditions, current as of the date of this Agreement. The Owner and the Architect each shall require appropriate similar waivers from their contractors, consultants and agents.

ARTICLE 12

SUCCESSORS AND ASSIGNS

12.1 The Owner and the Architect, respectively, bind themselves, their partners, successors, assigns and legal representatives to the other party to this Agreement and to the partners, successors, assigns and legal representatives of such other party with respect to all covenants of this Agreement. Neither the Owner nor the Architect shall assign, sublet or transfer any interest in this Agreement without the written consent of the other.

ARTICLE 13

EXTENT OF AGREEMENT

13.1 This Agreement represents the entire and integrated agreement between the Owner and the Architect and supersedes all prior negotiations, representations or agreements, either written or oral. This Agreement may be amended only by written instrument signed by both Owner and Architect.

ARTICLE 14

BASIS OF COMPENSATION

The Owner shall compensate the Architect for the Scope of Services provided, in accordance with Article 6, Payments to the Architect, and the other Terms and Conditions of this Agreement, as follows:

14.1   AN INITIAL PAYMENT of   dollars ($)

shall be made upon execution of this Agreement and credited to the Owner's account as follows:

14.2   BASIC COMPENSATION

14.2.1   FOR BASIC SERVICES, as described in Paragraphs 1.1 through 1.5, and any other services included in Article 15 as part of Basic Services, Basic Compensation shall be computed as follows:

(Here insert basis of compensation, including fixed amounts, multiples or percentages, and identify Phases to which particular methods of compensation apply, if necessary.)

14.2.2   Where compensation is based on a Stipulated Sum or Percentage of Construction Cost, payments for Basic Services shall be made as provided in Subparagraph 6.1.2, so that Basic Compensation for each Phase shall equal the following percentages of the total Basic Compensation payable:

(Include any additional Phases as appropriate.)

Schematic Design Phase:	percent (%)
Design Development Phase:	percent (%)
Construction Documents Phase:	percent (%)
Bidding or Negotiation Phase:	percent (%)
Construction Phase:	percent (%)

14.3   FOR PROJECT REPRESENTATION BEYOND BASIC SERVICES, as described in Paragraph 1.6, Compensation shall be computed separately in accordance with Subparagraph 1.6.2.

14.4   COMPENSATION FOR ADDITIONAL SERVICES

14.4.1   FOR ADDITIONAL SERVICES OF THE ARCHITECT, as described in Paragraph 1.7, and any other services included in Article 15 as part of Additional Services, but excluding Additional Services of consultants, Compensation shall be computed as follows:

(Here insert basis of compensation, including rates and/or multiples of Direct Personnel Expense for Principals and employees, and identify Principals and classify employees, if required. Identify specific services to which particular methods of compensation apply, if necessary.)

14.4.2   FOR ADDITIONAL SERVICES OF CONSULTANTS, including additional structural, mechanical and electrical engineering services and those provided under Subparagraph 1.7.21 or identified in Article 15 as part of Additional Services, a multiple of (   ) times the amounts billed to the Architect for such services.

(Identify specific types of consultants in Article 15, if required.)

14.5   FOR REIMBURSABLE EXPENSES, as described in Article 5, and any other items included in Article 15 as Reimbursable Expenses, a multiple of (   ) times the amounts expended by the Architect, the Architect's employees and consultants in the interest of the Project.

14.6   Payments due the Architect and unpaid under this Agreement shall bear interest from the date payment is due at the rate entered below, or in the absence thereof, at the legal rate prevailing at the principal place of business of the Architect.

(Here insert any rate of interest agreed upon.)

(Usury laws and requirements under the Federal Truth in Lending Act, similar state and local consumer credit laws and other regulations at the Owner's and Architect's principal places of business, the location of the Project and elsewhere may affect the validity of this provision. Specific legal advice should be obtained with respect to deletion, modification, or other requirements such as written disclosures or waivers.)

14.7   The Owner and the Architect agree in accordance with the Terms and Conditions of this Agreement that:

14.7.1   IF THE SCOPE of the Project or of the Architect's Services is changed materially, the amounts of compensation shall be equitably adjusted.

14.7.2   IF THE SERVICES covered by this Agreement have not been completed within

(   ) months of the date hereof, through no fault of the Architect, the amounts of compensation, rates and multiples set forth herein shall be equitably adjusted.

<u>ARTICLE 15</u>
OTHER CONDITIONS OR SERVICES

This Agreement entered into as of the day and year first written above.

OWNER   ARCHITECT

_____   _____

_____   _____

_____   _____

BY_____   BY_____

AIA DOCUMENT B141 • OWNER-ARCHITECT AGREEMENT • THIRTEENTH EDITION • JULY 1977 • AIA® • © 1977
THE AMERICAN INSTITUTE OF ARCHITECTS, 1735 NEW YORK AVENUE, N.W., WASHINGTON, D.C. 20006

THE AMERICAN INSTITUTE OF ARCHITECTS

AIA Document B141/CM

CONSTRUCTION MANAGEMENT EDITION

Standard Form of Agreement Between Owner and Architect

1980 EDITION

THIS DOCUMENT HAS IMPORTANT LEGAL CONSEQUENCES; CONSULTATION WITH AN ATTORNEY IS ENCOURAGED.

This document is intended to be used in conjunction with
AIA Documents B801, 1980; A101/CM, 1980; and A201/CM, 1980.

AGREEMENT

made as of the   day of   in the year of Nineteen
Hundred and

BETWEEN the Owner:

and the Architect:

For the following Project:
(Include detailed description of Project location and scope.)

the Construction Manager:

The Owner and the Architect agree as set forth below.

AIA DOCUMENT B141/CM • OWNER-ARCHITECT AGREEMENT • CONSTRUCTION MANAGEMENT EDITION • JUNE 1980 EDITION
AIA® • ©1980 • THE AMERICAN INSTITUTE OF ARCHITECTS, 1735 NEW YORK AVENUE, N.W., WASHINGTON, D.C. 20006 **B141/CM—1980 1**

TERMS AND CONDITIONS OF AGREEMENT BETWEEN OWNER AND ARCHITECT

ARTICLE 1
ARCHITECT'S SERVICES AND RESPONSIBILITIES

BASIC SERVICES

Unless modified by Article 15, the Architect's Basic Services shall be provided in conjunction with, and in reliance upon, the services of a Construction Manager as described in the Standard Form of Agreement Between Owner and Construction Manager, AIA Document B801, 1980 Edition. They shall consist of the five Phases described in Paragraphs 1.1 through 1.5, inclusive, and include normal structural, mechanical and electrical engineering services, and any other services included in Article 15 as part of Basic Services.

1.1 SCHEMATIC DESIGN PHASE

1.1.1 The Architect shall review the program furnished by the Owner to ascertain the requirements of the Project and shall review and confirm the understanding of these requirements and other design parameters with the Owner.

1.1.2 The Architect shall provide a preliminary evaluation of the program and the Project budget requirements, each in terms of the other, subject to the limitations set forth in Subparagraph 3.2.1.

1.1.3 The Architect shall review with the Owner and the Construction Manager site use and improvements; selection of materials, building systems and equipment; construction methods and methods of Project delivery.

1.1.4 Based on the mutually agreed upon program and the Project budget requirements, the Architect shall prepare, for approval by the Owner, Schematic Design Documents consisting of drawings, outline specifications and other documents illustrating the scale and relationship of Project components.

1.1.5 At intervals appropriate to the progress of the Schematic Design Phase, the Architect shall provide schematic design studies for the Construction Manager's review, which will be made so as to cause no delay to the Architect.

1.1.6 Upon completion of the Schematic Design Phase the Architect shall provide the drawings, outline specifications and other documents approved by the Owner for the Construction Manager's use in preparing an estimate of Construction Cost.

1.2 DESIGN DEVELOPMENT PHASE

1.2.1 Based on the approved Schematic Design Documents and any adjustments authorized by the Owner in the program or the Project budget, the Architect shall prepare, for approval by the Owner, the Design Development Documents consisting of drawings, outline specifications and other documents to fix and describe the size and character of the entire Project as to architectural, structural, mechanical and electrical systems, materials, and such other elements as may be appropriate.

1.2.2 At intervals appropriate to the progress of the Design Development Phase, the Architect shall provide de-sign development documents for the Construction Manager's review, which will be made so as to cause no delay to the Architect.

1.2.3 Upon completion of the Design Development Phase, the Architect shall provide the Construction Manager with drawings, outline specifications and other documents approved by the Owner for use in preparing a further estimate of Construction Cost, and shall assist the Construction Manager in preparing such estimate of Construction Cost.

1.3 CONSTRUCTION DOCUMENTS PHASE

1.3.1 Based on the approved Design Development Documents, and any further adjustments in the scope or quality of the Project or in the Project budget authorized by the Owner, the Architect shall prepare, for approval by the Owner, Construction Documents consisting of Drawings and Specifications setting forth in detail the requirements for the construction of the Project.

1.3.2 The Architect shall keep the Construction Manager informed of any changes in requirements or in construction materials, systems or equipment as the Drawings and Specifications are developed so that the Construction Manager can adjust the estimate of Construction Cost appropriately.

1.3.3 The Architect shall assist the Owner and the Construction Manager in the preparation of the necessary bidding information, bidding forms, the Conditions of the Contracts, and the forms of Agreement between the Owner and the Contractors.

1.3.4 The Architect shall assist the Owner and the Construction Manager in connection with the Owner's responsibility for filing documents required for the approvals of governmental authorities having jurisdiction over the Project.

BIDDING OR NEGOTIATION PHASE

1.4.1 The Architect, following the Owner's approval of the Construction Documents and the latest estimate of Construction Cost, shall assist the Construction Manager in obtaining Bids or negotiated proposals by rendering interpretations and clarifications of the Drawings and Specifications in appropriate written form. The Architect shall assist the Construction Manager in conducting pre-award conferences with successful Bidders.

1.5 CONSTRUCTION PHASE-ADMINISTRATION OF THE CONSTRUCTION CONTRACT

1.5.1 The Construction Phase will commence with the award of the initial Contract for Construction and, together with the Architect's obligation to provide Basic Services under this Agreement, will end when final payment to all Contractors is due, or in the absence of a final Project Certificate for Payment or of such due date, sixty days after the Date of Substantial Completion of the Project whichever occurs first.

1.5.2 Unless otherwise provided in this Agreement and incorporated in the Contract Documents, the Architect, in cooperation with the Construction Manager, shall provide administration of the Contracts for Construction as set forth below and in the 1980 Edition of AIA Document A201/CM, General Conditions of the Contract for Construction, Construction Management Edition.

1.5.3 The Architect and the Construction Manager shall advise and consult with the Owner during the Construction Phase. All instructions to the Contractors shall be forwarded through the Construction Manager. The Architect and the Construction Manager shall have authority to act on behalf of the Owner only to the extent provided in the Contract Documents unless otherwise modified by written instrument in accordance with Subparagraph 1.5.18.

1.5.4 The Architect shall visit the site at intervals appropriate to the stage of construction, or as otherwise agreed by the Architect in writing, to become generally familiar with the progress and quality of Work and to determine in general if Work is proceeding in accordance with the Contract Documents. However, the Architect shall not be required to make exhaustive or continuous on-site inspections to check the quality or quantity of Work. On the basis of such on-site observations as an architect, the Architect shall keep the Owner informed of the progress and quality of Work, and shall endeavor to guard the Owner against defects and deficiencies in Work of the Contractors.

1.5.5 The Architect shall not be responsible for, nor have control or charge of, construction means, methods, techniques, sequences or procedures, or for safety precautions and programs in connection with the Project, and shall not be responsible for Contractors' failure to carry out Work in accordance with the Contract Documents. The Architect shall not be responsible for, nor have control over, the acts or omissions of the Contractors, Subcontractors, any of their agents or employees, or any other persons performing any Work, nor shall the Architect be responsible for the Construction Manager's obligations as an agent of the Owner.

1.5.6 The Architect shall at all times have access to Work wherever it is in preparation or progress.

1.5.7 Based on the Architect's observations at the site, the recommendations of the Construction Manager and an evaluation of the Project Application for Payment, the Architect shall determine the amounts owing to the Contractors and shall issue a Project Certificate for Payment in such amounts, as provided in the Contract Documents.

1.5.8 The issuance of a Project Certificate for Payment shall constitute a representation by the Architect to the Owner that, based on the Architect's observations at the site as provided in Subparagraph 1.5.4 and on the data comprising the Project Application for Payment, Work has progressed to the point indicated; that, to the best of the Architect's knowledge, information and belief, the quality of Work is in accordance with the Contract Documents (subject to an evaluation of Work for conformance with the Contract Documents upon Substantial Completion, to the results of any subsequent tests required by or performed under the Contract Documents, to minor deviations from the Contract Documents correctable prior to completion, and to any specific qualifications stated in the Project Certificate for Payment); and that the Contractors are entitled to payment in the amount certified. However, the issuance of a Project Certificate for Payment shall not be a representation that the Architect has made any examination to ascertain how or for what purpose the Contractors have used the monies paid on account of the Contract Sums.

1.5.9 The Architect shall be the interpreter of the requirements of the Contract Documents and the judge of the performance thereunder by both the Owner and the Contractors. The Architect shall render interpretations necessary for the proper execution or progress of Work, with reasonable promptness and in accordance with agreed upon time limits. The Architect shall render written decisions, within a reasonable time, on all claims, disputes and other matters in question between the Owner and the Contractors relating to the execution or progress of Work or the interpretation of the Contract Documents.

1.5.10 All interpretations and decisions of the Architect shall be consistent with the intent of, and reasonably inferable from, the Contract Documents, and shall be in writing or in graphic form. In the capacity of interpreter and judge, the Architect shall endeavor to secure faithful performance by both the Owner and the Contractors, shall not show partiality, and shall not be liable for the result of any interpretation or decision rendered in good faith in such capacity.

1.5.11 The Architect's decision in matters relating to artistic effect shall be final if consistent with the intent of the Contract Documents. The Architect's decisions on any other claims, disputes or other matters, including those in question between the Owner and the Contractor(s), shall be subject to arbitration as provided in this Agreement and in the Contract Documents.

1.5.12 The Architect shall have authority to reject Work which does not conform to the Contract Documents, and whenever, in the Architect's reasonable opinion, it is necessary or advisable for the implementation of the intent of the Contract Documents, the Architect shall have authority to require special inspection or testing of Work in accordance with the provisions of the Contract Documents, whether or not such Work be then fabricated, installed or completed, but the Architect shall take such action only after consultation with the Construction Manager.

1.5.13 The Architect shall receive Contractors' submittals such as Shop Drawings, Product Data and Samples from the Construction Manager and shall review and approve or take other appropriate action upon them, but only for conformance with the design concept of the Project and with the information given in the Contract Documents. Such action shall be taken with reasonable promptness so as to cause no delay. The Architect's approval of a specific item shall not indicate approval of an assembly of which the item is a component.

1.5.14 The Architect shall review and sign or take other appropriate action on Change Orders prepared by the Construction Manager for the Owner's authorization in accordance with the Contract Documents.

1.5.15 The Architect shall have authority to order minor changes in Work not involving an adjustment in a Contract Sum or an extension of a Contract Time and which are not inconsistent with the intent of the Contract Documents. Such changes shall be effected by written order issued through the Construction Manager.

AIA DOCUMENT B141/CM • OWNER-ARCHITECT AGREEMENT • CONSTRUCTION MANAGEMENT EDITION • JUNE 1980 EDITION

1.5.16 The Architect, assisted by the Construction Manager, shall conduct inspections to determine the Dates of Substantial Completion and final completion and shall issue appropriate Project Certificates for Payment.

1.5.17 The Architect shall assist the Construction Manager in receiving and forwarding to the Owner for the Owner's review written warranties and related documents assembled by the Contractors.

1.5.18 The extent of the duties, responsibilities and limitations of authority of the Architect as a representative of the Owner during construction shall not be modified or extended without the written consent of the Owner, the Contractors, the Architect and the Construction Manager, which consent shall not be unreasonably withheld.

1.6 PROJECT REPRESENTATION BEYOND BASIC SERVICES

1.6.1 If the Owner and the Architect agree that more extensive representation at the site than is described in Paragraph 1.5 shall be provided, the Architect shall provide one or more Project Representatives to assist the Architect in carrying out such responsibilities at the site.

1.6.2 Such Project Representatives shall be selected, employed and directed by the Architect, and the Architect shall be compensated therefor as mutually agreed between the Owner and the Architect, as set forth in an exhibit appended to this Agreement, which shall describe the duties, responsibilities and limitations of authority of such Project Representatives.

1.6.3 Through the observations of such Project Representatives, the Architect shall endeavor to provide further protection for the Owner against defects and deficiencies in Work, but the furnishing of such Project representation shall not modify the rights, responsibilities or obligations of the Architect as described in Paragraph 1.5.

1.7 ADDITIONAL SERVICES

The following services are not included in Basic Services unless so identified in Article 15. They shall be provided if authorized or confirmed in writing by the Owner, and they shall be paid for by the Owner as provided in this Agreement, in addition to the compensation for Basic Services.

1.7.1 Providing analyses of the Owner's needs and programming the requirements of the Project.

1.7.2 Providing financial feasibility or other special studies.

1.7.3 Providing planning surveys, site evaluations, environmental studies or comparative studies of prospective sites, and preparing special surveys, studies and submissions required for approvals of governmental authorities or others having jurisdiction over the Project.

1.7.4 Providing services relative to future facilities, systems and equipment which are not intended to be constructed during the Construction Phase.

1.7.5 Providing services to investigate existing conditions or facilities, or to make measured drawings thereof, or to verify the accuracy of drawings or other information furnished by the Owner.

1.7.6 Providing services in connection with alternative designs for cost estimating or bidding purposes.

1.7.7 Providing coordination of work performed by separate contractors or by the Owner's own forces.

1.7.8 Providing services in connection with the work of separate consultants, other than the Construction Manager, retained by the Owner.

1.7.9 Providing interior design and other similar services required for or in connection with the selection, procurement or installation of furniture, furnishings and related equipment.

1.7.10 Providing services for planning tenant or rental spaces.

1.7.11 Making revisions in Drawings, Specifications or other documents when such revisions are inconsistent with written approvals or instructions previously given, are required by the enactment or revision of codes, laws or regulations subsequent to the preparation of such documents, or are due to other causes not solely within the control of the Architect.

1.7.12 Preparing Drawings, Specifications and supporting data and providing other services in connection with Change Orders. If Basic Compensation is to be adjusted according to adjustments in Construction Cost, to the extent that any Change Order not required by causes solely within the control of the Architect results in an adjustment in the Basic Compensation not commensurate with the services required of the Architect, compensation shall be equitably adjusted.

1.7.13 Making investigations, surveys, valuations, inventories, detailed appraisals of existing facilities, and services required in connection with construction performed by the Owner.

1.7.14 Providing consultation concerning replacement of any Work damaged by fire or other cause during construction, and furnishing services as may be required in connection with the replacement of such Work.

1.7.15 Providing services made necessary by the failure of performance, the termination or default of the Construction Manager; by default of a Contractor; by major defect or deficiencies in the Work of any Contractor; or by failure of performance of either the Owner or any Contractor under the Contracts for Construction.

1.7.16 Preparing a set of reproducible record drawings showing significant changes in Work made during construction based on marked-up prints, drawings and other data furnished to the Architect.

1.7.17 Providing extensive assistance in the utilization of any equipment or system such as initial start-up or testing, adjusting and balancing, preparation of operation and maintenance manuals, training personnel for operation and maintenance, and consultation during operation.

1.7.18 Providing services after issuance to the Owner of the final Project Certificate for Payment, or in the absence of a final Project Certificate for Payment, more than sixty days after the Date of Substantial Completion of the Project.

1.7.19 Preparing to serve or serving as a witness in connection with any public hearing, arbitration proceeding or legal proceeding.

1.7.20 Providing services of consultants for other than the normal architectural, structural, mechanical and electrical engineering services for the Project.

1.7.21 Providing any other services not otherwise included in this Agreement or not customarily furnished in accordance with generally accepted architectural practice.

1.8   TIME

1.8.1   The Architect shall perform Basic and Additional Services as expeditiously as is consistent with professional skill and care and the orderly progress of the Project. Upon request of the Owner, the Architect shall submit for the Owner's approval a schedule for the performance of the Architect's services which shall be adjusted as required as the Project proceeds, and which shall include allowances for periods of time required for the Owner's review and approval of submissions and for approvals of authorities having jurisdiction over the Project. The Architect shall consult with the Construction Manager to coordinate the Architect's time schedule with the Project Schedule. This schedule, when approved by the Owner, shall not, except for reasonable cause, be exceeded by the Architect.

ARTICLE 2
THE OWNER'S RESPONSIBILITIES

2.1   The Owner shall provide full information regarding requirements for the Project, including a program which shall set forth the Owner's design objectives, constraints and criteria, including space requirements and relationships, flexibility and expandability, special equipment and systems and site requirements.

2.2   The Owner shall provide a budget for the Project based on consultation with the Architect and the Construction Manager, which shall include contingencies for bidding, changes during construction and other costs which are the responsibility of the Owner. The Owner shall, at the request of the Architect, provide a statement of funds available for the Project and their source.

2.3   The Owner shall designate a representative authorized to act in the Owner's behalf with respect to the Project. The Owner, or such authorized representative, shall examine the documents submitted by the Architect and shall render decisions pertaining thereto promptly to avoid unreasonable delay in the progress of the Architect's services.

2.4   The Owner shall retain a construction manager to manage the Project. The Construction Manager's services, duties and responsibilities will be as described in the Agreement Between Owner and Construction Manager, AIA Document B801, 1980 Edition. The Terms and Conditions of the Owner-Construction Manager Agreement will be furnished to the Architect and will not be modified without written consent of the Architect, which consent shall not be unreasonably withheld. Actions taken by the Construction Manager as agent of the Owner shall be the acts of the Owner, and the Architect shall not be responsible for them.

2.5   The Owner shall furnish a legal description and a certified land survey of the site, giving, as applicable, grades and lines of streets, alleys, pavements and adjoining property; rights-of-way, restrictions, easements, encroachments, zoning, deed restrictions, boundaries and contours of the site; locations, dimensions and complete data pertaining to existing buildings, other improvements and trees; and full information concerning available service and utility lines both public and private, above and below grade, including inverts and depths.

2.6   The Owner shall furnish the services of soil engi-

neers or other consultants when such services are deemed necessary by the Architect. Such services shall include test borings, test pits, soil bearing values, percolation tests, air and water pollution tests, ground corrosion and resistivity tests including necessary operations for determining subsoil, air and water conditions, with reports and appropriate professional recommendations.

2.7   The Owner shall furnish structural, mechanical, chemical and other laboratory tests, inspections and reports as required by law or the Contract Documents.

2.8   The Owner shall furnish such legal, accounting and insurance counseling services as may be necessary for the Project, including such auditing services as the Owner may require to verify the Project Applications for Payment or to ascertain how or for what purposes the Contractors have used the monies paid by or on behalf of the Owner.

2.9   The services, information, surveys and reports required by Paragraphs 2.5 through 2.8, inclusive, shall be furnished at the Owner's expense, and the Architect shall be entitled to rely upon their accuracy and completeness.

2.10   If the Owner observes or otherwise becomes aware of any fault or defect in the Project, or nonconformance with the Contract Documents, prompt written notice thereof shall be given by the Owner to the Architect and the Construction Manager.

2.11   The Owner shall furnish the required information and services and shall render approvals and decisions as expeditiously as necessary for the orderly progress of the Architect's services and Work of the Contractors.

ARTICLE 3
CONSTRUCTION COST

3.1   DEFINITION

3.1.1   The Construction Cost shall be the total cost or estimated cost to the Owner of all elements of the Project designed or specified by the Architect.

3.1.2   The Construction Cost shall also include at current market rates, including a reasonable allowance for overhead and profit, the cost of labor and materials furnished by the Owner and any equipment which has been designed, specified, selected or specially provided for by the Architect. It shall also include the Construction Manager's compensation for services, Reimbursable Costs and the cost of work provided by the Construction Manager.

3.1.3   Construction Cost does not include the compensation of the Architect and the Architect's consultants, the cost of the land, rights-of-way, or other costs which are the responsibility of the Owner as provided in Article 2.

3.2   RESPONSIBILITY FOR CONSTRUCTION COST

3.2.1   The Architect, as a design professional familiar with the construction industry, shall assist the Construction Manager in evaluating the Owner's Project budget and shall review the estimates of Construction Cost prepared by the Construction Manager. It is recognized, however, that neither the Architect, the Construction Manager nor the Owner has control over the cost of labor, materials or equipment, over the Contractors' methods of determining Bid prices, or over competitive bidding, market or negotiating conditions. Accordingly, the Architect cannot and does not warrant or represent that

Bids or negotiated prices will not vary from the Project budget proposed, established or approved by the Owner, if any, or from the estimate of Construction Cost or other cost estimate or evaluation prepared by the Construction Manager.

3.2.2 No fixed limit of Construction Cost shall be established as a condition of this Agreement by the furnishing, proposal or establishment of a Project budget under Subparagraph 1.1.2 or Paragraph 2.2, or otherwise, unless such fixed limit has been agreed upon in writing and signed by the parties to this Agreement. If such a fixed limit has been established, the Construction Manager will include contingencies for design, bidding and price escalation, and will consult with the Architect to determine what materials, equipment, component systems and types of construction are to be included in the Contract Documents, to make reasonable adjustments in the scope of the Project, and to include in the Contract Documents alternate Bids to adjust the Construction Cost to the fixed limit. Any such fixed limit shall be increased in the amount of any increase in the Contract Sums occurring after the execution of the Contracts for Construction.

3.2.3 If Bids are not received within the time scheduled at the time the fixed limit of Construction Cost was established, due to causes beyond the Architect's control, any fixed limit of Construction Cost established as a condition of this Agreement shall be adjusted to reflect any change in the general level of prices in the construction industry between the originally scheduled date and the date on which Bids are received.

3.2.4 If a fixed limit of Construction Cost (adjusted as provided in Subparagraph 3.2.3) is exceeded by the sum of the lowest figures from bona fide Bids or negotiated proposals, plus the Construction Manager's estimate of other elements of Construction Cost for the Project, the Owner shall (1) give written approval of an increase in such fixed limit, (2) authorize rebidding or renegotiation of the Project or portions of the Project within a reasonable time, (3) if the Project is abandoned, terminate in accordance with Paragraph 10.2, or (4) cooperate in revising the Project scope and quality as required to reduce the Construction Cost. In the case of item (4) the Architect shall modify the Drawings and Specifications as necessary to comply with the fixed limit without additional cost to the Owner if the Architect has concurred in the Construction Manager's estimate of Construction Cost, but subject to compensation as an Additional Service under Subparagraph 1.7.11 if the Architect has not so concurred. The providing of such service shall be the limit of the Architect's responsibility arising from the establishment of such fixed limit, and having done so, the Architect shall be entitled to compensation for all services performed in accordance with this Agreement, whether or not the Construction Phase is commenced.

ARTICLE 4
DIRECT PERSONNEL EXPENSE

4.1 Direct Personnel Expense is defined as the direct salaries of all the Architect's personnel engaged on the Project, and the portion of the cost of their mandatory and customary contributions and benefits related thereto, such as employment taxes and other statutory employee benefits, insurance, sick leave, holidays, vacations, pensions and similar contributions and benefits.

ARTICLE 5
REIMBURSABLE EXPENSES

5.1 Reimbursable Expenses are in addition to the compensation for Basic and Additional Services and include actual expenditures made by the Architect and the Architect's employees and consultants in the interest of the Project for the expenses listed in the following Subparagraphs:

5.1.1 Expense of transportation in connection with the Project; living expenses in connection with out-of-town travel; long distance communications; and fees paid for securing approvals of authorities having jurisdiction over the Project.

5.1.2 Expense of reproductions, postage and handling of Drawings, Specifications and other documents, excluding reproductions for the office use of the Architect and the Architect's consultants.

5.1.3 Expense of data processing and photographic production techniques when used in connection with Additional Services.

5.1.4 If authorized in advance by the Owner, expense of overtime work requiring higher than regular rates.

5.1.5 Expense of renderings, models and mock-ups requested by the Owner.

5.1.6 Expense of any additional insurance coverage or limits, including professional liability insurance, requested by the Owner in excess of that normally carried by the Architect and the Architect's consultants.

ARTICLE 6
PAYMENTS TO THE ARCHITECT

6.1 PAYMENTS ON ACCOUNT OF BASIC SERVICES

6.1.1 An initial payment as set forth in Paragraph 14.1 is the minimum payment under this Agreement.

6.1.2 Subsequent payments for Basic Services shall be made monthly and shall be in proportion to services performed within each Phase of services, on the basis set forth in Article 14.

6.1.3 If and to the extent that the period initially established for the Construction Phase of the Project is exceeded or extended through no fault of the Architect, compensation for Basic Services required for such extended period of Administration of the Construction Contracts shall be computed as set forth in Paragraph 14.4 for Additional Services.

6.1.4 When compensation is based on a percentage of Construction Cost, and any portions of the Project are deleted or otherwise not constructed, compensation for such portions of the Project shall be payable to the extent services are performed on such portions, in accordance with the schedule set forth in Subparagraph 14.2.2, based on (1) the lowest figures from bona fide Bids or negotiated proposals, or (2) if no such Bids or proposals are received, the most recent estimate of Construction Cost for such portions of the Project.

6.2 PAYMENTS ON ACCOUNT OF ADDITIONAL SERVICES

6.2.1 Payments on account of the Architect's Additional Services, as defined in Paragraph 1.7, and for Reimbursable Expenses, as defined in Article 5, shall be made monthly upon presentation of the Architect's statement of services rendered or expenses incurred.

6.3 PAYMENTS WITHHELD

6.3.1 No deductions shall be made from the Architect's compensation on account of penalty, liquidated damages or other sums withheld from payments to Contractors, or on account of changes in Construction Cost other than those for which the Architect is held legally liable.

6.4 PROJECT SUSPENSION OR ABANDONMENT

6.4.1 If the Project is suspended or abandoned in whole or in part for more than three months, the Architect shall be compensated for all services performed prior to receipt of written notice from the Owner of such suspension or abandonment, together with Reimbursable Expenses then due and all Termination Expenses as defined in Paragraph 10.4. If the Project is resumed after being suspended for more than three months, the Architect's compensation shall be equitably adjusted.

ARTICLE 7
ARCHITECT'S ACCOUNTING RECORDS

7.1 Records of Reimbursable Expenses and expenses pertaining to Additional Services and services performed on the basis of a Multiple of Direct Personnel Expense shall be kept on the basis of generally accepted accounting principles and shall be available to the Owner or the Owner's authorized representative at mutually convenient times.

ARTICLE 8
OWNERSHIP AND USE OF DOCUMENTS

8.1 Drawings and Specifications as instruments of service are and shall remain the property of the Architect whether the Project for which they are made is executed or not. The Owner shall be permitted to retain copies, including reproducible copies, of Drawings and Specifications for information and reference in connection with the Owner's use and occupancy of the Project. The Drawings and Specifications shall not be used by the Owner on other projects, for additions to this Project, or for completion of this Project by others provided the Architect is not in default under this Agreement, except by agreement in writing and with appropriate compensation to the Architect.

8.2 Submission or distribution to meet official regulatory requirements or for other purposes in connection with the Project is not to be construed as publication in derogation of the Architect's rights.

ARTICLE 9
ARBITRATION

9.1 All claims, disputes and other matters in question between the parties to this Agreement arising out of or relating to this Agreement or the breach thereof, shall be decided by arbitration in accordance with the Construction Industry Arbitration Rules of the American Arbitration Association then obtaining unless the parties mutually agree otherwise. No arbitration arising out of or relating to this Agreement shall include, by consolidation, joinder or in any other manner, any additional person not a party to this Agreement except by written consent containing a specific reference to this Agreement and signed by the Architect, the Owner and any other person sought to be joined. Any consent to arbitration involving an additional person or persons shall not constitute consent to arbitration of any dispute not described therein or with any person not named or described therein. This agreement to arbitrate and any agreement to arbitrate with an additional person or persons duly consented to by the parties to this Agreement shall be specifically enforceable under the prevailing arbitration law.

9.2 Notice of the demand for arbitration shall be filed in writing with the other party to this Agreement and with the American Arbitration Association. The demand shall be made within a reasonable time after the claim, dispute or other matter in question has arisen. In no event shall the demand for arbitration be made after the date when institution of legal or equitable proceedings based on such claim, dispute or other matter in question would be barred by the applicable statute of limitations.

9.3 The award rendered by the arbitrators shall be final, and judgment may be entered upon it in accordance with applicable law in any court having jurisdiction thereof.

ARTICLE 10
TERMINATION OF AGREEMENT

10.1 This Agreement may be terminated by either party upon seven days' written notice should the other party fail substantially to perform in accordance with its terms through no fault of the party initiating the termination.

10.2 This Agreement may be terminated by the Owner upon at least seven days' written notice to the Architect in the event that the Project is permanently abandoned.

10.3 In the event of termination not the fault of the Architect, the Architect shall be compensated for all services performed to the termination date, together with Reimbursable Expenses then due and all Termination Expenses as defined in Paragraph 10.4.

10.4 Termination Expenses include expenses directly attributable to termination for which the Architect is not otherwise compensated, plus an amount computed as a percentage of the total Basic and Additional Compensation earned to the time of termination, as follows:

.1 20 percent if termination occurs during the Schematic Design Phase; or

.2 10 percent if termination occurs during the Design Development Phase; or

.3 5 percent if termination occurs during any subsequent Phase.

ARTICLE 11
MISCELLANEOUS PROVISIONS

11.1 Unless otherwise specified, this Agreement shall be governed by the law of the principal place of business of the Architect.

11.2 Terms in this Agreement shall have the same meaning as those in the 1980 Edition of AIA Document A201/CM, General Conditions of the Contract for Construction, Construction Management Edition.

11.3 As between the parties to this Agreement: as to all acts or failures to act by either party to this Agreement, any applicable statute of limitations shall commence to run and any alleged cause of action shall be deemed to have accrued in any and all events not later than the relevant Date of Substantial Completion of the Project, and as to any acts or failures to act occurring after the relevant Date of Substantial Completion of the Project, not later than the date of issuance of the final Project Certificate for Payment.

11.4 The Owner and the Architect waive all rights against each other, and against the contractors, consultants, agents and employees of the other, for damages covered by any property insurance during construction, as set forth in the 1980 Edition of AIA Document A201/CM, General Conditions of the Contract for Construction, Construction Management Edition. The Owner and the Architect shall each require appropriate similar waivers from their contractors, consultants and agents.

ARTICLE 12
SUCCESSORS AND ASSIGNS

12.1 The Owner and the Architect, respectively, bind themselves, their partners, successors, assigns and legal representatives to the other party to this Agreement, and to the partners, successors, assigns and legal representatives of such other party with respect to all covenants of this Agreement. Neither the Owner nor the Architect shall assign, sublet or transfer any interest in this Agreement without the written consent of the other.

ARTICLE 13
EXTENT OF AGREEMENT

13.1 This Agreement represents the entire and integrated agreement between the Owner and the Architect and supersedes all prior negotiations, representations or agreements, either written or oral. This Agreement may be amended only by written instrument signed by both the Owner and the Architect.

13.2 Nothing contained herein shall be deemed to create any contractual relationship between the Architect and the Construction Manager or any of the Contractors, Subcontractors or material suppliers on the Project; nor shall anything contained in this Agreement be deemed to give any third party any claim or right of action against the Owner or the Architect which does not otherwise exist without regard to this Agreement.

ARTICLE 14
BASIS OF COMPENSATION

The Owner shall compensate the Architect for the Scope of Services provided, in accordance with Article 6, Payments to the Architect, and the other Terms and Conditions of this Agreement, as follows:

14.1   AN INITIAL PAYMENT of   dollars ($) shall be made upon execution of this Agreement and credited to the Owner's account as follows:

14.2   **BASIC COMPENSATION**

14.2.1   FOR BASIC SERVICES, as described in Paragraphs 1.1 through 1.5, and any other services included in Article 15 as part of Basic Services, Basic Compensation shall be computed as follows:
(Here insert basis of compensation, including fixed amounts, multiples or percentages, and identify Phases or parts of the Project to which particular methods of compensation apply, if necessary.)

14.2.2   Where compensation is based on a Stipulated Sum or Percentage of Construction Cost, payments for Basic Services shall be made as provided in Subparagraph 6.1.2, so that Basic Compensation for each Phase shall equal the following percentages of the total Basic Compensation payable:

(Include any additional Phases as appropriate.)

Schematic Design Phase:	percent (%)
Design Development Phase:	percent (%)
Construction Documents Phase:	percent (%)
Bidding or Negotiation Phase:	percent (%)
Construction Phase:	percent (%)

14.3   FOR PROJECT REPRESENTATION BEYOND BASIC SERVICES, as described in Paragraph 1.6, compensation shall be computed separately in accordance with Subparagraph 1.6.2.
(Here insert basis of compensation which may be a stipulated sum for a given period of time or a Multiple of Direct Personnel Expense as defined in Article 4. If a Multiple of Direct Personnel Expense is used, the Multiple should be clearly stated.)

14.4   COMPENSATION FOR ADDITIONAL SERVICES

14.4.1   FOR ADDITIONAL SERVICES OF THE ARCHITECT, as described in Paragraph 1.7, and any other services included in Article 15 as part of Additional Services, but excluding Additional Services of consultants, compensation shall be computed as follows:
(Here insert basis of compensation, including rates and/or Multiples of Direct Personnel Expense for Principals and employees, and identify Principals and classify employees, if required. Identify specific services to which particular methods of compensation apply, if necessary.)

14.4.2   FOR ADDITIONAL SERVICES OF CONSULTANTS, including additional structural, mechanical and electrical engineering services and those provided under Subparagraph 1.7.21 or identified in Article 15 as part of Additional Services, a multiple of   (   ) times the amounts billed to the Architect for such services.
(Identify specific types of consultants in Article 15, if required.)

14.5   FOR REIMBURSABLE EXPENSES, as described in Article 5, and any other items included in Article 15 as Reimbursable Expenses, a multiple of   (   ) times the amounts expended by the Architect, the Architect's employees and consultants in the interest of the Project.

14.6   Payments due the Architect and unpaid under this Agreement shall bear interest from the date payment is due at the rate entered below, or in the absence thereof, at the legal rate prevailing at the principal place of business of the Architect.
(Here insert any rate of interest agreed upon.)

(Usury laws and requirements under the Federal Truth in Lending Act, similar state and local consumer credit laws and other regulations at the Owner's and Architect's principal places of business, the location of the Project and elsewhere may affect the validity of this provision. Specific legal advice should be obtained with respect to deletion, modification or other requirements such as written disclosures or waivers.)

14.7   The Owner and the Architect agree in accordance with the Terms and Conditions of this Agreement that:

14.7.1   IF THE SCOPE of the Project or the Architect's services is changed materially, the amounts of compensation shall be equitably adjusted.

14.7.2   IF THE SERVICES covered by this Agreement have not been completed within (   ) months of the date hereof, through no fault of the Architect, the amounts of compensation, rates and multiples set forth herein shall be equitably adjusted.

ARTICLE 15
OTHER CONDITIONS OR SERVICES

This Agreement entered into as of the day and year first written above.

OWNER   ARCHITECT

_____   _____

_____   _____

_____   _____

_____   _____

THE AMERICAN INSTITUTE OF ARCHITECTS

AIA Document B801

Standard Form of Agreement Between Owner and Construction Manager

1980 EDITION

THIS DOCUMENT HAS IMPORTANT LEGAL CONSEQUENCES; CONSULTATION WITH AN ATTORNEY IS ENCOURAGED.

This document is intended to be used in conjunction with
AIA Documents A101/CM, 1980; B141/CM, 1980; and A201/CM, 1980.

AGREEMENT

made as of the   day of   in the year of Nineteen
Hundred and

BETWEEN the Owner:

and the Construction Manager:

For the following Project:
(Include detailed description of Project location and scope.)

the Architect:

The Owner and the Construction Manager agree as set forth below.

AIA DOCUMENT B801 • OWNER-CONSTRUCTION MANAGER AGREEMENT • JUNE 1980 EDITION • AIA®
©1980 • THE AMERICAN INSTITUTE OF ARCHITECTS, 1735 NEW YORK AVE., N.W., WASHINGTON, D.C. 20006   **B801 — 1980 1**

TERMS AND CONDITIONS OF AGREEMENT BETWEEN OWNER AND CONSTRUCTION MANAGER

ARTICLE 1
CONSTRUCTION MANAGER'S SERVICES AND RESPONSIBILITIES

The Construction Manager covenants with the Owner to further the interests of the Owner by furnishing the Construction Manager's skill and judgment in cooperation with, and in reliance upon, the services of an architect. The Construction Manager agrees to furnish business administration and management services and to perform in an expeditious and economical manner consistent with the interests of the Owner.

BASIC SERVICES

The Construction Manager's Basic Services consist of the two Phases described below and any other services included in Article 16 as Basic Services.

1.1 PRECONSTRUCTION PHASE

1.1.1 Provide preliminary evaluation of the program and Project budget requirements, each in terms of the other. With the Architect's assistance, prepare preliminary estimates of Construction Cost for early schematic designs based on area, volume or other standards. Assist the Owner and the Architect in achieving mutually agreed upon program and Project budget requirements and other design parameters. Provide cost evaluations of alternative materials and systems.

1.1.2 Review designs during their development. Advise on site use and improvements, selection of materials, building systems and equipment and methods of Project delivery. Provide recommendations on relative feasibility of construction methods, availability of materials and labor, time requirements for procurement, installation and construction, and factors related to cost including, but not limited to, costs of alternative designs or materials, preliminary budgets and possible economies.

1.1.3 Provide for the Architect's and the Owner's review and acceptance, and periodically update, a Project Schedule that coordinates and integrates the Construction Manager's services, the Architect's services and the Owner's responsibilities with anticipated construction schedules.

1.1.4 Prepare for the Owner's approval a more detailed estimate of Construction Cost, as defined in Article 3, developed by using estimating techniques which anticipate the various elements of the Project, and based on Schematic Design Documents prepared by the Architect. Update and refine this estimate periodically as the Architect prepares Design Development and Construction Documents. Advise the Owner and the Architect if it appears that the Construction Cost may exceed the Project budget. Make recommendations for corrective action.

1.1.5 Coordinate Contract Documents by consulting with the Owner and the Architect regarding Drawings and Specifications as they are being prepared, and recommending alternative solutions whenever design details affect construction feasibility, cost or schedules.

1.1.5.1 Provide recommendations and information to the Owner and the Architect regarding the assignment of responsibilities for safety precautions and programs; temporary Project facilities; and equipment, materials and services for common use of Contractors. Verify that the requirements and assignment of responsibilities are included in the proposed Contract Documents.

1.1.5.2 Advise on the separation of the Project into Contracts for various categories of Work. Advise on the method to be used for selecting Contractors and awarding Contracts. If separate Contracts are to be awarded, review the Drawings and Specifications and make recommendations as required to provide that (1) the Work of the separate Contractors is coordinated, (2) all requirements for the Project have been assigned to the appropriate separate Contract, (3) the likelihood of jurisdictional disputes has been minimized, and (4) proper coordination has been provided for phased construction.

1.1.5.3 Develop a Project Construction Schedule providing for all major elements such as phasing of construction and times of commencement and completion required of each separate Contractor. Provide the Project Construction Schedule for each set of Bidding Documents.

1.1.5.4 Investigate and recommend a schedule for the Owner's purchase of materials and equipment requiring long lead time procurement, and coordinate the schedule with the early preparation of portions of the Contract Documents by the Architect. Expedite and coordinate delivery of these purchases.

1.1.6 Provide an analysis of the types and quantities of labor required for the Project and review the availability of appropriate categories of labor required for critical Phases. Make recommendations for actions designed to minimize adverse effects of labor shortages.

1.1.6.1 Identify or verify applicable requirements for equal employment opportunity programs for inclusion in the proposed Contract Documents.

1.1.7 Make recommendations for pre-qualification criteria for Bidders and develop Bidders' interest in the Project. Establish bidding schedules. Assist the Architect in issuing Bidding Documents to Bidders. Conduct pre-bid conferences to familiarize Bidders with the Bidding Documents and management techniques and with any special systems, materials or methods. Assist the Architect with the receipt of questions from Bidders, and with the issuance of Addenda.

1.1.7.1 With the Architect's assistance, receive Bids, prepare bid analyses and make recommendations to the Owner for award of Contracts or rejection of Bids.

1.1.8 With the Architect's assistance, conduct pre-award conferences with successful Bidders. Assist the Owner in preparing Construction Contracts and advise the Owner on the acceptability of Subcontractors and material suppliers proposed by Contractors.

1.2 CONSTRUCTION PHASE

The Construction Phase will commence with the award of the initial Construction Contract or purchase order and, together with the Construction Manager's obligation to provide Basic Services under this Agreement, will end 30 days after final payment to all Contractors is due.

1.2.1 Unless otherwise provided in this Agreement and incorporated in the Contract Documents, the Construction Manager, in cooperation with the Architect, shall provide administration of the Contracts for Construction as set forth below and in the 1980 Edition of AIA Document A201/CM, General Conditions of the Contract for Construction, Construction Management Edition.

1.2.2 Provide administrative, management and related services as required to coordinate Work of the Contractors with each other and with the activities and responsibilities of the Construction Manager, the Owner and the Architect to complete the Project in accordance with the Owner's objectives for cost, time and quality. Provide sufficient organization, personnel and management to carry out the requirements of this Agreement.

1.2.2.1 Schedule and conduct pre-construction, construction and progress meetings to discuss such matters as procedures, progress, problems and scheduling. Prepare and promptly distribute minutes.

1.2.2.2 Consistent with the Project Construction Schedule issued with the Bidding Documents, and utilizing the Contractors' Construction Schedules provided by the separate Contractors, update the Project Construction Schedule incorporating the activities of Contractors on the Project, including activity sequences and durations, allocation of labor and materials, processing of Shop Drawings, Product Data and Samples, and delivery of products requiring long lead time procurement. Include the Owner's occupancy requirements showing portions of the Project having occupancy priority. Update and reissue the Project Construction Schedule as required to show current conditions and revisions required by actual experience.

1.2.2.3 Endeavor to achieve satisfactory performance from each of the Contractors. Recommend courses of action to the Owner when requirements of a Contract are not being fulfilled, and the nonperforming party will not take satisfactory corrective action.

1.2.3 Revise and refine the approved estimate of Construction Cost, incorporate approved changes as they occur, and develop cash flow reports and forecasts as needed.

1.2.3.1 Provide regular monitoring of the approved estimate of Construction Cost, showing actual costs for activities in progress and estimates for uncompleted tasks. Identify variances between actual and budgeted or estimated costs, and advise the Owner and the Architect whenever projected costs exceed budgets or estimates.

1.2.3.2 Maintain cost accounting records on authorized Work performed under unit costs, additional Work performed on the basis of actual costs of labor and materials, or other Work requiring accounting records.

1.2.3.3 Recommend necessary or desirable changes to the Architect and the Owner, review requests for changes, assist in negotiating Contractors' proposals, submit recommendations to the Architect and the Owner, and if they are accepted, prepare and sign Change Orders for the Architect's signature and the Owner's authorization.

1.2.3.4 Develop and implement procedures for the review and processing of Applications by Contractors for progress and final payments. Make recommendations to the Architect for certification to the Owner for payment.

1.2.4 Review the safety programs developed by each of the Contractors as required by their Contract Documents and coordinate the safety programs for the Project.

1.2.5 Assist in obtaining building permits and special permits for permanent improvements, excluding permits required to be obtained directly by the various Contractors. Verify that the Owner has paid applicable fees and assessments. Assist in obtaining approvals from authorities having jurisdiction over the Project.

1.2.6 If required, assist the Owner in selecting and retaining the professional services of surveyors, special consultants and testing laboratories. Coordinate their services.

1.2.7 Determine in general that the Work of each Contractor is being performed in accordance with the requirements of the Contract Documents. Endeavor to guard the Owner against defects and deficiencies in the Work. As appropriate, require special inspection or testing, or make recommendations to the Architect regarding special inspection or testing, of Work not in accordance with the provisions of the Contract Documents whether or not such Work be then fabricated, installed or completed. Subject to review by the Architect, reject Work which does not conform to the requirements of the Contract Documents.

1.2.7.1 The Construction Manager shall not be responsible for construction means, methods, techniques, sequences and procedures employed by Contractors in the performance of their Contracts, and shall not be responsible for the failure of any Contractor to carry out Work in accordance with the Contract Documents.

1.2.8 Consult with the Architect and the Owner if any Contractor requests interpretations of the meaning and intent of the Drawings and Specifications, and assist in the resolution of questions which may arise.

1.2.9 Receive Certificates of Insurance from the Contractors, and forward them to the Owner with a copy to the Architect.

1.2.10 Receive from the Contractors and review all Shop Drawings, Product Data, Samples and other submittals. Coordinate them with information contained in related documents and transmit to the Architect those recommended for approval. In collaboration with the Architect, establish and implement procedures for expediting the processing and approval of Shop Drawings, Product Data, Samples and other submittals.

1.2.11 Record the progress of the Project. Submit written progress reports to the Owner and the Architect including information on each Contractor and each Contractor's Work, as well as the entire Project, showing percentages of completion and the number and amounts of Change Orders. Keep a daily log containing a record of weather, Contractors' Work on the site, number of workers, Work accomplished, problems encountered, and other similar relevant data as the Owner may require. Make the log available to the Owner and the Architect.

1.2.11.1 Maintain at the Project site, on a current basis: a record copy of all Contracts, Drawings, Specifications, Addenda, Change Orders and other Modifications, in good order and marked to record all changes made during construction; Shop Drawings; Product Data; Samples; submittals; purchases; materials; equipment; applicable handbooks; maintenance and operating manuals and instructions; other related documents and revisions which arise out of the Contracts or Work. Maintain records, in duplicate, of principal building layout lines, elevations of the bottom of footings, floor levels and key site elevations certified by a qualified surveyor or professional engineer. Make all records available to the Owner and the Architect. At the completion of the Project, deliver all such records to the Architect for the Owner.

1.2.12 Arrange for delivery and storage, protection and security for Owner-purchased materials, systems and equipment which are a part of the Project, until such items are incorporated into the Project.

1.2.13 With the Architect and the Owner's maintenance personnel, observe the Contractors' checkout of utilities, operational systems and equipment for readiness and assist in their initial start-up and testing.

1.2.14 When the Construction Manager considers each Contractor's Work or a designated portion thereof substantially complete, the Construction Manager shall prepare for the Architect a list of incomplete or unsatisfactory items and a schedule for their completion. The Construction Manager shall assist the Architect in conducting inspections. After the Architect certifies the Date of Substantial Completion of the Work, the Construction Manager shall coordinate the correction and completion of the Work.

1.2.15 Assist the Architect in determining when the Project or a designated portion thereof is substantially complete. Prepare for the Architect a summary of the status of the Work of each Contractor, listing changes in the previously issued Certificates of Substantial Completion of the Work and recommending the times within which Contractors shall complete uncompleted items on their Certificate of Substantial Completion of the Work.

1.2.16 Following the Architect's issuance of a Certificate of Substantial Completion of the Project or designated portion thereof, evaluate the completion of the Work of the Contractors and make recommendations to the Architect when Work is ready for final inspection. Assist the Architect in conducting final inspections. Secure and transmit to the Owner required guarantees, affidavits, releases, bonds and waivers. Deliver all keys, manuals, record drawings and maintenance stocks to the Owner.

1.2.17 The extent of the duties, responsibilities and limitations of authority of the Construction Manager as a representative of the Owner during construction shall not be modified or extended without the written consent of the Owner, the Contractors, the Architect and the Construction Manager, which consent shall not be unreasonably withheld.

1.3   ADDITIONAL SERVICES

The following Additional Services shall be performed upon authorization in writing from the Owner and shall be paid for as provided in this Agreement.

1.3.1 Services related to investigations, appraisals or evaluations of existing conditions, facilities or equipment, or verification of the accuracy of existing drawings or other information furnished by the Owner.

1.3.2 Services related to Owner-furnished furniture, furnishings and equipment which are not a part of the Project.

1.3.3 Services for tenant or rental spaces.

1.3.4 Consultation on replacement of Work damaged by fire or other cause during construction, and furnishing services in conjunction with the replacement of such Work.

1.3.5 Services made necessary by the default of a Contractor.

1.3.6 Preparing to serve or serving as a witness in connection with any public hearing, arbitration proceeding or legal proceeding.

1.3.7 Recruiting or training maintenance personnel.

1.3.8 Inspections of, and services related to, the Project after the end of the Construction Phase.

1.3.9 Providing any other services not otherwise included in this Agreement.

1.4   TIME

1.4.1 The Construction Manager shall perform Basic and Additional Services as expeditiously as is consistent with reasonable skill and care and the orderly progress of the Project.

ARTICLE 2
THE OWNER'S RESPONSIBILITIES

2.1 The Owner shall provide full information regarding the requirements of the Project, including a program, which shall set forth the Owner's objectives, constraints and criteria, including space requirements and relationships, flexibility and expandability requirements, special equipment and systems and site requirements.

2.2 The Owner shall provide a budget for the Project, based on consultation with the Construction Manager and the Architect, which shall include contingencies for bidding, changes during construction and other costs which are the responsibility of the Owner. The Owner shall, at the request of the Construction Manager, provide a statement of funds available for the Project and their source.

2.3 The Owner shall designate a representative authorized to act in the Owner's behalf with respect to the Project. The Owner, or such authorized representative, shall examine documents submitted by the Construction Manager and shall render decisions pertaining thereto promptly to avoid unreasonable delay in the progress of the Construction Manager's services.

2.4 The Owner shall retain an architect whose services, duties and responsibilities are described in the agreement between the Owner and the Architect, AIA Document B141/CM, 1980 Edition. The Terms and Conditions of the Owner-Architect Agreement will be furnished to the Construction Manager, and will not be modified without written consent of the Construction Manager, which consent shall not be unreasonably withheld. Actions taken by the Architect as agent of the Owner shall be the acts of the Owner and the Construction Manager shall not be responsible for them.

2.5 The Owner shall furnish structural, mechanical, chemical and other laboratory tests, inspections and reports as required by law or the Contract Documents.

2.6 The Owner shall furnish such legal, accounting and insurance counseling services as may be necessary for the Project, including such auditing services as the Owner may require to verify the Project Applications for Payment or to ascertain how or for what purposes the Contractors have used the monies paid by or on behalf of the Owner.

2.7 The Owner shall furnish the Construction Manager a sufficient quantity of construction documents.

2.8 The services, information and reports required by Paragraphs 2.1 through 2.7, inclusive, shall be furnished at the Owner's expense, and the Construction Manager shall be entitled to rely upon their accuracy and completeness.

2.9 If the Owner observes or otherwise becomes aware of any fault or defect in the Project, or nonconformance with the Contract Documents, prompt written notice thereof shall be given by the Owner to the Construction Manager and the Architect.

2.10 The Owner reserves the right to perform work related to the Project with the Owner's own forces, and to award contracts in connection with the Project which are not part of the Construction Manager's responsibilities under this Agreement. The Construction Manager shall notify the Owner if any such independent action will in any way compromise the Construction Manager's ability to meet the Construction Manager's responsibilities under this Agreement.

2.11 The Owner shall furnish the required information and services and shall render approvals and decisions as expeditiously as necessary for the orderly progress of the Construction Manager's services and the Work of the Contractors.

ARTICLE 3
CONSTRUCTION COST

3.1 Construction Cost shall be the total of the final Contract Sums of all of the separate Contracts, actual Reimbursable Costs relating to the Construction Phase as defined in Article 6, and the Construction Manager's compensation.

3.2 Construction Cost does not include the compensation of the Architect and the Architect's consultants, the cost of the land, rights-of-way or other costs which are the responsibility of the Owner as provided in Paragraphs 2.3 through 2.7, inclusive.

3.3 Evaluations of the Owner's Project budget and cost estimates prepared by the Construction Manager represent the Construction Manager's best judgment as a professional familiar with the construction industry. It is recognized, however, that neither the Construction Manager nor the Owner has control over the cost of labor, materials or equipment, over Contractors' methods of determining Bid prices or other competitive bidding or negotiating conditions. Accordingly, the Construction Manager cannot and does not warrant or represent that Bids or negotiated prices will not vary from the Project budget proposed, established or approved by the Owner, or from any cost estimate or evaluation prepared by the Construction Manager.

3.4 No fixed limit of Construction Cost shall be established as a condition of this Agreement by the furnishing, proposal or establishment of a Project budget under Subparagraph 1.1.1 or Paragraph 2.2, or otherwise, unless such fixed limit has been agreed upon in writing and signed by the parties to this Agreement. If such a fixed limit has been established, the Construction Manager shall include contingencies for design, bidding and price escalation, and

shall consult with the Architect to determine what materials, equipment, component systems and types of construction are to be included in the Contract Documents, to suggest reasonable adjustments in the scope of the Project, and to suggest alternate Bids in the Construction Documents to adjust the Construction Cost to the fixed limit. Any such fixed limit shall be increased in the amount of any increase in the Contract Sums occurring after the execution of the Contracts for Construction.

3.4.1 If Bids are not received within the time scheduled at the time the fixed limit of Construction Cost was established, due to causes beyond the Construction Manager's control, any fixed limit of Construction Cost established as a condition of this Agreement shall be adjusted to reflect any change in the general level of prices in the construction industry occurring between the originally scheduled date and the date on which Bids are received.

3.4.2 If a fixed limit of Construction Cost (adjusted as provided in Subparagraph 3.4.1) is exceeded by the sum of the lowest figures from bona fide Bids or negotiated proposals plus the Construction Manager's estimate of other elements of Construction Cost for the Project, the Owner shall (1) give written approval of an increase in such fixed limit, (2) authorize rebidding or renegotiation of the Project or portions of the Project within a reasonable time, (3) if the Project is abandoned, terminate in accordance with Paragraph 10.2, or (4) cooperate in revising the scope and quality of the Work as required to reduce the Construction Cost. In the case of item (4), the Construction Manager, without additional compensation, shall cooperate with the Architect as necessary to bring the Construction Cost within the fixed limit.

ARTICLE 4
CONSTRUCTION SUPPORT ACTIVITIES

4.1 Construction support activities, if provided by the Construction Manager, shall be governed by separate contractual arrangements unless otherwise provided in Article 16.

ARTICLE 5
DIRECT PERSONNEL EXPENSE

5.1 Direct Personnel Expense is defined as the direct salaries of all of the Construction Manager's personnel engaged on the Project, excluding those whose compensation is included in the fee, and the portion of the cost of their mandatory and customary contributions and benefits related thereto such as employment taxes and other statutory employee benefits, insurance, sick leave, holidays, vacations, pensions, and similar contributions and benefits.

ARTICLE 6
REIMBURSABLE COSTS

6.1 The term Reimbursable Costs shall mean costs necessarily incurred in the proper performance of services and paid by the Construction Manager. Such costs shall be at rates not higher than the standard paid in the locality of the Project, except with prior consent of the Owner. Reimbursable Costs and costs not to be reimbursed shall be listed in Article 16.

AIA DOCUMENT B801 • OWNER-CONSTRUCTION MANAGER AGREEMENT • JUNE 1980 EDITION • AIA®
©1980 • THE AMERICAN INSTITUTE OF ARCHITECTS, 1735 NEW YORK AVE., N.W., WASHINGTON, D.C. 20006

6.2 Trade discounts, rebates and refunds, and returns from sale of surplus materials and equipment shall accrue to the Owner, and the Construction Manager shall make provisions so that they can be secured.

ARTICLE 7

PAYMENTS TO THE CONSTRUCTION MANAGER

7.1 PAYMENTS ON ACCOUNT OF BASIC SERVICES

7.1.1 An initial payment as set forth in Paragraph 15.1 is the minimum payment under this Agreement.

7.1.2 Subsequent payments for Basic Services shall be made monthly and shall be in proportion to services performed within each Phase of Services, on the basis set forth in Article 15.

7.1.3 If and to the extent that the time initially established for the Construction Phase of the Project is exceeded or extended through no fault of the Construction Manager, compensation for Basic Services required for such extended period of Administration of the Construction Contract shall be computed as set forth in Paragraph 15.3 for Additional Services.

7.1.4 When compensation is based on a percentage of the total of the Contract Sums of all the separate Contracts, and any portions of the Project are deleted or otherwise not constructed, compensation for such portions of the Project shall be payable to the extent services are performed on such portions, in accordance with the schedule set forth in Subparagraph 15.2.1, based on (1) the lowest figures from bona fide Bids or negotiated proposals, or (2) if no such Bids or proposals are received, the most recent estimate of the total of the Contract Sums of all the separate Contracts for such portions of the Project.

7.2 PAYMENTS ON ACCOUNT OF ADDITIONAL SERVICES AND REIMBURSABLE COSTS

7.2.1 Payments on account of the Construction Manager's Additional Services, as defined in Paragraph 13, and for Reimbursable Costs, as defined in Article 16, shall be made monthly upon presentation of the Construction Manager's statement of services rendered or costs incurred.

7.3 PAYMENTS WITHHELD

7.3.1 No deductions shall be made from the Construction Manager's compensation on account of penalty, liquidated damages or other sums withheld from payments to Contractors, or on account of the cost of changes in Work other than those for which the Construction Manager is held legally liable.

7.4 PROJECT SUSPENSION OR ABANDONMENT

7.4.1 If the Project is suspended or abandoned in whole or in part for more than three months, the Construction Manager shall be compensated for all services performed prior to receipt of written notice from the Owner of such suspension or abandonment, together with Reimbursable Costs then due and all Termination Expenses as defined in Paragraph 10.4. If the Project is resumed after being suspended for more than three months, the Construction Manager's compensation shall be equitably adjusted.

7.4.2 If construction of the Project has started and is stopped by reason of circumstances not the fault of the Construction Manager, the Owner shall reimburse the Construction Manager for the costs of the Construction Manager's Project-site staff as provided for by this Agreement. The Construction Manager shall reduce the size of the Project-site staff after 30 days' delay, or sooner if feasible, for the remainder of the delay period as directed by the Owner and, during that period, the Owner shall reimburse the Construction Manager for the costs of such staff prior to reduction plus any relocation or employment termination costs. Upon the termination of the stoppage, the Construction Manager shall provide the necessary Project-site staff as soon as practicable.

ARTICLE 8

CONSTRUCTION MANAGER'S ACCOUNTING RECORDS

8.1 Records of Reimbursable Costs and costs pertaining to services performed on the basis of a Multiple of Direct Personnel Expense shall be kept on the basis of generally accepted accounting principles and shall be available to the Owner or the Owner's authorized representative at mutually convenient times.

ARTICLE 9

ARBITRATION

9.1 All claims, disputes and other matters in question between the parties to this Agreement arising out of or relating to this Agreement or the breach thereof, shall be decided by arbitration in accordance with the Construction Industry Arbitration Rules of the American Arbitration Association then obtaining unless the parties mutually agree otherwise. No arbitration arising out of or relating to this Agreement shall include, by consolidation, joinder or in any other manner, any additional person not a party to this Agreement except by written consent containing a specific reference to this Agreement and signed by the Construction Manager, the Owner, and any other person sought to be joined. Any consent to arbitration involving an additional person or persons shall not constitute consent to arbitration of any dispute not described therein or with any person not named or described therein. This agreement to arbitrate and any agreement to arbitrate with an additional person or persons duly consented to by the parties to this Agreement shall be specifically enforceable under the prevailing arbitration law.

9.2 Notice of demand for arbitration shall be filed in writing with the other party to this Agreement and with the American Arbitration Association, and a copy shall also be filed with the Architect. The demand shall be made within a reasonable time after the claim, dispute or other matter in question has arisen. In no event shall the demand for arbitration be made after the date when institution of legal or equitable proceedings based on such claim, dispute or other matter in question would be barred by the applicable statute of limitations.

9.3 The award rendered by the arbitrators shall be final, and judgment may be entered upon it in accordance with applicable law in any court having jurisdiction thereof.

ARTICLE 10

TERMINATION OF AGREEMENT

10.1 This Agreement may be terminated by either party upon seven days' written notice should the other party fail substantially to perform in accordance with its terms through no fault of the party initiating the termination.

10.2 This Agreement may be terminated by the Owner upon at least fourteen days' written notice to the Construction Manager in the event that the Project is permanently abandoned.

10.3 In the event of termination not the fault of the Construction Manager, the Construction Manager shall be compensated for all services performed to the termination date together with Reimbursable Costs then due and all Termination Expenses.

10.4 Termination Expenses are defined as Reimbursable Costs directly attributable to termination for which the Construction Manager is not otherwise compensated.

ARTICLE 11
MISCELLANEOUS PROVISIONS

11.1 Unless otherwise specified, this Agreement shall be governed by the law in effect at the location of the Project.

11.2 Terms in this Agreement shall have the same meaning as those in the 1980 Edition of AIA Document A201/CM, General Conditions of the Contract for Construction, Construction Management Edition.

11.3 As between the parties to this Agreement: as to all acts or failures to act by either party to this Agreement, any applicable statute of limitations shall commence to run, and any alleged cause of action shall be deemed to have accrued, in any and all events not later than the relevant Date of Substantial Completion of the Project, and as to any acts or failures to act occurring after the relevant Date of Substantial Completion of the Project, not later than the date of issuance of the final Project Certificate for Payment.

11.4 The Owner and the Construction Manager waive all rights against each other, and against the contractors, consultants, agents and employees of the other, for damages covered by any property insurance during construction, as set forth in the 1980 Edition of AIA Document A201/CM, General Conditions of the Contract for Construction, Construction Management Edition. The Owner and the Construction Manager shall each require appropriate similar waivers from their contractors, consultants and agents.

ARTICLE 12
SUCCESSORS AND ASSIGNS

12.1 The Owner and the Construction Manager, respectively, bind themselves, their partners, successors, assigns and legal representatives to the other party to this Agreement, and to the partners, successors, assigns and legal representatives of such other party with respect to all covenants of this Agreement. Neither the Owner nor the Construction Manager shall assign, sublet or transfer any interest in this Agreement without the written consent of the other.

ARTICLE 13
EXTENT OF AGREEMENT

13.1 This Agreement represents the entire and integrated agreement between the Owner and the Construction Manager and supersedes all prior negotiations, representations or agreements, either written or oral. This Agreement may be amended only by written instrument signed by both the Owner and the Construction Manager.

13.2 Nothing contained herein shall be deemed to create any contractual relationship between the Construction Manager and the Architect or any of the Contractors, Subcontractors or material suppliers on the Project; nor shall anything contained in this Agreement be deemed to give any third party any claim or right of action against the Owner or the Construction Manager which does not otherwise exist without regard to this Agreement.

ARTICLE 14
INSURANCE

14.1 The Construction Manager shall purchase and maintain insurance for protection from claims under workers' or workmen's compensation acts; claims for damages because of bodily injury, including personal injury, sickness, disease or death of any of the Construction Manager's employees or of any person; from claims for damages because of injury to or destruction of tangible property including loss of use resulting therefrom; and from claims arising out of the performance of this Agreement and caused by negligent acts for which the Construction Manager is legally liable.

ARTICLE 15
BASIS OF COMPENSATION

The Owner shall compensate the Construction Manager for the Scope of Services provided, in accordance with Article 7, Payments to the Construction Manager, and the other Terms and Conditions of this Agreement, as follows:

15.1 AN INITIAL PAYMENT of   dollars ($) shall be made upon execu-
tion of this Agreement and credited to the Owner's account as follows:

15.2   **BASIC COMPENSATION**

15.2.1 FOR BASIC SERVICES, as described in Paragraphs 1.1 and 1.2, and any other services included in Article 16 as part of Basic Services, Basic Compensation shall be computed as follows:

For Preconstruction Phase Services, compensation shall be:
(Here insert basis of compensation, including fixed amounts. multiples or percentages.)

For Construction Phase Services, compensation shall be:
(Here insert basis of compensation, including fixed amounts, multiples or percentages.)

15.3   **COMPENSATION FOR ADDITIONAL SERVICES**

15.3.1 FOR ADDITIONAL SERVICES OF THE CONSTRUCTION MANAGER, as described in Paragraph 1.3, and any other services included in Article 16 as Additional Services, compensation shall be computed as follows:
(Here insert basis of compensation, including fixed amounts, multiples or percentages.)

15.4 FOR REIMBURSABLE COSTS, as described in Article 6 and Article 16, the actual costs incurred by the Construction Manager in the interest of the Project.

15.5 Payments due the Construction Manager and unpaid under this Agreement shall bear interest from the date payment is due at the rate entered below, or in the absence thereof, at the legal rate prevailing at the principal place of business of the Construction Manager.
(Here insert any rate of interest agreed upon.)

(Usury laws and requirements under the Federal Truth in Lending Act. similar state and local consumer credit laws, and other regulations at the Owner's and Construction Manager's principal places of business, the location of the Project and elsewhere may affect the validity of this provision. Specific legal advice should be obtained with respect to deletion, modification or other requirements such as written disclosures or waivers.)

15.6 The Owner and the Construction Manager agree in accordance with the Terms and Conditions of this Agreement that:

15.6.1 IF THE SCOPE of the Project or the Construction Manager's Services is changed materially, the amounts of compensation shall be equitably adjusted.

15.6.2 IF THE SERVICES covered by this Agreement have not been completed within
(   ) months of the date hereof, through no fault of the Construction Manager, the amounts of compensation, rates and multiples set forth herein shall be equitably adjusted.

ARTICLE 16
OTHER CONDITIONS OR SERVICES

(List Reimbursable Costs and costs not to be reimbursed.)

This Agreement entered into as of the day and year first written above.

OWNER   CONSTRUCTION MANAGER

_____   _____

_____   _____

_____   _____

INDEX